The Market and the Masses in Latin America

What do ordinary citizens in developing countries think about free markets? Conventional wisdom views globalization as an imposition on unwilling workers in developing nations, concluding that the recent rise of the Latin American Left constitutes a popular backlash against the market. Andy Baker marshals public opinion data from eighteen Latin American countries to show that most of the region's citizens are enthusiastic about globalization because it has lowered the prices of many consumer goods and services while improving their variety and quality. Among recent free-market reforms, only privatization has caused pervasive discontent because it has raised prices for services like electricity and telecommunications. Citizens' sharp awareness of these consumer consequences informs Baker's argument that a new political economy of consumption has replaced a previously dominant politics of labor and class in Latin America. Baker's research clarifies the sources of voters' connection to new left-wing parties and helps account for their leaders' moderation and nuanced approach to economic policymaking, embracing globalization while stalling or reversing privatization.

Andy Baker is Assistant Professor of Political Science at the University of Colorado at Boulder. His research on mass political behavior, political economy, and electoral systems has been published in the *American Journal of Political Science*, *DuBois Review*, *Electoral Studies*, *World Politics*, and various edited volumes. He has also been a contributor on two National Science Foundation grants and a recipient of two Social Science Research Council fellowships. He received his Ph.D. from the University of Wisconsin–Madison in 2001 and previously taught at the University of Houston and Northeastern University.

Cambridge Studies in Comparative Politics

General Editor
Margaret Levi *University of Washington, Seattle*

Assistant General Editor
Stephen Hanson *University of Washington, Seattle*

Associate Editors
Robert H. Bates *Harvard University*
Torben Iversen *Harvard University*
Stathis Kalyvas *Yale University*
Peter Lange *Duke University*
Helen Milner *Princeton University*
Frances Rosenbluth *Yale University*
Susan C. Stokes *Yale University*
Sidney Tarrow *Cornell University*
Kathleen Thelen *Northwestern University*
Erik Wibbels *Duke University*

Other Books in the Series

Continued after the Index

The Market and the Masses in Latin America

POLICY REFORM AND CONSUMPTION IN LIBERALIZING ECONOMIES

ANDY BAKER

University of Colorado at Boulder

CAMBRIDGE
UNIVERSITY PRESS

CAMBRIDGE UNIVERSITY PRESS
Cambridge, New York, Melbourne, Madrid, Cape Town, Singapore, São Paulo, Delhi

Cambridge University Press
32 Avenue of the Americas, New York, NY 10013-2473, USA

www.cambridge.org
Information on this title: www.cambridge.org/9780521899680

First published 2009

Printed in the United States of America

A catalog record for this publication is available from the British Library.

Library of Congress Cataloging in Publication Data
Baker, Andy, 1972–
    The market and the masses in Latin America : policy reform and consumption in
    liberalizing economies / Andy Baker.
       p.   cm. – (Cambridge studies in comparative politics)
    Includes bibliographical references and index.
    ISBN 978-0-521-89968-0 (hardback)
    1. Globalization – Latin America – Public opinion.   2. Neoliberalism –
    Latin America – Public opinion.   3. Consumption (Economics) – Latin America.
    4. Public opinion – Latin America.   I. Title.
    HC125.B22 2009
    339.4'7098–dc22   2008030558

ISBN 978-0-521-89968-0 hardback

To Lila

Contents

Figures and Tables

Tables

Acknowledgments

By one measure, I began writing this book from scratch in April 2005. More accurately (and perhaps shamefully), the writing process began more than a decade before that when, during my first semester of graduate school at the University of Wisconsin–Madison, my advisor, Leigh Payne, suggested to me the idea of studying Latin Americans' beliefs about free-market reforms. Though I finished a dissertation on the topic in 2001, I was not at all confident that I had anything new and interesting to say to scholars beyond my dissertation committee. Besides, two of the more exemplary and definitive books in comparative politics were published on that very topic in the few months following my defense (Susan Stokes's *Mandates and Democracy* and Kurt Weyland's *The Politics of Market Reform in Fragile Democracies*). What more did I have to add? My dissertation ended up in a circular file somewhere in Madison. Without even a single useful paragraph to cut and paste from it, I began from scratch again four years later. Much to my relief, the reader holds the final product of this lengthy process in her or his hands.

If I have finally added something, it is due heavily to many individuals who helped me along the way. Needless to say, one accrues many debts while writing two book-length manuscripts over a decade and a half. When I consider the long list of individuals who read and gave me constructive comments on earlier drafts, I am reminded of the wonderful collegiality of my profession and of why I have the best job on the planet . . . save playing shortstop for the Chicago White Sox (which never quite worked out). Four individuals were generous enough to read the entire manuscript: Maureen Donaghy, Wendy Hunter, Kenneth Greene, and Ethan Scheiner. Ken, in particular, read multiple drafts and gave very thorough comments that improved immensely the book's intellectual merit and readability. The following individuals read and commented on individual or multiple chapters: Jason Barabas, Adam Berinsky, Carew Boulding, Ernesto Calvo, Michele Claibourn, Jonathan Graubart, Jennifer Jerit, Robert Kaufman, Daniel Kono, Chappell Lawson, David Leblang, Raúl Madrid, William Mayer, James McCann, Maria Victoria Murillo, Timothy Power, Sybil Rhodes, Joel Rosenthal, Kenneth Scheve, and Kurt Weyland. It is impossible to overestimate the extent to which this final product was improved by their input. I also thank the following individuals for other forms of assistance (everything from data sharing to translations to free baby-sitting to endorsements of me as I searched for publishers): Isabella Alcañiz, Dinah Berland, Phil Bolduc, Kenneth Greene, Robert Huckfeldt, Diana Mutz, Kenneth Roberts, Jonathan Rodden, Guillermo Rosas, Liliana Rosenthal, David Samuels, Ethan Scheiner, Neil Willenson, and Jennifer Wolak.

I am grateful to the David Rockefeller Center for Latin American Studies (Harvard University) for inviting me to present the project and receive feedback. Some paragraphs and figures in Chapters 2, 3, 4, and 7 are heavily revised excerpts from "Why Is Trade Reform So Popular in Latin America? A Consumption-Based Theory of Trade Policy Preferences," *World Politics* 55(3): 423–455.

A number of organizations funded my research at different stages. Diana Mutz and the Institute for the Study of Citizens and Politics at the Annenberg Public Policy Center as well as the Research and Scholarship Development Fund at Northeastern University provided funding for the 2005 wave of the four-city Brazil survey. Also, I am very grateful to Diana for funding an excellent research assistant (Danielle Dougherty). The Social Science Research Council International Dissertation Fellowship funded the 1999 wave of the four-city survey. Small grants from the University of Colorado (Dean's Fund for Excellence) and the University of Houston (New Faculty Research Grant and Small Grants Program) helped with the purchase of survey data and other expenses.

In graduate school, this project was funded by the Social Science Research Council Predissertation Fellowship, the University of Wisconsin Graduate School, the University of Wisconsin Global Studies MacArthur Fellowship, and the Rio Branco Institute in Brazil. I am also grateful for the mentorship provided at the University of Wisconsin by my advisors, Leigh Payne and Charles Franklin. It was not through any lack of guidance that my dissertation never saw the light of day. Finally, the following individuals and institutions provided assistance, friendship, and academic

Acknowledgments

support while I was in the field in Brazil and Mexico: Ulissis Bazílio, Henrique de O. de Castro, Plínio Dentzien, Federico Estévez, Cristiano Ferraz, Ney Figuereido, Rodrigo Giacomet, Alejandro Moreno, Sonia Ranicheski, Antônio Carlos Réa, Lúcia Leme Réa, Paulo Zerbati, Centro de Estudos de Opinião Pública in Campinas, and the Instituto Tecnológico Autónomo de México in Mexico City.

In the end, my family deserves more thanks than anyone. My parents, Robert and Susan Baker, never pressured me to pursue any career other than the one of my choosing, and their financial support is still remembered and appreciated. My wife's parents, Joel and Liliana Rosenthal, have always taken a genuine interest in my research, and they provided crucial assistance on this project. Finally, an author does not devote fifteen years to a book project without frequently calling on the patience and support of his immediate family. I began the second, and more successful, phase of this book project in the foggy weeks surrounding my daughter Della's birth in April 2005. I hope I was a good enough father to make her oblivious to the occasional frustration and stress caused by the writing process. My wife, Lila Rosenthal, made many sacrifices during the writing of this book (e.g., enduring a cross-continental relationship, baby-sitting "Tobin Tax"), and they are not forgotten. A book dedication falls far short in expressing the extent of my love and gratitude, but never has one been more deserved.

The Market and the Masses in Latin America

PART I

Introduction and Theory

1

Consuming the Washington Consensus

> A clear majority in all [Latin American] countries favour a market economy rather than a closed, state-directed one.
> – *The Economist*, in the November 5, 2005, issue (*Economist* 2005a, 11)

> There is disillusion [among Latin Americans] with free-market reforms that are seen as having been sponsored by the United States.
> – *The Economist*, in the same issue (*Economist* 2005b, 41)

On October 27, 2002, Luiz Inácio Lula da Silva became the first candidate from a left-wing party to be elected Brazil's president. Lula's poor, working-class upbringing was also a first for a Brazilian president and made him a rarity in Latin America's political history. His personal victory after three failed attempts and the ascendancy of the Brazilian Workers' Party (PT) to the presidency seemed to many observers the electorate's repudiation of the free-market policies implemented by his predecessor, Fernando Henrique Cardoso (1995 to 2002). Cardoso had initiated and overseen eight years of newfound price stability and expanded consumption, but in the 2002 election the increase in unemployment and deindustrialization that had occurred during his two terms seemed to weigh more heavily on voters' minds. Opponents of the incumbent party received 76% of the presidential vote.

The election in Latin America's largest country of a left-leaning president seemed the high point of a regionwide trend that began during the recessionary "lost half-decade" of 1998 to 2002. During and after these difficult five years, voters in most Latin American countries – Argentina, Bolivia, Brazil, Chile, Ecuador, Guatemala, Nicaragua, Paraguay, Peru, Uruguay, Venezuela – either elected presidents from leftist parties or chose ones that openly criticized the market orthodoxy of the "Washington Consensus." Well into its second decade as the region's development strategy, journalists, scholars, and politicians alike spoke of mass fatigue with the various elements of the market reform package: privatization, trade and capital account liberalization, and fiscal discipline. Market advocates feared that election mandates would translate into policy reversals: a re-nationalization of privatized enterprises, higher protectionist barriers, and fiscal profligacy. Socialists and other opponents of market liberalization felt vindicated in their belief that voters had finally figured out the hazards of "neoliberalism."

This seemingly straightforward interpretation of voters' beliefs about economic reform, however, is simplistic. Consider Lula's election victory. Lula and the PT did emerge on the national scene as committed socialists in the 1980s, with roots in some of the country's most radical labor and social movements. In his first presidential bid in 1989, the party's platform proposed nationalization of the financial sector and suspension of foreign debt payments. By 2002, however, Lula had moderated his views on economic policy, calling himself "Little Peace and Love Lula" (Hunter 2007; Samuels 2004). The PT platform did not contain the word "socialism." Lula promised not to reverse any major privatizations. He criticized developed countries not for trading too much with Brazil but for trading too little. The most well-publicized line from his "Letter to the Brazilian People," released near the start of his campaign, was the commitment to honor standing contracts with foreign creditors. In short, voters did not elect an outspoken antimarket candidate in 2002.

Moreover, after his inauguration, Lula pursued many fiscal and macroeconomic measures that largely matched those of his predecessor. He implemented an austere reform of the state-provided pension system, maintained a tight monetary policy, and sustained a large budgetary surplus. These were all policies that the PT had strictly opposed during the preceding eight years. By the end of his first year, many observers were referring to Lula's administration as "Fernando Henrique's third term." However, rather than feeling betrayed by Lula and the PT's pro-market about-face, Brazilians rewarded him with high presidential approval ratings and eventually a second term.

Lula's steady move to the ideological center thus raises a series of crucial questions about his mandate and mass beliefs about economic reform. Was the victory of a leftist in Brazil a popular mandate for reversing market reform, an "unraveling of the so-called Washington consensus" (Samuelson 2002, A25)? Or was Lula's necessitated moderation a mandate for continuing the extant economic model? In other words, did Brazilians choose a leftist in 2002 because they were experiencing "reform fatigue"? Or did they choose a *former* leftist because of his promises to keep market policies in place? In short, did most voters in Brazil want to see the continuation or reversal of market reforms?

Similar questions surround interpretations of leftist victories and reform reversal elsewhere in the region. Besides the election of left-of-center candidates, privatizations have been blocked or reversed at the behest of demonstrators in numerous countries, including Bolivia (water), Colombia (telecommunications), Costa Rica (electricity and telecommunications), Dominican Republic (electricity), El Salvador (hospitals), Guatemala (water), Mexico (electricity and petrochemicals), and Peru (electricity) (Harris et al. 2003). Few Latin American countries have *not* seen such movements, with some pro-privatization observers bemoaning "mob rule" in countries where protest has been successful in changing policy (*Economist* 2005c). Some reversals have even occurred at the behest of broader public opinion, as evidenced by the results of national referenda in Bolivia and Uruguay that blocked privatizations or foreign investment in their energy sectors.

Despite these events and the oft-touted leftward swing in voters' preferences after 1998, some observers have spoken of an "ideological pruning" (Colburn 2002, 5) and a "diminishing latitude for economic policy choice" (Weyland 2004, 145) because large-scale reform reversal has not appeared to be a viable political option (Domínguez 1998). Successful presidential candidates from a variety of party types and political backgrounds have railed against neoliberalism during their campaigns: from Nicanor Duarte (Paraguay, 2003) to Néstor Kirchner (Argentina, 2003) to Evo Morales (Bolivia, 2005). Outside of Venezuela, however, only limited policy change has occurred in this direction (Castañeda and Navia 2007; Lora and Panizza 2003). Most "reversals" have been mere tweaks, especially when compared to the state-led policies predominating before reform implementation: "The greatest achievement of the right is that it no longer matters who governs. Yesterday's revolutionaries have ended up administering the model that best suits the right" (*Economist* 2005d, 38; see also Castañeda 2006).

As in Brazil, the implications of these conflicting tendencies for election mandates and for mass preferences are fraught with ambivalence. In Chile, the 2000 victory of Socialist President Ricardo Lagos (2001 to 2006) may have been a sign of popular discontent with the incumbent liberal economic policies. His party's reelection to the presidency in 2005, however, may have indicated widespread approval of the free trade agreement he signed with the United States and his unwillingness to reverse the country's market orthodoxy. In Bolivia, the 2005 victory of Morales (2006 to the present) may have represented widespread approval of his platform to nationalize the country's natural gas sector, yet his high approval ratings even as he pushed for enhanced commercial ties with the European Union may have suggested that voters endorsed freer trade. Even in Venezuela, the many electoral affirmations of Hugo Chávez (1999 to the present) may signify the electorate's wholehearted embrace of his fiery socialist and anti-imperialist rhetoric as well as his strict rules on foreign ownership in the petroleum sector. Alternatively, they may represent an endorsement of Venezuela's relative openness to world trade and its growing import volumes from the United States and Europe.

In short, amid the "left wave," leaders have kept most market reforms intact. Does this indicate that voters would consider undesirable a spate of re-nationalizations and increased tariff barriers? Or have voters used their discretion to grant statist mandates to their governments, only to be betrayed not by moderate leaders but by the economic policy straitjackets imposed by international financial institutions, global market competition, and budgetary constraints? Existing answers to these questions are almost completely speculative. It remains extremely unclear what Latin America's citizens actually think of the nearly two-decade-old experiment with market orthodoxy.

Scholarly Dissensus over the Washington Consensus

These ambiguities make it difficult to reach any clear conclusions about the nature of the Left's mandate and the overall reasons for the "left turn." Reading the election-result tea leaves is a highly imperfect science. Voting behavior and the issue preferences of candidates expressed during campaigns are at best ambivalent proxies for the balance of citizen attitudes, so imputing mass beliefs about market reforms using the ideological stance of election victors can be misleading (Armijo and Faucher 2002; Dore 2003; Roberts and Arce 1998; Stokes 2001a).[1] For example, while conventional

[1] For example, elections may not always be contested on the grounds of economic policies, as other issues such as candidates' personalities, democratization, or corruption may dominate. Alternatively, the leftward shift in leadership after 1998 may have been the natural result of anti-incumbent, not antimarket, voting during tough times.

wisdom in the early 2000s interpreted the success of left-of-center parties as a sign of voters' statism, by 2006 some observers claimed that the reelection of these same parties was an electoral affirmation of the market-oriented status quo (Castañeda and Navia 2007).[2] Overall, the election mandates of recent years have provided enough imprecision and leeway for ideological observers to find what they are looking for in citizen sentiment: Socialists see mass outrage at continued market liberalization, while capitalists see diffuse acceptance of a market model.

Imputing mass beliefs from the preferences of small but vocal civil society organizations and protestors can be equally misleading (Forero 2002, 2005; Johnson 2004; Petras 1999; SAPRIN 2004; Walton and Ragin 1990; Wise et al. 2003). Privatizations have often been greeted with protests, and many have turned violent. Arequipa, Caracas, Cochabamba, and San Salvador have been among the sites of violent antiprivatization or antiglobalization protests in recent years, and in 2003 protests in Bolivia even overthrew a president (Gonzalo Sánchez de Lozada). While it is tempting to conclude that these protests represent widespread distaste for market liberalization, they may be misleading measures of the entire electorate's pulse. The impact of economic reforms may feature concentrated costs for relatively small but highly vocal groups and diffuse gains for a silent majority. As a result, relying too heavily on the preferences of protestors may lead scholars and other observers to overpredict opposition to the Washington Consensus.

Moreover, many observers assume that any given citizen holds equivalent opinions about each of the varied policy elements of the Washington Consensus. In other words, attitudes toward potentially different issues, such as privatization, trade liberalization, and pension reform, are presumed to be unidimensional, as exemplified by the conclusion that Latin Americans in the new millennium have expressed a "massive rejection of the International Monetary Fund and the Washington Consensus" (Rohter 2005, A3). These policies, however, were often implemented separately and have each exerted very different effects on citizens' livelihoods. Assuming that citizens evaluate them as a monolithic whole may oversimplify and mislead. Some reforms may be more popular than others.

---

[2] Consider the following interpretation of the region's slate of elections in 2006: ". . . incumbency strength should . . . be considered as an endorsement of the policies implemented by the outgoing leaders – for the most part committed to free trade" (Castañeda and Navia 2007, 52).

Even scholarly accounts that rely on survey or other kinds of data have added to the confusion. After more than a decade of research, a persistent division remains. On one side is the "reform-is-popular" school:

There has . . . been a conversion to free market open economy policies among ordinary people. (Hojman 1994, 210)

Public opinion surveys . . . generally show that a majority of Latin Americans prefer markets and the private enterprise system to government control. (Rodrik 2001, 12)

. . . [T]here is still broad-based support for the market economy in general. (Graham and Sukhtankar 2004, 365)

Latin Americans show few signs of being eager to abandon the market economy. (Shifter and Jawahar 2005, 52)

Many Latin American voters – in some cases solid majorities – continue to support neoliberal economic policies. (Castañeda and Navia 2007, 53)

On the other side is the "reform-is-unpopular" school:

. . . [O]rdinary citizens and social movements were taking fervent issue with free-market dogma and its inequitable outcomes. (Smith 2000, 345)

Across the region only [a small minority] of the people believe that the state should leave economic activity to the private sector. (Mahon 2003, 61)

In general, Latin American public opinion on the reforms has not been favorable. (IDB 2004, 137)

If neoliberal policies are not causally responsible for Latin America's economic problems, the political fact remains that they have become associated with them in the popular mind. (Kurtz 2004, 287)

A large political backlash to privatization has been brewing for some time, and public opinion and policymakers in Latin America . . . have now turned against privatization. (Chong and López-de-Silanes 2005, 57)

Ambivalence also abounds over the contours of group-level differences in opinion, especially regarding the extent to which the poor are disproportionately harmed by, and thus are the group most vehemently opposed to, market reforms. The prevailing opinion is that wealth is the most important correlate of attitudes: The poor are less pro-market than the rich (Castañeda 2006; SAPRIN 2004). Many observers have greeted the victories of left-leaning candidates as a political triumph for the poor and their demands to overturn exploitative market policies. However, most left-of-center presidents were elected by broad cross-class coalitions (Dix 1989;

Roberts 2002). In fact, several reform-implementing presidents were elected and reelected with disproportionately high support from the poor (Roberts and Arce 1998; Singer 1990). Moreover, well-heeled rent-seeking groups, such as public-sector workers and subsidized business owners, were often the main beneficiaries of state intervention, not the poor (Weyland 1996).

Scholarly findings on wealth and economic attitudes are highly contradictory. The prevailing opinion has some empirical support:

... [P]rivate ownership was supported by 77 per cent of the upper class, but by only 49 per cent of the lower class. (Turner and Elordi 1995, 484)

... [S]upport for pro-market positions declined monotonically with social class. (Stokes 2001a, 148)

Not surprisingly, wealth levels ... had positive and significant effects on pro-market attitudes. (Graham and Pettinato 2002, 85)

Yet, the countervailing claim also has adherents:

[Neoliberalism] appeals to unorganized, largely poor people in the informal sector. ... Better off groups offer the most powerful resistance to neoliberal reforms. (Weyland 1996, 10, 13)

In much of Latin America, the lower classes have given their electoral consent ... to neoliberal projects. (Roberts and Arce 1998, 218)

... [T]he staunchest foes of privatization tend to be found among the middle class. (Lora and Panizza 2003, 124)

Educated people are ... less likely to be satisfied with how the market is working. ... Wealth is *negatively* correlated with favouring lower taxes, as are years of education. (Graham and Sukhtankar 2004, 264, 367)

Needless to say, the confusion over *whether* Latin Americans are neoliberals – that is, whether market reforms are largely popular or unpopular throughout the region – and *which* Latin Americans are neoliberals – that is, how wealth and other individual-level characteristics relate to mass beliefs about market reforms – has muddled the picture about *why* Latin Americans think the way they do about the Washington Consensus. Labor markets have tightened in the new market era, so scholars who think reforms are unpopular presume that citizens evaluate them by considering their impact on job opportunities and wages: "Undoubtedly, the widely held perception that the reforms were detrimental to workers is behind the opposition of the public to the so-called neoliberal agenda" (Lora et al. 2004, 14). In contrast, the market-friendly era has also been one of relatively low inflation, so scholars who believe that markets are popular often presume that citizens evaluate them by thinking more about their consequences for consumers: ". . . [T]he biggest reason for popular support of reformist politicians . . . is that market reforms have ended inflation" (Armijo and Faucher 2002, 29; see also Gervasoni 1995). Still others claim that concrete economic consequences matter less than the long-standing political biases that color citizens' perceptions of economics or the rhetorical efforts of elites to shape these mass beliefs (Kaufman and Zuckermann 1998; Przeworski 1991; Stokes 2001b).

Summary of Theory and Findings

Descriptive Findings

This book moves beyond these vague and contested impressions of public opinion in Latin America by taking a microscope to citizens' beliefs about the policies that have transformed their economies in recent decades. To provide a more empirically sound basis for understanding Latin Americans' attitudes, I analyze cross-national surveys administered in eighteen nations between 1990 and 2007 and conduct an in-depth case study of Brazil. A central task of the book is thus descriptive: I set the record straight on two seemingly straightforward but to date poorly answered sets of questions.

First, what is the balance of aggregate opinion about various elements of the market-oriented development strategy? In other words, are Latin Americans neoliberals? Or, more precisely, *how many* Latin Americans are neoliberals? This question remains a hotly debated topic, typically because so little public opinion data are consulted when answering it. Even when such data are used, inappropriately worded questions and a failure to recognize that Latin Americans do not evaluate all policy elements of the Washington Consensus as a unidimensional set have led to confusing and contradictory findings.

Figure 1.1 provides a preliminary answer to the "how many" question by demonstrating that most Latin Americans are enthusiastic about globalization and unenthusiastic about privatization. The figure reports some exemplary results from the cross-national survey datasets used throughout this book. The four diamonds in the figure (ignoring momentarily the curved horizontal lines) represent the percentage of respondents in eighteen Latin American countries that supported each of four different market policies (measured between 1996 and 2001). From left to right, they are trade liberalization, enticements to foreign investors, privatization in general, and the privatization of pensions. (Question wordings for these and all other survey items are reported in the Survey Data Appendix at the end of the book. All survey questions are given italicized variable names that can be used to locate their wordings in the Appendix.) The two leftmost diamonds are much higher than the two rightmost diamonds, an indication of the first central finding: Majorities supported free trade and foreign investment, while far fewer citizens supported privatization in general and pension privatization. In other words, a "popularity gap" existed between globalization and privatization. Moreover, this implies that a certain degree of "unpacking" took place when citizens evaluated

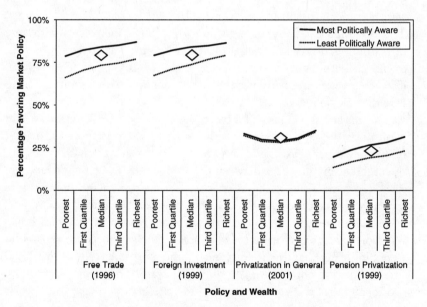

Figure 1.1 Support for Four Market Reforms in Eighteen Latin American Countries by Wealth and Political Awareness, 1996–2001.
Note: Lines are predicted values from four different ordered probit regressions with the following dependent variables: *Free trade helps country* (LB) in 1996, *Foreign investment should be encouraged* (LB) in 1999, *Privatization is good for country* (LB) in 2001, and *Privatization by sectors: Pensions* (LB) in 1999. Diamonds represent the simple observed percentages. "Poorest" are the 5th percentile of wealth, and "Richest" are the 95th percentile.
Source: LB.

various market reforms. Latin Americans did not evaluate the market reform package as a monolithic whole but rather discriminated among its various elements, supporting some more than others.

Second, which groups or types of individuals in Latin America are enthusiastic about market reforms and which are not? In other words, *which* Latin Americans are neoliberals? Figure 1.1 portrays some of the book's main claims regarding this question: (1) the rich were only slightly more supportive of market policies than the poor, and (2) elites forged important group-level divergences in beliefs about the Washington Consensus. The lines (ignoring now the diamonds) show the percentage of Latin Americans supporting each policy at five different levels of wealth. For each policy, wealth is arrayed from the poorest respondents (the leftmost or starting point of each line) to the richest ones (the rightmost or ending point of each line). Sharp upward slopes to these lines would indicate that the wealthiest were far more favorable toward a particular market policy than the poorest. The two different lines for each policy represent individuals with very high (solid) and very low (dotted) levels of "political awareness" – that is, attentiveness to the discourse of political elites.[3] At any point, the vertical distance between the two lines thus represents the impact of attention to elite rhetoric on market beliefs.

The upward-sloping lines for three of the four policies demonstrate that wealth was typically associated with higher levels of support for market reforms. In other words, the rich were more pro-market than the poor, yet the difference in attitudes between the two groups was only moderate in size. The rich were typically only about ten percentage points more favorable toward reforms than the very poor, and no such "wealth gap" existed at all in attitudes toward privatization. Moreover, the wealth gap was typically matched or exceeded in size by the gaps between those who were highly exposed to elite discourse – the most politically aware – and those who were not – the least politically aware. The former were more pro-market than the latter. In other words, the "awareness gap" was just as

[3] The lines represent predicted percentages from four different ordered probit models (one for each policy). The dependent variable in each model is support for the market policy. The independent variables are income, income squared, and political awareness (measured with the respondent's performance in a short "quiz" of objective political facts). I report these predicted percentages instead of the raw observed percentages merely to aid visual interpretation: The predicted values smooth over some irregularities, or departures from the overall pattern, that exist because some groups are represented by a small sample size. More sophisticated and fully specified model results are the subject of Chapter 5.

large as the wealth gap. In the 1990s, elite discourse was just as important as wealth in forging group-level divergences in beliefs about the Washington Consensus. However, elites' ability to do so, according to the privatization results, had disappeared by 2001.

The most striking overall conclusion from these two sets of descriptive findings is that *the best predictor of support for the Washington Consensus is not wealth but the policy being evaluated.* The poor generally agree with the rich that globalization has been a positive change and that privatization has been a negative one. Thus, the key to understanding mass responses to the market in Latin America is to start from the fact that there is far greater variation in beliefs across different issues than there is across groups on the same issue.

Theoretical Argument

These descriptive findings are important, but the primary goal of this book is to derive a theoretical explanation for them. They present numerous theoretical puzzles. Why is globalization so popular, especially when economic studies generally find that it has been detrimental to job availability? Why is privatization so unpopular, especially considering the widely accepted scholarly claim that it has had a negligible net impact on labor markets? Why are poor, low-wage laborers only slightly less enthusiastic about globalization than wealthy and highly educated ones, despite the fact that freer trade and more foreign investment have increased the disparity in wages between skilled and unskilled workers? Finally, what explains the gap in attitudes between less and more politically aware citizens? This book provides answers to these questions by reconsidering theories about politics and public opinion in Latin America in two crucial ways.

First, it recalibrates the widely used "bottom-up" public opinion approach, which holds that citizens have autonomous and economically self-interested preferences about economic policy. I develop a new bottom-up approach that reorients theory away from commonly considered producer- and labor-market-oriented interests, instead pointing scholarship toward consumer-oriented interests. I claim that citizens' interests as consumers, not as workers or producers, now drive their beliefs about economic policy because the impacts of market policies on consumption interests have been far more visible in everyday lives than their consequences for labor markets.

As a result, consumer, and not labor-market, interests explain why some policies are more popular than others and why some groups are more supportive of reforms than others. On the one hand, Latin Americans support globalization because it has led to a wider availability of less expensive but higher-quality goods. Moreover, the rich have benefited from this "consumer revolution" more than the poor because the former have been more likely than the latter to consume the types of goods and services that have undergone the greatest cost and quality improvements. These wealth-related differences in consumption patterns, however, are actually relatively small. As a result, the discrepancy in attitudes between rich and poor is also small. On the other hand, privatization is unpopular because it has raised prices for crucial utility services, such as potable water, electricity, and telecommunications. These price hikes have been a heavier burden on middle-income consumers than on the poor or the rich because of wealth-related differences in consumption patterns. Again, however, citizens across wealth levels are largely united in opposition to them. (See Figure 1.1.)

Second, this book finds a role for widely ignored "top-down" influences on public opinion. The mass politics of reform is not exclusively about the economics of consumption. It is also about elites' sometimes-successful efforts to shape public opinion. Upon implementation, politicians had to rhetorically "sell" market reforms to electorates who had grown accustomed to decades of state-led development. By the mid-1990s, such persuasive rhetoric flowed from a political elite that had reached a consensus in favor of market policies, so the balance of elite rhetoric throughout Latin America was favorable toward the Washington Consensus. This exerted a "hegemony effect" on mass attitudes (Gramsci 1971): Citizens who were highly aware of elite discourse were more likely to share these pro-market opinions than citizens who consumed little elite discourse. By the late 1990s, however, this elite consensus had broken down. Many left-leaning parties, movements, and candidates levied sharp criticisms against the new economic orthodoxy. The revitalization of the Left meant that elites grew more polarized as some market reforms became issues of intense partisan contestation. As a result, high levels of political awareness no longer meant greater exposure to pro-market discourse by 2001. (See Figure 1.1.) Instead, partisan divisions among elites led to partisan divisions among citizens who had enough political cognition and awareness to hear and accept the relevant arguments made by elites from their preferred political camp.

Implications

This book thus claims that citizens are "consuming the Washington Consensus" on two fronts. Most importantly, reforms have produced material consequences for consumers' welfare by visibly shifting the affordability, availability, and quality of many goods and services, and these effects have been much more evident to citizens than the effects of reforms on wages and employment opportunities. In this sense, citizens consume the economic effects of reforms, and they do so in ways that strongly influence their evaluation of market policies. But citizens are also political beings, selectively listening to the persuasive efforts of political elites and doing so with predispositions about their credibility and merit. In this sense, citizens also consume elite rhetoric, and they do so in ways that reflect the overall balance of elite discourse about market reforms.

These findings carry some crucial implications for Latin American politics. First, consumer interests unify citizens with contrasting wealth levels more than they divide them. Labor-market assets and interests differ far more markedly across individuals, and especially across income levels and classes, than consumer interests do: All social classes are largely unified in their preferences for lower prices on goods and services. As a result, the rise of consumer interests and their predominant role in shaping opinions has contributed to the disappearance of wealth- and class-based cleavages in the region's politics. While industrialization forged highly politicized class identities in the era of state-led development, market liberalism and the rise of consumerism, or *consumismo*, have eroded them. Second, *consumismo* has both empowered and constrained the region's new Left. While mass outrage over postprivatization price increases has certainly contributed to the rise of the Left, the new leftist leadership is constrained in its ability to resurrect protectionist barriers against imports and foreign investors because such measures would stoke inflationary pressures. In short, the average voter's obsession with prices in Latin America has created the left turn, but it has also constrained the Left from pursuing unfettered statism in all policy realms while in power. Finally, politicians' rhetorical appeals matter, but only in a limited way. Elites can shape mass cleavages by dictating the extent to which citizens' attitudes divide along partisan or informational lines. The overall volume and balance of their rhetoric, however, play only a minor role in influencing the aggregate level of popularity for market reforms. The objective economic consequences of reforms matter more for their mass popularity than elites' rhetoric about them.

Scope and Outline of the Book

The primary goal of this book is to describe and explain Latin American citizens' specific support for the market policies that have either been implemented or been seriously considered, and thus widely debated, by the region's political leadership in recent decades (Easton 1965). It thus analyzes public opinion toward the kinds of policies that, since the 1980s, have had the most important economic consequences – by visibly affecting citizen welfare – and political consequences – by providing heated fodder for elite debate, partisan division, and candidate contestation. In particular, I focus on the set of "first-generation" Washington Consensus reforms. This has three central pillars: (1) *privatization*: the transfer of state-owned enterprises (SOEs) to private actors; (2) *globalizing policies*: measures such as trade and capital account liberalization that increase foreigners' access to various aspects of the domestic economy; and (3) *fiscal reform*: welfare state and tax reforms designed to improve the state's financial health (Naím 1994; Navia and Velasco 2003).

Under the first pillar, broadly described as "privatization," I consider attitudes toward (1) privatization in general, (2) privatization of utility sectors, (3) privatization of natural resource sectors, and (4) privatization of various service sectors. I broadly define the second pillar as "globalizing policies" or, for ease of exposition, "globalization." I consider beliefs about (1) free trade in general; (2) the various South–South regional trade pacts, such as Mercosul (Southern Cone Common Market), the Andean Pact, and the Central American Common Market (CACM);[4] (3) the potential Free

---

[4] Are these regional trade agreements (RTAs) part of the market liberalization package? There is a general consensus among economists (the scholarly group most inclined to skepticism of RTAs) that the answer to this question is "yes"; Latin America's trade pacts are wholly compatible with and actually expand free trade and other market policies. First, Latin America's "new regionalism" contrasts markedly with the "old regionalism" of the import-substitution era, in which lower intra-RTA barriers were coupled with higher barriers to extra-RTA trade partners (Bulmer-Thomas 1994). New regional trade pacts have worked in tandem with lower barriers to imports from all countries. Indeed, extra-RTA partners must lower their prices on exports to Latin American countries in order to compete with intra-RTA trade (Chang and Winters 2002). Second, regional trade pacts have locked in and reinforced other market-friendly trends and reforms. For example, regional trade pacts have encouraged inward foreign investment, and their relative depth and permanence have signaled the region's commitment to trade liberalization (Blomstrom and Kokko 1997). Finally and most simply, regional pacts have increased trade volumes in Latin America (IDB 2002a). Some scholars express concerns that detrimental "trade diversion" effects – the substitution of exchange with inefficient intra-RTA partners for

Trade Agreement of the Americas (FTAA); and (4) foreign investment. Finally, although I do on occasion describe citizens' general beliefs about the welfare state, I focus on pension reform as the most pertinent case of the fiscal reform pillar. Reform and privatization of retirement pension systems represent the only widespread example of fiscal retrenchment in the social area (Kaufman and Segura-Ubiergo 2001). Despite many portrayals to the contrary, state spending on education, health care, and even targeted antipoverty programs has actually increased since 1990 in Latin America, a regional trend that is wholly consistent with the original prescriptions of the Washington Consensus (see the list in Williamson 1990; see also Avelino et al. 2005 and Birdsall et al. 2001). Because of this, I focus only on pension reform attitudes.

The following chapter (Chapter 2) builds the theoretical infrastructure for the book. It reorients the standard bottom-up approaches to public opinion formation in the Latin Americanist literature by stressing the role of consumption-based interests over producer-oriented ones. It also describes a framework for understanding elite-based, top-down influences on public opinion. Chapter 2 also establishes the need to analyze market reforms in a disaggregated manner – that is, to focus on individual policies and individual-level differences in beliefs rather than on the macro-level popularity of entire reform packages.

Part II of the book contains three chapters that describe and explain regionwide public opinion patterns using cross-national opinion polls. Chapter 3 sets the context for the analysis of public opinion data by describing the two primary independent variables: the economic consequences of reforms (the key bottom-up variable) and the contours of elite opinion on market reforms (top-down). Chapter 4 examines questions of aggregate support for individual policies, establishing the basic descriptive facts regarding patterns and trends in the popularity of the various reforms and applying the consumption-based theory to explain differences in average beliefs across policies, countries, and time. Chapter 5 explains differences in beliefs across individuals, focusing especially on the role of wealth and how it relates to consumer interests and differences in receptivity to elite rhetoric.

---

exchange with efficient extra-RTA partners – outrun beneficial "trade-creating" effects (Kono 2007; Yeats 1998). Most evidence, however, suggests that the new regionalism in Latin America does not suffer from this problem (IDB 2002a). Moreover, even if trade diversion does occur, it is still globalization because it entails exchange with foreigners instead of compatriots.

The cross-national survey data used in Part II provide unparalleled measures of overall regional beliefs, but they sacrifice depth and at times measurement precision for geographical breadth. To allay some of these concerns and to provide new findings on public opinion in the region's largest country, Part III is a single-country case study of Brazil. Chapters 6, 7, and 8 are collectively organized to parallel the three chapters in Part II. Chapter 6 sets the main independent variables by presenting an historical overview of Brazil's reform process, describing the economic consequences of market liberalization as well as the balance of elite efforts to rhetorically sell or sink the new policies. Chapter 7 addresses the aggregate question for the Brazilian case, reporting the proportion of Brazilians that support each policy and analyzing how survey respondents justify their beliefs about different market policies. Chapter 8 explains variation in beliefs across different types of Brazilians, focusing again on wealth and the role of elite opinion leadership.

The arguments and findings made throughout this book have implications that help scholars understand Latin America's new social and political cleavages as well as the recent electoral success of the Left. I summarize these interpretations in a concluding chapter in Part IV.

2

Theoretical Framework

THE TOP-DOWN AND BOTTOM-UP SOURCES OF PUBLIC OPINION

Who knew shopping would turn out to be so important?
– Charles Fishman in *The Wal-Mart Effect* (Fishman 2006)

... [T]he rupture between producer and consumer has become nearly complete.
– Arnold J. Bauer in *Goods, Power, History* (Bauer 2001, 7)

What explains Latin Americans' beliefs about market liberalization? The extraordinary economic policy changes that have occurred since the early 1980s have been drastic enough to have exerted noticeable material impacts on citizens' everyday lives. Among other changes, jobs have disappeared, prices have changed, new transfer-payment programs have been created, and state-funded benefits have been taken away. Because the consequences of economic policies have so obviously "hit people over the head," I claim that citizens have formulated policy beliefs partially out of economic self-interest. Amid these turbulent and obvious economic shifts, however, politicking has persisted. Politicians have continued to sell themselves and their preferred policies, making promises and other rhetorical attempts to sway voters' opinions about the new market economics. Moreover, many citizens have clung to long-standing political affinities that bias their perceptions of elite discourse and objective economic consequences. In other words, political predispositions *and* politicians' rhetoric have colored voters' self-interested calculus of the region's drastic economic policy transformation.

This chapter develops a theoretical framework that incorporates elements of both economic self-interest, the basis of bottom-up influences on public opinion, and elite persuasion, also referred to as top-down influences. First, I argue that scholars of Latin America have miscast the nature of citizens' self-interest. I reorient what has been a nearly exclusive focus on citizens-as-producers to a theory of citizens-as-consumers. Most encounters that Latin Americans have had with market reforms and their impact have occurred as they have gone about the everyday activity of being consumers. The most visible effects of market reforms have been on the affordability, availability, and quality of many goods and services. As a result, citizens have evaluated the various elements of the Washington Consensus more by assessing each policy's influence on consumer options than by considering its influence on labor-market opportunities or overall personal welfare. Second, I argue that scholars of Latin American politics have underestimated the impact that politicians have had on mass opinion. Elites have shaped citizens' perceptions with persuasive rhetorical appeals, although these top-down influences have occurred only among citizens who have been exposed and receptive to certain politicians' pronouncements.

In the end, I argue that the material interests of citizens-as-consumers can account for differences in mass beliefs across individuals and policies, two sources of variation that scholars have either ignored or explained in unsatisfactory ways. At the same time, citizens' exposure to and acceptance of elite rhetoric can explain additional attitudinal differences across individuals who have otherwise identical consumer interests.

This chapter establishes the need for this new framework by first describing shortcomings in existing research. The first section discusses the absence of consumer-oriented and top-down understandings of Latin American public opinion in older scholarship, which existed before survey data were widely available. The second section describes the unsatisfactory treatment of these two theoretical avenues in recent studies that have employed survey research, examining in particular their tendency to treat public opinion in an overly aggregated manner. The remaining three sections describe the strategies used in this book to assess bottom-up and top-down influences.

In Search of Consumers and Elites: Latin American Public Opinion Before Surveys

Until the 1990s, scholarship on mass attitudes toward economic policies in Latin America was strictly wedded to bottom-up, producer-oriented notions of individuals' interests and beliefs. In this section, I describe scholarly conceptions of mass economic issue beliefs prior to the widespread adoption of survey research in the 1990s. In doing so, I demonstrate the need to introduce consumption-based interests and elite-led, top-down influences into scholarship on Latin American politics.

Do Citizens Think as Producers or as Consumers?

Economically active individuals engage in economic exchange both as producers and as consumers. As producers, workers apply their employable assets in the labor market to earn wages and investors deploy capital in search of profits. These economic returns from production are then used to acquire goods and services that have certain costs.

This oversimplified statement about the fundamental nature of economic activity in nonsubsistence economies nonetheless highlights the basic fact that individual well-being is based on *real* economic returns: the ratio of returns to prices. The prices one must pay dictate well-being as much as one's nominal wages or profit rates. Economic interests are set by a combination of production- and consumption-oriented concerns.

Despite this economic truism, scholarship on Latin American politics has privileged the producer side of this equation when making assumptions about mass preferences over economic policies. The spate of scholarly approaches that predominated from the 1950s through the 1980s all featured this bias. Marxist and neo-Marxist perspectives emphasized ownership of the means of production (Cardoso and Faletto 1979; Waisman 1982; Wallerstein 1976), structuralist perspectives stressed workers' and investors' economic roles and interests (Collier 1979; Evans 1979; O'Donnell 1973; Prebisch 1950), and the study of corporatism focused on the political organization of groups that were defined by occupational functions (Collier and Collier 1991; Malloy 1977; Stepan 1978). These approaches fixed scholars to the assumption that actors' self-interested assessments of economic policy rested largely on the characteristics of their employment or income source and not on the prices, quality, and affordability of the goods and services they bought or wished to buy. Characteristics of workers' sector of employment (e.g., urban or rural, export-oriented or domestically oriented, public- or private-sector) dictated their economic policy interests. Aspects of capitalists' and landowners' investments and assets determined their interests. While consumer interests were implicit in these studies, lingering under the surface merely because actors produced in order to consume, they were rarely analyzed explicitly as independent sources of economic policy preferences.[1]

---

[1] Moreover, during this era, a persistent "export-centered" approach characterized many studies of Latin American economic history. Historians categorized the region's trade policy history, its various economic eras, and its class politics by export and production

This propensity to overlook consumer-oriented concerns in mass policy preferences was not without reason. During the corporatist era, Latin America's most important interest groups were employer and worker associations that were organized by economic sector. Governments even granted many welfare-state benefits and often set wages according to occupational status (Mesa-Lago 1978). Corporatist structures themselves thus politicized production and not consumption.

Moreover, before the 1990s, the lack of survey data from Latin America forced scholars to perform a "drunkard's search" by looking for mass preferences where they were most readily revealed: instances of overt political mobilization and organization. This inclination focused scholars' attention on the obvious production-based groups around which political mobilization occurred rather than on the latent consumption-based preferences that for two reasons largely failed to instigate political action.

First, consumer interests unify citizens' preferences across classes and wealth levels more than they divide them. Citizens in all income groups prefer lower and more stable prices to higher and less stable ones, whereas demands for higher wages create divisions between capital and labor and between all consumers and the workers making such demands. Furthermore, differences in consumption patterns across economic groups are smaller than differences in labor-market criteria, such as skills and geographical location. For example, recent research demonstrates that shifts in wage inequality translate into much smaller changes in consumption inequality: ". . . [A]n increase in the volatility of income . . . *always* leads to a *smaller* increase in consumption inequality" (Krueger and Perri 2006, 164). The wealthy devote their extra income to savings, which does not influence present consumption, or to goods (such as large televisions, luxury automobiles, and gourmet food) that differ from those consumed by the poor merely in terms of quality.[2] Second, the costs and benefits of an economic policy are often diffusely spread across all consumers but concentrated

patterns and *not* by consumer preferences for certain imported goods (Bulmer-Thomas 1994; Estevadeordal et al. 2004; Rogowski 1989). "By emphasizing production over consumption and by stressing industrial capitalism as a key dynamic force in world history, many writers have directed attention toward the exports of raw materials from Latin America and away from the imports of goods into Latin America. . . . Some tendencies within the social sciences and history have contributed to making imports a long-known but little-examined topic within Latin American studies" (Orlove and Bauer 1997, 1).

[2] These claims about the relative homogeneity of consumer vis-à-vis labor-market interests are wholly consistent with the well-known "magnification effect" from international trade theory: The impact of a change in a good's consumer price on the wages of workers who

among small and (as a result) well-organized producer groups (Haggard and Kaufman 1995; Olson 1982). In the end, the scholarly inclination before the 1990s to focus on highly organized producer groups meant that most conclusions about public opinion in Latin America were determined by the preferences of small groups experiencing concentrated costs or gains.

The first central claim of this book is that consumption-based interests and concerns have been the primary shapers of public opinion toward market reforms in Latin America. I present survey data that demonstrate the primacy of consumption and consumer interests in Latin America's new market-oriented era. Although the consumer-oriented gains and costs of market policies have been diffuse (i.e., thinly spread over a large number of people), citizens have noticed them more readily than they have observed the labor-market consequences of economic reform, making producer and particularly labor-market concerns of secondary importance.

Do Politicians Influence Mass Beliefs?

Both the consumer- and producer-oriented explanations are examples of bottom-up approaches to mass opinion formation. In bottom-up approaches, citizens' opinions about economic issues are responses to relevant economic information that is *not biased by political elites*. In other words, bottom-up opinion formation occurs when individuals develop conclusions through an assessment of economic information that is largely accurate – because it is gathered through personal experience or politically balanced media outlets and conversation partners – and not replete with bias implanted by partisan and politically minded elites.

In contrast, top-down approaches identify political elites and their rhetorical attempts to persuade mass publics as the central agents of public opinion formation (Berinsky 2007; Brody 1991; Zaller 1992). In other words, this view holds that citizens learn about economic events, proposals, and policies by listening to political elites and other sources that have a partisan bias. Rather than reflecting on and responding to more objective sources of economic information gathered through direct observation in their personal lives or from balanced mass media outlets, citizens follow cues from elites about what to believe. According to top-down models,

produce that good exceeds the magnitude of the original price change (Stolper and Samuelson 1941).

23

citizens typically defer to leaders from the parties or political camps with which they sympathize (Sniderman et al. 1991).

Top-down models of mass preference formation have been prevalent in some areas of scholarship on Latin America, such as the study of racism (Marx 1998), national identity (Anderson 1983), partisan and charismatic bonds (Madsen and Snow 1991), working-class consciousness (Cornelius 1973), and regime support (Cohen 1989). Oddly, however, scholarship on mass preferences toward economic policy has held exclusively to a bottom-up conception of public opinion formation.[3] In most models, political elites take citizens' economic policy preferences as a given and seek not to shape interests but to mobilize certain groups by appealing to their interests (Collier and Collier 1991; Waisman 1982). In other words, the political class attempts to persuade groups to participate and organize but not to think differently about their interests vis-à-vis economic policy. This bottom-up bias was certainly evident in structuralist and Marxist approaches, but the new leading paradigm in scholarship on Latin American politics, "new institutionalism," also betrays it. In this school of thought, political institutions, and in particular political parties, do not shape economic policy preferences. They merely aggregate, channel, and adjudicate among them (Mainwaring and Scully 1995). The following quote from a leading institutionalist study of economic liberalization exemplifies this sentiment: "We do not make the strong claim that institutions affect the underlying preferences of social actors, but they do affect their strategies and capabilities" (Haggard and Kaufman 1995, 370).

This exclusive focus on bottom-up modes of mass preference formation misses much about the reform process and about Latin American politics more broadly. Most importantly, it divorces citizens from their political environments and their political affinities. Political elites are constantly engaged in argumentation to persuade citizens about the relative merits of policies they have proposed, implemented, blocked, or opposed. Such attempts are *heightened* in eras of stark economic transformation because major policy initiatives force elites into rhetorical battles that have much higher stakes than those occurring in less transformative times. Moreover, citizens view such argumentation through politically biased lenses. Mass-level symbolic or ideational predispositions, such as partisanship or ideology, color citizens' perceptions of elite discourse and incline them to trust the rhetoric of some elites more than others (Zaller 1992). In short, it

---

[3] See Geddes and Zaller (1989) for one exception.

would be surprising if elite influence were wholly absent from mass economic policy preferences.

The second central claim of this book is that elites in Latin America have shaped mass responses to the market in important ways. Elites' persuasive appeals to the masses have frequently fallen on attentive and receptive ears, but only among certain individuals at certain times: Citizens' varying political predispositions and degrees of *political awareness* – that is, the extent to which they are exposed to and cognizant of elite discourse – have conditioned their propensities to accept pro-market rhetoric. As a result, elites have influenced the shape of mass cleavages over market reforms, and these cleavages have adhered to mass-level differences in political predispositions and political awareness.

Aggregation Problems: Shortcomings in Survey-Based Studies

Consumer orientations and top-down effects have not been absent from all scholarship on Latin American public opinion. The advent of survey research in the region has enabled scholars in recent years to explore potentially more concealed causes of mass beliefs, such as the consumer interests that may not inspire political action and the deeply subjective partisan lenses through which citizens view the economic world. However, despite the newfound ability to investigate consumption- and elite-based sources of mass opinions, survey-based studies still cling to producer-oriented and bottom-up biases.

First, they emphasize the labor-market rather than the consumption side of beliefs toward market reforms (Graham and Pettinato 2002; Graham and Sukhtankar 2004; IDB 2004; Kaufman and Zuckermann 1998; Seligson 1999).[4] Various scholars speculate that the allegedly weak support for reforms in the region is due to their impact on labor markets (Bucndia 2001; IDB 2004; Lora et al. 2004). Qualitative analyses of attitudes toward reforms among the poor in Latin America also share a labor-market bias (Narayan-Parker and Petesch 2002; SAPRIN 2004). Beyond the region as well, general research on mass support for market policies emphasizes employable assets and other labor-market variables over consumption behavior (Gabel 1998; Hiscox 2002; Mayda and Rodrik 2005;

---

[4] Many recent comprehensive analyses of the Washington Consensus and its economic consequences are also silent about consumer-channel effects (Berry 1998; Bulmer-Thomas 1996; IDB 1997, 2004; Stallings and Peres 2000).

Rogowski 1989; Scheve and Slaughter 2001, 2004). For example, one assumption in models of trade policy preferences is that while trade liberalization initially shifts the relative prices of goods and services that foreign and domestic consumers encounter, its most serious impact occurs once the resulting changes in consumer behavior cause a reshuffling of demand for particular types of employable assets.

Second, most of the public opinion studies overlook top-down influences, stressing the relationship between objective macroeconomic indicators and shifts in aggregate opinion toward market reform packages (Stokes 2001a, 2001b; Weyland 1998a, 2002). In other words, citizens, as described in this new literature, are oriented toward concrete economic events and trends, adjusting their opinions toward free-market policies as their nation's and their own well-being shift. With but a few exceptions, elites are effectively silent in these studies, powerless to convince the electorate to see things their way. Ruling elites who fail to deliver material well-being know this all too well, as they typically pay with their jobs (Remmer 1991).

Admittedly, some recent studies of public opinion data do consider certain aspects of the long-overlooked consumption-based and top-down influences. For example, a few studies find that consumer price inflation and, in particular, hyperinflationary crises have had significant effects on the *aggregate* popularity of market reform packages or structural adjustment plans. Latin American citizens greeted the initial broad-based structural adjustment and stabilization plans of the late 1980s and early 1990s with an unexpected enthusiasm that seemed to contradict the new policies' immediate economic costs. Market reform packages were popular at the national level when the old heterodox policies failed to stem the hyperinflationary spirals of the 1980s and early 1990s and when leaders implemented them in response to these economic crises (Weyland 1998a, 2002). They were also popular when they precipitated the end of hyperinflationary crises (Gervasoni 1995; Roberts and Arce 1998; Stokes 2001b). Thereafter, aggregate support for market policies grew when inflation fell and fell when inflation grew in a familiar "retrospective voting" pattern that indicated that citizens were using past macroeconomic performance to evaluate incumbent policies (Fiorina 1981; Stokes 2001b; Weyland 2000, 2002). In short, to some scholars, inflation, and thus consumer concerns, were the key determinants of national-level support for reform packages.

Some studies in this new literature also allude to potential top-down influences. For example, a few find evidence of "intertemporal" posturing toward market reforms by Latin American citizens. Soon after reform implementation, many citizens believed that economic downturn actually signaled better times ahead, based on the presumption that a market-induced austerity was superior in the long run to the statist status quo (Przeworski 1991, 1993; Stokes 2001b). According to some scholars, this willingness to accept intertemporal trade-offs may have occurred at the behest of reforming elites. For instance, Argentine President Carlos Menem (1989 to 1999) repeatedly employed intertemporal language, invoking "no-pain, no-gain" rhetoric by referring to his drastic reform program of June 1989 as "surgery without anesthesia" (Echegaray and Elordi 2001). Other scholars hint at possible top-down influences by showing a correlation between citizens' partisanship and their beliefs about market reforms (Kaufman and Zuckermann 1998; Luna and Zechmeister 2005; Magaloni and Romero 2008).

However, these studies of consumption-based and top-down influences are unsatisfying because they suffer from two types of "aggregation problems." First, they fail to "unpack" reform because they aggregate beliefs about a variety of different market policies into single indicators of overall support. Second, they focus on explaining the aggregate popularity of reforms at the national level, frequently ignoring cross-individual variation in beliefs about reforms or, at best, providing a weak theoretical grounding for understanding whether and why attitudes are stratified by important individual-level factors such as wealth, political awareness, and partisanship. In the following two subsections, I describe each of these problems in turn.

Unpacking Reform

Because the different elements of market-reform packages yield cross-cutting effects on national and, especially, individual welfare, citizens in Latin America surely unpack the new set of reforms, appreciating some free-market policies while being suspicious of others. The Washington Consensus is not a single policy but rather a list of different market-oriented measures. Privatization, trade liberalization, fiscal prudence, and other market-friendly policies can work at cross-purposes with one another: "Market-oriented reform involves a multi-dimensional and, potentially, not fully coherent process of policy change" (Remmer 1998, 7; see also Arce 2005; Brooks and Kurtz 2007; Stallings and Peres 2000). For example, different policies can have contradictory macroeconomic effects:

The privatization of firms provides an infusion of revenue that can improve a government's fiscal position, yet lower taxes on imports and foreign investments countervail this trend by decreasing the state's intake. At a microeconomic level, trade liberalization lowers the prices a consumer pays for tradable goods, yet utility privatization typically results in higher telephone and electricity bills.

Despite the multidimensional nature of the Washington Consensus, existing studies of public opinion in Latin America largely fail to consider that citizens do not think about different market policies as a monolithic whole. Scholars typically group potentially diverse policies under the single "neoliberal" or "structural adjustment" rubric, invoking the questionable assumption that citizens have a high degree of "issue constraint" – that is, a tendency to exhibit a high correlation between beliefs about different, but ideologically related, issues (Converse 1964). Some authors disregard potential attitudinal divergences across varied policy items by creating a singular measure of citizen placement on a market-versus-statist dimension compiled from different survey items about distinct reforms (Duch 1993; Graham and Pettinato 2002; Kaufman and Zuckermann 1998). Others force the aggregation of diverse policies by using as indicators mass evaluations of particular stabilization plans, structural adjustment packages, and even presidents (Stokes 2001a, 2001b; Weyland 2002). A few also look at general support for abstract values such as "freedom," "market economy," "productivity," or "individual initiative" (Graham and Pettinato 2002; Graham and Sukhtankar 2004; Turner and Elordi 1995).

Admittedly, mass attitudes toward the various market-oriented policies are candidates for exhibiting a high degree of issue constraint. The term "Washington Consensus" itself refers to a broad set of market measures supported by developed-world economists and policy experts (Williamson 1990). A common ideological rationale underlies most of its various elements: State intervention in the economy creates distortions that lead to suboptimal welfare outcomes. In part for this reason, different policies share overlapping patterns and consequences. For example, many state-owned enterprises were sold to foreign investors, and foreign-owned firms are much more export-oriented than locally owned ones (ECLAC 2000a). Moreover, throughout the 1990s, Latin American leaders typically implemented various reform elements either as single legislative packages or as a succession of policy measures.

These hints of issue constraint among political elites, however, do not necessarily translate into cohesion in belief systems among mass publics

(Converse 1964; Jennings 1992). In general, public opinion scholars find issue constraint to be weak; most citizens do not hold to logically consistent organizing principles, such as equality, justice, or freedom, that coherently structure their beliefs toward individual policies (Luskin 1987). Instead, citizens "morselize" their issue attitudes, approaching different policy issues, even if related, in a piecemeal and stand-alone fashion (Lane 1962).

In the end, I argue that issue constraint is weak and abstract values are nearly irrelevant to specific policy beliefs in Latin American for several reasons. First, leaders adopted market reforms "more by default than by conviction," so reform implementation was rarely accompanied by grandiose rhetoric about "economic freedom" or "individual responsibility" that might provide a unifying rationale for different policy beliefs (Manzetti 1999, 164; see also Stokes 2001b). Few market advocates, be they Latin American politicians or economists in international financial institutions, have espoused the libertarian ideal of complete individual responsibility for personal well-being and development. Moreover, I show in Chapter 3 that elite attitudes have not been as constrained or unidimensional as scholars typically presume: Latin American politicians have supported some policies with more vigor and unity than they have supported others. Second, the presumed trade-off between, on the one hand, the abstract capitalist values of economic productivity and individual responsibility and, on the other hand, statist values of economic equality and collective responsibility actually bears little resemblance to the reality of Latin America's political economy and policy alternatives. Statist economic policies often had regressive effects on income equality. Moreover, Latin America's state-led development era was characterized by rapid improvements in economic productivity *and* rising inequality. Indeed, the efficiency/equality trade-off is a false one in *all* developing countries because they do not fully utilize all factors of production: "In most developing and transitional economies well inside the production frontier there is no *necessary* tradeoff between increasing efficiency and resulting economic growth, on the one hand, and increasing equity on the other" (Birdsall and Nellis 2003, 1619). Finally, Latin America's economic reforms were drastic enough to exert concrete and visible impacts on national economies and citizens' everyday lives. Personal experiences have usurped abstract values.

For these reasons, unifying ideological principles do not drive Latin Americans' beliefs about the distinct ingredients of the Washington

Consensus.[5] Instead, the varied consequences of fundamentally different policies, and even varied elite rhetoric about them, lead citizens to approach the menu of market reforms on a piecemeal basis. I demonstrate in this book that citizens hold remarkably different opinions about the varying elements of the Washington Consensus. The existence of these varying beliefs stems from the fact that distinct elements of the market reform package have had different inflationary consequences. Some policies have raised the prices of certain goods and services, while other policies have lowered them.

Clarifying Individual-Level Differences in Support for Reforms

Besides yielding varied consequences through its different policy elements, the Washington Consensus has influenced different groups and individuals in varied ways. In other words, reforms have created winners and losers, so some citizens are surely more supportive of certain market policies than are others. Moreover, individuals vary in their attention to elite discourse and in their political predispositions, so elite rhetoric about reforms has also affected citizens and their opinions in highly varied ways. Despite these seemingly obvious facts about cross-individual variation in mass beliefs, leading studies of public opinion in Latin America typically fail to separate out attitudes across different individuals. When they do, scholars focus almost exclusively on the impact of relevant variables, such as wealth, political knowledge, and partisanship, without providing clear and convincing theoretical explanations for why attitudes are stratified by these factors.

Most studies of mass beliefs toward market reforms in Latin America focus on macroeconomic and national-level opinion trends (Stokes 2001a, 2001b; Weyland 1998, 2002). These studies are based on empirical evidence of covariance between, on the one hand, macroeconomic indicators and, on the other hand, aggregate support for market-friendly reforms, candidates, parties, or presidents. Such analyses are certainly useful in their own right: Macro-level trends in public opinion are of utmost relevance in democratic systems. They provide, however, a deceivingly narrow

---

[5] While a study of "diffuse" support for liberal ideals and values might itself be useful, scholars have yet to show that such concepts resonate with Latin American citizens or have any relevance for political cleavages or more concrete issue beliefs (Easton 1965; Graham and Pettinato 2002; Lora et al. 2004; Turner and Elordi 1995).

portrayal of mass political behavior because their findings are largely shaped by changes "at the margin" – that is, among a small and perhaps unrepresentative share of the population (Stimson 1999, 2004): "Great movements . . . to approval or disapproval are produced by the systematic change of quite a small number of people" (Stimson 2004, 158–159).

Despite this implied focus on a minority of individuals, studies with a macro-level orientation betray a characterization of the citizenry as homogeneous, overlooking within-nation or individual-level differences in political behavior. These studies are not clear about which citizens change their beliefs in response to past economic trends or expectations about the future, leaving the impression that causal variables shift every citizen's probability of supporting reform by an equivalent amount. Portrayals rarely move beyond a simple depiction of citizens robotically shifting preferences with the macro-economy's ebbs and flows, revealing a strictly "sociotropic" understanding of mass political behavior that assumes that citizens are oriented solely toward national, not personal, well-being (Kinder and Kiewiet 1979, 1981).

Aggregate-level studies exhibit these shortcomings despite the fact that the theories they apply have obvious implications for intranational behavioral patterns. For example, retrospective voting theory posits material gains and losses as the primary cause of policy evaluations, yet many applications fail to exploit the variations in individual-level changes in welfare that have occurred in the wake of reforms. Likewise, while intertemporal theory claims that reform-minded presidents have the rhetorical ability to induce an optimistic prospective orientation among citizens, analysts making this claim overlook the massive variation within mass publics in (1) attention to elite discourse and (2) politically motivated propensities to accept arguments made by the chief executive.

Admittedly, a few studies investigate relationships between individual-level traits and market attitudes. Some even consider the impact of bottom-up factors, such as wealth, and potential top-down variables, such as political awareness and mass partisanship (Graham and Pettinato 2002; Graham and Sukhtankar 2004; Kaufman and Zuckermann 1998; Stokes 2001a). These studies leave behind, however, a murky and unconvincing theoretical basis for understanding the impact of these individual-level variables.

Consider first the standard approach to wealth. Studies that do stratify attitudes by wealth proceed with little or no theoretical justification for the widely held assumption, although slightly less frequent finding, that wealth is positively correlated with pro-market beliefs in Latin America. Scholars typically assume that the theoretical underpinnings of the standard "wealth hypothesis" or "class hypothesis" are self-evident. A closer examination, however, reveals some potential problems in applying these standard assumptions to public opinion in the Latin American context.

The fundamental assumption underlying the wealth hypothesis – that the poor benefit disproportionately from state interventions in the economy because modern states redistribute resources from rich to poor – may have limited applicability to Latin America. For several reasons, the state throughout Latin American history has often had a regressive impact on income distribution. First, during the import-substitution years, state intervention often favored politically powerful and typically well-heeled rentier groups (Evans 1979; Weyland 1996). Protectionist measures were rarely targeted toward bolstering the welfare of marginalized groups, and they were particularly detrimental to the rural poor who had agricultural assets. Well-connected industrialists and formal-sector urban workers in the most powerful unions were the greatest beneficiaries of trade protection (Frieden 1991). Second, employment in SOEs was used only rarely as a means to correct economic injustices. More typically, office-seeking politicians saw SOE jobs and funds as clientelistic resources to be distributed to achieve personal political goals rather than collective economic ones (Greene 2007). Finally, Latin American welfare states were *far* less extensive, effective, and progressive than their counterparts in Western Europe. Many of the region's poor were outside the welfare state's reach. Moreover, many state-sponsored benefits, such as retirement pensions and free tertiary education, were highly regressive because middle- and upper-income groups disproportionately enjoyed them. Some studies have actually concluded that overall taxing and expenditure patterns in many Latin American countries have historically exacerbated income inequality (IDB 1998). Furthermore, even if welfare states had been progressive, full-scale welfare state retrenchment was *never* part of the market reform package. Most forms of social spending have actually *increased*, with several countries introducing targeted antipoverty programs in the 1990s and 2000s (Brown and Hunter 1999). Only retirement pension programs, which were in fact the most regressive form of welfare state spending, have seen some retrenchment (Kaufman and Segura-Ubiergo 2001).

In short, the notion that reforms have hurt the poor by dismantling a historically progressive state is categorically wrong. As a result, it is not automatic or obvious that poor Latin Americans should be less supportive of market reforms than the wealthy. The statist policies that were reversed by reform were playing a highly mixed role in redistributing wealth. The poor cannot point to the glory days of yore in which state institutions provided them with an economic safety net. Most have *always* gotten by with only a minimal state presence, relying on personal entrepreneurship and social networks to survive (de Soto 1989). Such experiences may actually endow the poor with a *greater* sense of self-reliance and "rugged individualism" than the rich (Powers 2001). This is not to assert that the reform process has been progressive, or that there are no reasons to expect the poor to be less enthusiastic about reforms than the wealthy. Rather, it is to suggest that the most common assumptions about wealth and the reform process may not hold.

The fact that scholars typically overlook potential top-down influences further beclouds research on the impact of wealth. Many scholars purport the existence of a "neoliberal hegemony" among Latin American elites – that is, a pro-market consensus within the region's political class. Even if this is only partly true, then most elite statements about the region's new economic model are favorable toward markets. As a result, the failure to account for the top-down factor of mass-level political awareness may produce a spurious positive correlation between wealth and pro-market beliefs. After all, political awareness, and thus the degree of exposure to elite discourse, is highly correlated with wealth: Middle- and high-income individuals tend to be more politically aware than lower-income ones (Moreno 1999; Price and Zaller 1993). Therefore, observed individual-level differences in issue attitudes may derive not from variation in wealth-based interests but from the fact that the highly aware are more attentive to and more persuaded by the pro-market discourse of political elites.

Finally, in the rare instances in which scholars do explore the role of top-down factors, such as political awareness and partisanship, they produce theoretically unsatisfying results. Regarding awareness, scholars interpret evidence of a positive correlation between political awareness and pro-market attitudes as a sign that greater knowledge of policies enhances support for them (Bratton et al. 2004; Kaufman and Zuckermann 1998). This argument is problematic, however, as its logic is both nonobvious (why does knowledge of a policy and its outcomes necessarily yield support for it?) and self-contradictory (what if a citizen is highly knowledgeable about two conflicting policies?). Regarding partisanship, numerous studies observe a correlation between political predispositions and policy attitudes: Right-leaning citizens and supporters of market-friendly presidents tend to be more favorable toward market policies than leftists and opponents of pro-market incumbents (Kaufman and

Zuckermann 1998; Luna and Zechmeister 2005; Magaloni and Romero 2008). Again, however, scholars do not derive the precise reason for these relationships. In particular, they are agnostic about whether citizens (1) move to a new party because of their beliefs about market policies (bottom-up) or (2) adopt views about market policies by unthinkingly absorbing the beliefs of their preferred party (top-down). Intertemporal theorists are also noncommittal, suggesting that citizens may derive optimism about the future not from elites but from intuitions about economic trade-offs.

I demonstrate in this book that beliefs about market reform vary across individuals. More importantly and less obviously, the top-down and bottom-up models I develop and employ provide a new and concrete theoretical infrastructure for understanding and explaining why some individuals are more enthusiastic about the Washington Consensus than others. First, I move beyond previous consumption-based arguments and their focus on hyperinflation by recognizing that the inflationary consequences of policies differ across individuals because individuals have varying consumer preferences. Every citizen consumes a slightly different set of goods and services, so policy-induced price changes do not affect citizens uniformly. Citizens are sensitive to these facts about inflation and derive their preferences toward each policy accordingly. Second, I demonstrate how top-down influences vary across individuals. Besides having different partisan predispositions, citizens vary in the extent to which they are even attentive to political elites. Politicians' effectiveness in persuading the masses is far from uniform across all citizens.

Thus far, this chapter has established the fact that existing scholarship either completely overlooks consumption- and elite-based influences on Latin Americans' economic policy preferences or does so in highly aggregated, and thus oversimplifying, ways. The remainder of this chapter provides a theoretical architecture for understanding and applying the bottom-up, consumption-oriented and the top-down, elite-oriented explanations of public opinion in Latin America.

Bottom-Up Influences: Why Latin Americans Think about Reforms as Consumers

The bottom-up bias in studies of Latin American politics and public opinion toward market reforms sits uneasily with some of the central findings from mass political psychology about the cognitive limitations of mass publics. Many of the bottom-up studies hold unexpressed and

34

unrealistic expectations about the cognitive capacities of citizens and their propensity to strike self-interested positions on issues of economic import. I claim that a bottom-up and even a self-interest approach is useful and applicable for understanding how Latin Americans have responded to market reforms, but only because reforms have exerted extremely visible welfare impacts that citizens have learned about through their everyday activities. This visibility, however, does not make citizens omniscient about market policies. The manner in which citizens perceive the impact of reforms on their livelihoods shapes the way in which they evaluate them. In the end, I claim that citizens in Latin America have been more likely to perceive the consequences of reforms through their consumer activities than through their labor-market activities. In turn, they have evaluated reforms more for their influence on consumption than for their influence on their employment situation. The section concludes by providing an analytical framework for understanding how consumption-based interests are translated into policy beliefs.

Cognition in Extraordinary Times: The Citizen in Partial Equilibrium

The causal mechanisms of mass preference formation in the standard bottom-up models of Latin American politics are unspecified, leaving the impression that objective economic interests are robotically converted into policy attitudes. Studies in mass political psychology, however, show little evidence that citizens are calculating, utility-maximizing individuals who formulate well-reasoned political opinions after seeking out extensive information (Kinder and Kiewiet 1979; Sears et al. 1980). Rather, most citizens are "cognitive misers" who only episodically gather political information from sources that are easy to find (Delli Carpini and Keeter 1996; Popkin 1991). One such avenue is when policy-relevant information becomes available as a by-product of normal everyday activities (Brody and Sniderman 1977; Downs 1957; Popkin 1991). In other words, even if citizens do not intentionally seek out information on policies and their outcomes, such information often inadvertently reaches their perceptual screens as they go about their quotidian behaviors. The ubiquity of politics suggests that, even in normal times, individuals will inevitably happen upon politically relevant information through everyday scenarios, such as encounters with members of another racial or ethnic group, withholdings from a paycheck, unplanned pregnancies, or hospital visits.

In less developed economies undergoing fundamental restructuring, such scenarios are extremely prevalent. Market reforms in Latin America abruptly reversed an economic strategy that had been entrenched for over two generations. As a result, they have exerted a very intense and visible impact on economic well-being and daily life. By causing vast and visible changes to consumer options, prices, employment opportunities, entitlements, infrastructure quality, and other economic criteria, reforms have evoked ideas and reactions within citizens merely as they have gone about their daily lives: "It's hard to escape some knowledge of politics and policy when they are so relentlessly determinant of one's day-to-day welfare" (Stokes 2001a, 191; see also Duckett and Miller 2006). Because of the intensity and visibility of economic change in such extraordinary times, scholars should suspend for these contexts the standard pessimism about the degree of political knowledge citizens have.

Major economic developments, however, do not make citizens omniscient regarding the new policies. Instead, citizens remain susceptible to issue "frames" that narrowly define the essence of an issue and how one should think about it. Political psychologists typically talk of "rhetorical frames" that politicians use to describe an issue in order to yield a desired effect on public opinion (Lakoff 2004; Nelson and Kinder 1996). Policy-relevant information that individuals encounter through everyday activities also comes packaged with frames because citizens come across only one facet of an issue or one aspect of a policy's impact on their material welfare (Gamson 1992; Just et al. 1996, 134). These "by-product frames" highlight *certain aspects* of a policy's impact while masking others, inducing citizens to form perceptions that are based on partial and biased information (Kahneman et al. 1982). The manner in which the individual stumbles upon the policy and its impact determines the content of the by-product frame and, as a result, her or his opinion about the issue. For example, consider a city with a new foreign-owned manufacturing plant that employs 1,000 workers. Residents in the city observe the new plant and its many employees and conclude that foreign investment is beneficial because it provides jobs. Unknown to them, however, is the fact that competition from the plant closed down a less efficient, more labor-intensive firm of 1,500 employees in another city. The residents' everyday experiences expose them to workers employed by the foreign firm rather than workers laid off from the inefficient one, so they approve of foreign investment. The content of the by-product frame shapes the way they think about the issue and ultimately their opinion.

Theoretical Framework

This by-product approach indicates an avenue by which self-interest can play a role in crafting opinions. The more information citizens have about a policy and its effects, the more likely they are to construct a response based on self-interest (Gomez and Wilson 2006; Mutz 1993). Because their consequences are so immediate and visible, the changes caused by drastic economic policy shifts often overcome the informational barriers to the politicization of self-interest. In other words, major reforms in transitional economies bring the consequences of economic policies to citizens' doorsteps, providing many with the information needed to formulate self-interested policy positions.

Given the imperfections in the information provided through by-product frames, however, extraordinary economic times do not turn each citizen into *homo economicus*. Citizens are still unable to omnisciently calculate the welfare impact of each policy and convert it into a self-interested preference. For most citizens, such a calculation would have to be based on a consideration of real returns to their labor (the ratio of wages to prices), which is in turn altered by tax outlays, receipt of state-funded services, returns from investments, and other miscellaneous factors. In other words, the *overall* welfare effects of reforms must be calculated in, using the parlance of economics, a "general equilibrium" perspective – that is, one that considers the total impact summed over all of these possible "channels." As this suggests, citizens occupy multiple roles as economic actors: workers, consumers, investors, taxpayers, borrowers, transfer-payment recipients, and others. Economic policies have multivalent consequences, including many that are indirect and unintended. As a result, a single policy influences well-being through a variety of these channels. Citizens occupy and perceive a variety of these economic roles, yet the information they receive as a by-product of everyday activities often speaks to just one of them.

Moreover, because economic policies yield multivalent consequences, a single policy may influence well-being vis-à-vis each role differently. For example, politicians frequently find fiscal austerity and welfare state retrenchment to be unpopular even when the costs are diffusely spread (Pierson 1996). Citizens as transfer-payment recipients and users of public services are more likely to notice the disappearance of these benefits than they are to recognize the beneficial impact of austerity on inflation or their economy's international competitiveness. In sum, the role through which citizens assess a policy's impact on their well-being depends on the nature

37

of the policy's impact and in turn determines how favorably the policy is viewed.

The narrowness of by-product frames indicates that scholars would view citizens more fruitfully from a "partial equilibrium" perspective, one that accounts for a single welfare channel. The argument that citizens morselize their different economic roles, not making linkages among them and not averaging over the roles to create an overall summary judgment of utility, is thus bad economics; yet it is sound political psychology (Lane 1962). When evaluating policy options, citizens use, say, a consumer frame in one instance and a taxpayer frame in another. How the policy influences one's life – that is, which economic roles are most *visibly* influenced by the policy shift – determines which frame is activated. Like the proverbial blind men and the elephant, individuals notice how a policy influences well-being through one particular channel while being largely ignorant of the effect on their overall welfare. Extraordinary times make citizens more "rational" in the strict utility-maximizing sense, but their rationality remains "bounded" by informational and cognitive limitations (Simon 1957; Weyland 2007).

The Overlooked Latin American Consumer

Due to certain characteristics of the reform process in Latin America, I argue that market reforms have exerted much more *visible*, even if not necessarily more important, impacts on consumer options than on labor markets. The impacts of globalization and privatization have been most evident to citizens as consumers, while these policies have had crucial yet rather opaque influences on labor markets. The reasons for these trends are rooted in economic realities that have important consequences for how citizens learn about and assess market reforms.

In a variety of ways, the impacts of market policies on consumer options in Latin America have created ready-made, policy-relevant pieces of information that have been a by-product of daily life, so citizens have had little choice but to be influenced by and to notice the consumer consequences of the Washington Consensus. First, consider the cognitive aspects of consumption for beliefs about globalization. Domestic monopolies or oligopolies filled demand in many product markets during the protectionist decades, so consumers chose among a relatively small number of low-quality alternatives that cost more than the world's market price (Frieden 1991). The relaxation of import tariffs and restrictions on foreign investment inflows thus had an immediate and obvious impact on consumer choice. With liberalized foreign investment inflows and an influx of imports (combined in many countries with an overvalued exchange rate), consumer options exploded (Broda and Weinstein 2006; Guedes and Oliveira 2006). The quality, variety, and affordability of many goods expanded in a short time and in a process that consumers noticed through the ordinary act of shopping. Second, almost all citizens are consumers of at least one utility service that was privatized in recent years. Most electricity, water, and telecommunications companies in the region were public-sector monopolies at the beginning of the 1980s. When privatization occurred, it exposed such firms to market forces and (often) to new regulations that obliged the private-sector owners to change the prices, the availability, and the quality of such services (Ugaz and Price 2003). Privatization thus exerted impacts on the welfare of all utility customers in ways that were visible when they paid monthly bills, confronted a breakdown in their electricity or telephone service, or signed up for newly available services. Finally, these policy-induced changes to welfare affected a citizenry that was already keenly sensitized to its consumer interests because of the hyperinflationary episodes of the 1980s and early 1990s (Remmer 1991; Weyland 1998b). These crises led to a variety of new consumer behaviors, such as hoarding, frequent shopping, and paying acute attention to price shifts (O'Dougherty 2002). Consumer concerns, particularly the influence of economic trends and policies on prices, were thus the top economic priority of many citizens as market economics unfolded.

These consumer consequences are more likely than labor-channel effects to shape overall public opinion because every citizen is a consumer, while only 60% to 70% of Latin America's adult population is even in the labor market (Jacobs 2005; World Bank 2006). Moreover, only a minority of the population in Latin America ever worked in sectors whose employment opportunities and wages were directly and visibly touched by market reforms. The share of the workforce employed in SOEs prior to privatization rarely exceeded 5% (Chong and López-de-Silanes 2005). Likewise, the share of the population in tradable goods sectors (manufacturing, mining, and agriculture) has been a shrinking minority, with the remaining majority either employed in the service sector or not even in the economically active population (EAP). Admittedly, workers employed in or laid off from a tradable goods sector probably know whether they are benefiting from increased exports or losing from greater import competition, and SOE employees are likely to have a reasonably clear sense of privatization's impact on their potential wage and employment status in the newly privatized firm. However, workers who are directly influenced by reforms' direct and immediate ("primary") effects comprise only a slim portion of the population (Stokes 2001a, 86). To the remaining individuals, the cause-and-effect impact of reforms on their employment, their employment potential (for the unemployed and students), or the employment of their main income providers (for homemakers and the retired) is "secondary," or indirect and therefore less obvious.

Other aspects of the region's labor markets also make it difficult for most workers to perceive the precise impact of reforms on their wages and employment opportunities. The natural volatility of labor markets in the new market economies far outdistances that caused by systematic policy changes or macroeconomic shocks, so isolating the impact of policy on labor-market criteria can be difficult. Job and worker turnover are large and have increased in recent years because of reforms (Haltiwanger et al. 2004). Incredibly, 25% of all jobs are either created or destroyed in a given year, and the vast majority of this is due merely to "normal job churning" – that is, to idiosyncratic decisions by workers and firms and not to policy shifts or even macroeconomic trends (IDB 2004, 217, 244). Furthermore, worker turnover is actually *higher* than job turnover, so average job tenure is typically less than five years for Latin American workers (IDB 2004, 50, 176). Workers are now more likely to be employed as temporary or subcontracted workers, making their labor-market skills less "specific" to a particular sector or job (Hiscox 2002; IDB 2004). As worker turnover has increased in the market-friendly era, membership has declined in the trade unions and other employment associations that forged obvious linkages between national economic policy and the well-being of workers (IDB 2004; Kurtz 2004).

Because of these trends, fewer Latin American citizens than in the past have their interests and identities defined by employment in a particular job or sector. As a result, the visibility of reforms' consequences for one's job, and thus the availability of information linking policy to personal employment situation, is limited. Increased labor-market volatility might incline one to think that citizens' sensitivities toward the impact of policies on their wages and job prospects would be heightened, and in fact, low wages and unemployment are widely regarded by the region's residents as its most important problems (IDB 2004; Rodrik 2001; Saavedra 2003). However, cognition and perceptions, not objective economic consequences, determine public opinion. Extreme levels of labor market fluidity make it difficult for workers to pinpoint the precise influence of reforms on their wages and employment opportunities. Even a leading academic study of the region's labor markets admits that ". . . it is difficult to identify precisely who is losing from reforms" (IDB 2004, 176). In short, Latin American citizens are extremely concerned about labor markets, but they have a hard time linking market policies and their impacts to labor-market outcomes.

In sum, the traditional bottom-up models of Latin American politics, which featured clearly delineated classes, sectors, and functional interest groups, are defunct. Workers now shift fluidly in and out of careers, sectors, and labor organizations, so their interests are less specific to and therefore less defined by a particular employment situation than they were in the statist era. As a result, consumer interests are now the primary determinants of beliefs about incumbent economic policies, especially because the effects of the Washington Consensus have drastically and visibly shifted the prices, availability, and quality of goods and services. This argument does not necessarily imply that citizens were unconcerned with these consumption criteria before the market era. Because real incomes are determined in part by prices, there is surely nothing new about the fact that citizens have consumption-related economic concerns. What is new, however, is the highly visible manner in which economic policies have jolted consumer prices and options. Because of this, consumer criteria play an enhanced role in shaping mass beliefs about the main economic issues of the day.[6]

A Framework for Analyzing Consumer-Driven Responses to Market Reforms

When citizens think as consumers, they convert the observed or potential impact of a policy on the quality, availability, and prices of goods and

---

[6] Is the claim that consumer interests now outrun labor-market interests a mere methodological artifact? Perhaps the advent of survey research in the region has shed new light on otherwise diffuse, and thus previously hard-to-measure, mass consumer interests that have *always* existed and even always predominated. Evidence from social movements, however, contradicts this claim. While scholars' attention to public opinion has not been constant because of measurement limitations, their awareness of social movements and economic interest groups has. Thus, the noted rise in recent years of consumer protection movements is the best indication that the new consumer focus is genuine (Rhodes 2006). Moreover, some structuralist studies of economically defined groups under import substitution industrialization *did* find evidence of consumer defined interests, although only among one group in one country (O'Donnell 1978). Were consumption-based interests more widely present, scholars presumably would have found them.

services they purchase or wish to purchase into a belief about that policy. The degree of impact on their policy beliefs depends on the importance to them of the affected goods and services. To develop a framework for analysis that incorporates these simple propositions, I define the impact of a policy on consumer i's welfare (W_i) as follows:

$$\Delta W_i = \left[\frac{U_t}{P_t}(Q_{it}) - \frac{U_{t-1}}{P_{t-1}}(Q_{it-1})\right] \times R_i, \tag{1}$$

where U is a measure of the quality of all relevant goods and services (those that are affected by the policy), P is their price, Q is the quantity available to consumer i, and R is the share of i's total consumption devoted to the relevant goods and services. The subscript $t-1$ denotes the time prior to the policy's implementation, and t denotes the time after its implementation.

According to this framework, four criteria define the impact of a policy reform on consumer welfare (and thus mass beliefs about that policy). First is the policy's impact on the price of relevant goods and services: A policy that lowers prices is better for a consumer than one that raises or has no effect on prices. Second, the policy's impact on the quality of goods and services has an independent effect; reform-induced quality improvements add to consumer welfare. Third, the policy's impact on the availability of goods and services is also crucial. A policy that introduces previously unavailable goods and services to a consumer enhances welfare more than a policy that fails to do so.[7] Finally, the combined effect of these three elements can by magnified or diminished by the share of the relevant goods and services in the consumer's total consumption bundle, which is the set of all goods and services the consumer purchases in a given time period. If the relevant goods and services comprise a large share of the consumer's consumption budget, then the joint effect on welfare of changes in price, quality, and availability is substantial. If such goods and services comprise a small share of the consumer's consumption budget, then the combined effect are less so.[8]

This model yields predictions about public opinion toward market policies at two different levels: the aggregate and the individual level. First,

[7] Consider two scenarios. The first scenario is when the policy does *not* introduce previously (and still) unavailable relevant goods and services to consumer i. In this instance, the equation yields no change in consumer welfare because Q_t and Q_{t-1} are both zero. The second scenario is when the policy does introduce relevant goods and services to the consumer. In this instance, all terms indexed by $t-1$ drop out (because $Q_{t-1} = 0$), so the resulting change in consumer welfare is necessarily positive.
[8] For simplicity's sake, R is the average share of consumption bundles across the time periods.

expectations about the aggregate popularity of market policies are straightforward.[9] Mass support for a market policy depends on how the policy influences the price, quality, and availability of relevant goods and services. Reforms that lower prices, improve quality, or expand access are more popular than reforms that accomplish the opposite. Second, individual-level predictions stem from the fact that the framework allows consumption budgets to vary across individuals (R_i). Economic policies affect different consumers in different ways because individuals have "nonhomothetic tastes" – that is, the share of relevant goods and services in total expenditures varies across consumers (Harsanyi 1953; Hunter and Markusen 1988). Economists and political scientists typically overlook the impact of variation in consumption budgets, but I argue in this book that these differences are meaningful not only for economic welfare but also for public opinion.

Trade policy affects citizens heterogeneously through the consumer channel. Consumer-welfare gains from trade vary positively with the share of income that a consumer devotes to imports and import-competing goods (Deaton 1989). Trade liberalization leads to relative declines in the prices of *foreign imports* (M_F) and *locally* produced goods that compete with *imports* (M_L). Prices for these goods fall relative to those for *nontraded* (NT_L) goods and services as well as *locally* produced goods in *export*-oriented sectors (X_L). Moreover, imports and import-competing goods also undergo more rapid quality improvements, and trade liberalization, almost by definition, enhances the availability of new imports (Irwin 2005; Murphy and Shleifer 1997). Overall, consumers are increasingly disadvantaged by protectionism as the share of M_F and M_L in their consumption budgets rises and as the share of NT_L and X_L decreases. Technically speaking, the consumer gains from trade for consumer i vary with $R_{(trade)}$, which is the proportion of expenditures devoted to imports and import-competing goods:[10]

$$R_{(trade)i} = \frac{M_{F_i} + M_{L_i}}{M_{F_i} + M_{L_i} + X_{L_i} + NT_{L_i}}. \tag{2}$$

Privatization exerts its most poignant consumption-channel impact by effecting changes in the prices, quality, and availability of services provided

---

[9] These can be derived taking average beliefs over all consumers i.

[10] The terms on the right-hand side of the equal sign are the amount of expenditure for each type of good or service.

by formerly state-owned utility monopolies. In contrast to trade liberalization, however, privatization typically yields cross-cutting effects on consumers by counterbalancing price increases with expanded access. (The impact on quality is more mixed.) Regarding prices, consumers who commit a large share of their expenditures to newly privatized services are more disadvantaged by the price increases than consumers who commit a smaller share. Consumer gains from privatization for consumer i thus vary in part with $R_{(priv)}$, which is the proportion of expenditures devoted to the newly privatized (A) service:

$$R_{(priv)i} = \frac{A_i}{A_i + \tilde{A}_i}, \tag{3}$$

where $\tilde{A}$ is the amount of expenditure on all goods and services that are not produced by the newly privatized company. The impact of privatization on access and availability, however, can vary across individuals independently of these price-change burdens. Newly privatized firms extend their services to consumers who did not have access to them under state ownership (e.g., individuals who did not have telephone or electricity hookups). As a result, consumer welfare benefits also vary with whether individuals gain access to the relevant service after privatization occurs: Individuals who gain access after privatization should be more supportive of the policy than those who either had access before privatization or who do not gain access even after it occurs.

While interesting in their own right, these individual-level consumption patterns (represented by equations 2 and 3) are closely related to wealth. For example, the consumption budgets of poor individuals in Latin America feature a smaller share of import and import-competing goods than those of wealthy individuals; the poor tend to consume fewer skill-intensive luxury items. Also, poor consumers are more likely than wealthy ones to experience newfound access to privatized services because the latter typically already had access. In the end, I claim that mass-level attitudinal cleavages over market policies are correlated with wealth solely because of wealth-related differences in consumption patterns.

Top-Down Influences: How Elites Shape Public Opinion

Basing the bottom-up approach on cognition rather than strict self-interest leaves the door open for noneconomic criteria to influence public opinion as well. In particular, even in extraordinary times, many citizens are swayed by elite rhetoric or defer to their favorite politician when they know little about a policy. In this section, I present the framework used for analyzing top-down effects on public opinion. To maintain the clear distinction between bottom-up and top-down approaches, I describe the top-down framework in its theoretically purest form, which holds that "creative" elites are the *only* source of mass issue beliefs (Selznick 1951; Zaller 1992). This places the two approaches at obvious tension with one another, but at the end of this chapter I describe how I integrate the two.

Scenarios of Elite Opinion Leadership

According to the standard top-down approach, two individual-level factors forge differences across citizens in issue beliefs: (1) their propensity to pay attention to elite discourse and (2) their predispositions regarding which politicians and/or party to trust on policy matters (Zaller 1992).[11] Attention to elite discourse matters because politicians can only influence citizens who listen to them. Political predispositions matter because citizens tend to absorb the rhetorical arguments only of politicians from parties that they support. Because of these simple micro-level facts, the distribution and divisiveness of elite opinion on any given issue have major consequences for the contours of mass opinion. To establish predictions for mass-level patterns, top-down theory describes the impact of two different elite opinion scenarios: one for united elites and one for divided elites.

The first hypothetical scenario is one in which elites are united, unanimously favoring market policies. In this "neoliberal hegemony" scenario, the pro-market elite consensus is the "mainstream" opinion, and persuasive information about market reforms emanating from elites is "one-sided" (Zaller 1992). According to top-down theory, a neoliberal hegemony among elites has a "hegemony effect" on some citizens, inducing many politically attentive individuals to support policies they might not otherwise support. As a result, citizens who are the most attentive to and knowledgeable about elite discourse are more supportive of free-market policies than citizens who pay little attention to elites. Panel A of Figure 2.1

---

[11] By assumption, these mass-level political predispositions are formed exogenously, not because of issue positions or policy-related interests but because of arational forces of political socialization (Achen and Bartels 2006; Campbell et al. 1960). This purges the theoretical model of the bottom-up possibility that partisan predispositions are the result of issue attitudes.

graphically depicts this theoretical relationship. Attention to elite discourse, also called "political awareness," is on the x-axis and support for the pro-market consensus is on the y-axis. The line illustrates the simple positive relationship between an individual's expected level of support for a market policy and political awareness. In quantitative terms, the size of the hegemony effect, or "awareness gap," is equal to the difference in the probability of supporting the market policy between the least aware and the most aware.

The second hypothetical scenario is one in which elites are divided into two equally sized partisan camps that disagree sharply on the merits of market policies. Rhetoric is characterized by a "balanced, two-sided" information flow. The partisan nature of elite rhetoric exerts a "polarizing effect" that, unlike united elites, does forge a mass partisan cleavage over market reforms, *but it does so only among politically aware citizens* (Zaller 1992). Panel B of Figure 2.1 portrays the top-down theory's predictions when elite opinions about market reforms are divided between a "Right Party" that favors market policies and a "Left Party" that opposes them. Both parties are of roughly equal size at the elite level, so the volumes of the two competing information flows are similar. Unlike united elites, divided elites activate mass-level partisan predispositions. Political awareness increases the probability that citizens' policy opinions match those of their preferred party because awareness both (1) exposes citizens to greater amounts of discourse from leaders of their preferred party and (2) equips citizens with the knowledge to accept messages that come from their preferred leaders and reject those from leaders of opposing parties. As a result, support for the Washington Consensus is higher among Right Party sympathizers (solid black line with "**R**" labels) who have high levels of political awareness than it is among copartisans with low levels of political awareness. In contrast, increased political awareness has the mirror opposite effect among Left Party sympathizers (dotted black line with "**L**" labels). The extent of polarization between Right and Left partisans is thus a direct function of political awareness. The model also makes predictions for independents (solid gray line with "**I**" labels), who lack strong political predispositions. By definition, independents have no inclinations to accept one party's message over that of another. They thus accept all (or, more accurately, a random sample) of the elite messages to which they are exposed.[12] Because the

---

[12] In the original formulation of the elite opinion leadership model, independents were ignored (Zaller 1992). Extending the model to independents is important, however, especially

Theoretical Framework

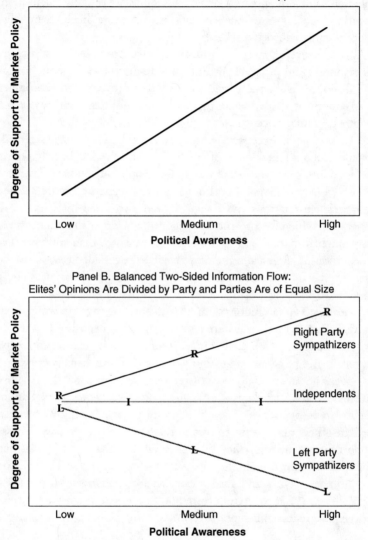

Panel A. One-Sided Information Flow: Elites are United in Support of Market Policy

Panel B. Balanced Two-Sided Information Flow:
Elites' Opinions Are Divided by Party and Parties Are of Equal Size

Figure 2.1   Theoretical Patterns of Mass Support for Market Policies under Two Different Top-Down Scenarios.
Note: "**R**": Right Party sympathizers. "**L**": Left Party sympathizers. "**I**": Independents.

amounts of anti- and pro-market elite discourse are roughly balanced in this scenario, highly aware independents are no more likely than unaware independents to absorb market-friendly attitudes.

Although useful, these two ideal-type patterns are not sufficient for understanding all possible patterns of elite discourse. In some instances, elite discourse is characterized by something in between the one-sided and balanced two-sided scenarios. If one elite political camp is larger than the other, as might occur in a dominant-party or soft authoritarian system, then an intermediate scenario exists (Geddes and Zaller 1989; Greene 2007; Scheiner 2006). The volume of communication flows is heavily skewed in one direction, yet advocates of the minority opinion still have a voice.

To address this possibility, I define a third scenario. Figure 2.2 depicts theoretical expectations under this "skewed, two-sided-information-flow" scenario, in which the pro-market elite camp is larger than the antimarket camp and pro-market information flows are heavier than antimarket ones. Expectations diverge from the more balanced two-sided case in two ways. First, among independents, the relationship between awareness and pro-market attitudes is positive (rather than flat). Because independents uncritically accept a random sample of all elite messages to which they are exposed, higher levels of awareness yield greater exposure to the overall pro-market slant of elite discourse.[13] Second, the relationship between awareness and pro-market attitudes among Left partisans is not negative. Two scenarios are actually possible among Left partisans. Because overall information flows are skewed, exposure to the largely pro-market discourse of elites may overwhelm the predispositions of even highly aware Left partisans. This may create a positive relationship between awareness and support for the market policy, as in scenario 1.[14] Even when most rhetoric is pro-market, however, highly aware Left partisans may still be able to seek out antimarket elites and absorb their rhetoric, as in scenario 2 (Geddes and Zaller 1989). If so, an inflection point occurs in which the relationship between awareness and support reverses.

because Latin American countries feature many new or highly transitional party systems that have weak roots in the electorate (Baker et al. 2006; Mainwaring and Scully 1995).

[13] Awareness does expose independents to some antimarket messages, which they uncritically accept. Therefore, their slope is not as steep as that for Right partisans.

[14] Moderately and highly aware Left partisans are not as prone to accept uncritically all pro-market messages as Right partisans, so the slope on awareness in scenario 1 is not as steep as that for Right partisans.

Theoretical Framework

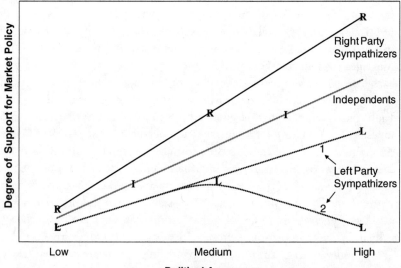

Figure 2.2 Theoretical Patterns of Mass Support for Market Policies under a Skewed Two-Sided Information Flow: Elites' Opinions Are Divided by Party and the Right Party Is Larger.
Note: "**R**": Right Party sympathizers. "**L**": Left Party sympathizers. "**I**": Independents.

The skewed, two-sided-information-flow scenario illustrates how the one-sided and the balanced, two-sided scenarios (Figure 2.1) are not exhaustive but rather are opposite ends of a continuum of possible elite-discourse arrangements. This has two important implications. First, when elite opinion is skewed but not unanimous, a partisan cleavage among the politically aware and an awareness gap can exist simultaneously. In Figure 2.2, awareness has a positive impact on the propensity to support the market policy among Right partisans and independents, who (because the Left Party is of minority size) collectively comprise a majority of the citizenry. Therefore, across all citizens, the politically aware have a higher average propensity to support the policy than the politically unaware do. Despite this, highly aware Left partisans are not as enthusiastic about the policy as highly aware Right partisans: Left partisans listen to antimarket elites, so a partisan gap at high levels of awareness still exists.

Second, because independents accept a random sample of elite communications, one can interpret the slope of the awareness line among

49

independents as a "barometer" of the relative effectiveness of competing political camps. If the balance of messages emanating from elites is skewed in a pro-market direction, then independents will absorb more pro-market messages than antimarket ones, *but only to the extent that they are exposed to elite communications.* When the line for independents is positively and steeply sloped, matching or nearly matching the slope of the line among Right partisans, pro-market elites are far more effective than antimarket elites at disseminating their messages and persuading the attentive masses. As the relative effectiveness of the pro-market camp declines, so too does the steepness of the awareness line for independents. When pro-market elites are matched in their effectiveness by antimarket ones, the line collapses to the flat line of the balanced two-sided scenario. A negative slope is also possible and would indicate that antimarket elites are more rhetorically effective than pro-market ones. In short, the more positive the slope among independents, the more dominant and effective are pro-market elite communications.

The application of this top-down framework indicates that I derive my conclusions about the merits of a top-down explanation by assessing how political predispositions condition the impact of political awareness rather than by assessing the impact of political predispositions alone. Other scholars merely do the latter, noting a correlation between attitudes and partisanship (Kaufman and Zuckermann 1998; Luna and Zechmeister 2005; Magaloni and Romero 2008). Their finding, however, is consistent with predispositions as both cause and effect, so scholars do not arrive at any definitive or convincing conclusions about whether elites do influence mass opinion. The application and testing of a more rigorous and theoretically grounded framework will clarify the extent of elite influence over mass beliefs in Latin America.

A Neoliberal Hegemony?

Which of the three information-flow scenarios best describes elite opinion toward market reform in Latin America? According to some scholars, the united elites scenario may be the most relevant. Many political scientists pinpoint the early to mid-1990s as a time in which a neoliberal hegemony emerged among the Latin American political elite (Armijo and Faucher 2002; Biersteker 1995; Munck 2003; Murillo 2002; Weyland 2002). This claim regarding the emergence of a consensus or a *pensée unique* among elites is well summarized in the following quotation:

Theoretical Framework

Neoliberalism began to claim hegemonic status in the sense that it defined what could be said (believed?) and not said by opinion leaders who wanted to be taken seriously. To say that a new economic hegemony was forged in this period should not be taken as saying that there were no real, responsible policy alternatives available to leaders with distinct constituencies and priorities. . . . Yet certain forms of expression about the economy that had been common only a decade or two earlier now nearly disappeared. . . . [C]learly one of the greatest achievements of those who pressured for [the shift to neoliberal policies] was the consequent rise of a neoliberal hegemony. (Stokes 2001a, 195)

Perceived changes within the Latin American Left were crucial in driving these scholarly perceptions. Many left-leaning elites themselves had moderated their economic policy beliefs because statist policies seemed so discredited by the region's economic crises in the 1980s. Left-of-center parties with roots in urban labor movements espoused and implemented market-friendly policies in some countries, and the Left acquiesced or gave only token resistance in many others (Bruhn 2004; Hunter 2007; Levitsky 2003; Murillo 2001; Murillo and Martinez-Gallardo 2007; Samuels 2004). Moreover, in the 1990s, the Left's presence was diminutive as it struggled to attract voters. A leading study of the Left concludes that its capacity to mobilize and shape public opinion in the 1990s against free market orthodoxy was "neutralized and dissolved":

. . . [T]he Latin American Left has had [difficulties] in crafting a viable economic alternative to neoliberalism.. . . [T]he sweep of the market revolution reflects the remarkable capacity of neoliberalism to neutralize and dissolve its opposition or countervailing forces. (Roberts 1998, 12, 270)

Other scholarship and empirical trends suggest, however, that claims of a neoliberal hegemony are exaggerated or have grown less accurate through time, making a divided elites scenario potentially more applicable to the Latin American case. As a set of ideologically charged issues with concrete distributional consequences, market policies have been a principal axis of elite and partisan contestation in most countries throughout the new market era (Rosas 2005). Moreover, many scholars allege the existence of an elite fatigue with reform, one that settled into the region in the late 1990s and remained thereafter (Lora et al. 2004). Since 1998, the traditionally statist Left has been reinvigorated, winning various presidencies and greater representation in national legislatures, thereby potentially increasing the share of antimarket discourse in the region's information flows. Indeed, since then, the reform process has slowed or even been partially reversed, with some leaders blocking or reversing certain privatizations, exiting regional trade pacts, and halting their countries' involvement in negotiations over the FTAA.

In the end, and in the spirit of unpacking reforms, I demonstrate that the contours and balance of elite opinion, and thus mass opinion, have varied across different policy elements and through time. Elite rhetoric concerning most forms of trade liberalization has been one-sided and pro-market, while politicians' discourse about privatization and foreign investment has been two-sided but skewed in a pro-market direction. For these reasons, *elites have induced hegemony effects for most issues at most times*. However, while one-sided information flows about trade have produced equally sized awareness gaps among right-partisans, left-partisans, and independents, two-sided information flows about privatization and foreign investment have produced polarizing effects among highly aware partisans. Still, the balance of elite discourse on some issues varied through time. In particular, elite support for privatization began to decline in the late 1990s. The greater balance between pro- and antimarket elite messages diminished the hegemony effects among citizens. It also ignited a newfound distaste for market reforms among many highly aware citizens. The late 1990s shift in the balance of elite discourse to a stance more critical, and thus more balanced, of the market-oriented status quo weakened the strong hegemony effects associated with one- and skewed, two-sided patterns in the 1990s.

Top-Down and Bottom-Up Influences Compared

Although I argue that both matter, this book specifies a crucial division of labor between the top-down and bottom-up frameworks. I argue that aggregate support for market policies is mostly established by the bottom-up, material consequences of reforms and not by the top-down, elite pronouncements about them. This argument contrasts with a purist top-down explanation, in which elite rhetoric is the *sole* source of all mass opinion. I claim that the overall popularity of economic policies, which varies substantially across policies, countries, and time, is almost exclusively a function of the concrete economic consequences that citizens experience. Top-down factors shape individual-level differences, or mass cleavages, in beliefs about reforms (as do bottom-up factors), but elites have only a minor impact on the overall popularity of market reforms.

Figure 2.3 clarifies the varied roles of these two different approaches. The two leftmost cells represent the two theoretical approaches or sets of

Theoretical Framework

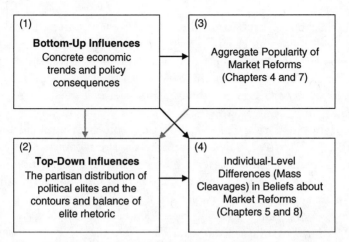

Figure 2.3. Hypothesized Role of Bottom-Up and Top-Down Factors.

independent variables: bottom-up (cell 1) and top-down influences (cell 2). The two right-hand cells show the two dependent variables or, more accurately, two different levels of public opinion: the aggregate level (cell 3) and the individual level (cell 4). The three black arrows represent the relationships that are analyzed, described, and argued in this book. First, the horizontal arrow from cell 1 to cell 3 represents the argument that bottom-up factors are the primary cause of the aggregate popularity of market reforms. This is the focus of Chapters 4 (on Latin America) and 7 (on Brazil). Second, the diagonal black arrow from cell 1 to cell 4 demonstrates that bottom-up factors, such as individual-level differences in consumption behavior, structure individual-level attitudinal differences, also called "mass cleavages," over market reforms. This is the focus of Chapters 5 and 8. Third, the horizontal arrow from cell 2 to cell 4 suggests that top-down factors also structure mass cleavages, explaining attitudinal differences across individuals who otherwise have equivalent consumer interests. Chapters 5 and 8 also examine this relationship. However, *the lack of a black arrow from cell 2 to cell 3 conveys the crucial claim that top-down factors have only a weak impact on aggregate public opinion toward market reforms.* In other words, bottom-up, and especially consumption-based, economic concerns are more influential than elite rhetoric in setting *aggregate* patterns. The aggregate levels of support are exogenous to elite rhetoric, set instead by economic trends and material consequences.

In this book, I demonstrate the veracity of these patterns with data, but the lack of a strong causal influence from elite discourse to aggregate popularity also has a sound theoretical grounding. First, the purist version of the top-down framework is self-contradictory because it admits that a large swath of mass publics in all societies is mostly unexposed to elite rhetoric. Elites have little ability to shape the beliefs of these politically unaware individuals, so other influences must fill this void (Zaller 1992). Second, the enormous literature within political science on retrospective voting patterns points to a strong correlation between objective economic conditions and a variety of mass political evaluations and behaviors, such as vote choice, presidential approval, and issue beliefs (Fiorina 1981; Remmer 1991; Stokes 2001b; but see Hellwig and Samuels 2007). These findings demonstrate not only that economic conditions directly shape citizens' perceptions but also that the aggregate distribution of elite rhetoric itself is endogenous to these perceptions. Finally, countless empirical examples demonstrate a disjuncture between elite opinion and mass opinion. For example, early public opinion studies showed that the masses were far less tolerant than elites (McClosky 1964). More recently, many Europeans, especially referendum voters in France, Ireland, and the Netherlands, have rejected the proposed European Union (EU) constitution despite a broad consensus among elites in its favor. Rigorous empirical research on this issue has demonstrated that EU elites are largely powerless to shape aggregate levels of mass support for integration (Gabel and Scheve 2007). In short, elites have a very weak capacity to make substantial portions of the electorate perceive economic results that simply do not exist.

Two other relationships in Figure 2.3 are represented by grayed-out arrows. They are grayed out because they depict causal claims that have a plausible empirical basis but are not the focus of this book. First, the vertical arrow from cell 1 to cell 2 represents the standard retrospective voting claim: The partisan distribution of elites and thus the balance of pro-market discourse result from economic trends and economic policy consequences. Second, the diagonal arrow from cell 3 to cell 2 represents an "issue voting" relationship, whereby aggregate trends in the mass popularity of market reforms establish the balance of elite configurations. Surprisingly, scholars have largely failed to test empirically whether this link exists, yet many assume that it does. For example, when scholars proclaim that a leftist victory represents a mandate for reform reversal, they posit the nature of (unknown) cell 3 from (observed) cell 2 based on the assumption that this causal link exists. After all, the conventional explanation for the rise of the Left in Latin America is that voters' growing disappointment with market reforms after 1998 led them to increase the relative size and importance of the Left among the region's political elite. My argument in this book does not directly address whether this link exists. However, by establishing with empirical data some facts about the aggregate mass preferences of cell 3, I create a sounder basis than previous studies have for arriving at some conclusions about the nature of the Left's mandate in Latin America.

Conclusion

By analyzing the bottom-up and top-down aspects of public opinion formation, this book applies a more realistic approach to mass political behavior than any application of a single theoretical construct could. It eschews the heroic assumptions of strict economic rationality, yet it adopts numerous hypotheses from political economy theory for the bottom-up view and applies them with a limited-information rationality approach. In doing so, it also shuns the purist top-down depictions of unthinking citizens who reactively follow the cues of political elites, yet it recognizes that politicians may often be able to persuade substantial portions of the population.

In the end, the theoretical and methodological contributions of this book are threefold. First, although scholarship on Latin American politics has a long and rich bottom-up tradition for understanding mass preferences over economic policy, it has focused on producer-based interests to the near exclusion of consumption-oriented ones. This book systematizes a consumption-based notion of interests, and it shows how these have been primarily responsible for shaping Latin Americans' beliefs about the Washington Consensus. Second, the literature on Latin American politics largely ignores top-down influences on public opinion, typically assuming that elites take mass preferences as a given. This book provides a framework and evidence to show that elite rhetoric is frequently persuasive. Finally, the specific literature on public opinion toward the market reform process fails to unpack attitudes toward different policies and to explain why some market policies are more popular than others. It also fails to provide a convincing descriptive and theoretical statement of why some individuals are more pro-market than others. This book develops such a picture that is based on both bottom-up and top-down notions of public opinion.

To derive specific expectations from these new theoretical and methodological approaches, the following chapter establishes the context in which Latin American citizens have forged beliefs about the Washington Consensus. To do so, it depicts the contours of the main independent variables: the economic consequences so crucial to the bottom-up approach and the content of elite rhetoric for the top-down approach.

PART II
_____

Mass Beliefs about Market Policies in Latin America

3

The Economic Consequences and Elite Rhetoric of Market Reform in Latin America

In the bottom-up theoretical framework, the source of mass responses to market reforms is the impact of these policies on material well-being. In the top-down framework, the source of mass beliefs is elite rhetoric about market policies. This chapter describes the nature and content of these two independent variables in Latin America throughout the 1990s and early 2000s. In the first section, I describe the most important and visible microeconomic consequences of privatization, globalizing policies, and pension privatization. For most policies, the two most important and visible economic channels through which reforms have influenced individual welfare have been the labor-market channel and the consumption channel. I address labor-channel effects by describing how each policy has affected employment availability, wages, and other aspects of job quality. I describe consumer-channel effects by clarifying how each policy has influenced the quality, availability, and affordability of goods and services. In doing so, I explicate each policy's aggregate impact on labor markets and consumer welfare as well as its distributional consequences (i.e., varied effects across individuals) through each of these channels. In the second section, I describe the contours of elite opinion toward reforms. In both sections, I describe regionwide averages and trends. While cross-national differences certainly exist, the goal of this and the subsequent two chapters on mass opinion is to highlight and explain regionwide, not country-level, patterns.

The first section has four sets of findings. First, privatization has had mostly negative consequences for consumers because it has resulted in utility price increases. In contrast, globalizing policies, such as trade and capital account liberalization, have had almost exclusively positive consumer consequences because relative prices for relevant goods and services have declined dramatically as availability and quality have improved. Second, privatization has had a limited impact on labor markets because, while it did typically result in immediate layoffs, the number of job losses was small relative to the size of the entire labor market. In contrast, globalizing policies have had a mostly negative impact on labor markets because firm restructuring has caused a rise in unemployment and job turnover.

Third, privatization and globalization have had distributional consequences. Privatization has had progressive, albeit minimal, distributional consequences through the labor channel. Globalization has had a largely regressive impact because it has increased the gap in wages between skilled and unskilled workers. Both policies have exerted important distributional consequences through the consumer channel. Privatization has had a nonlinear (with respect to income) impact on consumer welfare, helping the poor who did not have access to utility services before privatization but hurting middle-income groups that have seen price increases in services that they already had. The wealthy also had access before privatization, but they have been better positioned to absorb price increases than middle-income groups. In contrast, the impact of globalization through the consumption channel has been regressive because middle- and upper-income groups have been more likely than the poor to consume the high-value-added imports and import-competing goods that underwent relative price declines. Finally, I discuss the impact of pension privatization in a different light. Although consumption- and labor-channel effects have been present, they have been largely invisible to most citizens. Instead, the most visible consequences of pension privatization have occurred through changes in citizens' transfer payments and tax burdens, and these consequences have been largely negative.

The second section describes politicians' opinions toward market reforms and arrives at three main conclusions. First, Latin American elites have been, on balance, favorable to market policies. Second, this sentiment has not been unanimous or uniform across all policies. In particular, issues such as privatization and foreign investment have been partisan, dividing left-leaning politicians from right-leaning ones. In contrast, trade liberalization has been a less polarizing issue. Finally, elite support for market policies has shifted through time. Enthusiasm peaked in the late 1990s, falling thereafter as elites of both the Left and the Right grew slightly more critical of the Washington Consensus.

The Economic Consequences of Market Reforms

Privatization

Technical studies generally agree that the privatization of SOEs made the newly privatized firms more efficient and profitable. Privatization also improved governments' fiscal positions by providing an immediate cash infusion and by offloading indebted firms (Birdsall and Nellis 2003; Chong and López-de-Silanes 2005; Megginson and Netter 2001). Such trends, however, are unlikely to resonate in public opinion. Firm efficiency and profitability directly affected only a small number of people, and privatization's implications for fiscal and macroeconomic criteria were not readily visible to most citizens (Chong and López-de-Silanes 2005; Pierson 1996).

Instead, more likely to have produced widespread impacts on citizens is the extent to which newly privatized firms (1) streamlined by sacking workers and cutting labor costs and (2) managed the enhanced productivity by passing it on to consumers in the form of lower prices, higher quality, and greater access. The fact that newly privatized firms experienced improved efficiency and profitability confirms the long-held suspicion that SOEs ignored market signals for political reasons. They typically engaged in deliberate overemployment or "labor hoarding," with managers and politicians using jobs as sources of patronage. Moreover, rates for state-owned utility services often did not reflect cost structures. Many electricity, water, and telecommunications firms set prices to subsidize residential users at the expense of commercial ones. I describe the impact of privatization on employment and consumption criteria in turn.

The privatization process resulted in immediate job losses, a sign that overemployment was extensive. Even privatization proponents agree: ". . . the evidence indicates that more people have lost jobs than gained them through privatization" (Birdsall and Nellis 2003, 1626; Foster et al. 2005). Cutbacks were large in former SOEs, with the typical Latin American country reducing its SOE workforce by about one-quarter to one-half and some firms firing as many as 75% of their employees (Chong and López-de-Silanes 2005; Li and Xu 2004). Many of these sacked workers were absorbed into the private sector, and some were even rehired by the privatized firm. Even in such cases, however, workers typically began their new jobs with lower wages (Galiani et al. 2005; IDB 2004; McKenzie and Mookherjee 2005).

A crucial fact, however, should temper this pessimism when considering privatization's longer-term, aggregate impact on labor markets: Labor-market shifts caused by postprivatization layoffs have been dwarfed by normal job churning, macroeconomic trends, and other influences. SOE employees prior to reform initiation comprised *at most* 4% of the work-force in Latin American countries. Overemployment was not a generalized means of providing a social safety net, so layoffs directly affected only a slim slice of the population. For example, only 13% of Argentina's rise in unemployment from 1989 to 1997 was due to layoffs in SOEs and former SOEs (McKenzie and Mookherjee 2005).

Although the impact of privatization through the labor-market channel has not been large in the aggregate, most economic studies find that the distributional consequences of privatization layoffs have been progressive, even if slightly so. Prior to the privatization wave, most SOE employees were white-collar workers with moderate to high degrees of formal education, so layoffs were more heavily concentrated among skilled workers than among unskilled workers (Graham and Pettinato 2002; IDB 2004).

While economists downplay privatization's impact on labor markets, they find the impact of privatization on consumers to be far more extensive: "Privatization's most widespread effects are on consumers of essential utility services" (McKenzie and Mookherjee 2005, 76; see also Foster et al. 2005). In particular, privatization has affected welfare through the consumer channel by changing the degree of access to utility networks, tariffs for utility services, and the quality of services provided.

By far the most impressive accomplishment of utility privatization has been a rapid expansion of the infrastructure that enables consumer access to utility networks. Opponents of utility privatization feared that it would retard the extension of networks to rural and poor areas because of these areas' lower profitability (Bayliss 2002; SAPRIN 2004). In the end, however, new investment, improved technology, and higher prices made it affordable for firms to expand existing water, electricity, and telephone service networks. Moreover, many privatization contracts contained "universal service obligations" that required the new firms to establish service in previously underserved areas (Birdsall and Nellis 2003; Omar et al. 2003; Ramamurti 1996). Increased network availability also dramatically lowered the connection fees charged to establish consumer access. As a result, by the mid-2000s, well over 95% of urban residents throughout Latin America had water and electricity service, and their availability in rural areas had also increased (Kuczynski 2003). Telephone usage also grew. In the years following telecommunications privatization, the number of people with fixed-line access rose by 25% to 100% as many firms cleared their years-long waiting lists (ITU 2005; McKenzie and Mookherjee 2005). Mobile phone networks and usage also grew exponentially in the post-privatization era.

Although expanded access is proponents' favorite success story, three other important consumer-related trends have mitigated this beneficial impact. First, Latin America's remaining state-owned utilities *also* increased network coverage during the 1990s and 2000s. For example, access to telephone networks grew in countries like Colombia and Uruguay that never privatized their providers (ITU 2005). Similarly, comparisons within countries of subnational regions that pursued divergent policies in their water sectors reveal that privatized firms expanded network access at only a slightly faster rate, one that was probably imperceptible to most citizens (Galiani et al. 2005; McKenzie and Mookherjee 2005).

Second, the impact of privatization on the quality of utility services has also been mixed. Quality improvements on the decrepit infrastructure of the 1980s have been obvious, supporting advocates' claims that privatization is the solution to frequent blackouts, dropped phone calls, and dead fixed lines (Estache 2005; Kuczynski 2003). Despite these improvements, Latin America's recent history is rife with visible and contentious failures in service delivery by newly privatized firms (Estache and Goicoechea 2005). For example, electricity blackouts in the Dominican Republic led to protests in which nine people were killed, and complaints of dirty drinking water in Argentina contributed to the annulment of a foreign company's contract.

Third and most important, postprivatization utility rate hikes have been common due to "tariff rebalancing." Cross-subsidies from industrial to residential users were commonplace when SOEs provided services, so liberalization necessitated a correction that in most cases caused a price increase for the vast majority of citizens. Since pro-privatization governments were desperate to raise as much revenue from sell-offs as possible, they were more concerned with luring investors than with protecting consumers. Policymakers often promised weak regulatory regimes or no competition as enticements to investors. Motivated by this fiscal logic, governments promised potential buyers that they could rebalance tariffs upon purchasing the SOE (Rhodes 2006; Ugaz 2003). Moreover, private firms often made universal service obligations contingent on permission to eventually raise prices.

63

Figure 3.1 demonstrates that tariff hikes were the norm. It plots the evolution of mean pre- and postprivatization real prices (that is, relative to overall inflation) for residential telephone usage (Panel A) and electricity services (Panel B) in seventeen Latin American countries. The solid lines (labeled "Real Price Index" and corresponding to the left y-axis) represent an index of the mean price across all countries that privatized.[1] (Telephone service rates are the cost of a monthly "price basket" of fixed-line residential services, while electricity rates are the cost to residents of a single unit of electricity.[2]) In both utility sectors, the mean price rose in the years following the sell-off. The increase was especially sharp in the telecommunications sector, with prices rising over 500% faster than overall inflation in the decade pursuant to the sale. Real electricity rates also rose, although more modestly.

The dotted lines in Figure 3.1 identify privatization itself as the main force behind these price increases. Simple pre/post comparisons, as depicted by the solid lines, do not isolate the impact of the change in ownership itself. For example, real mean prices also increased steadily from 1985 to 2005 in the pool of countries that did *not* privatize their telephone or electricity firms, and prices may have increased faster than in countries with a privatized utility. As a fairer point of comparison, the dotted lines entitled "Ratio" (corresponding to the right y-axis) represent the ratio of the real price indices among countries that privatized to those among countries that did not. These ratios quantify the counterfactual of how much higher (if greater than 1) or lower (if less than 1) prices would have been had privatization never occurred. The dotted line in Panel A indicates that telephone service prices continued to rise in countries after privatization at a *much* faster rate than in countries that did not privatize. After nine years, prices had risen four times higher in the former than they had in the latter. The results on electricity rates in Panel B also confirm that privatization contributed to price hikes, although these results are less stark. In sum, prices in both sectors clearly rose after privatization, and the change in ownership itself caused these rate changes. New owners did *not* pass on the labor productivity and efficiency

---

[1] Means were smoothed with lowess to iron out idiosyncrasies.
[2] Telephone service rates are measured with a standard price basket of fixed-line services that estimates average monthly costs in constant U.S. dollars for residential users in each country. The price basket is comprised of the cost of a monthly subscription plus the per-unit cost of thirty three-minute local calls (ITU 2007; World Bank 2006). Electricity rates are the cost of 1 kWh of electricity in constant U.S. dollars (Estache and Goicoechea 2005).

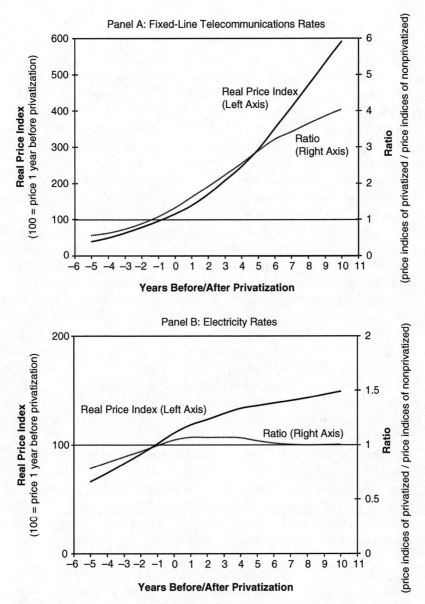

Figure 3.1 The Evolution of Pre- and Postprivatization Utility Prices in Latin America.
Note: Lines are produced with a lowess smoother.
Sources: Estache and Goicoechea (2005); ITU (2007).

gains from utility privatizations to consumers in the form of lower prices (Estache and Rossi 2004).

Besides these aggregate effects, privatization-induced changes to consumer welfare have produced important distributional consequences because consumption patterns are nonhomothetic, differing across individuals. The separate developments of access expansion and price increases have yielded distinct cross-cutting effects on relative well-being. The expanded access to telephone, electricity, and potable water networks has had a progressive effect because it occurred most rapidly among the rural and urban poor (Foster et al. 2005; McKenzie and Mookherjee 2005; Ugaz and Price 2003). Prior to privatization, a much higher proportion of middle- and upper-income consumers already had network access and was able to afford services. In contrast, the impact of tariff rebalancing has not been progressive. Price increases in utility services have created a greater burden for lower- and lower-middle-income users because such services already commanded a relatively high share of their consumption budgets (Chisari et al. 2003). Moreover, the process of tariff rebalancing in most countries almost always raised monthly subscription charges more quickly than it raised per-unit (by-the-minute or by-the-call) costs, thus penalizing low-usage and typically less wealthy subscribers more than high-usage ones (Foster et al. 2005; Ugaz 2003, 85). The standard trend in the postprivatization structure of Latin American telephone charges has been a rapid increase in the monthly subscription fee and a slightly slower increase in the cost of a local call (McKenzie and Mookherjee 2005; Ugaz and Price 2003).[3]

The two consumer-channel effects of expanded access and increased prices have combined to yield a nonlinear distributional result. First, poor individuals have been the most likely to experience gains because of new access. Second, existing low-usage customers, who tend to be of middle-income status, have been the most negatively affected. Many middle-income users were privileged enough to have access before privatization (i.e., existing customers) yet not privileged enough to be able to afford high usage. The cross-subsidization that took place when utilities were state-owned benefited middle-income and not poor consumers because the latter were less likely to have access: "After privatization, rather than the rich, it was the middle groups [that] were squeezed in order to reduce (partially) the price of access" (Rhodes 2006, 139; see also Estache 2005;

---

[3] The per-unit cost of long-distance calls, however, has fallen.

Irwin and Brook 2003; Murillo 2009; Murillo and Martinez-Gallardo 2007). Finally, existing high-usage consumers, who tend to be wealthy, have experienced smaller relative price increases and therefore have been less negatively affected. Income differences themselves have reinforced the distributional effects occurring among middle- and high-income groups; existing middle-income users devote a higher share of their overall expenditures to these services and the subsequent price changes than high-income users. In sum, the consumer channel effects of privatization have been nonlinear, exerting their most negative influence on lower-middle and middle-income groups while exerting their least negative influence on the poor and the rich.

Globalizing Policies

Prior to the reform wave, many economists sold globalization as a way to turn Latin America into an East Asia–like economic success story. Because they assumed that the region had a comparative advantage in unskilled labor, pro-market economists claimed that trade liberalization would lead to higher living standards for most workers and a progressive redistribution of wealth through export-led job creation and growth. An infusion of foreign investment was supposed to aid the process, introducing advanced technologies to more efficiently and productively employ the region's natural resources and human capital (Edwards 1995; Wood 1997). Unfortunately, the lowering of protectionist barriers to foreign goods and the opening of capital accounts to foreigners have not sent Latin America on a rapid path to prosperity. The revealed comparative advantage of most countries in the region is not unskilled labor, especially vis-à-vis other recent successful entrants to the global economy such as China and India (Leamer 1984; Wood 1997). Instead, it is primary products, leaving the region in globalization's "missing middle": squeezed by knowledge economies from above and low-wage economies from below (Garrett 2004).

Liberalization has thus exposed the region's vulnerabilities in labor-intensive manufacturing. During the import substitution years, many private firms depended on protection from international competition for their very existence. Although they sold expensive goods and were detrimental to economic efficiency, these "hothouse" economies allowed many workers to share in the rents enjoyed by the tradable goods sector. With increased trade inflows, imports have replaced many locally produced inputs and finished consumer goods (Berg et al. 2006). Instead of achieving export-led growth, most Latin American countries initially saw imports increase at a much faster rate than exports.[4] Restructuring due to import competition has decimated many manufacturing firms and even entire sectors in some countries.

Similarly, a boom in foreign direct investment has not yielded the widely expected increases in employment opportunities in Latin American economies. Foreign-owned firms have introduced laborsaving techniques that are capital-intensive (Reardon and Berdegué 2002; Stallings and Peres 2000). In many countries, foreign investment inflows have largely occurred through the acquisition of existing assets, in part through the job-deleting privatization process. Even when inflows have gone toward asset creation or "greenfield" investment, new jobs and the infusion of capital have often crowded out existing jobs and domestic capital; net capital formation has not necessarily expanded as a percentage of gross domestic product (GDP) (Berg et al. 2006). Moreover, although capital inflows have grown, they have also become more volatile due to the increase in foreign *portfolio* investment, whereby foreigners merely lend to domestic borrowers but do not directly participate in the creation of assets. In the end, foreign investment may have lowered wages: Findings in economics demonstrate that openness to inflows grants mobile capital enhanced bargaining power vis-à-vis immobile labor (IDB 1998; Rodrik 1997).

Overall, the results of these increases in trade and capital inflows for labor markets have been largely negative, as many workers have given up the rents they enjoyed under import substitution: "... Latin American countries generally suffered from stagnant wages, rising unemployment, and increasing wage inequality" (IDB 2004, 179). High-quality formal sector jobs have steadily disappeared, and many discouraged workers have dropped out of the labor market altogether (Berg et al. 2006; Haltiwanger et al. 2004). Job creation has been concentrated in the informal sector, which has lower average wages and no labor contracts to provide safety regulations, retirement pensions, or unemployment benefits. Historically a primary source of stable formal sector jobs, manufacturing as a share of GDP has declined. Remaining formal sector jobs have also become more precarious and less lucrative. Job turnover and the number of temporary contracts have increased, and the share of unionized jobs has

---

[4] The overvalued exchange rates of the 1990s (an anti-inflationary maneuver) contributed to this trend. I consider overvaluation a trade liberalization measure itself, however, as it exposes domestic industries to severe import competition.

fallen: ". . . [T]he proportion of workers with 'secure' jobs has declined practically in all of the countries of the region" (Rodrik 2001, 13). Wages have stagnated or declined, and unemployment rates have increased in nearly every country (ECLAC 2000b; IDB 1997, 2004; Stallings and Peres 2000).[5]

Moreover, rather than improving the relative wages and welfare of unskilled workers, precisely the *opposite* has occurred in most cases: Relative returns to skill have increased because of globalization. Evidence abounds that demonstrates an increase in the Latin American "skill premium" (Graham and Pettinato 2002; IDB 2004, 179). On average, the wage returns for an extra year of schooling increased by 7% from 1990 to 2000, and most of this increase was concentrated among those with at least some college education (Behrman et al. 2003). Scholars disagree on why policies encouraging international trade and foreign investment have increased this wage gap, but the consensus is that they did (Berg et al. 2006; Ferranti 2003; Morley 2001; Robbins and Gindling 1999; Stallings and Peres 2000).

These observations about the relationship between wealth and the labor-market effects of trade refer to Latin America's enhanced trade with developed countries – that is, North–South trade. Trade with other developing countries and especially with other Latin American neighbors has also grown since 1990. This increase in South–South trade, however, has not yielded the major distributional consequences for workers that expanded North–South trade has. Countries trading within Latin America's South–South trade pacts, such as Mercosul and the Andean Pact, often have low trade "complementarities" (IDB 2002a; Kono 2007). They specialize in and export similar types of goods with matching skill intensities, so the distributional consequences of these pacts do not relate to workers' overall skill or wealth levels.

Amid the rather bad news about workers and globalization in Latin America, a quiet revolution in consumer welfare has occurred (Guedes and Oliveira 2006). Standard trade theory holds that a protected industry

---

[5] Of course, these aggregate trends in job quality and availability were not solely the result of Latin America's new trade and capital account laws. Rigid labor laws, macroeconomic shocks, and the exchange rate blunders of the 1990s certainly contributed to slow job creation. A number of scholars, however, have linked these negative trends to increased trade: "[Reforms] have slowed the pace of employment growth and may have been one cause of the rise in unemployment rates. . . . Employment rates have declined, and that has happened more forcefully where the structural reforms, and particularly trade and finance reforms, have been deepest" (IDB 1997, 58; see also Currie and Harrison 1997; Goldberg and Pavcnik 2004; Saavedra 2003; Stallings and Peres 2000).

decreases aggregate national income by increasing consumer prices for its goods and services (Smith 1776; Tullock 1967). Consumers are charged extra for the industry's inefficiencies, so only owners and employees in that sector benefit from protectionism. As a result, consumers experience net benefits from trade liberalization. Under import substitution, Latin America's many hothouse firms offered few alternatives at low quality above the world's market price. The relaxation of import tariffs in the 1980s and 1990s had an immediate and obvious impact on consumer choice. The affordability, quality, variety, and availability of many goods expanded in a short time (Irwin 2005; Murphy and Shleifer 1997; Reardon and Berdegué 2002; Romer 1994).

Figure 3.2 demonstrates the positive effects of trade liberalization on affordability. The setup of the figure is similar to that of Figure 3.1 (which reported privatization-related price changes). Figure 3.2 plots, as a function of time, the smoothed means of real price indices for three classes of tradable goods in seventeen Latin American countries. Time on the x-axis is expressed as the number of years before or after trade liberalization began.[6] Data are normalized so that the price in each country one year prior to liberalization is equivalent to 100. The three categories of tradable goods are "Food and Beverages" (solid line); "Household Durables," such as electronic appliances and furniture (dashed line); and "Clothing" (dotted line). Real prices fell after trade liberalization for all three classes of tradable goods. The real price of food, however, did not fall as quickly as the real prices of the other two types of goods. In sum, the cost of tradable goods relative to prices of other goods and services (and especially utilities) fell sharply throughout the 1990s in Latin America.

While yielding a net positive impact for all consumers, globalization has had a regressive distributional effect through the consumption channel because of wealth-related differences in consumer tastes (Deaton 1989; Houthakker 1957). In Latin America, the propensity to consume imports and import-competing goods is positively correlated with wealth. I describe why this is so in two different ways. First, generally speaking, high-income countries tend to produce and export goods that fit the consumption budgets of high-income consumers, and less developed countries tend to produce and export goods that low-income individuals

---

[6] To determine the first year of trade liberalization, I consulted the commercial policy reform index in "Indexes of Structural Reform" (Morley et al. 1999). The precise years are available from the author upon request.

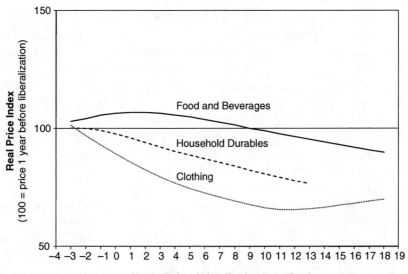

Figure 3.2   The Evolution of Pre- and Postliberalization Prices for Three Classes of Tradable Goods in Latin America.
Note: Lines are produced with a lowess smoother. Although the original mean values are 100 for the real price index one year prior to privatization (−1 on the *x*-axis), these values are not precisely achieved in these figures because of the smoothing.
Source: ECLAC (2001).

have a higher propensity to consume (Broda and Romalis 2008; Stewart 1977). Stated differently, "poor countries export necessities, and rich export luxuries" (Dalgin et al. 2008, 771). As a result, Latin America's wealthy consumers have a higher propensity to consume its imports and import-competing goods, and its poor consumers have a higher propensity to consume its exportable goods (Baker 2005; O'Donnell 1978). Second and more specifically, Latin American exports are resource-intensive and its imports are capital- and skilled-labor-intensive (Berg et al. 2006; IDB 2004; Ventura-Dias et al. 1999). On average, capital- and skilled-labor-intensive goods comprise a higher share of high-income consumption bundles than they do of low-income bundles (Leonardi 2003). It is a widely established cross-national fact that poor consumers spend a higher share of their incomes than wealthy consumers on resource-intensive necessities like food, beverages, and low-quality clothing (Engel 1857; Houthakker 1957; Selvanathan and Selvanathan 2003). In contrast, wealthy individuals consume capital- and skill-intensive goods like motor vehicles, electronic appliances, and fashionable clothing at a higher rate than poor consumers (Gregory et al. 2007). As a result, poor Latin Americans consume imports and import-competing goods at lower rates than the wealthy.

Three points merit emphasis. First, the strength of the linear, positive relationship between income and the propensity to consume imports and import-competing goods may be mitigated somewhat by the fact that extremely wealthy individuals in Latin America devote a large share of their incomes to nontraded items, especially services such as health, education, and savings (Baker 2003). Second, these findings on the positive relationship between wealth and consumer-channel benefits should not becloud the following fact: The average prices and quality of tradable goods that lower-income groups tend to purchase *have declined* with free trade. After all, food prices have fallen following trade liberalization episodes. The average prices and quality of items that middle- and upper-income consumers tend to purchase, however, have undergone *greater* improvements because household durables prices have fallen *faster* than those for food.[7] (Revisit Figure 3.2.) Third, these claims about the relationship between consumption-channel gains and wealth again refer to the consequences of North–South, not South–South, trade. The wealth-related distributional consequences of South–South trade for consumers have been limited because trade with other developing countries involves an exchange of similar types of goods.

Another mechanism through which nonhomothetic tastes might affect attitudes is via differences in the propensity to consume foreign culture, especially popular entertainment. The explosion of and attraction to foreign entertainment options, such as movies, music, television, and sports, have certainly been among the most visible consequences of globalization in Latin America and have thus been vehicles for transporting pro-trade norms (Barber 1995). For consumers, foreign entertainment goods and services are luxury purchases. Such items are likely to comprise a greater share of high-income consumption baskets than low-income ones (Bourdieu 1986).

Qualitative researchers working in extremely different traditions and on very different historical periods provide further backing for these findings

---

[7] Baker (2003) presents more detailed consumption budget data to show that the share of durable goods and clothing in one's consumption budget varies almost monotonically with wealth.

about wealth and the propensity to consume imports. Foreign purchases have a particular hold over individuals with high levels of disposable income:

... [T]he patterning of imports [throughout Latin American history] shows more complex divisions than the bifurcation between a small elite heavily committed to foreign goods and the masses of the population, consuming only a few basic imported goods. There were a number of intermediate strata (urban middle classes strongly oriented toward imports appear again and again). (Orlove and Bauer 1997, 12)

... [T]he quest for foreign goods and travel unifies the Brazilian middle class. (O'Dougherty 2002, 126)

Foreign direct investment has also yielded consumption-related distributional consequences. A strict focus on purely tradable goods is not necessary when considering foreign direct investment. Foreign investment inflows to Latin America have been largely concentrated in the service sector (59%), such as retailing, banking, and entertainment, outdistancing those in the manufacturing (28%) and agricultural sectors (13%) (ECLAC 2005). Like imports, services also comprise a higher share of high-income consumption budgets than they do of low-income ones. The consumption-channel effects of foreign investment are thus also regressive (Gregory et al. 2007).

A case study of postliberalization developments in the retail food sector exemplifies some of the influences of globalization on workers and consumers in Latin America. Besides being a particularly illustrative example of the aggregate and distributional consequences of trade and capital account liberalization policies, food retailing is an important sector because Latin Americans devote 30% to 35% of their consumption budgets to food and beverages. Moreover, food as a share of consumption budgets is stratified by wealth.

The most important trend in food retailing during the 1990s was a globalization-induced "supermarket revolution," with the supermarket share of the entire sector growing from about 10% in 1990 to 50% by 2000 (Schwentesius and Gómez 2002). Foreign investors and international trade directly spurred the rise of supermarkets. Most supermarkets are owned by foreign conglomerates, with Carrefour (French), Royal Ahold (Dutch), and Wal-Mart (American) among the leaders. These foreign investments have also stimulated the expansion of domestically owned supermarkets, such as Pão de Açucar (Brazil) and Soriana (Mexico). Supermarkets are also more likely to sell imported foods than their competitors.

The consequences of supermarket growth through the labor-market channel have been mostly negative and regressive. The growth of supermarkets came at the expense of small retail grocers (also called "mom-and-pop" stores) and to a lesser extent informal-sector traditional markets (also called "plaza markets" or "street fairs") specializing in fresh fruits and vegetables. For example, 65,000 small shops in Argentina closed between 1984 and 1993, and 5,240 did so in Chile between 1991 and 1995 (Reardon and Berdegué 2002). More efficient because of economies of scale and access to laborsaving technologies, supermarkets have caused net job losses in the food retailing sector. Moreover, supermarkets require more skilled workers than small retailers to manage larger inventories and larger (and often more foreign) suppliers. With greater bargaining power than individual and family vendors, supermarkets also tend to buy from medium- and large-scale agribusiness suppliers who can deliver large quantities at lower cost while maintaining formal sector accounting practices. This has squeezed out small farmers because they typically demand higher per-unit prices (Reardon and Berdegué 2002).

Despite these labor-market concerns, the rise of supermarkets has been a major impetus behind the consumer revolution in Latin America. Most obviously, many consumers favor supermarkets, a preference that clearly drove the quintupling of their market share. Supermarkets can be more convenient because they are conducive to large-volume shopping trips. In fact, for this reason, many consumers flocked to supermarkets during the hyperinflationary years. The larger scale of supermarkets also enables greater product variety and differentiation, and they offer more nonperishable and processed food options, many of them imported, than traditional markets and small stores. Finally, supermarkets offer lower prices for many products along with higher standards of cleanliness and quality (Reardon and Berdegué 2002).

Distributional implications, however, lurk behind these developments. Supermarkets were initially established as niche-market players in upper-income urban neighborhoods. While they eventually spread to middle- and even some lower-income urban neighborhoods by the late 1990s, for several reasons supermarket customers were still more likely to be from the upper half of the income scale (Rodríguez et al. 2002). Large-volume shopping trips require cars and large refrigerators, amenities that poor citizens are less likely to own. Middle- and upper-income women with full-time employment prefer the convenience of processed foods.

Moreover, 25% of agricultural production is exported, and food comprises a relatively high proportion of Latin American exports. Local agribusinesses sell their goods in international markets if unable to find a high enough price at home. Similarly, many of the highest-quality products are exported to satisfy the more discriminating demands of developed-country consumers. Because food comprises a much higher share of low-income consumption budgets, negative consumer-welfare trends such as these resonate more strongly among the poor.

This does not negate the fact, however, that the poor have experienced net gains as consumers from the supermarket revolution. The small stores and markets that have survived have lowered prices and improved quality (often by expanding imported options) to remain competitive with supermarkets. In sum, the supermarket revolution has provided net benefits to all consumers, but these benefits have accrued most heavily to middle-income groups and the wealthy.

Fiscal Reform: Pension Privatization

In 1981, Chile enacted a sweeping reform of its state-run pension system. The country's military regime pioneered the implementation of pension privatization by requiring almost all future entrants into the labor force to contribute to privately managed individual retirement savings accounts. Workers' eventual retirement benefits were subsequently based on the accumulated savings they held in personal accounts to which they made mandatory contributions. By 2007, nine other Latin American countries had also established mandatory individual retirement accounts as one means to fund and provide old-age pensions.[8]

The new approach has created social security systems in Latin America that have multiple "pillars," such that logically distinct pension regimes exist simultaneously within the same country (World Bank 1994). None of the ten countries that established a privately funded pillar has completely eliminated the extant "pay-as-you-go" (PAYG) pillar, which finances current retirees from a pool of public funds collected through the taxation of active workers. In the most ambitious cases, the PAYG pillar is to remain

---

[8] The countries that did so were Argentina, Bolivia, Colombia, Costa Rica, Dominican Republic, El Salvador, Mexico, Peru, and Uruguay (Gill et al. 2005).

open but only to fund the pensions of already-retired workers. Moreover, most countries maintain a trimmed-down PAYG system that guarantees a minimum antipoverty pension to supplement payouts from the new privately funded accounts. Some countries even offer workers a choice between the existing publicly funded and the new privately funded systems. Therefore, Latin America's pension regimes have not been completely privatized, but the region is unique in the fervor with which it has adopted a privately funded pillar (Weyland 2007).

To encourage implementation, privatization advocates listed a variety of reasons for shifting pension provision to individually funded accounts. The primary motivations invoked macroeconomic rationales, citing alleged improvements in fiscal health and in the financial sector rather than in social and antipoverty outcomes (Madrid 2003; Müller 2000; Weyland 2007). First, pension privatization would allow Latin American states to offload, at least partially, a budgetary line item that was perennially indebted. The exclusively PAYG "defined-benefits" systems enabled individuals' benefits to outrun their contributions because the latter did not necessarily constrain the former. Evasion, low retirement ages, and growing life expectancies reduced the financial solvency of many countries' PAYG systems and cast doubt on governments' ability to provide pensions in the long term. Second, privately funded accounts could potentially raise national savings rates and spur the development of financial markets in Latin America. Privatization advocates feted both trends as promoters of economic growth.

To be sure, advocates also argued that pension privatization would yield social benefits. They claimed that individualized accounts would grant "pride of ownership" to workers by allowing them to accrue personal wealth. This would encourage the millions of informal sector workers, who by definition lacked old-age pension coverage, to participate (James 1998; Piñera 1996). Also, eventual payouts from the accounts were expected to exceed those provided by PAYG because the latter were indexed to inflation or real wages and not to (presumably faster-growing) returns from capital investments.

In the end, however, pension privatization as implemented was intended "to serve macroeconomic goals (such as savings and investment)" (Mesa and Montecinos 1999, 8). In countries where pension privatization occurred, some of these fiscal and financial goals have been partially realized. The long-term fiscal sustainability of governments' pension commitments has improved dramatically. Moreover, the need to develop privately administered pension funds has expanded and has diversified

Latin America's capital markets, possibly encouraging faster economic growth (Gill et al. 2005).

Recall, however, the cognitive underpinnings of the theory of public opinion employed in this book. Citizens are not likely to notice or link macroeconomic benefits with pension reform per se. The link between, on the one hand, welfare-state reform and, on the other hand, macroeconomic growth, capital-market development, or long-term fiscal health is not one that is visible to most citizens (Pierson 1996). However, the consumer- and labor-market channel effects of pension privatization are also not highly visible. On the consumption side, the shift to private accounts, even if partial, has entailed inflationary "transition costs"; the state maintains its obligations to current retirees, who were "grandfathered in" to the PAYG system even when privatization occurred, while foregoing many contributions from the active labor force. Government borrowing and deficit spending to cover these costs may have increased consumer prices. On the labor-market side, pension privatization in some countries has lowered payroll taxes, potentially encouraging higher employment rates. In both instances, because the cause–effect linkages are distant, diffuse, and opaque, common citizens are unlikely to be aware of their existence.

Rather, the most crucial and visible microeconomic consequences of pension privatization in Latin America have occurred through changes to citizens' actual or expected transfer payments and to their tax burdens. Some of these consequences have been positive: Returns in the private accounts have matched expectations, exceeding 6% per year (in real terms) in most countries (Gill et al. 2005; Madrid 2006). Most outcomes, however, have been decidedly negative. First, returns in the individual accounts have been volatile. Financial crises struck numerous countries in the second half of the 1990s and in 2001, causing massive swings in most privately managed pension funds. Second, individual accounts hold a finite amount of funds, in contrast to the PAYG defined-benefits schemes that paid in perpetuity. As a result, individuals who live longer can exhaust their funds and effectively outlive their privately accrued pensions (Bertranou 2001). Third, administration costs have been much higher and more visible in the private funds than in the PAYG systems. Estimates show that costs paid to private fund administrators have exceeded 15% of contributions, a high rate induced by the muted competition among oligopolistic fund managers (Huber and Stephens 2000; Mesa-Lago 2005). High administrative costs have cut deeply into the annual returns of private accounts. Finally, policymakers often implemented pension privatization alongside laws that tightened eligibility requirements by raising the retirement age or the minimum number of contribution years (Madrid 2003). Even though such measures have helped to relieve fiscal burdens, they have required individuals to work longer before retiring.

For these reasons, pension reforms "have not . . . significantly improved benefits" (Bertranou 2001, 912). For example, average pensions from the public system in Chile exceeded those from the private system by 25% in 2001, and half of all workers with private accounts will not be able to fund even the state-mandated minimum pension (Mesa-Lago 2005). Moreover, private accounts have left workers more exposed to risk, evoking uncertainty and anxiety about the standard of living one can obtain in retirement. Such concerns may weigh heavily because, as much research demonstrates, human beings tend to be risk-averse (Kahneman and Tversky 1979).

Pension privatization has also led to potentially visible distributional consequences through the transfer-payment and tax channels. First, privatization has had age-related distributional effects. Advocates of private accounts argued that future retirees would prefer a privatized system because they had reason to doubt the long-term solvency of existing PAYG plans (World Bank 1994). This oddly assumes, however, that current workers (1) know and actively care about, or at least fail to discount, the future PAYG system's financial health and (2) prefer the current risks of private accounts to the future risk of an insolvent PAYG system. Moreover, it also presumes that abstract concerns about the future are not outweighed by the more immediate and concrete transition costs that are incurred most heavily by these current and future workers – that is, those who must fund the pensions of current retirees *and* themselves (Mesa and Bertranou 1997). Overall, future retirees have disproportionately absorbed risk (that was previously held by all taxpayers) and the fiscal costs of transition. Despite these concrete distributional consequences, current retirees themselves have had reasons to be skeptical of privatization because it has weakened the fiscal position of the PAYG funding pool.

Second, pension privatization has had gender-related distributional effects. Under strictly PAYG systems, monthly retirement benefits were based on workers' salaries in their final few years (usually three to five) of employment. Because of their longer life expectancies and (as was typical under PAYG systems) lower retirement ages, retired women received monthly pensions that were similar in size to those of men for a longer period. The establishment of individual private accounts reversed these advantages for women (Mesa and Bertranou 1997; Mesa and Montecinos

1999). Women enter and exit the labor market more frequently than men, and women also have lower average wages. Individual retirement accounts reflect these gender-related differences in the active labor market because women are unable to contribute as much to their accounts during their working years. To match the contributions of men, women must retire later and/or start contributing earlier. Moreover, women receive lower monthly benefits because their individual accounts must stretch over longer retirement times.

Finally, pension privatization has reinforced income inequalities. First, private systems are no more likely than PAYG systems to redistribute wealth because they, like PAYG systems, effectively mandate more generous retirement benefits for higher-wage individuals: PAYG systems linked monthly payouts to the size of one's wages, while private systems link benefits to the size of one's contributions. Second, while advocates believed that individual accounts would encourage informal-sector, and on average poorer, workers to participate in the pension regime, labor-force coverage has actually declined (IDB 2004; Mesa-Lago 2005). Third, informal-sector workers bear the transition costs, through increased tax burdens and/or deficits, of a system from which they do not benefit. Fourth, while PAYG systems were prone to rent-seeking, many groups, such as the military and other public-sector employees that enjoyed higher benefits under PAYG systems, have held on to their privileges. Finally, extremely well-heeled groups have been among the primary beneficiaries of reforms: Employers in many countries have seen their contribution requirements fall and bankers have gained access to more capital (Madrid 2003).

Elite Opinion toward Market Reforms

Citizens may certainly learn about policies and their impact on prices, jobs, and entitlements through their everyday activities. To the extent that concerns over less tangible concepts such as budget deficits and national sovereignty shape mass opinions, however, citizens are expressing attitudes that originated elsewhere. The ultimate sources are often political elites – that is, high-profile elected or appointed government officials whose policy statements are disseminated through the mass media.[9] This section describes

[9] This definition of "elite" admittedly overlooks numerous types of potential opinion leaders, such as journalists, political commentators, civil society leaders, and even pop culture icons. Research in political behavior, however, has shown this narrow definition

patterns in the economic policy attitudes and public rhetoric of Latin America's political class, describing the two criteria that determine the nature of top-down effects: (1) the relative balance of pro- versus antimarket opinion and (2) the contours of partisan cleavages, if any, over economic issues.

Scholarly statements about the contours of elite opinion in Latin America are generally made without the benefit of systematic, cross-national evidence. Researchers typically use the strength of the Left or vague impressions of rhetoric from presidential campaigns as proxies for the balance of elites' economic policy beliefs. Potential shifts in beliefs among nonleftist politicians are ignored. Moreover, all scholarly conclusions about the contours of elite opinion and rhetoric are marked by the ongoing failure to unpack attitudes toward different policies. To address these shortcomings and, in doing so, to provide concrete expectations for the top-down influences on mass opinion, I briefly summarize relevant findings from opinion surveys of national legislators in eighteen Latin American countries from 1994 to 2004. I use the elite survey data collected by the Latin American Parliamentary Elites Project (PELA) (Alcántara 2005).

Figure 3.3 graphically summarizes the extent of (1) overall elite support and (2) partisan divisiveness for three sets of market policies: privatization of public services (Panel A), trade liberalization (Panel B), and foreign investment (Panel C). To convey these attitudes, each of the panels in Figure 3.3 plots three types of lines. First, the thick gray solid lines represent the "Mean (Weighted by Party Size) Across All Countries," a yearly estimate of the overall balance of elite opinion throughout Latin America toward the particular policy. These means take into account party size, so that large parties (based on seat shares in the lower house) weigh more heavily than small ones in estimating a country's balance of elite opinion. For example, the relative balance of elite opinion would grow increasingly antimarket in a country in which (1) each party's mean attitude remains constant while (2) the relative size of an antimarket leftist party grows at the expense of a pro-market rightist party through time. Of course, attitudinal or personnel changes within a party can also drive shifts in this relative balance. The opinions of mass independents (the group also depicted with gray solid lines in Figures 2.1 and 2.2) with high levels of political awareness should be sensitive to this mean elite opinion across all countries because independents accept a random sample of all elite discourse.

to be sufficient for defining the relative balance and, especially, the partisan nature of elite discourse (Zaller 1992).

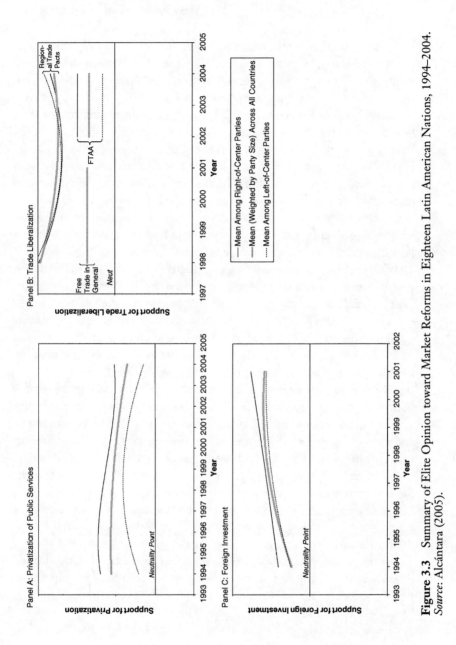

Figure 3.3 Summary of Elite Opinion toward Market Reforms in Eighteen Latin American Nations, 1994–2004. *Source:* Alcántara (2005).

Second, the thin black solid lines represent the "Mean Among Right-of-Center Parties," which for each year is the overall mean of all Right and Center-Right parties' mean scores.[10] Because they seek information from rightist elites, the opinions of mass rightists (the group also depicted with black solid lines in Figures 2.1 and 2.2) with high political awareness should be sensitive to this mean opinion among right-of-center elites. Finally, the thin black dotted lines represent the "Mean Among Left-of-Center Parties," or the yearly mean of all Left and Center-Left parties' mean scores. Because they seek information from leftist elites, the opinions of mass leftists (the group also depicted with black dotted lines in Figures 2.1 and 2.2) with high awareness should be sensitive to this mean opinion among left-of-center elites. The Survey Data Appendix contains details on how these three means were calculated.

With these definitions in mind, each panel of Figure 3.3 can be used to determine the relative balance and the divisiveness of elite opinion toward each policy. First, the extent of overall elite support for the policy is evident by comparing the gray, mean-across-all-countries line to the "Neutrality point" on the y-axis. This neutrality point is the score at which, according to the survey question wording, a respondent was expressing neutrality, neither favoring nor opposing the market policy. Lines above this neutrality point indicate a pro-market bias to elite opinion, and lines below this point indicate an antimarket leaning. (The y-axis sweeps out the entire range of the survey question. The numerical scales of the survey questions, and thus of these y-axes, are themselves not relevant, so I do not report them.) That said, I treat conclusions about aggregate elite opinion as suggestive rather than definitive because, for reasons spelled out in the Survey Data Appendix, the available response categories are not fairly balanced between pro- and antimarket sentiments. For example, respondents were not offered an *explicit* antiprivatization option, so results undoubtedly overestimate elite support for this policy.

Second, the degree to which these policies divided elites along partisan lines is evident in the size of the *vertical gaps* between the two thin lines – that is, between the "Mean Among Right-of-Center Parties" and the "Mean Among Left-of-Center Parties" lines. Large gaps indicate that a particular policy divided elites along partisan, left/right lines. Small or

---

[10] Ideological labels are assigned using Coppedge (1998). Coppedge does not assign ideological labels to most Central American countries. To fill these in, I use the labels from Roberts and Wibbels (1999).

nonexistent gaps indicate that differences of opinion did not follow partisan lines.

According to Panel A of Figure 3.3, two straightforward conclusions about *Elite support for privatization of public services* are evident: Beliefs were divided along partisan lines, and aggregate support for privatization declined after 1998. First, privatization was clearly a partisan issue, dividing the pro-market Right from the more skeptical Left. This polarization was sharpest in the mid-1990s. The partisan gap remained but was smaller by the late 1990s, shrinking mainly because left-of-center parties moderated their stance on privatization during the second half of the decade. Second, aggregate elite support declined steadily from the 1990s to the 2000s. The Left's moderation of the late 1990s was short-lived, as leftist politicians grew more critical of privatization after 1999. Moreover, right-of-center politicians *also* grew less enthusiastic toward privatization throughout the late 1990s and early 2000s. In other words, *changes among right-leaning politicians* drove the overall decline in support for privatization through time as much as changes among left-leaning ones.

A third conclusion regarding the precise balance of elite opinion toward privatization is harder to pinpoint. The mean across all countries is above the neutrality point at all time points, suggesting a persistent pro-privatization leaning to elite discourse. The location of this neutrality point, however, is probably misleading. Antiprivatization responses were coded by interviewers, but this option was not explicitly mentioned to interviewees. Therefore, the results in relation to the neutrality point surely overestimate support for privatization. Moreover, according to the question's wording, the midpoint of the y-axis, where the mean-across-all-countries line tends to be, reflects support for privatization in *some* sectors. In the end, I treat the first two conclusions as more definitive than the third.

Panel B of Figure 3.3 depicts elite beliefs about the following three aspects of trade liberalization: *Elite support for free trade in general* (1998 to 2001), *Elite support for regional trade pacts* (1998 to 2004), and *Elite support for the FTAA* (2002 to 2004). The results diverge substantially from those in Panel B, thus highlighting the importance of unpacking attitudes toward the Washington Consensus. First, the most definitive finding speaks to the degree of divisiveness of each policy. Free trade in general was *not* a partisan issue: The mean-across-countries line falls on the same points as the two partisan lines (which for this reason are not even visible). Leftist and rightist politicians were united in their beliefs about free trade. Moreover, these beliefs were largely favorable toward trade liberalization, as all lines lie above the neutrality point. (In fact, these results probably *underestimate* support for free trade because the alternative responses were not necessarily protectionist. See the Survey Data Appendix for details.) Second, opinions toward regional trade pacts were similar in that the pacts were extremely popular and nonpartisan. Support for regional trade pacts was nearly unanimous, declining only slightly through time. Moreover, politicians from both camps supported regional trade pacts to equal degrees. Finally, the configuration of opinions toward the FTAA was more similar to that of privatization opinions. Like privatization, the FTAA was a partisan issue. Right-leaning politicians were more favorable toward the hemispheric-wide trade area than left-leaning ones. On balance, Latin American elites favored the FTAA, but the issue was clearly more polarizing than the other two trade-related issues.[11] In sum, trade liberalization was quite popular and for the most part nonpartisan. Only the Left's skittishness about the FTAA made the hemispheric-wide trade pact a partisan issue.

Finally, I depict *Elite support for foreign investment* (1994 to 2001) in Panel C of Figure 3.3. First, the issue of foreign investment was a partisan one, persistently dividing Right from Left. Second, attitudes toward foreign investment grew more favorable through time. On average, elites were more favorable toward foreign investment in the late 1990s than they had been in the mid-1990s, although the available evidence hints that this increase was arrested in the early 2000s. Finally, foreign investment was seemingly popular, with the mean-across-countries line appearing well above the neutrality point.

To summarize these findings, I point out three general conclusions. First, scholarly claims of a neoliberal hegemony exaggerate elite support for the Washington Consensus. To be sure, Latin American elites were on balance favorable to market policies, even well into the 2000s. The degree of support, however, varied across policies: Regional trade pacts were almost unanimously popular, but many politicians opposed privatization, foreign investment, and the FTAA. Second, some issues evoked more partisan division than others. Privatization, the FTAA, and foreign investment were issues that divided Left from Right, while free trade in general and regional trade pacts did not. This mix of policies

---

[11] If it seems surprising that the eventually failed FTAA was popular among elites, recall that by 2007 only a minority of Latin American countries did *not* have bilateral free trade arrangements with the United States.

thus provides wide variation in the balance and divisiveness of elite opinion flows, a fact that proves advantageous when testing to see if politicians have influenced mass beliefs. Finally, although data limitations make such a conclusion tentative, the scholarly consensus that a "hegemonic" era in the 1990s gave way to a "posthegemonic" one in the 2000s contains some important grains of truth. Time series for privatization, foreign investment, and regional trade pact beliefs show that support for market policies peaked in the late 1990s. Enthusiasm for reforms trailed off thereafter, coinciding with the economic lost half-decade and the electoral rise of the Left. Contrary to conventional wisdom, however, shifts in beliefs among right-leaning politicians drove this decline as much as the electoral reinvigoration and increased opposition of the Left.

Conclusions

The goal of this chapter has been to describe the economic and political contexts in which Latin Americans formulated their opinions toward the Washington Consensus. The market-friendly era has been one of tightened and less egalitarian labor markets, caused in large part by heightened competition from foreign goods, services, and capital. Workers, however, have seen these losses compensated for somewhat by substantial relative declines in the prices of the products made by these new foreign competitors. While these price shifts have benefited middle- and upper-income groups disproportionately, the poor have also reaped the benefits of this consumer revolution. Still, the news has not been completely positive for Latin America's consumers, as privatization has resulted in utility rate hikes. Again, however, the poor have not been entirely sold short: Increased access to electricity and telecommunications networks has disproportionately benefited lower-income groups.

As these economic consequences have taken hold, politicians have chattered. Most elites were favorable toward market reforms in the 1990s, yet partisan divisions lurked behind this weak neoliberal hegemony. Moreover, politicians of all stripes have seemingly lost some enthusiasm for the Washington Consensus since 2000. The next two chapters turn to mass opinion, using the facts laid out in this chapter to explain Latin Americans' beliefs about the market.

4

Are Latin Americans Neoliberals?

It's like Sweden with sunshine.
– Cícero Péricles de Carvalho, professor of economics at the Federal
University of Alagoas (Brazil), on the welfare state and weather of his
home state (*Economist* 2008, 39)

By the time Fernando Lugo ascended to the Paraguayan presidency in 2008, only one South American electorate (Colombia's) had *not* elected a left-of-center president in the new millennium.[1] Many observers spoke with certainty that this trend indicated a "massive rejection of the International Monetary Fund and the Washington Consensus" (Rohter 2005, A3), yet most made such assertions in lieu of actual data on what voters thought about market reforms. While a few scholars have conducted studies of public opinion data, they have focused on attitudes in the reform initiation stage toward broad-based structural adjustment packages. The result is a muddled understanding of whether market reforms evoke enthusiasm, outrage, or something in between.

In this chapter, I settle these questions by describing and explaining the contours of aggregate support for various market reforms in Latin America between 1990 and 2007. I do so as part of a series of hypothesis tests regarding the macro-level implications of the bottom-up and top-down theoretical arguments central to this book. The most important finding is that Latin Americans have been persistently favorable toward globalizing policies yet rather unenthusiastic about privatization. The consumer consequences (described in the previous chapter) of each

---

[1] This count excludes Guyana, Suriname, and French Guiana, and it classifies Hugo Chávez (Venezuela), Lula (Brazil), Michelle Bachelet (Chile), Tabaré Vazquez (Uruguay), Evo Morales (Bolivia), Alan García (Peru), Rafael Correa (Ecuador), Fernando Lugo (Paraguay), and Néstor Kirchner (Argentina) as left of center.

policy explain this popularity gap: Globalization has benefited consumers, while privatization has harmed them. Producer-oriented factors cannot account for these cross-policy attitudinal differences because globalization has yielded mostly negative consequences for labor markets.

A number of other empirical patterns presented in this chapter confirm the consumer orientation in Latin Americans' beliefs about the Washington Consensus. First, general attitudes toward privatization have been driven by specific preferences about the private ownership of utilities. Preferences about private ownership of sectors that have great symbolic, fiscal, or employment importance have been less relevant than preferences about utility sector privatization, a policy that has greatly influenced consumer welfare. Second, variation in utility-price changes across countries and time has determined the aggregate popularity of privatization. Postprivatization utility rate hikes have led to declines in support for privatization, and these declines have been more rapid in countries with more dramatic price increases. Third, Latin Americans have been notably more positive about the impact of trade on prices than they have been about its impact on unemployment or wages. Finally, support for globalization has been higher in countries with small economies – that is, those with a limited ability to produce their own consumer goods and services – than in those with large economies.

This chapter also accomplishes two other goals. First, it tests for the influence of top-down factors – the balance of elite opinion and discourse – on aggregate opinion. The findings reveal that elites have had limited influence over the aggregate popularity of economic policies. Bottom-up material consequences, and not the rhetorical ploys of elites, have dictated why mass beliefs have varied across policies, countries, and time. Second, I address a series of speculations by economists about why privatization, which they presume to be universally beneficial, has been so unpopular. This supposed "privatization paradox" has a simple solution: the obvious utility price increases that have occurred in the wake of privatization.

The following section lists the hypotheses tested in this chapter. I then describe the average levels of support for different market policies across the entire region of Latin America and describe how these are compatible with the consumption-based model of interests. Subsequent sections test further hypotheses regarding cross-country and cross-temporal differences in beliefs.

Hypotheses for Aggregate Beliefs about Market Reforms

The theoretical infrastructure in Chapter 2 and the review of empirical facts in Chapter 3 combine to produce numerous hypotheses about the causes and contours of aggregate support for market reforms in Latin America. Recall from Chapter 3 that globalization has improved consumer welfare far more than privatization has, yet globalization has had far more negative consequences for labor markets than privatization. Therefore, the most important hypotheses are as follows: If Latin Americans do view reforms through a consumption lens, then they should be much more enthusiastic about globalization than about privatization. In contrast, if citizens evaluate policies as producers and workers, then globalization should be especially unpopular and privatization should evoke indifference or middling levels of support.

I also test specific hypotheses about the causes of beliefs toward each policy. First, I test a number of theoretical expectations about privatization beliefs. If consumer concerns dominate privatization beliefs, then beliefs about public ownership of important utility sectors, namely electricity and telecommunications, should drive beliefs about privatization in general. Privatization has occurred throughout Latin America in a variety of sectors: airlines, banking, defense, electricity, fertilizer, fishing, mining, natural gas, highways, mail delivery, petroleum, ports, potable water, rail transport, sanitation, sewerage, steel, telecommunications, and others. However, "privatization's most widespread effects are on consumers of essential utilities," so beliefs about ownership in electricity, water, and telecommunications sectors should be particularly germane when citizens construct overall opinions about the merits of privatization (McKenzie and Mookherjee 2005, 76). In contrast, if privatization evokes symbolic values of national sovereignty, economic redistribution, and shared ownership, then thoughts about natural resource sectors, such as mining and petroleum, should drive general beliefs about privatization. Moreover, if consumer concerns matter, then average support for privatization should (1) be higher in countries with lower postprivatization utility rate increases and (2) vary inversely with utility price changes through time. In contrast, if labor markets matter, then citizens should be more sensitive to layoffs and shifting employment patterns in newly privatized industries.

Second, I test several hypotheses about the causes of globalization beliefs. If indeed free trade is popular because of its beneficial consumer effects, then citizens should believe that trade is more beneficial for the availability and price of consumer goods than it is for wages and employment opportunities. Moreover, if citizens think about globalization as consumers, then national-level mass support for globalization should vary inversely with a country's ability to produce its own goods and services. The beneficial effects of trade liberalization and foreign direct investment on consumer options are more pronounced and more visible in countries (like Nicaragua) that historically have not produced a wide variety of manufactured goods and services than in countries (like Brazil) with large and diversified economies.

Finally, I test hypotheses about pension privatization, which Chapter 3 describes as a stand-alone issue that does not cue consumer or, for that matter, labor-market concerns. To maintain consistency with the consumer-oriented focus, I might hypothesize that, because the transitional costs of pension privatization place inflationary pressures on the region's macro-economies, the policy should be unpopular. This hypothesis, however, takes the consumer argument beyond what the cognitive aspects of my overall argument allow. The impact of these transitional costs on consumer prices does not qualify as a visible economic incident that citizens observe as a by-product of their daily activities. Instead, I hypothesize that pension privatization should be unpopular not because of inflationary pressures but because it has exposed citizens to greater risk, higher administrative costs, and stricter eligibility requirements. If citizens consider the absolute returns in their private accounts or the (mostly positive) macroeconomic effects of pension privatization, then this reform should be popular.

The Popularity Gap: Regionwide Support for Market Policies

Have market reforms been popular in Latin America? I answer this question differently than previous scholars by unpacking the distinct elements of the Washington Consensus. I analyze separately beliefs about privatization, globalization, and pension reform. By unpacking in this way, I find that the answer to this question is "it depends." The survey data compiled here, for the years 1990 to 2007, illustrate a fundamental and persistent popularity gap between globalizing policies and privatization. Latin Americans have largely supported globalization in its various forms while opposing privatization.

To demonstrate this claim, I compile results from the following cross-national public opinion surveys of Latin American citizens: the annual eighteen-nation Latinbarometer (LB) series that began in 1995; the fourteen-nation *Wall Street Journal Americas* (*WSJA*) survey conducted in 1998;

the World Values Surveys (WVS) of 1990 to 1992, 1995 to 1997, and 1999 to 2001; the Pew Global Attitudes Projects (Pew) of 2002 and 2007; and the Globescan International Survey of 2003. Viewing data from so many sources provides two distinct methodological advantages. First, it provides a robustness check on question-wording effects and changes in sampling frames. The wording of survey questions can influence the aggregate (marginal) distribution of attitudes (Sniderman and Theriault 2004). Presenting results from differently worded questions that query attitudes toward the same policy helps to isolate underlying popularity levels that are unadulterated by question wording and framing effects. Likewise, these cross-national surveys did not sample the same pool of countries, and a few only sampled subsets of national populations.[2] I describe broad patterns that are not due to mere methodological decisions. Second, the wide array of data provides a time series of attitudes that demonstrates how attitudes have evolved in the market-oriented era.

Figures 4.1 through 4.4 present the aggregate results. Figures 4.1 and 4.2 report beliefs about privatization, and Figures 4.3 and 4.4 report attitudes toward free trade and foreign investment. Each figure plots the percentage of opinionated respondents supporting the market-oriented reform.[3] These numbers are calculated by first obtaining the pro-market percentages for each country, then taking the average of these percentages. Therefore, each country is weighted equally when calculating these numbers. (This is based on the presumption that large countries or countries with more respondents should not be more important when depicting regionwide trends and patterns.) Rather than presenting overly nuanced country-specific findings, the figures reveal general patterns that are common to most countries and can thus characterize the region as a whole. Each figure combines results from all relevant items in the cross-national surveys. Results for differently worded items are represented with different symbols. Lines connect responses from questions that were repeated or similarly worded. The figures give an

---

[2] In some of its 1990s surveys, the Latinbarometer only sampled urban residents in many countries. This does not, however, skew or bias the aggregate percentages reported in this chapter in any major way because, as demonstrated in Chapter 5, the attitudinal gap between urban and rural residents is minimal.

[3] This means that the answers "don't know" and "no response" were dropped when calculating these percentages, although ambivalent responses such as "depends" or "I both disagree and agree" were not. In other words, the percentages in the figures are as follows:

Frequency of Positive Responses

Frequency of Positive Responses + Frequency of Negative Responses + Frequency of Ambivalent Responses

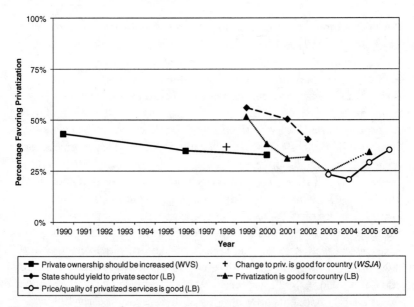

Figure 4.1 Support for Privatization in Latin America, 1990–2006.
Sources: LB, *WSJA*, and WVS.

abbreviated account of survey question wordings, but the full wordings for these and all other questions used throughout this book are in the Survey Data Appendix. The list of countries covered by each cross-national survey is also in this appendix.

Results

Two central patterns characterize Latin Americans' beliefs about privatization in general between 1990 and 2006, and, as shown in Figure 4.1, these two findings are robust to survey question wording. First, in most years, privatization commanded support only from a minority of citizens. At the beginning of two Latinbarometer time series in 1999, proponents did slightly outnumber opponents, as supporters in two different questions were between 50% and 55% of the population.[4] More commonly,

---

[4] Readers familiar with the Latinbarometer time series might be surprised to see a reference to the 1999 version of the survey. In fact, this is the wave that the Latinbarometer organization and other authors refer to as the "1998" wave. However, I classify it as 1999 data to fill in a gap between the 1998 *WSJA* survey and the 2000 Latinbarometer wave. (The

91

however, support existed only among minorities of 20% to 45%. As early as 1990 only 43% of citizens favored privatization, and aggregate support was as low or even lower in almost every other instance.

Second, support for privatization unequivocally trended downward throughout most of the period depicted. Privatization steadily lost proponents during the decade and a half following the initiation of reform. According to the WVS question series (*Private ownership should be increased*) occurring in 1990, 1996, and 2000, support for the idea of greater private ownership fell by about one percentage point per year in the 1990s. The ranks of privatization proponents declined even more precipitously from 1999 to 2003, shrinking by half (according to the *Privatization is good for country* series), from 52% to 24% at a rate of seven percentage points *per year*. Attitudes toward the quality and price of newly privatized services (*Price/quality of privatized services is good*) also blipped downward from 2003 to 2004. Two different time series hint that support may have rebounded slightly in 2005 and 2006. Overall, however, it is beyond refute that the number of privatization opponents grew steadily in the 1990s and early 2000s.

Figure 4.2 confirms these two central findings, even though it approaches the privatization issue differently. It reports the percentage of citizens that favored private or public ownership in eleven different economic sectors. The layout of Figure 4.2 departs slightly from that of Figure 4.1 because it arrays sectors, rather than time, from left to right. They are arrayed roughly in ascending order of enthusiasm for private ownership. Within each sectoral category, I list results for each of the three years chronologically. First, only a minority of citizens typically supported private ownership in these economic sectors. Across all sectors in all three years, 31% of respondents favored private ownership. Second, the share of citizens favoring privatization fell through time: Average support for private ownership in all sectors fell by three percentage points over this four-year span.

These two central tendencies, however, mask important variance across the eleven sectors. Most importantly, these are the first indications that citizens did unpack reforms, as differences in support across varying sectors

organization refers to this latter wave as the "1999/2000" wave, although no interviews occurred in 1999.) While this may appear misleading, it is in fact sensical for two reasons. First, a quarter of the countries in the "1998" wave actually carried out their interviews in March 1999. Second, the remaining interviews in the "1998" wave occurred in November and December 1998, a full ten months after the January 1998 *WSJA*. As a result, classifying all of these as 1999 data actually better represents their time gap between the *WSJA* and the 2000 Latinbarometer.

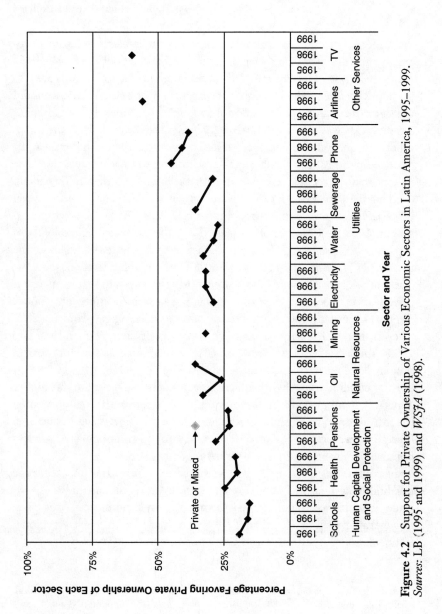

Figure 4.2 Support for Private Ownership of Various Economic Sectors in Latin America, 1995–1999.
Sources: LB (1995 and 1999) and *WSJA* (1998).

93

are evident. For example, airline privatization elicited a more favorable re-action than did water utility privatization. Proponents of the former out-numbered those of the latter by 2:1. Other differences across sectors are also pronounced, a general indication that a large number of Latin Americans did not think of and assess privatization as a monolithic good or evil but rather as a policy that was more appropriate for some economic activities than for others. In general, the aggregate differences across sectors followed well-reasoned patterns, clustering together according to logical categories. The sectors that citizens were most hesitant to commit to private ownership (ranging between 15% and 28%) were those in the human capital and social protection category. Utility (ranging from 29% to 45%) and natural re-source (26% to 36%) sectors clustered together at intermediate levels of support, and citizens were most enthusiastic about private ownership of the two "other" service sectors (56% to 60%): airlines and television.

Figure 4.2 also contains the findings on aggregate support for pension privatization, showing that the policy was generally quite unpopular. Support for private operation of retirement pensions ranged from just 23% to 28%, falling from the latter to the former between 1995 and the late 1990s. On average, citizens saw private ownership to be less appropriate only in the education and health sectors. The percentage of citizens sup-porting either a privately run system or a *mixed* pension system was higher at 36%, a number that is more relevant because reforms typically entailed the introduction of a private system alongside the preexisting public one. Overall, however, pension privatization was not only unpopular, it was less popular than privatization in most other sectors.

In contrast to the lackluster mass support for privatization, free trade was highly popular in Latin America. Figure 4.3 reports attitudes toward trade liberalization, dividing the issue into North–South trade – free trade in general and the FTAA (Panel A)[5] – and South–South trade – regional trade pacts and Latin American economic integration (Panel B).[6]

---

[5] I designate free trade in general and the FTAA as North–South trade with some hesitation, but this seems a plausible contrast to draw with the South–South policies. Trade liberal-ization in general has expanded Latin America's trade with wealthy countries relative to less developed ones, and the FTAA would be dominated by the U.S. economy. It is thus plausible that, when asked about free trade in general and the FTAA, most Latin American citizens think about North–South trade. This is not definitive, but it is also not crucial to my overall argument.

[6] Panel A connects with lines two items each from *WSJA* and Latinbarometer. These are questions with similar rather than equivalently worded queries.

Are Latin Americans Neoliberals?

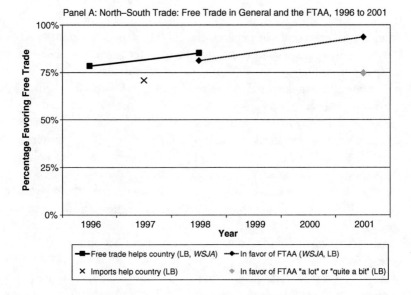

Panel A: North–South Trade: Free Trade in General and the FTAA, 1996 to 2001

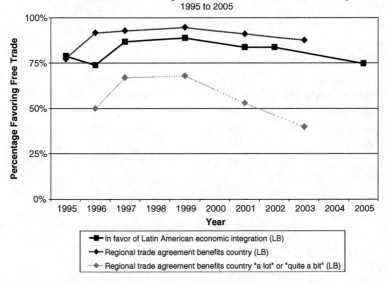

Panel B: South–South Trade: Regional Trade Pacts and Latin American Integration, 1995 to 2005

Figure 4.3 Support for Trade Liberalization in Latin America, 1995–2005.
Sources: LB and *WSJA*.

According to Panel A, between 70% and 95% of respondents declared support for free trade in general, the FTAA, and even imports. At two different times, large majorities of around 80% believed that free trade had helped the country. Over 70% of Latin Americans believed that imports were good for the country. More than 80% in 1998 even supported the eventually beleaguered FTAA, and in 2001 almost 95% claimed that the proposed FTAA would help their country "a little," "quite a bit," or "a lot" (as indicated by the black *In favor of FTAA* diamond). The intensity of support for FTAA was even quite high, as 75% chose the "quite a bit" or "a lot" options to this question (depicted by the gray diamond). Moreover, as of 2001 the popularity of free trade showed no signs of trending downward.

Panel B demonstrates that citizens also enthusiastically embraced regional trade pacts and Latin American economic integration. Support for Latin American integration was never lower than 74% and was typically in the 80% to 95% range. Support did decline slightly after 1999, but it occurred at a slow rate and failed to make more than a small dent in the impressive levels of overall support for Latin American integration.[7] Similarly, beliefs about the new regional trade pacts in the region were overwhelmingly and persistently positive.[8] *Almost all* (typically more than 90%) Latin American citizens evaluated their country's regional trade pact as a success. The intensity of support for regional trade pacts, however, did decline after 1999. While citizens did not register greater opposition to their regional trade pact after 1999, fewer expressed observations of extensive benefits. (The gray dotted line reports the percentage of respondents saying that they thought the regional trade pact had benefited the country "a lot" or "quite a bit," in contrast to the black, dotted line's portrayal of the percentage saying "a lot," "quite a bit," or "a little." Panel B thus indicates an increase in the percentage of respondents choosing the "a little" category.) Still, the overall finding that regional trade pacts, and South–South trade more generally, were popular holds.

Finally, foreign investment was also popular in Latin America, commanding support from 60% to 80% majorities. Figure 4.4 shows aggregate beliefs about foreign investment from 1995 to 2007. Between 1995 and 2001, majorities of more than 75% believed that foreign investment was good for the country and should be encouraged, and, as in the case of trade

[7] The upward blips seen in the mid-1990s were likely due to changes in question wording that are detailed in the Survey Data Appendix.
[8] These results exclude Mexico, since it is a member of a North–South trade pact.

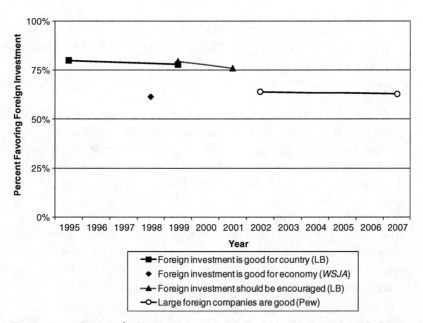

Figure 4.4. Support for Foreign Investment in Latin America, 1995–2007. *Sources:* LB, *WSJA*, and Pew.

liberalization, no downward trend occurred during this time. Foreign investment and, more specifically, foreign-owned companies remained popular well into the 2000s, drawing support from a stable two-thirds of respondents in 2002 and 2007.

These results on the popularity of free trade and foreign investment are corroborated by other cross-national surveys querying support for "globalization" or "growing international trade and business ties." Because these wordings subsume both free trade and foreign investment, I cite them briefly here instead of plotting them in the figures. The 2002 and 2007 Pew Global Attitudes surveys were conducted in eight Latin American countries and contained three pertinent questions (Pew Research Center 2003, 2007). Two different questions asked whether "growing trade and business ties between your country and other countries" were a good thing for (1) the country (*Globalization's impact on the country*) and for (2) the respondent's family (*Globalization's impact on my family*). Eighty percent responded affirmatively to both questions in 2002 and 81% did so to the former question (the only one of the two asked) in 2007. Moreover, 66% in

2002 agreed that globalization was a good thing. Likewise, in a 2003 Globescan survey, two-thirds of respondents in five Latin American nations claimed that globalization had a positive impact on themselves and their families (*Globalization's effect on my family*) (Globescan Research Partners 2003).

In sum, the most important finding that emerges from these surveys is the existence of a popularity gap between globalizing policies and privatization. *Latin Americans have been neither strict neoliberals nor rigid statists. Rather, they have been much like Swedes, desiring open economies strongly tied to international markets that still maintain a large state presence in the provision of many basic services.* Figures 4.1 through 4.4 demonstrate that this finding is robust to question wording and to time. It is also consistent across countries.[9] The figures are not cluttered with reports of spread around the central tendencies because cross-national heterogeneity, especially with respect to the central substantive findings, is minimal.[10] Free trade and foreign investment were more popular than privatization *in every country* in the 1998 *WSJA* survey. Moreover, support for free trade was not lower than 60% in any country, while a majority opposed foreign investment in just one country (Argentina). The countries that were least favorable toward free trade (62% in Paraguay, 1996) and foreign investment (59% in Uruguay, 1998) still featured pro-globalization majorities in the Latinbarometer surveys. By contrast, in not a single country in any year after 2000 did a majority of citizens favor privatization. Overall, the means plotted in the figures accurately depict the central patterns and trends regionwide: The popularity gap existed in every country, and it grew through time.

---

[9] This claim regarding a popularity gap between globalization and privatization beliefs is confirmed in the results of the few national referenda on questions of economic policy that have occurred in the region. Between 1992 and 2007, four referenda occurred in Latin American countries on questions of privatization and one occurred on a question regarding trade. The privatization-related referenda resulted in votes against the expansion of private ownership, while the one trade-related referendum confirmed support for the expansion of North–South trade. A majority of Uruguayans voted to (1) repeal a law authorizing the privatization of the state-owned telephone company (1992), (2) reject a law ending the monopoly of their state-owned oil company (2003), and (3) require that drinking water and sewerage be provided by the state (2004). Similarly, a large majority of Bolivians in 2004 agreed to increase state control in the country's gas and oil sector. In contrast, in 2007 a majority of Costa Ricans approved their country's entry into the Central American Free Trade Agreement with the United States.

[10] Across the eighteen countries, the standard deviations of the reported percentages in any given year were typically just ten percentage points.

Understanding the Popularity Gap

The evidence that citizens have unpacked the reform process is overwhelming in these aggregate findings. Between 1990 and 2007, citizens had starkly opposing views of privatization and globalization, indicating a tendency to separate these distinct elements of the Washington Consensus. Majorities embraced open international markets by supporting policies that enabled greater inflows of foreign goods, services, and capital. In contrast, far fewer citizens were enthusiastic about the sale of state-owned assets to private investors and the privatization of retirement pension systems. Moreover, support for privatization steadily waned during the 1990s and fell sharply between 1999 and 2004, while the taste for globalizing policies showed no signs of disappearing. Overall, by the early 2000s, privatization was about as unpopular as free trade was popular. In this subsection, I consider some methodological challenges to and implications of the popularity gap.

Have quirks of language artificially induced this gap between globalization and privatization? One possible counterargument to the claim that the data reflect a real gap in popularity between globalization and privatization is the fact that globalization was defined in some of the survey questions as free trade, with the word "free" having a positive connotation that could induce an artificially favorable response. In contrast, the word "privatization" may have implied to respondents that a collectively owned asset is being given away to benefit a few private business owners. In fact, however, only a few of the globalization survey questions did contain the word "free," and some even cued citizens to assess the enhanced power of foreigners over their local economy. Moreover, it is not clear why Latin Americans would have considered the "private business" connotation of privatization to be worse than the "state" connotation of public ownership. For example, in these same cross-national surveys, Latin American respondents invariably expressed more confidence in "big business" and large entrepreneurs than in state and political institutions, such as the congress, courts, police, political parties, and public administration. Furthermore, just 20% of respondents to the 2005 Latinbarometer survey were confident that tax revenues were well managed and well distributed, and over 80% thought that half or more of all public-sector employees were corrupt. In other words, Latin Americans have not held their states' veracity and capacity in high regard, nor have they exhibited widespread suspicion of big business. Overall, semantic reasons alone have not inclined citizens to express more support for globalization than privatization.

Table 4.1. *Pairwise Correlations in Individual-Level Reform Attitudes in Fourteen Latin American Countries, 1998*

	Privatization in General	Pension Privatization	Free Trade
Pension Privatization	+.23		
Free Trade	+.22	+.07	
Foreign Investment	+.25	+.07	+.33

Note: Entries are maximum likelihood polychoric correlation coefficients (Kolenikov and Angeles 2004). *N* is slightly different for each coefficient, varying between 10,403 and 10,777. $p < .001$ for all correlations, one-tailed. Variables are *Change to privatization is good for country, Privatization by sectors: Pensions, Free trade helps country*, and *Foreign investment is good for country*. *Source: WSJA.*

The roots of the aggregate-level gap in attitudes between privatization and globalization lie in a lack of issue constraint at the individual level (Converse 1964; Domínguez and McCann 1996). Weak correlations among individuals' attitudes toward the various policies indicate that citizens have not viewed them jointly through a rigid ideological lens. Instead, they have approached the list of Washington Consensus policies in a piecemeal fashion. Table 4.1 shows the correlations in individual-level attitudes for six possible pairwise combinations of four different policies. All are positive and statistically significant, yet all are weak to moderate in size. Only the correlation between free trade and foreign direct investment exceeds + .25. Attitudes toward globalization and pension privatization have almost no relationship whatsoever.

These findings on how citizens have unpacked the Washington Consensus carry two important theoretical implications. First, to speak of a uniform level of popularity for all market reforms, as observers so frequently do, is misleading. For example, claims of a "massive rejection of the Washington Consensus" in the new millennium clearly tell a highly distorted story. Moreover, the erroneous sentiments in the following scholarly ruminations about citizens' opposition to privatization are common:

... [T]he public commonly lumps privatization together with other promarket reforms, such as fiscal contraction and trade liberalization, which collectively constitute the Washington Consensus.. . . Such negative associations may cause citizens to overlook the benefits of privatization. (McKenzie and Mookherjee 2005, 76)

... [P]rivatization shares in the criticism directed at the entire liberalization process. (Barja et al. 2005, 123)

The evidence presented in this chapter indicates the clear inaccuracy of these statements: Citizens liked their trade unfettered and their utilities and safety nets state-owned. As a result, privatization received support from only a minority *precisely because citizens did not lump it with trade liberalization*. Privatization was not "guilty by association" but rather had a life of its own in the mind of the Latin American citizen.

Second, citizens have been more discerning about the different policies than the commonly held sociotropic model would expect. The standard claim that support for incumbent market policies is a function of the health of the existing macroeconomy offers only a limited explanation of policy attitudes (Magaloni and Romero 2008; Panizza and Yáñez 2005; Stokes 2001a, 2001b; Weyland 2002). Macroeconomic health can potentially explain temporal shifts and cross-national differences in aggregate support. The macroeconomy, however, is constant across policies, so it alone cannot explain why some policies have been more popular than others.

In the end, the existence of the popularity gap supports the consumption-oriented explanation of economic policy attitudes. Because of the boom in consumer options, trade liberalization and foreign investment have had visible and positive impacts through the consumption channel and have therefore been quite popular. This has been the case despite their overall negative implications for labor markets. By contrast, privatization has yielded mostly negative effects on consumer welfare, therefore receiving middling to negative levels of popular support. *Citizens have been inconsistent in their inclinations toward the different market policies, yet they have been fiercely consistent in their obsession with prices.*

A comparison of two different survey questions that ask respondents to assess only the consumption-channel aspects of free trade and privatization solidifies this claim. In 1997 Latinbarometer registered respondents' thoughts on whether imports were beneficial (*Imports help country* in Figure 4.3, Panel A), and from 2003 to 2006 it queried evaluations of the price and quality of newly privatized services (*Price/quality of privatized services is good* in Figure 4.1). The results indicate that citizens were much more positive toward free trade in this regard than they were toward privatization. Only 27%, on average, were "more satisfied" or "satisfied" with the price and quality of newly privatized services. The remaining respondents were either "less satisfied" or "much less satisfied." In contrast, over 70% were favorable toward imports. Favorability toward imports thus outdistanced satisfaction with newly privatized services by almost 3:1. In other words, citizens were much more favorable toward the consumption-channel effects of trade than toward those of privatization.

The lack of enthusiasm for pension privatization is part of the popularity gap. The finding that privately run or even mixed pension systems were unpopular indicates that the greater risk, higher administrative costs, and stricter eligibility requirements of private pension funds outweighed their reasonably high returns in the minds of most citizens. This is not a consumption-based explanation, yet it is more in line with the cognitive limitations of citizens. It is not likely that citizens noticed the inflationary pressures exerted by the fiscal transition costs of pension reform. For example, if citizens thought in this way, then privatization in other sectors would have been popular because it provided large cash infusions to indebted governments, thus potentially mitigating inflationary pressures. In the end, however, the data at hand do not provide substantial verification of the reasons for pension privatization's unpopularity; further research is needed to reach conclusions that are more convincing.

Further Evidence of Consumption-Channel Effects

The popularity gap provides support for a consumption-oriented, rather than a labor-market- or sociotropic-oriented, explanation of popular attitudes toward market reforms. In the remainder of this chapter, I further investigate the validity of a consumer-channel theory. To do so, I test competing hypotheses regarding the source of variation in aggregate beliefs across different aspects of a single policy, across countries, and through time.

Sectoral Correlates of General Privatization Attitudes

Scholars of privatization conclude that its most important consequences have been the changes in the prices, quality, and availability of essential utility services. If such consumer concerns have predominated in the minds of citizens, then beliefs about the public ownership of important utility sectors, and not other sectors, should drive attitudes toward privatization in general.

To discern which sectors have been the most important in determining citizens' attitudes, I investigate the relationship between general privatization attitudes (presented in Figure 4.1) and batteries of sector-specific beliefs about private versus public ownership (presented in Figure 4.2). I use two general attitude measures, *Change to privatization is good for the country (WSJA)* and *Privatization is good for the country* (LB), as dependent variables (DVs) in two statistical models. The full batteries of sectoral items comprise the independent variables. Figure 4.5 graphically depicts the most important substantive results. (The details of the statistical models and the numerical results are reported in the Chapter 4 Appendix.) The figure quantifies the impact of each sectoral attitude by plotting the difference in the probability of expressing general support for privatization between a pro-private-ownership individual and a pro-public-ownership individual. Each black circle is the independent impact (that is, while holding attitudes about all other sectors constant) of support for private ownership in the denoted sector on the probability of supporting privatization in general. The vertical lines centered on each circle sweep out the 95% confidence interval of these estimated probabilities.[11]

The central finding in Figure 4.5 is that attitudes toward two utility sectors, telecommunications and electricity, correlate most strongly with general privatization beliefs. When considering the telecommunications sector, the difference in the probability of supporting privatization in general between pro-private-ownership and pro-public-ownership individuals was nine percentage points in 1998. The difference created by attitudes toward the electricity sector was eleven percentage points. In contrast, commitments to private ownership in the remaining sectors boosted general privatization beliefs by only about two to six percentage points. In 1999, beliefs about telecommunications again yielded a nine-point difference in the dependent variable, the largest impact of any sector.

These correlations between beliefs about utilities and overall privatization attitudes at the individual level hold up when opinions are aggregated up to the national level. I created three new variables to conduct a country-level analysis. First, the *Percent supporting privatization in general* uses the dependent variables from Figure 4.5 to calculate the share of respondents in each country that agreed that privatization was good for the country. Second, the *Average percent supporting private ownership of utilities* is the average of the following two proportions in each country: the share of respondents preferring telephone- and electricity-sector privatization. Third, the *Average percent supporting private ownership of nonutility sectors* is

---

[11] Throughout this book, all confidence intervals for predicted probabilities were generated with Clarify 2.1 (King et al. 2000; Tomz et al. 2003).

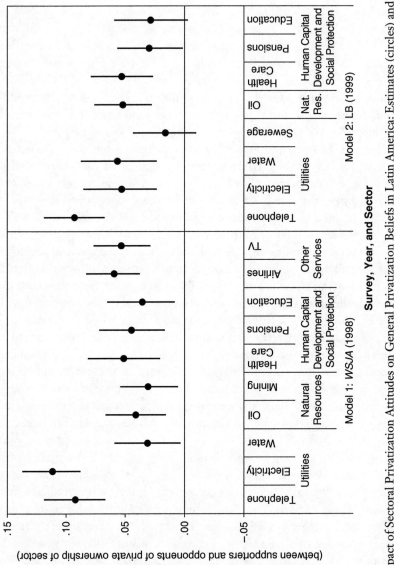

Figure 4.5 The Impact of Sectoral Privatization Attitudes on General Privatization Beliefs in Latin America: Estimates (circles) and 95% Confidence Intervals (vertical lines).
Note: Estimates are from the ordered probit regressions reported in Table 4.2.
Sources: Dependent variable is *Privatization is good for country* (*WSJA* 1998 and LB 1999).

the average of the percentages of respondents supporting private owner-ship in the seven (1998) or four (1999) nonutility sectors. If specific utility sectors drove overall privatization beliefs, then the correlation between the first and second variables should be stronger than that between the first and third variables.

This is indeed the case. The zero-order correlations between the two-sector utility variable and overall privatization support is a statistically significant $+.56$ in 1998 ($p < .02$, $N = 14$) and $+.50$ in 1999 ($p < .02$, $N = 17$). In contrast, the zero-order correlations with the nonutility-sectors variable are smaller and have larger p-values: $+.43$ in 1998 ($p < .07$) and $+.31$ in 1999 ($p < .12$). Partial correlations (defined as the correlation between two variables when holding other independent variables constant) are even more revealing. The correlation between general privatization beliefs and utility-sector beliefs, holding constant nonutility-sector beliefs, is $+.47$ in 1998 ($p < .05$) and $+.48$ in 1999 ($p < .03$). In contrast, the correlation between general privatization beliefs and nonutility-sector attitudes, controlling for utility-sector beliefs, is $+.27$ in 1998 ($p < .20$) and $-.28$ in 1999 ($p < .85$).

In short, to the Latin American masses, the politics of privatization has been the politics of utility-sector privatization and, in particular, sell-offs in the telecommunications and electricity sectors. Attitudes toward private ownership in these two sectors drove much of the observed individual- and country-level differences in support for privatization in general. The rel-ative unimportance of beliefs about highly symbolic natural resource sec-tors (petroleum and mining) is noteworthy. Historically, natural resource sectors in many countries had a symbolic and in some cases mythical importance that drew on appeals to national sovereignty and anti-imperialism. Former presidents such as Lázaro Cárdenas in Mexico and Getúlio Vargas in Brazil have been heroes in their respective countries partly because of their decisions to nationalize their countries' petroleum sectors. State-owned natural resource companies in many Latin American countries have also played an important fiscal role, with company revenues comprising a large share of government receipts in countries such as Mexico and Venezuela. Despite this, general privatization attitudes were much more closely associated with beliefs about electricity and telecommunications, even in countries with large petroleum sectors.[12]

---

[12] These separate analyses on the oil-rich countries are available from the author upon request.

Most citizens had some firsthand consumptive experience with electricity or telecommunications, so they understood the influence of state owner-ship or privatization on prices, quality, and access. Consumer-oriented concerns explain why attitudes toward these two sectors were the primary correlates of general privatization beliefs.

Although revealing, these findings on the correlation between sector-specific and general privatization attitudes do not provide a rigorous causal explanation of the latter because they use one type of privatization attitude to predict another type of privatization attitude. The following subsection discusses the relative merits of theoretically distinct independent variables.

Utility Prices and Country-Level Support for Privatization

What explains differences in privatization attitudes through time and across countries? Recall that a central finding in Figures 4.1 and 4.2 was the downward trend in support for privatization. The trend was especially precipitous between 1999 and 2004. Moreover, although cross-national differences in beliefs were not especially stark, they did exist. To explain the sources of these cross-temporal and cross-national variations in beliefs about market reforms, I combine survey data with economic indicators in a pooled time series dataset with 119 (17 countries × 7 years) observations.

The goal of the analysis is to explain the percentage of respondents in each country that supported privatization between 1999 and 2005. To accomplish this, I use as a dependent variable the *Percent agreeing that privatization is good for the country* (LB), a question that was asked annually in nearly every Latin American country during these years. I group inde-pendent variables into four theoretical categories. First, I assess bottom-up consumption-channel effects. In particular, I test the impact of utility price changes on attitudes toward privatization. I measure telephone service rates with the price basket introduced in the preceding chapter: The var-iable *Percent change in residential fixed-line price basket* is the percentage change in this price basket from the previous year to the current year. I also include changes in end-user electricity fees: The variable *Percent change in residential electricity rates* captures these annual shifts in prices.

These variables alone, however, do not suffice. In years after the pri-vatization of a particular utility occurred, the correlation between prices and support for privatization should be negative, with rate increases causing less enthusiasm for privatization and rate decreases leading to greater support. In years before privatization and in countries where privatization never occurred, the correlation between rate changes and support for privatization should be positive; this would indicate that citizens saw privatization as a solution to rate increases by their state-owned providers. To allow for these potentially different patterns, I parse each of the utility price variables into two: one for contexts in which the particular utility was state-owned and another for contexts in which it was privately owned.[13]

Second, I measure bottom-up labor-market factors by including the annual *Percent change in employment in the telecommunications sector*. Crossnational data on the yearly number of privatization-induced layoffs are not available, and more widely available national-level unemployment data do not capture the precise impact of privatization. I use employment patterns in the most relevant utility sector as a measure of privatization's labor-market consequences. If labor-channel effects influenced privatization attitudes, then this variable should be positively correlated with the dependent variable. Third, I test the influence of bottom-up macroeconomic factors. In the late 1990s and early 2000s, many observers attributed lagging support for privatization to economic slowdown throughout the region. I include, therefore, standard measures of *GDP growth* and *Inflation*. If these sociotropic arguments are correct, then the aggregate support for privatization should have a positive correlation with GDP growth and a negative correlation with inflation. Finally, I evaluate the impact of topdown factors by testing whether *Elite support for privatization of public services* influenced the aggregate level of support for privatization in each country. This variable is constructed from the elite opinion data presented in Chapter 3: The value for each country in each year is the mean (weighted by party size) score elites gave to the privatization of public services question in the PELA survey.

Readers interested in the full numerical results of the statistical models as well as a detailed discussion of all methodological decisions (especially those related to the pooled nature of the data) are again directed to the Chapter 4 Appendix. In the remainder of this subsection, I describe the main substantive findings in the text.

The most important finding to emerge from the pooled time series analysis is that utility price changes caused shifts in public support for

---

[13] To properly isolate these interactive effects, I include the dummy variables *Telecommunications privately owned* and *Electricity privately owned*, which are 0 when the sector is stateowned and 1 when privately owned.

privatization. In contexts where fixed-line utilities were privately owned, price hikes caused declining support for privatization while price decreases yielded higher support. For example, privatization support was ten percentage points (a full standard deviation) higher when prices fell by 30% than when they rose by 30%, a relationship that is statistically significant. Electricity price changes caused similar, although slightly weaker and not statistically significant, changes in public opinion. The results of utility price changes in state-owned contexts are equally revealing. Price increases levied by publicly owned telephone and electricity firms raised support for privatization, while decreases lowered it. (This relationship was statistically significant in the electricity but not the telecommunications sector.) Rate hikes of 30% by publicly owned electricity firms caused support for privatization to be ten percentage points higher than did rate drops of 30%.

Only one other factor, annual change in GDP, had an impact on privatization attitudes. A country enjoying rapid economic expansion was more likely to support privatization than a country experiencing sluggish growth or a recession. All remaining variables, labor-market and top-down factors, had no statistically significant effect. Moreover, overall price inflation did not influence attitudes in the expected direction, demonstrating that Latin American citizens were discerning enough to pinpoint utility rate changes rather than overall price shifts.

Overall, these results support the consumption-based framework and explain the sharp decline in support for privatization throughout the lost half-decade of 1998 to 2002. Slowing macroeconomies certainly contributed, but postprivatization price increases, especially in the telecommunications sector, played a leading role in driving down support for privatization. What happened, however, in countries in which neither the electricity nor the telecommunications sector was privatized? In many cases, prices fell in these state-owned contexts, leading citizens to reject the prospect of privatization. For example, Uruguay was one of just four countries to privatize neither its electricity nor its telecommunications sector. The real price of a residential fixed-line price basket fell by 45% between 1998 and 2003, and the price of a unit of electricity fell by more than a third. Meanwhile, support for privatization in Uruguay fell by half, from 30% to 15%.

Globalization and Consumption

This final subsection tests a number of hypotheses regarding attitudes toward globalizing policies, namely, free trade and foreign investment. I first test whether citizens have been more favorable toward the consumption-channel impact of trade than toward the labor-channel consequences. If free trade has been popular because of its beneficial consumer effects, then citizens should believe that trade has been more beneficial for the availability and prices of consumer goods than for wages and employment opportunities.

In a 1998 battery of questions entitled *Regional trade bloc's effects*, respondents in thirteen countries were asked if the regional trade bloc of which their country was a member had helped or harmed, in succession, (1) the price of consumer goods, (2) employment, and (3) wages. I compare responses across these three questions to determine whether citizens were more appreciative of trade's impact on prices than they were of its impact on the two labor-market criteria.[14] To accomplish this, I conduct difference of mean t-tests that compare whether (1) the evaluation of the impact on prices was more positive than the evaluation of the impact on wages and whether (2) the evaluation of the impact on prices was more positive than the evaluation of the impact on employment. I set up the t-tests so that positive differences equate to citizens evaluating the consumer-channel effects more favorably than the labor-channel effects. In Figure 4.6, each t-test result is plotted with a "+" or "–" marker. Markers above the gray dotted line represent a statistically significant difference, meaning that citizens were more favorable toward the bloc's impact on prices than toward its impact on a labor-market criterion. The two markers in the leftmost column indicate the results for the aggregated data across all thirteen countries. Countries are grouped by trade bloc thereafter.

In the region as a whole, citizens thought that their regional trade bloc had exerted a much more beneficial impact on prices than on employment and wages. This is evidenced by the strongly positive and highly statistically significant results in the leftmost column. The country-level results show the depth of this sentiment across countries. In all but two countries, citizens were more favorable toward their bloc's impact on prices than they were toward their bloc's impact on wages. Similarly, the difference in

---

[14] The fact that these questions refer to regional trade blocs, and not trade liberalization in general, may seem problematic because the former may not have been central to citizens' conceptualizations of the latter. This is, however, a methodological opportunity. If consumer concerns predominated in shaping attitudes about a single, and potentially a secondary, aspect of globalization, then it is likely that such findings would pertain to attitudes toward most or all aspects of trade liberalization.

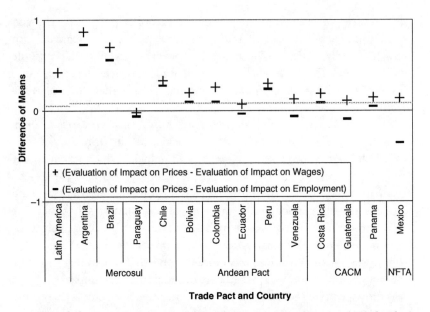

Figure 4.6 Latin Americans' Comparative Assessments of Regional Trade Bloc's Effects on Prices and Labor-Market Criteria.
Note: The gray line is the critical value at $p < .05$. Markers above the gray line are statistically significant. Questions are the *Regional trade bloc's effects* battery. NAFTA (North American Free Trade Agreement.)
Source: WSJA (1998).

means between the assessment of the bloc's impact on prices and on employment is positive and statistically significant in seven of thirteen cases and highly negative in only one case.[15] In sum, these results confirm the claim that citizens viewed favorably the effects of trade liberalization on consumer interests, especially when compared to labor-market interests.

Finally, I test competing explanations for cross-national differences in globalization attitudes. I evaluate a consumption-based hypothesis founded on the following premises. Consumers living in countries with a small, highly concentrated manufacturing sector have far fewer domestically made tradable goods options available to buy than consumers whose countries have a large, diversified manufacturing sector. Likewise, consumers in small

---

[15] This case, Mexico, is easily explained when one considers that Mexico was the only country experiencing considerable success with export-led job creation through its main regional trade agreement (Berg et al. 2006; Stallings and Peres 2000).

economies have fewer domestically made consumer products to choose from, whether tradable or not, than those in large economies. As a result, citizens in small economies should be more supportive of globalizing policies, such as free trade and foreign investment, than citizens in large economies.

Is this inquiry about a country's economic size truly a consumption-oriented hypothesis? Political economists have known for years that small economies in the developed world tend to be more open to foreign imports and investment, yet these scholars commonly overlook the consumption-based reasons for this (Katzenstein 1985). As is known, small economies prefer openness because they rely on foreign inputs to their own production processes – that is, investors' "consumption." However, they also choose openness because their size prohibits them from producing every good and service that citizens demand – that is, mass consumption. Small economies are not open so that they can export a large share of their GDP; exports are not an end in and of themselves (Krugman 1996). Instead, small open economies export so that they can acquire the inputs and imports that their consumers demand. Moreover, in Latin America, cognition underlies the claim that an economy's size is a consumption-oriented variable. The beneficial effects on consumer options of lowered barriers to imports and foreign investment should be more pronounced and more visible in countries that did not produce a wide variety of manufactured goods and services than in countries that already had large, diversified economies.

I assess this and competing hypotheses with a 1998 cross section of fourteen countries. (No pooled time series of North–South trade or foreign investment attitudes exists.) I use *Percent agreeing that free trade helps the country* and *Percent agreeing that foreign investment is good for the economy* as dependent variables in two different statistical models. The consumption-oriented hypothesis requires a slightly different measure of economic size for each model. For the free trade model, I create a variable entitled *Tradables GDP*, which is the size of each country's agriculture and manufacturing sectors. (Alternatively, one might think of this variable as the GDP of the nonservice sector.[16]) For the foreign investment model, I use *Overall GDP*.[17] It is important to clarify that these two independent variables are not percentages or per capita figures but rather measures of the sheer amount of these two types of economic activity.

[16] These figures were logged (natural), and data are for 1998 (World Bank 2006).
[17] This is in constant 2000 US$ at purchasing power parity (logged) (World Bank 2006).

I also gauge alternative explanations. To test for labor-market factors, I assess the impact of the national *Unemployment rate* and *Exports as a percent of GDP* (although the latter is included only in the model of trade attitudes). Citizens in countries with high unemployment rates might be more skeptical of globalization. Also, countries with large export-oriented sectors have a large number of individuals employed in globally competitive sectors: Citizens in such Latin American countries might be more pro-trade for this labor-market reason. To test for other macroeconomic effects, I also include *GDP growth*: Citizens in countries with booming economies might attribute these economic successes to globalization. Finally, I also include as a control variable *Distance to Washington, D.C.*: the distance in kilometers between each country's capital and the U.S. capital. A large amount of evidence links transport costs to trade volumes and overall economic well-being (Gallup et al. 2003; Leamer 1997). Countries that are closer to the epicenters of world economic activity have advantages because the transaction costs of trade flows are lower. Latin American countries that are close to the United States may for these reasons have more pro-trade citizens than those that are far away (Baker 2005). Again, I report the full numerical results and other details of the two statistical models in the Chapter 4 Appendix.

The most important finding is the importance of economic size and, thus, consumption. Citizens in small economies were on average more enthusiastic about both aspects of globalization than those in large ones. The substantive impacts of tradables GDP and overall GDP were large in magnitude and statistically significant. Citizens in small economies were more enthusiastic about globalization than those in large ones. A comparison of the region's smallest economy (Nicaragua) and its largest (Brazil) exemplifies this trend. Because of the differences in the size of their tradable goods sectors, the percentage of Nicaraguans supporting free trade was twelve points (more than two standard deviations and 70% of the entire range) higher than the percentage of pro-trade Brazilians. Moreover, the partial correlation between tradables GDP and the percentage supporting free trade is $-.70$ ($p < .02$). The impact of the size of the economy on beliefs about foreign investment was equally impressive. Nicaraguans were sixteen percentage points (greater than half of the range and equal to two standard deviations) more supportive of foreign investment than Brazilians. The partial correlation between overall GDP and support for foreign investment is $-.60$ ($p < .04$).

The only other variable that shows a statistically significant impact on globalization attitudes is distance from the U.S. market. Mexicans and Central Americans were about seven percentage points more enthusiastic about trade than Southern Cone residents merely because of the difference in proximity to the world's largest market. More importantly, labor-market factors (unemployment and exports as a percent of GDP) and economic growth did not have the expected influence on country-level attitudes. In both models, all three variables are "wrongly signed." The partial correlation between free trade attitudes and unemployment is +.30 and that between foreign investment attitudes and unemployment is +.28. The partial correlation between GDP growth and free trade attitudes is −.21, and it is −.09 between foreign investment attitudes and GDP growth.[18] The variable measuring exports as a percent of GDP has a −.61 partial correlation with support for free trade, a high but again wrongly signed result. In sum, a consumption-based variable, economic size, is the most important and meaningful determinant of cross-national beliefs about globalizing policies.

Discussion and Conclusion

This chapter demonstrates the importance of consumer interests in determining mass attitudes toward market policies. Consumer interests have been at the forefront of Latin Americans' minds when evaluating the Washington Consensus; labor-market interests have taken a back seat. The primacy of consumption concerns highlights the role of cognitive limitations, or the boundedness of rationality, in public opinion toward market reforms. Citizens' perceptions of relevant interests stem from a narrowly defined economic role – that of consumer. While labor-market or producer roles maintain their importance as determinants of objective economic welfare, policy shifts and their consequences in the new market era have primed consumer-oriented concerns and interests.

Combining these political psychology elements with notions of self-interest resolves some of the problems that other scholars have in understanding Latin Americans' responses to the Washington Consensus. Most

---

[18] Alternative measures of the labor-market and macroeconomic factors, such as change in unemployment and nonlagged effects, performed no better.

importantly, the results presented in this chapter cast considerable doubt on the conventional wisdom of the economists who have speculated about the causes of mass opinions toward certain reforms. In particular, several studies on the microeconomic consequences of state divestment wrestle with the apparent puzzle known as the "privatization paradox": Why is privatization so unpopular when it has been so beneficial (IDB 2002b; see also Macedo 2005; McKenzie and Mookherjee 2005; Nellis et al. 2004; Shirley 2005)? In other words, since privatization has yielded greater firm efficiency and expanded infrastructure networks, why do so many Latin Americans oppose it?

The standard answer posits misinformation or bias on the part of citizens. Citizens may have a psychological sensitivity to extremely visible negative cases, such as the Water War in Cochabamba, electricity blackouts in Brazil, or massive layoffs everywhere (IDB 2002b; Macedo 2005; McKenzie and Mookherjee 2005). Furthermore, privatization may have yielded diffuse consumption benefits that have been too small to reach citizens' radar screens. "Popular views are shaped by extreme cases that invite media attention, while widely diffused benefits are rarely noticed. Many benefits accrue to a wide range of customers, each of whom may benefit moderately; their improved welfare is overshadowed, however, by the dramatic losses of a few workers or customers" (McKenzie and Mookherjee 2005, 75; see also Haggard and Kaufman 1995; Nellis et al. 2004). For example, citizens may have "collective amnesia" about the poor quality of and lack of access to utility services under the state-led development era: "The key point is that the standards applied today to assess the effects of reform are significantly higher than those used to gauge the delivery systems under which people were living in the early 1980s" (Estache 2005, 284–285; see also Reel 2006).

The empirical results presented in this chapter cast considerable doubt on this standard diffuse-gains/concentrated-costs claim. The diffuse benefits of trade through the consumption channel *have* reached citizens' perceptual screens and *have* influenced public opinion. In fact, in retrospect, it is obvious that consumers prefer lower prices to higher prices and thus have been an obvious constituency for trade liberalization. Moreover, given Latin American citizens' support for foreign investment and free trade, it is unlikely that the rejection of privatization in recent years has been due to exaggerations of a few negative events. If citizens overemphasized negative events, then they would have done the same with pessimistic anecdotes about globalization and, for that matter, *any* policy.

These economists misread how the economic consequences of utility privatization for consumers are mapped on to policy preferences. The presumption behind the privatization paradox is that citizens should be more sensitive to changes in access than to price changes. The standard conclusion from economists' empirical studies is that the positive impact of expanded access to utility services has outweighed any detrimental impact from tariff increases (Nellis et al. 2004, 4; Ugaz and Price 2003). Some interpretations of mass opposition betray a sentiment that rate hikes have been a smoke screen that has hidden the real success story, improved access: "Higher tariffs partially blurred the favorable effects of a major expansion of telecommunications services" (Macedo 2005, 256).

However, presuming that citizens should be more responsive to changes in access than to prices is itself a judgment call, and it is a judgment call that rests on shaky ground. Network expansion has benefited citizens who lacked access prior to privatization, yet before privatization a large majority already had access to electricity and water services and a sizable minority had access to telecommunications services (Murillo and Martinez-Gallardo 2007). Likewise, even when considering those who *did* receive access after privatization occurred, the intimation that access expansion should have trumped price increases presumes that these citizens were indifferent to subsequent increases in their utility bills. A new telephone line or electricity hook-up surely provides a one-off boost in support for privatization. As new costumers, however, such individuals respond to subsequent price shifts in the same manner as long-standing customers (Kahneman and Tversky 1979). In fact, because individuals with newly acquired services tend to be poor, utility service charges comprise a higher share of their consumption budgets and thus make them *more* politically sensitive to ensuing fee changes (Chisari et al. 2003). Although counter-intuitive, expanded access therefore has *contributed* to falls in aggregate support for privatization when rate hikes have occurred. In a perverse way, the most important benefits of privatization have sowed the seeds for precipitous declines in popular support.

Are citizens amnesiacs for not remembering the poor service quality and limited access of the 1980s? Perhaps, but such a stance harbors unrealistic and even arbitrary expectations of human psychology. Individuals do not use such (relatively) distant history as a point of comparison or reference. Rather, relevant time horizons for comparing shifts in well-being are much shorter: one or two years (Kiewiet 1983). Therefore, citizens are likely to consider whether a telephone rate hike is justified by quality or access improvements in the past year, not by improvements in the past twenty years. Overall, Latin Americans have not been misinformed or misled into opposing privatization. Far from "not able to identify fully the benefits of privatization," citizens have been closely tracking recent price changes (Anuatti-Neto et al. 2005, 170). The fact that privatization typically led to price increases makes the rising levels of antiprivatization sentiment after 1998 perfectly logical. Moreover, the apparent uptick in privatization support starting in 2005 (see Figure 4.1) is potentially a sign that citizens have adapted to the new market-based prices; the immediate post-privatization price increases of the late 1990s and early 2000s have faded from memory.

Latin American citizens thus *have* been aware of diffuse costs (in the case of privatization) and diffuse gains (in the case of globalization) accruing to consumers. Whether a policy's impact resonates in public opinion depends not on how diffuse or concentrated its impact is but on whether the impact is easily observable in everyday activities. Latin American citizens have been particularly attuned to policy-induced changes occurring through the consumption channel, even when these changes have been diffuse.

Chapter 4 Appendix: Methodology and Full Statistical Model Results

Results: Sectoral Correlates of General Privatization Attitudes

The estimates reported in Figure 4.5 are generated from two different ordered probit models. The maximum likelihood coefficients and their standard errors are reported in Table 4.2. The two dependent variables are ordinal, with higher values representing greater support for privatization. (See the Survey Data Appendix for the exact wordings.) The independent variables are ordered choice variables, with respondents expressing a preference for (1) state, (2) mixed, or (3) private ownership. Country fixed effects (dummy variables for all but one country in the sample) are also included but not shown.

Results: Utility Prices and Country-Level Support for Privatization

The pooled time series results discussed in the "Utility Prices and Country-Level Support for Privatization" subsection are reported in Table 4.3.

116

Table 4.2. *Sectoral Correlates of General Privatization Attitudes in Eighteen Latin American Countries, 1998 and 1999*

	WSJA (1998)	*LB* (1999)
	DV: Change to Privatization Is Good for Country	DV: Privatization Is Good for Country
Telephone	.138** (.029)	.117** (.022)
Electricity	.139** (.020)	.063** (.018)
Water	.047* (.021)	.069** (.022)
Sewerage		.015 (.026)
Oil	.043* (.024)	.066** (.017)
Mining	.043* (.021)	
Health Care	.058** (.016)	.064** (.016)
Pensions	.052* (.021)	.042* (.022)
Education	.038** (.018)	.023 (.025)
Airlines	.083** (.016)	
Television	.058** (.016)	
N of countries	14	17
N of respondents	11,239	16,051

Note: Entries are ordered probit maximum likelihood estimates with robust standard errors in parentheses. Each model also contains a constant, country fixed effects, and two cutpoint parameters that are not shown. Results are from twenty multiply imputed data sets (King et al. 2001). ** $p < .01$, * $p < .05$. Directions of hypotheses are all positive. Some predictions from these regressions are plotted in Figure 4.5.

Sources: *WSJA* (1998) and LB (1999).

This table reports the results of two different pooled time series models, each with a different specification to check the robustness of the central substantive findings. The predicted values discussed in the text are generated from model 1 ("Fixed Effects"). The dependent variable in the pooled time series models represents an aggregate measure of citizens' opinions. Rather than wholly reinventing their opinions at each period, the economic information measured with the independent variables in these models is likely to lead citizens to adjust their standing opinions – that is, to deviate in a certain direction from their previous attitudes. In other words, the dependent variable is probably dynamic; opinions are somewhat contingent on previous beliefs. As a result, a model with a lagged dependent variable is preferred (Keele and Kelly 2006).

Table 4.3. *Determinants of Country-Level Support for Privatization: Pooled Time Series Analysis of Seventeen Latin American Countries, 1999–2005*

DV: Percentage (in Country) Agreeing That *Privatization is good for the country*		
	(1) Fixed Effects	(2) Random Effects
Bottom-Up Factors: Consumer Interests		
When utility was privately owned		
Percent change in residential fixed-line price basket	−1.079* (.613)	−.829* (.501)
Percent change in residential electricity rates	−.367 (.800)	−.162 (.597)
When utility was publicly owned		
Percent change in residential fixed-line price basket	.373 (.650)	.064 (.597)
Percent change in residential electricity rates	1.879* (.820)	1.246* (.680)
Bottom-Up Factors: Labor-Market Interests		
Percent change in employment in telecoms. sector	−1.174 (5.679)	−1.180 (4.480)
Bottom-Up Factors: Macroeconomy		
GDP growth$_{(t-1)}$	.541 (.863)	1.165* (.795)
Inflation$_{(t-1)}$	1.413 (1.490)	1.907 (.992)
Top-Down Factors		
Elite support for privatization of public services	−2.757 (11.873)	6.125 (6.661)
Other		
Telecommunications privately owned	−11.165 (8.620)	.694 (2.176)
Electricity privately owned	NA	−1.671 (2.177)
Dependent variable$_{(t-1)}$	.333** (.093)	.384** (.074)
Constant	24.498 (11.925)	6.817 (6.434)

Note: Entries are regression coefficients with standard errors in parentheses. Results are from twenty multiply imputed data sets (King et al. 2001; Royston 2004). * $p < .05$, ** $p < .01$. Directions of hypotheses are mentioned in the text.

Sources: Estache and Goicoechea (2005); ITU (2007); LB; World Bank (2006).

For utility price variables, the percent changes are logged (natural) when such changes are positive. To achieve symmetry about the origin, the negative of the absolute value's natural log is used when the percent change is negative. For telephone service rates, the price basket concept is that used by the World Bank (2006), and price data (originally expressed in constant US$) are from ITU (2007). Data on employment in the telecommunications sector are also from ITU (2007). I use Murillo and Martinez-Gallardo (2005) to identify whether and when fixed-line privatization occurred in the seventeen countries. Macroeconomic figures are lagged one year and logged in the symmetrical manner described for the utility price changes. Data are from the World Bank (2006)

Figure 4.1 shows that the dependent variable used in these models is missing in 2004: Latinbarometer did not ask the general privatization question in that year. The missing values from 2004, as well as those contained in the macroeconomic and utility price data, are filled in with standard multiple imputation procedures (King et al. 2001; Royston 2004). The 2004 imputations for the dependent variable are especially reliable since Latinbarometer did have a question that year about the price and quality of privatized services. This same question was also asked along with the main privatization question in 2003, so the common cross-national variance they share in that year is used to fill in the 2004 missing values.

Results: Globalization and Consumption

The regression results discussed in the "Globalization and Consumption" subsection are reported in Table 4.4. A number of different model specifications are reported to convince readers of the robustness of the findings. In particular, besides the standard ordinary least squares (OLS) results, results from robust regression analyses, which are less sensitive to outliers, are also reported. These robust regressions are "bounded influence estimators" that weight each case by the inverse of its influence (Cook's distance) on the OLS regression coefficients. The free trade models are also run with five independent variables ("Unrestricted Models") and with just three ("Restricted Models"), the latter dropping statistically insignificant independent variables. The partial correlations reported in the text are based on the unrestricted (five-variable) specification.

Table 4.4. *Determinants of Country-Level Globalization Attitudes in Fourteen Latin American Countries, 1998*

DV: Percentage (in Country) Agreeing That *Free trade helps country*

	Unrestricted Models		Restricted Models	
	(1) OLS	(2) Robust Regression	(3) OLS	(4) Robust Regression
Tradables GDP	−2.721** (.786)	−2.995** (1.083)	−2.605** (.727)	−2.626** (.786)
Exports as a percentage of GDP	−.279 (.059)	−.271 (.086)	−.269 (.050)	−.270 (.068)
Distance to Washington, D.C. (km/1000)	−1.365* (.583)	−1.164* (.720)	−1.368* (.531)	−1.397* (.5156)
GDP growth$_{(t-1)}$	.462 (3.038)	.537 (3.362)	—	—
Unemployment rate$_{(t-1)}$	−.000 (.218)	−.073 (.295)	—	—
Constant	163.100 (18.448)	168.926 (25.522)	160.819 (17.876)	161.415 (19.999)
R^2	.71	—	.72	—

DV: Percentage (in Country) Agreeing that *Foreign investment is good for economy*

	OLS	Robust Regression
Overall GDP	−3.417* (1.404)	−3.453* (1.765)
GDP growth$_{(t-1)}$	−3.558 (4.778)	−3.343 (6.946)
Unemployment rate$_{(t-1)}$	−.026 (.448)	.000 (.579)
Constant	152.951 (36.760)	153.387 (44.121)
R^2	.39	—

Note: Entries are regression coefficients with standard errors in parentheses. Results are from twenty multiply imputed data sets (King et al. 2001; Royston 2004). Directions of hypotheses are mentioned in the text. * $p < .05$, ** $p < .01$. $N=14$.

Sources: World Bank (2006) and *WSJA* (1998).

5

Are the Poor Neoliberals?

> Formed by authentic representatives of indigenous people, peasants, and
> workers, the Movement toward Socialism is currently the expression of
> all marginalized sectors of society that, oppressed by the neoliberal model
> and by globalization, struggle for their demands, their identity, their
> self-determination, their sovereignty and their dignity.
>   – *Movimiento al Socialismo*, in a press release issued during Evo Morales's
>   successful 2005 presidential campaign (*MAS* 2005, 1)

The average Latin American citizen embraces globalization while dis-
approving of privatization, but this average Latin American is surrounded by
massive variation in attitudes toward the Washington Consensus. In other
words, some people are more enthusiastic about market reforms than others.
Of course, this observation is not at all novel or controversial. For example,
many scholars, journalists, and even politicians assume that the politics of
neoliberalism *is* the politics of class and inequality: The poor are ravaged by
the region's newfound taste for rugged individualism and savage capitalism,
while the local rich and foreign investors benefit at their expense. (See this
chapter's epigraph for an example.) Beliefs about market policies are widely
thought to be stratified along class lines. Indeed, in countries with such
unequal distributions of wealth, many of which experienced violent struggles
over economic ideologies and resources during the Cold War, it would be
surprising if the poor were *not* more likely to favor state-sponsored protections from marketization.

In this chapter, I consider whether wealth and other factors that vary
across individuals explain why some Latin Americans are more enthusiastic
about market reforms than others. In other words, I describe and explain
the nature of mass attitudinal cleavages over market policies. I do so by

testing a series of hypotheses derived from the bottom-up and top-down theoretical frameworks.

I first show with some simple descriptive results that, as is widely believed, the affluent in Latin America have typically been more supportive of market policies than the poor. The size of this wealth gap in pro-market attitudes, however, has been modest: The richest citizens have typically been just five to fifteen percentage points more likely than the poor to support privatization and globalization. At times, they have even been no more favorable toward these policies than the poor. Moreover, these wealth gaps have typically been matched in size by hegemony effects – that is, attitudinal gaps between the politically aware and the politically unaware. I then estimate a series of statistical models to determine the theoretical sources and precise contours of these wealth gaps and hegemony effects and to discern whether other factors have been responsible for individual-level variation in beliefs about reforms. In doing so, I test a large number of hypotheses to discern the explanatory power of the consumption-based, labor-market-oriented, and top-down theoretical frameworks.

Three sets of findings are central. First, bottom-up, consumer-interest considerations have played a leading role in forging mass cleavages in beliefs about market reforms. Variations in consumer tastes and behaviors have caused some individuals to view globalization and privatization with more enthusiasm than others. They have also accounted for the existence, and occasional nonexistence, of wealth gaps. Second, elite discourse has fashioned important attitudinal cleavages. The pro-market bias on most issues among elites has created the hegemony effect, yet this effect has disappeared in the instances where elites have soured on the merits of a particular market policy. Moreover, elites have even activated partisan cleavages among the politically aware in instances when they themselves have been divided. Finally, labor-market interests, such as skill, social class, and job insecurity, have played a minimal role in determining individual-level differences in beliefs about market reforms.

Hypotheses for Individual-Level Differences in Support for Reforms

Differences across individuals in economic policy beliefs may stem from the fact that consumers have nonhomothetic tastes – that is, people consume relevant goods and services to varying degrees. I test three sets of hypotheses to determine whether this consumption-based framework can explain attitudinal cleavages among Latin Americans. First, privatization support should be highest among individuals (1) who experienced new-found access to utility services because of privatization and (2) who already had access but were well positioned financially to absorb privatization-induced price increases. Individuals in the first category tend to be poor, while those in the second category tend to be wealthy. As a result, I expect privatization beliefs to follow a U-shaped pattern with respect to wealth: Middle-income individuals should be less enthusiastic about privatization than the poor and the rich. The existence of this pattern, however, should be contingent on some degree of utility privatization having already occurred.

Second, individuals with a high propensity to consume imported and import-competing goods should be more likely to support trade liberalization than individuals with a low propensity to consume such goods. Latin America's imports from developed countries tend to be luxury durable goods, so I expect relatively heavy consumers of such goods, the wealthy, to be more enthusiastic about North–South trade than are light consumers of such goods, the poor. Similarly, heavy consumers of goods and services produced by foreign firms on domestic soil, the wealthy, should be more enthusiastic about foreign investment than are light consumers of such goods and services, the poor. In short, beliefs about these aspects of globalization should be positively related to wealth, although (for reasons described in Chapter 3) this relationship may be weaker toward the top of the income scale. In contrast, I expect beliefs about South–South trade to be *less* stratified by wealth because imports to Latin America from neighboring, less-developed countries tend to be primary products that are not disproportionately consumed by the wealthy.

Third, I evaluate the role of "consumption security," defined as the extent to which individuals believe they can meet their basic consumption needs. Individuals with a high degree of consumption insecurity should be less likely to support market reforms of all kinds because these reforms may have weakened state protections against vicissitudes in the ability to meet basic needs.

I also test whether elites influence public opinion and, in particular, shape mass cleavages over reforms. Chapter 3 showed that legislative elites in Latin America have been, on balance, favorable toward market policies. As a result, if elites influence mass beliefs, then highly aware individuals should have a greater propensity to support market reforms than highly unaware ones. Not all policies, however, have been popular among elites.

For attitudes toward policies that have steadily declined in popularity among legislators, namely privatization, the size of hegemony effects should also decline through time. Chapter 3 also showed that some issues, namely privatization, foreign investment, and the FTAA, have been divisive and partisan at the elite level, while others, namely free trade in general and regional trade pacts, have unified elites. Mass beliefs toward the former list of policies should thus show evidence of a polarizing effect, with highly aware leftists less supportive of the policy than highly aware rightists. Beliefs toward the latter list should reflect not a polarizing effect but rather a hegemony effect.

Finally, I test two sets of alternative hypotheses. First, I assess the influence of labor-market interests on public opinion. I test whether labor-market skills influence mass beliefs, hypothesizing that higher skill levels should increase support for globalization but decrease enthusiasm for privatization. Furthermore, if labor-market interests matter, then job insecurity should increase opposition to the incumbent market policies. I also test whether social class, the degree to which an individual controls the means of production, influences support for market policies. Second, I test whether capitalist values, expressed beliefs about principles such as economic equality and market efficiency, are positively correlated with more specific beliefs about privatization and globalization. Public opinion scholars often employ such measures of capitalist values as meaningful indicators of beliefs about the actual market policies implemented in recent years, so a test of whether they are actually relevant to beliefs about on-the-ground policies is overdue.

Wealth Gaps and Hegemony Effects

Before turning to a fully specified model of individual-level support for market reforms, I first describe the simple net impact of the two most important independent variables: wealth and political awareness. This provides a first-cut test of some of the consumption-based and top-down hypotheses, but it also establishes some important descriptive facts. First, because so many observers (typically without having looked at public opinion data) claim that wealth has been the primary stratifier of mass attitudes toward the market in Latin America, I clarify the precise impact of this bottom-up factor by quantifying the "wealth gap," the size of the gap in pro-market sentiment between the richest and poorest. Second, I quantify the "hegemony effect," the size of the gap in pro-market attitudes between the most politically aware and the least aware citizens. The hegemony effect, also called an "awareness gap," quantifies the extent to which a pro-market skew in elite discourse (if any) influences opinions among politically engaged and attentive citizens.

To unpack the reform process, I define and report in Figure 5.1 the wealth gap and the hegemony effect for each policy in each available year between 1990 and 2003. (I discuss in the following section how wealth and awareness are measured.) The darkened circles in the left half of Figure 5.1 quantify the wealth gap for each policy. This is the estimated difference in the probability of taking a pro-market stance between an individual at the 95th percentile of wealth and one at the 5th percentile of wealth. The right half of the figure shows hegemony effects, or the estimated differences in the probability of pro-market support between individuals at the 95th percentile of awareness and those at the 5th percentile. The figure groups estimates by policy and sorts them by year, joining estimates for the same policy (but different years) by a diagonal line. Each estimate is generated from a regression model containing only wealth and awareness as independent variables.[1] (The dependent variables are many of the attitudinal measures described in Chapter 4.) The vertical lines running through each circle represent the 95% confidence intervals of each effect. Confidence intervals that cross the horizontal line (which corresponds to zero on the y-axis) denote an effect that is not statistically distinguishable from zero. For example, the leftmost circle indicates that the wealthy were about .18, or eighteen percentage points, more likely than the poor to support privatization in 1990. The vertical line through this circle indicates that the 95% confidence interval for this estimate runs from .15 to .22. Because the confidence interval does not cross zero, this wealth gap is statistically distinguishable from zero.

The left half of Figure 5.1 definitively shows the inaccuracy of the claim that market beliefs are heavily stratified by wealth in Latin America. Instead, *wealthy citizens are only slightly more favorable toward market reforms than poor citizens.* In other words, Latin America counts many pro-reform poor as well as many antireform rich among its residents. According to Figure 5.1, wealthy citizens have typically been less than ten percentage points more likely than poor ones to support each market reform. While statistically significant, these wealth gaps are modest in size. In the 1990s,

---

[1] The models also contain country fixed effects. The full results of these models are available from the author upon request.

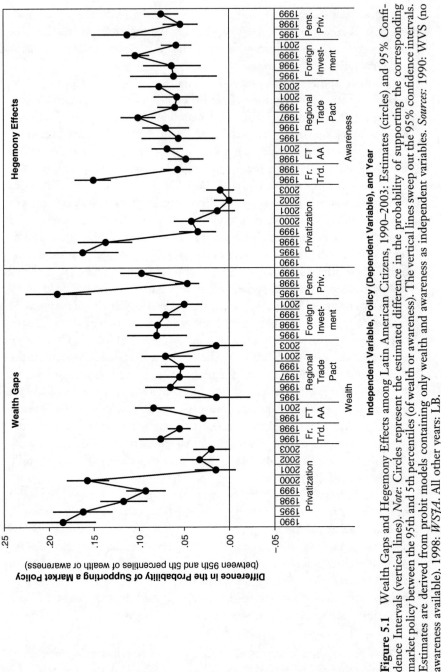

Figure 5.1 Wealth Gaps and Hegemony Effects among Latin American Citizens, 1990–2003: Estimates (circles) and 95% Confidence Intervals (vertical lines). *Note:* Circles represent the estimated difference in the probability of supporting the corresponding market policy between the 95th and 5th percentiles (of wealth or awareness). The vertical lines sweep out the 95% confidence intervals. Estimates are derived from probit models containing only wealth and awareness as independent variables. *Sources:* 1990: WVS (no awareness available). 1998: *WSJA*. All other years: LB.

126

wealth gaps for the privatization issue were in the teens, but these were the only policies (with the exception of pension privatization in 1995) for which the gaps exceeded ten percentage points.

In fact, the often studied and frequently cited effect of wealth was matched in size by the typically ignored effect of elite discourse. *In most cases, the hegemony effect, or the gap in pro-market beliefs between the politically aware and unaware, was just as large as the wealth gap.* The pro-market tinge to elite discourse throughout the 1990s and even the early 2000s trickled down and had a persuasive impact on the moderately to highly aware individuals who were recipients of it. The hegemony effect is statistically significant in all but three instances.

In sum, almost every wealth gap and hegemony effect fits a similar description: statistically significant but modest (about five to fifteen percentage points) in size. The most consistent set of exceptions fall under the privatization issue. Wealth gaps and hegemony effects on the privatization issue fell dramatically between 1998 and 2000. Privatization attitudes were stratified by wealth throughout the 1990s, but wealth gaps were effectively zero after 2000. Likewise, the hegemony effect on privatization attitudes was in the teens in the 1990s, only to shrink to zero after 2000.

These simple findings provide some initial insights into the relevance of consumption-based and top-down influences. As hypothesized, wealth gaps in globalization attitudes existed and were largely constant, yet no gaps existed in privatization attitudes after the late 1990s once most utility privatizations took hold. Also, hegemony effects existed in nearly every instance except, again as expected, for the privatization issue after the late 1990s, when elite discourse became more unfavorable. To test these and other hypotheses more rigorously, I turn to more fully specified statistical models.

Explaining Individual-Level Attitudes: Measurement and Theoretical Expectations

The finding that wealth gaps have been persistently positive yet modest in size is informative, yet it leaves many questions unanswered. When considering wealth, most scholarship on Latin American public opinion toward market reforms notes the existence (or occasional nonexistence) of a correlation between wealth and attitudes but fails to provide a causal explanation for why such a correlation exists (Graham and Pettinato 2002; Graham and Sukhtankar 2004; Stokes 2001a). This is problematic, as a large number of theoretically and conceptually distinct causal factors are tightly related to wealth.

First, wealth, which itself is the total value of one's assets, is related to a set of varying demand patterns or *consumer tastes*. Because food is a human necessity, poor consumers *must* devote a relatively large share of their incomes to consumption of food. Mostly because of this, they devote a small share to durable luxury items and services. The share of expenditures on other relevant categories of goods and services, such as foreign entertainment and utilities, also varies systematically with wealth. Similarly, wealth is related to who has access to certain utility services (Chisari et al. 2003). Wealth thus may be related to beliefs about market reforms because of these nonhomothetic tastes.

Second, wealth is correlated with different degrees of economic security. Assets and income determine one's ability to consume. With limited assets and low income, poor individuals are uncertain about whether they will be able to consume basic necessities. In contrast, wealthy individuals are relatively worry-free about their provision (Sen 2000). Thus, a sense of economic or *consumption insecurity* accompanies poverty, potentially inclining poorer citizens to favor government interventions that ensure consumption of necessities (Hoogeveen 2002).

Third, wealth is closely related to human capital assets or *skill level*. Many citizens are members of a certain income group precisely because of their skill sets. Because skill determines overall productivity and especially the extent to which workers can enhance output through technology and capital equipment, a primary determinant of wages is workers' level of human capital (Bound and Johnson 1992). Moreover, policy changes influence the relative demand for various skills, so attitudes may derive from these economic consequences.

Fourth, wealth is related to *social class*. I use "class" not in the vague but commonly used sense of income categories – lower class, middle class, and upper class – but in the strict Marxist sense: "common positions within social relations of production" (Wright and Perrone 1977, 33; Poulantzas 1973). To Marxian scholars, social class indicates the degree to which individuals own the means of production (Wright 1979). Individuals with control over the factors of production, the bourgeoisie, should be more favorable toward capitalism and market policies than individuals with little or no control, the proletariat.

Finally, wealth is often related to the main determinants of elite influence: *political awareness* and *political predispositions*. In most societies, wealth

128

is correlated with one's centrality to the political system, and thus with citizen attention to politics and elite discourse (Verba et al. 1978). Moreover, partisan cleavages, and thus political predispositions, often divide rich from poor (Lipset and Rokkan 1967).

Because of their interrelatedness, teasing out the independent impact of the various correlates of wealth on individual-level attitudes toward privatization and globalization is a daunting task. Statistical control, however, can provide insights into these cause-and-effect relationships. In the remainder of this section, I discuss how I measure these and other factors, which I then include as independent variables in a series of statistical models. I group the variables by the theoretical framework to which they correspond: consumer interests, labor-market interests, and elite influence. (Precise question wordings and codings for all variables are described in the Survey Data Appendix.)

Consumption-Based Interests

Precise measures of the consumption patterns, or the nonhomothetic tastes, deemed in Chapter 3 to be a main source of attitudinal variation at the individual level are expensive and time-consuming to collect. Household budget surveys, which require a sample of families to record expenditure patterns for at least a week (and often longer), are scant and have yet to be coupled with attitudinal surveys in Latin America. Moreover, a precise test of some of the hypotheses relating to changes in access to utility services would require panel data. Indeed, the absence of such consumption data indicates the extent to which scholars have ignored consumer-oriented explanations of economic policy preferences.

I address these shortcomings in a number of ways. First and most generally, I measure varying consumer tastes with an "asset index" of wealth (Filmer and Pritchett 2001). In Latinbarometer surveys, respondents are queried for ownership and consumption information about eleven goods (such as cars and computers) and services (such as sewerage and drinking water). I define *Wealth* as the total number of these that each respondent owned/used.[2] Admittedly, this variable does not measure

[2] Filmer and Pritchett (2001) and Kolenikov and Angeles (2004) recommend using principal components analyses to assign different weights to each item in the index. These weights would indicate the extent to which ownership of each item is correlated with an underlying dimension of long-term wealth. I conducted a number of analyses using these methods, and the resulting wealth indices were always highly correlated (+.95 or greater) with the simpler

consumer tastes directly. For example, it does not capture the precise percentage of a respondent's consumption budget that is devoted to utility expenditures or whether the respondent gained newfound access to telecommunications services in the last year. However, it does classify individuals into groups with identifiable and similarly defined consumer preferences. As discussed in Chapter 3, poor individuals with few assets have a higher propensity to consume primary products (and thus a lower propensity to consume luxury durables). They are also more likely than the wealthy to have gained newfound access to utility networks. Moreover, I assess the impact of wealth *when controlling for labor-market characteristics and the subjective accompaniments of well-being* (all discussed subsequently), so contamination from nonconsumption-related factors is unlikely to occur. After all, wealth itself does not measure alternative hypotheses, especially those regarding labor-market interests, because wealth is not a labor-market asset per se. Individuals peddle their skills in the labor market and only rarely receive meaningful returns on the material assets listed in the Latinbarometer battery.[3] In contrast, differences in demand patterns across wealth levels are stark, meaningful, and persistent. Finally, while differences across individuals in consumer tastes are certainly interesting, using wealth as the measure of nonhomothetic tastes links the latter to a variable of much broader interest.

If consumer interests drive public opinion toward market reform, then wealth should be positively correlated with pro-globalization attitudes because richer individuals are more likely to benefit from the influx of (typically) skill-intensive foreign goods and services. Beliefs about regional trade pacts, however, should not be correlated with wealth because expanded South–South trade does not increase the availability of goods with greater skill intensity. Wealth should have a nonlinear impact on attitudes toward firm privatization, but only after utility privatization became widespread in the late 1990s. Individuals at the extremes of

---

additive index that is used in my analyses. The asset index is unavailable in the *WSJA* and WVS surveys, so I use their income scales to measure wealth. See the Survey Data Appendix for details.

[3] This is especially so in a region where title to and profit from home ownership are not widespread (de Soto 2000). Moreover, it is not entirely obvious how the value of such potential returns is influenced by privatization and globalization. Wealthier individuals certainly have more assets to fall back on in the face of market-induced volatility, but the resulting sense of microeconomic vulnerability is captured in the consumption security variable.

wealth, the poor and the rich, should be less opposed to privatization than individuals in the middle of the wealth scale. Therefore, I test the statistical significance of $Wealth^2$, which should have a positive coefficient.[4]

Second, I use a more direct measure of relevant nonhomothetic tastes in a model of free-trade attitudes by constructing an indicator of each respondent's *Preference for durable goods*. In every year, Latinbarometer respondents were asked if they owned or consumed five different luxury durable goods items (such as washing machines and computers), the very types of capital- and skill-intensive goods that are imported or import-competing in Latin America. I sum up the number of such items each respondent owned and include it in a model that predicts beliefs about free trade in general. This variable, when controlling for overall wealth, is a measure of nonhomothetic tastes that should be positively correlated with pro-trade attitudes. Including both wealth and the propensity to consume durables in the same model helps to decipher whether wealth is correlated with trade beliefs because of its close relationship to consumer tastes or for other reasons.

Finally, I capture the degree of insecurity about the capacity to meet basic consumption needs with a variable called *Consumption security*. This survey question measures the degree to which respondents perceived that their family income allowed them to cover basic necessities. Individuals with a greater sense of insecurity may be more opposed to liberalizing reforms that expand the role of free-market forces and potentially weaken state protections against vicissitudes in the ability to meet consumption needs. If so, then this variable should be positively correlated with support for the various market reforms.

Labor-Market Interests

I test the main alternative hypotheses within the bottom-up tradition with a set of variables that measures labor-market characteristics. In contrast to consumption criteria, numerous indicators of labor-market interests are available in the cross-national surveys. First, I measure skill level as years of formal *Education* (Scheve and Slaughter 2001). Scholars widely agree that globalization in Latin America has widened the skill premium, so more

---

[4] I also test for a negative coefficient on $Wealth^2$ in models of globalization beliefs. This would indicate that the relationship between pro-trade attitudes and wealth is less positive at high levels of wealth than at low levels. (See Chapter 3.)

highly skilled individuals should be more enthusiastic about free trade and foreign investment. Moreover, relative returns to postsecondary education have increased especially rapidly. The effect of skill on attitudes may thus be nonlinear, so I also include *Education^2*. If labor-market interests drive globalization attitudes, then both of these variables should have positive coefficients. In contrast, education should have a negative coefficient in models of privatization beliefs; SOEs were more likely to employ, and thus sack upon being privatized, skilled workers.

Because the impact of labor-market factors is likely to work through family units, I include the skill level of multiple family members. In particular, individuals may be attuned to the labor-channel effects that market policies have had on the wages and employment of their family's "chief wage earner," particularly when they themselves are not in the EAP or, at the very least, are not the highest wage earner in the family. I control for *Chief wage earner's education* and *Chief wage earner's education^2*, and expect the same relationships as described in the previous paragraph.[5]

Second, to measure Marxian notions of social class, I classify individuals by the degree to which they control the three factors of production: (1) investment resources, (2) physical capital, and (3) labor power. To create a *Class* variable, I recode respondents' descriptions of their occupations into an ordered scale that ranges from "proletariat," the class with no control over any of the three factors of production, to "bourgeoisie," the class with full control over all three. Between these two extremes are seven other class categories, such as semiautonomous employees, middle managers, and small employers, which fall at intermediate levels of control. If social class explains policy attitudes, then support for market reforms should gradually increase as one moves up this scale from proletariat to bourgeoisie.[6] (The Survey Data Appendix contains an extensive discussion of how this variable is constructed.)

Again, family units are relevant. This type of class analysis raises the question of how to categorize the noneconomically active population (homemakers, students, and retirees) and the unemployed. Homemakers and students have "mediated class locations" through family ties, so I classify them according to the class location of the chief wage earner in

[5] Because it does not make sense to estimate the impact of these variables when respondents themselves are the chief wage earners, these variables are equal to zero for such respondents and I include a dummy variable to indicate when respondents are chief wage earners.
[6] The measure of occupational status in the *WSJA* survey does not allow one to code with this level of detail, so *WSJA* models do not contain any measures of social class.

their families. Retirees and the unemployed have a "postclass" location, so I classify them according to the class location of their most recent job (Wright 1979).

Third, I include a dummy variable for *Unemployed* respondents, expecting the unemployed to blame the incumbent market policies for their fate. Fourth, I include a dummy variable to indicate each *Public-sector employee* and test whether this status makes workers think differently about privatization. The literature is ambivalent about the impact that this variable might have on economic self-interest and thus privatization attitudes. Public-sector employees might be less supportive of privatization because it typically resulted in layoffs of SOE employees. Those who maintained their employment, however, often enjoyed wage and benefit increases, so this variable may actually capture, especially by the late 1990s and thereafter, the happy survivors of privatization. To allow for both possibilities, I conduct a two-tailed hypothesis test of the coefficients for this variable.

Finally, I contrast the aforementioned measure of consumption security with *Employment insecurity*. This survey item measures how worried respondents were about losing their jobs in the subsequent year. Higher values indicate greater degrees of concern about job loss, so if labor-market interests matter, this variable should have a negative impact on support for the incumbent market policies. This measure of labor-market interests is only meaningful as a possible predictor of policy attitudes among members of the EAP, so I estimate the impact of this variable only among this group.[7]

Unfortunately, the existing cross-national datasets do not contain measures of respondents' sector of employment. Such measures would be useful for gauging whether workers in competitive, export-oriented sectors are more pro-globalization than workers in import-competing sectors (Frieden 1991). Although sectoral affiliation is unavailable for cross-national testing, I do test for its effect in the case study of Brazilians' attitudes in Part III.

Elite Influence

Tests of top-down effects require the measurement of three factors: (1) each respondent's level of attention to elite discourse, (2) each

---

[7] Employment insecurity is thus zero for all individuals not in the EAP, and I include a dummy variable for EAP.

respondent's preferred party or political camp, and (3) the position of each party or political camp on relevant issues. I measure the first variable, attention to elite discourse, with *Political awareness*. Political behavior scholars widely agree that the optimal way to measure exposure to elite discourse is with political awareness – that is, respondents' objective knowledge of politics (Delli Carpini and Keeter 1996; Price and Zaller 1993). In most instances, this is a count (usually from zero to ten) of the number of various political and economic entities (like Mercosul, the FTAA, the World Bank, the International Monetary Fund, and the EU) about which citizens had "heard enough to form an opinion."[8]

In most instances, I measure the second variable, mass political predispositions, with the following survey question: "If elections were held this Sunday, for which party would you vote?" I specify the third variable, the stance of each Latin American party on market reform, by categorizing each party according to its *Party ideology*: left, center-left, center, center-right, and right. I use party ideology classifications from a leading survey of country experts to assign one of these five labels (Coppedge 1998). I create a sixth category for *Independents* to indicate those respondents who expressed no partisan preference.[9]

---

[8] The optimal way to measure awareness of politics and elite discourse is with a short quiz of objective political facts. Unfortunately, only one of the surveys (the *WSJA* in 1998) contains such a battery. The measure I use in most instances thus has the disadvantage of relying on respondent self-reports rather than on objective tests of knowledge. It does have the advantage, however, of capturing "domain-specific" knowledge of economic policy, since many of these entities are closely linked to market reforms (Alvarez and Brehm 2002). In the end, the measure has a high degree of reliability and construct validity: It correlates with known covariates of objective political knowledge like education, political interest, and media attention, and results reported later conform to plausible expectations.

[9] Measuring predispositions in this manner automatically incorporates cross-national party system differences into the statistical models. For example, in countries that have not had viable leftist parties or movements (such as most of those in Central America), no respondents are classified as leftists (Roberts forthcoming). Independents are individuals who said they "did not know" or "would not vote" if elections were held the following Sunday. Coppedge does not assign ideological labels to most Central American countries. To fill these in, I use the labels from Roberts and Wibbels (1999). The WVS, the *WSJA* survey, and the 2000 and 2003 LB survey contained either no or incomplete party codes for the simulated vote choice question. To measure political predispositions in these cases, I use the standard left–right ideological self-placement scale, which ranges from zero (*Leftist*) to ten (*Rightist*). Individuals who said they "did not know" or "would not vote" if elections were held on Sunday (based on responses to the aforementioned question) are *Independents*, as are individuals not self-placing on the 0 to 10 scale.

Are the Poor Neoliberals?

To test for elite influence, I assess the impact of awareness within each political group. If awareness does exert a statistically significant impact on attitudes within a particular politically defined group (and if the relationship is in the expected direction), then I conclude that elite influence has occurred. I do not necessarily conclude the opposite, however, when awareness has no impact. At times, the top-down model predicts no relationship between awareness and attitudes among certain groups. Instead, I weigh the totality of findings across all political groups to assess whether and how elite influence has occurred. That said, if awareness has no impact among any political groups, then it is safe to conclude that elites and top-down theory are irrelevant.

Capitalist Values

Because scholars and journalists so often use core values as indicators of support for the Washington Consensus, I examine the extent to which approval of capitalist principles correlates with specific support for particular policies. These *Capitalist values* questions vary substantially by survey year. In most years, however, the Latinbarometer included at least one question that gauged respondents' priorities by posing a trade-off between values such as individual versus state responsibility, market versus state superiority in solving problems, or equity versus productivity. Values questions such as these are often good predictors of economic policy beliefs in the United States and Western Europe, but their relevance for explaining and understanding mass responses to market reforms in Latin America is dubious. Regardless, I test their causal impact, hypothesizing that capitalist values should be associated with support for privatization, free trade, and foreign investment.

Results

To test these hypotheses, I estimate twenty-nine different statistical models. The list of dependent variables is similar to that used to create Figure 5.1. To avoid clutter and maintain a substantive focus, I present the most important results in text and in figures by reporting model-generated predicted probabilities. The full statistical results, along with technical notes, are in Tables 5.1 through 5.6 in the Chapter 5 Appendix.

Consumer Tastes and Interests

Figure 5.2 conveys the most interesting findings on the role of wealth and consumer tastes between 1990 and 2003. The figure plots the models' predictions of support for free trade and privatization, as measured with a variety of question wordings, as a function of wealth. I group wealth into five categories: "Poorest" (5th percentile of wealth), "First Quartile" (25th percentile), "Median" (50th percentile), "Third Quartile" (75th percentile), and "Richest" (95th percentile). Lines trace out the *independent* impact of wealth – that is, the impact of wealth while holding all other measured variables constant.[10]

First, the figure lends support to the consumption-based explanation of privatization sentiments (all depicted in the lower half of Figure 5.2). The critical test of the consumption-based hypothesis is whether patterns were nonlinear, following a U-shaped form, *after the widespread adoption of utility privatization in the mid- to late 1990s.* The figure clearly shows that wealth as a determinant of privatization attitudes had two distinct stages: a stage prior to 1999, in which the impact of wealth was positive and mostly linear, and a stage after 1999, in which U-shaped patterns emerged. Whereas the poorest were the most skeptical of privatization in every instance before 1998, support for privatization was at its nadir among middle-income groups in nearly every year thereafter. By 2001, *the very poor were as likely to support privatization as the very rich.* The statistical tests confirm this temporal shift and the consumption-based hypothesis. Before 1999, the coefficient on $Wealth^2$ is statistically significant in zero of five models. After 1998, the coefficient is significant in six of seven models.[11] (See Tables 5.1 and 5.2.)

The temporal process by which the nonlinear pattern emerged further supports a consumer-tastes argument. Between 1990 and 2003, support for privatization fell most quickly among middle- and upper-income groups, the two groups who had the highest degrees of access to these services before privatization and were therefore the most negatively affected by the resulting tariff hikes. In contrast, enhanced access to newly privatized

---

[10] I hold all other variables constant at their sample means.

[11] The WVS series is particularly useful because it straddles both eras with the same question wording. In 1990 and 1996, attitudes toward privatization were stratified rather sharply by wealth, with the wealthiest being about eighteen percentage points more likely than the poorest to support increased private ownership. By 2000, however, this wealth gap had disappeared entirely, morphing into the nonlinear pattern predicted earlier.

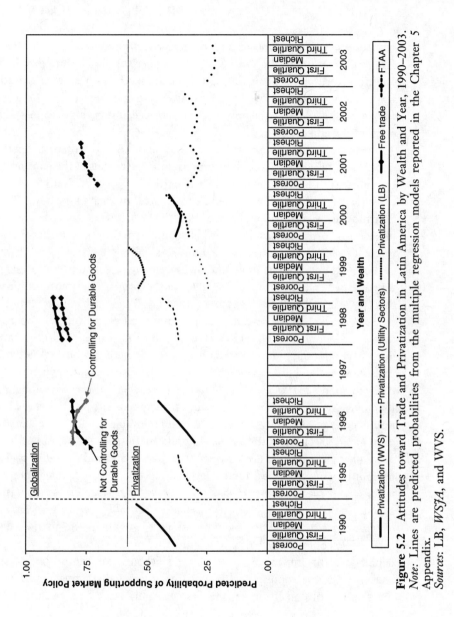

Figure 5.2 Attitudes toward Trade and Privatization in Latin America by Wealth and Year, 1990–2003.
Note: Lines are predicted probabilities from the multiple regression models reported in the Chapter 5 Appendix.
Sources: LB, *WSJA*, and WVS.

services prevented declines in support for privatization among the poorest groups. According to the WVS results, which are useful because they hold question wording constant through time, the level of support for privatization among the rich fell by almost twenty percentage points between 1990 and 2000. Among the poor, it did not budge during this decade, and it even increased between 1996 and 2000.[12]

Second, patterns of support for free trade and the FTAA (depicted in the upper half of Figure 5.2) also conform to the expectations of the consumer-based theory. The benefits of trade, and particularly North–South trade, to consumers have accrued more heavily to the wealthy than to the poor. In all four models, wealth had a positive, statistically significant (see Table 5.3) impact on pro-trade attitudes. The black lines with diamond markers in the top half of Figure 5.2 depict these upward-sloping effects.

To quell any doubts about the measurement of consumer interests, I estimate two statistical models of 1996 trade attitudes that jointly confirm that (1) wealth does indeed measure relevant differences in consumer tastes and *only* consumer tastes and (2) consumer tastes mattered. The two models differ only in their inclusion of respondents' propensity to consume durable goods (and thus imports and import-competing goods). When this variable is not included, the effect of wealth is positive, as shown with the black diamond-marked line in Figure 5.2 (labeled "Not Controlling for Durable Goods"). When this variable *is* included, two crucial statistical results emerge. The propensity to consume durable goods had a statistically ($p < .001$) and substantively significant impact on attitudes. The attitudinal gap between the heaviest (95th percentile) and the lightest (5th percentile) consumers of durable goods was thirteen percentage points, *which is twice the size of the originally defined wealth gap* (see Figure 5.1). Just as important, *wealth itself had no impact when controlling for the propensity to consume durable goods.* The downward-sloping, gray diamond-marked line in the 1996 column (labeled "Controlling for Durable Goods") shows what happens to the impact of wealth once I account for the propensity to consume durable goods. Wealth actually had a negative impact, although this slope is not statistically distinguishable from zero. The inclusion of the

---

[12] Most of the survey-based studies conducted by previous scholars (reviewed in Chapter 2) are based on data from the 1990s. This explains why the conventional wisdom has held to a belief that wealth gaps in Latin America are large. It remains unclear, however, why attitudes were so stratified by wealth prior to 1999. Perhaps the wealthy, the main users of (mostly) state-owned utilities at the time, were wooed by promises of improved service quality through privatization.

propensity to consume durable goods causes the wealth variable to drop out. In sum, accurate measures of consumer demand patterns reveal the important substantive impact of varying consumer tastes, yet they also reveal that *trade attitudes were stratified by wealth solely because consumer tastes were correlated with wealth*.

Third, although not depicted in Figure 5.2 to avoid clutter, wealth had a statistically significant impact on foreign investment attitudes in four out of four years, again confirming the importance of consumer tastes. (See Table 5.4.) Individuals who were more likely to consume the skill-intensive products sold by foreign firms were most supportive of encouraging investment inflows. Fourth and by contrast, attitudes toward regional trade pacts were less likely to be stratified by wealth than attitudes toward free trade in general, the FTAA, and foreign investment. Of the six different models of South–South trade beliefs, the impact of wealth was positive and statistically significant in only two (See Table 5.5.) The coefficient on wealth is negative for one year (1995) and zero for three others (1996, 1997, and 2003). Moreover, even in the two years in which wealth had a positive impact (1999 and 2001), its impact was small relative to that exerted by wealth on other globalization attitudes. The near absence of a wealth effect in South–South trade attitudes is thus the exception that proves the rule. Imports from regional trading partners did not disproportionately benefit one income group through the consumption channel, and mass beliefs reflect this.

Finally, for every policy in nearly every year, consumption security had a positive and statistically significant impact on support for market reforms. For fifteen of the available eighteen tests of this hypothesis, a sense of insecurity about the ability to fulfill basic consumption needs made individuals more skeptical of market reforms. The attitude gap between the secure and the insecure was typically about five to ten percentage points. Most importantly, consumption security had a positive, statistically significant effect on privatization attitudes in every available instance; the inability to fulfill one's needs encouraged negative assessments of privatization because it caused price increases for basic services.

Labor-Market Interests

The effects of labor-market factors were more modest. The models test myriad labor-oriented hypotheses, and to report one indicator of their relevance, they return statistically significant results in just 30 of 141 hypothesis tests. Moreover, no single factor had a persistent effect, as statistical significance for any single variable is sporadic.

First, education, the measure of labor-market skills, played a convincing role in predicting only some globalization attitudes. Education had a positive and statistically significant impact on support for free trade in general (in two of two tests), the FTAA (in one of two tests), and foreign investment (in three of four tests). (See Tables 5.3 and 5.4.) According to the statistical models, however, education had a negative and statistically significant impact on the propensity to express pro-privatization beliefs in only one of twelve hypothesis tests. (See Tables 5.1 and 5.2.) If anything, education was more likely to increase support for privatization, although this finding is sporadic (five of twelve hypothesis tests). Moreover, the education level of chief wage earners was irrelevant; across all policies, this variable had a statistically significant impact no more frequently than chance would dictate.[13]

Second, class had a statistically significant impact only sporadically. On five of ten occasions, members of the bourgeoisie and individuals with bourgeois characteristics were more supportive of privatization than members of the proletariat. In contrast, class had a statistically significant effect on globalization attitudes in just three of eleven occasions, and it was not relevant to North–South trade attitudes or, except in one instance, beliefs about foreign investment.

Third, the impact of unemployment and job security was also weak. Throughout the 1990s and 2000s, these two problems frequently topped the list of citizens' economic and political concerns, so one might expect individuals who were unemployed or concerned about future unemployment to blame incumbent economic policies. Just ten of forty-four statistical tests, however, indicate that this was the case. The impact of unemployment was inconsistent across policies. Being unemployed soured individuals on (1) privatization in just three of twelve hypothesis tests and (2) globalization in just two of fourteen tests. The impact of employment insecurity was only slightly more relevant. This variable is statistically significant in three of seven tests for privatization and two of eleven tests

---

[13] The fact that education works only at the individual, not the family, level could be an indication that the occasional statistical significance of this variable is due to criteria unrelated to labor market or even economic self-interest, such as economic knowledge or tolerance of foreign cultures (Hainmueller and Hiscox 2006; Inglehart 1990).

for globalization. The substantive and statistical impact of employment insecurity was far weaker than that of consumption security.

Finally, public sector employees did not differ from other respondents in their attitudes toward privatization. There was a slight tendency for the former to be more pro-privatization than the latter, and this finding is even statistically significant in one test. In general, however, the finding is not robust. In sum, the commonly held view that market policy beliefs have been driven by, and unpopular because of, self-interested labor-market criteria receives only weak empirical support (IDB 2004; Lora et al. 2004).

Patterns of Elite Influence

The portrayal of awareness gaps in Figure 5.1 confirmed the existence of hegemony effects for most issues at most times. This alone indicates that elites did exert some impact on public opinion and, in particular, did forge a mass-level cleavage between the politically aware and the unaware. The simple results from Figure 5.1, however, revealed nothing about the extent to which citizens' political predispositions conditioned elite influence. They also raised questions about why the size of hegemony effects shifted through time and varied across different policies. In this subsection, I consider what the more complete statistical models reveal about top-down effects.

Figures 5.3 through 5.5 convey the main results graphically. I plot the results so that those for each policy within each year can be directly compared to the three possible patterns of elite opinion leadership portrayed and discussed in Chapter 2: one-sided, balanced two-sided, and skewed two-sided. The lines in each figure show how the predicted probabilities of pro-market attitudes changed as a function of political awareness among three different political groups. Gray lines (with "**I**" or "i" labels) represent the attitudes of independents. Black lines represent the attitudes of the following two partisan groups: rightists (solid dark lines with "**R**" or "r" labels) and leftists (dotted dark lines with "**L**" or "l" labels). Although "Center-left," "Center," and "Center-right" partisans are included in the statistical analysis, lines for these groups are not plotted to reduce clutter. Lines trace predicted values from low awareness (5th percentile) to high awareness (95th percentile). Lines whose linear trends are statistically distinguishable from zero (according to the regression results) are thick and labeled with bold capital letters. Lines

141

whose linear trends are statistically indistinguishable from zero are thin and labeled with lowercase letters.[14]

What patterns would confirm the existence of top-down influences? To generate expectations, I resummarize the relevant findings from the elite opinion data reported in Chapter 3. I first analyze privatization attitudes and recall four main findings from Chapter 3. First, privatization divided legislators along partisan lines throughout the eleven years between 1994 and 2004: Rightists were more pro-privatization than leftists. Second, a decline in support occurred gradually among rightist party legislators throughout the entire period. Third, among leftist party legislators, support for privatization increased from 1994 to 1998 and fell thereafter. Finally, average support for privatization among all Latin American legislators fell gradually during this period. Pro-privatization sentiments among elites were at their peak in 1995, constituting a skewed, two-sided, information flow that on balance portrayed the market policy in a favorable light. Elite sentiment shifted toward a more balanced direction after 1998, however, as rightist elites grew less enthusiastic about privatization and leftist elites grew more numerous and more opposed to privatization. If these attitudinal, and presumably rhetorical, patterns among partisan elites influenced mass opinions toward privatization, then the statistical results should indicate the following about the relationship between awareness and pro-privatization beliefs: (1) it was more positive among mass rightists than among mass leftists, (2) it gradually grew less positive among mass rightists, (3) it grew more positive in the late 1990s and then more negative again in the 2000s among mass leftists, and (4) it gradually grew less positive among mass independents.

Figure 5.3 shows that mass attitudes, and in particular individual-level cleavages over market reforms, followed these four predicted patterns to an incredibly close degree. First, in every year, the relationship between awareness and pro-privatization sentiment was more positive among rightists than it was among leftists. Highly aware rightists were more pro-privatization than their unaware copartisans, and highly aware leftists were less pro-privatization than their unaware copartisans. In fact, in a number of years (1995, 1999 to 2001), the two relationships were oppositely signed

[14] The threshold for statistical significance is $p < .10$. For readers following the numerical results in the Chapter 5 Appendix, the most relevant and revealing hypothesis tests are those reported in the figures, not in the tables. This is because the various interaction coefficients reported in the tables do not directly reveal the statistical significance of relationships *within* each group.

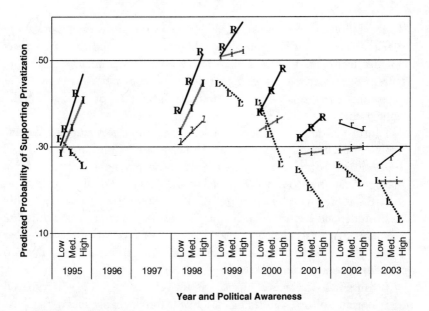

Figure 5.3   Attitudes toward Privatization in Latin America by Political Predispositions, Awareness, and Year, 1995–2003.
Note: Lines are predicted probabilities from statistical models reported in Tables 5.1 and 5.2. Lines labeled with bold and uppercase letters have slopes that are statistically distinguishable from zero. "R" and "r": right-partisans. "L" and "l": left-partisans. "I" and "i": independents.
Sources: *WSJA* (1998) and LB (all other years).

and roughly equal in magnitude. Because privatization was a partisan issue among legislators, elite rhetoric had a polarizing effect, indicative of a two-sided information flow, on mass opinion among highly aware partisans.

The departures from this polarizing pattern also follow expected patterns. In particular, the severity of this polarization changed through time because of the rhetorical shifts among rightist and leftist politicians. These are indicated by the second and third findings. Second, as expected, the strength of the relationship between pro-privatization attitudes and awareness fell markedly among rightists after 1998, eventually becoming statistically insignificant by 2002. Attitudinal gaps of sixteen percentage points between highly aware and highly unaware rightists disappeared in just four years. Third, the ability of leftist party elites to generate anti-privatization sentiments among their mass partisans subsided momentarily in 1998, the year in which leftist elites were most moderate on the issue.

Their ability returned, however, in 1999 and remained impressive every year thereafter, as they induced gaps between aware and unaware leftists ranging from five to fifteen percentage points. In sum, the polarizing pattern disappeared for a year in 1998 because of moderation by leftist elites and then again in 2002 and 2003 because of moderation by rightist elites.

Fourth and finally, the impact of political awareness among independents did decline through time. Sharp positive relationships in 1995 and 1998, nearly equivalent in strength to those among rightists, became nonsignificant by 1999 and remained so thereafter. The shift among elites toward a more critical view of privatization after 1998 meant that highly aware independents were no longer exposed to an overall body of elite discourse that was so heavily biased in a pro-privatization direction – that is, one that would induce them to think differently from independents who had no exposure to elite discourse.

Because independents comprised about 40% of the sample, they played an important role in establishing nationwide trends. In particular, the shifts in the impact of awareness among independents help to account for the shifting hegemony effects reported in Figure 5.1. The hegemony effect fell from fourteen percentage points in 1998 to three percentage points in 1999 and then to zero by 2001. The timing of this shift corresponds almost perfectly to the timing of the decline in elite support for privatization (as reported in Chapter 3), and it matches the shifts that took place among independents.

In contrast to privatization, trade policy was a more unifying economic issue among Latin American legislators. Chapter 3 demonstrated that, between 1994 and 2004, elites from the leftist and rightist parties were largely united in favor of overall trade liberalization and regional trade pacts. Only the FTAA divided elites along partisan lines. Because elite discourse about trade was more one-sided than discourse about privatization, the evidence regarding relationships among trade attitudes, predispositions, and political awareness should diverge from that characterizing beliefs about privatization. In particular, the results should indicate that elites forged the mainstreaming effect, indicative of a one-sided information flow, on beliefs about regional trade pacts and free trade in general; the observed relationship between awareness and pro-trade sentiment should be positive among rightists, leftists, *and* independents. In contrast, as a partisan issue over which legislative elites disagreed, the results on mass opinions toward the FTAA should show evidence of a polarizing effect, indicating that awareness had a positive impact among rightists and a negative impact among leftists. Among independents, however, I expect to find that awareness had a positive impact because, despite the partisan nature of the issue, the balance of elite opinion was favorable toward the hemispheric-wide trade agreement.

Figure 5.4 depicts patterns of individual-level support for these three different trade liberalization policies and confirms that elites had an important impact on public opinion. Panel A shows configurations in beliefs about free trade in general (left half) and the FTAA (right half), while Panel B shows them for regional trade pacts. The results for free trade in general contrast sharply with those for privatization. Awareness had a positive impact on pro-trade attitudes among all three groups at both times, and its impact is statistically significant in five of these six cases. In 1996, awareness increased support for free trade at a nearly equivalent rate among both rightists and leftists: Highly aware partisans of each stripe were about ten percentage points more favorable toward free trade than their unaware copartisans. The results in Panel B on regional trade pacts show similar signs of mass influence by united elites. All slopes but one are positive. Moreover, twelve of the eighteen are statistically significant, and the departures from statistical significance follow no temporal or partisan trend (each group's slope is significant four of six times).

As expected, however, patterns of support for the FTAA in 1998 and 2001 followed a more two-sided logic. According to Panel A, the divisions among elites on this issue induced a polarizing effect among mass partisans because awareness had a positive effect among rightists and a negative effect among leftists (three of these four slopes are statistically significant). The extent of this polarizing effect was substantial in 2001. Highly unaware rightists were about three percentage points *less* enthusiastic toward the FTAA than highly unaware leftists. Among highly aware partisans, however, rightists were eighteen percentage points more likely to favor the FTAA than were leftists. Moreover, as expected, awareness sloped upward among independents, a sign that the pro-FTAA bias in the overall balance of elite discourse induced many highly aware independents to favor the trade pact.

Finally, recall from Chapter 3 the contours of elite opinion toward foreign investment between 1994 and 2004. First, like privatization and the FTAA, foreign investment was a partisan issue. Second, unlike privatization, support for foreign investment among rightist party legislators increased through time. Third, among left party legislators, support for foreign investment increased from 1994 to 1998 but leveled off thereafter.

Panel A: Free Trade and FTAA

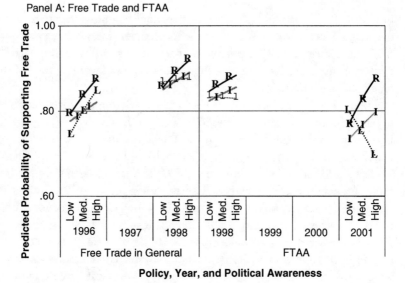

Policy, Year, and Political Awareness

Panel B: Regional Trade Pacts

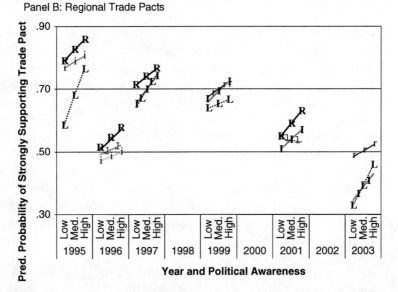

Year and Political Awareness

Figure 5.4 Attitudes toward Trade Liberalization in Latin America by Political Predispositions, Awareness, and Year, 1995–2003.

Note: Lines are predicted probabilities from statistical models reported in Tables 5.3 and 5.5. Lines labeled with bold and uppercase letters have slopes that are statistically distinguishable from zero. "**R**" and "r": right-partisans. "**L**" and "l": left-partisans. "**I**" and "i": independents.

Sources: WSJA (1998) and LB (all other years).

Finally and similarly, net support for foreign investment among Latin American legislators increased from 1994 to 1999 and remained steady thereafter. These elite-level patterns generate the following mass-level expectations. The observed relationships between awareness and pro-privatization beliefs should (1) be more positive among mass rightists than among mass leftists, (2) gradually grow more positive among rightists, (3) initially grow more positive and then remain stable among leftists, and (4) initially grow more positive and then remain stable among independents.

Figure 5.5 shows that patterns of support for foreign investment matched some but not all of these expectations. First, because it was a partisan issue at the elite level, awareness had a stronger positive impact among rightists than among leftists. A convincing polarizing effect, however, occurred in only two years (1998 and 2001) and was statistically significant in just one of them (1998). Second, the impact of awareness among rightists was positive and statistically significant in every year, although it did not necessarily increase in strength through time. Third, patterns among leftists were the most divergent from expectations. The impact of awareness jumped from nonexistent in 1995 to negative in 1998 to positive in 1999 and then back to negative in 2001. Finally, attitudes among independents *did* conform to expectations: Awareness had no impact in 1995 but did have a positive impact every year thereafter.

These mixed results, and in particular the Left leadership's ambivalent success in shaping opinion among politically aware left-partisans, perhaps stem from the fact that foreign investment is an issue that overlaps heavily with both privatization, about which there were two-sided information flows, and globalization, about which there were mostly one-sided information flows. Many privatizations were controversial because assets were sold to foreign investors, yet foreign investment itself is part of the globalization process. At times, left-partisans may have received negative messages from leftist elites about privatizations and the foreign investors that owned and operated the new firms. At other times, they may have received more positive statements about the benefits of economic exchange with foreigners.

In sum, the interaction between mass predispositions and political awareness confirms the existence of substantial elite influence over mass opinion and, especially, mass attitudinal cleavages over market reforms. Where party elites led, their politically aware mass copartisans followed. Politically aware independents were also sensitive to the overall balance of

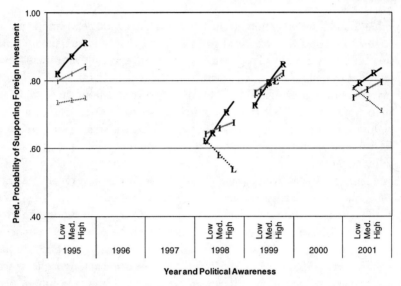

Figure 5.5 Attitudes toward Foreign Investment in Latin America by Political Predispositions, Awareness, and Year, 1995–2001.

Note: Lines are predicted probabilities from statistical models reported in Table 5.4. Lines labeled with bold and uppercase letters have slopes that are statistically distinguishable from zero. "**R**": right-partisans. "**L**" and "l": left-partisans. "**I**" and "i": independents.

Sources: *WSJA* (1998) and LB (all other years).

elite discourse, and their positioning largely accounted for the size of hegemony effects. In most years, elites did induce awareness gaps among Latin American independents (with the important exception of the privatization issue after 1999). Although not pictured in the figures to ensure readability, the awareness gaps among mass partisans of *centrist* parties were very similar (in size and statistical significance) to those among independents. This is important, as it indicates that the center of gravity of party systems in most Latin American countries was pro-market and thus tended to contribute to overall hegemony effects.

Capitalist Values

The findings on the relevance of core capitalist values strongly suggest that scholars are ill-advised to use them as proxies for more specific beliefs about actual implemented policies. Just eight of thirty-six hypothesis tests return statistically significant results. Capitalist values were only rarely associated with attitudes toward Washington Consensus policies. Beliefs about privatization were more frequently related to these abstract values (statistically significant in six of eighteen hypothesis tests) than were globalization beliefs; capitalist values had a statistically significant impact only slightly more often than chance would dictate (two of eighteen tests). Particularly damning of claims that expressions of capitalist values represent meaningful policy attitudes is the frequent *negative* correlation between the respondents' trust in the ability of the state to solve all the problems of society and support for market policies. Individuals with low degrees of trust in the state's ability to solve problems were, almost without exception, *less favorable* toward all aspects of privatization and globalization. In sum, attitudes toward privatization and globalization were clearly *not* generated by abstract beliefs about the general merits of state intervention.

Cleavages over Pension Privatization

Pension privatization is a stand-alone issue because its consequences have been more likely to cue fiscal-channel effects than consumption-channel effects. Precise measures of the impact of pension privatization are unavailable: The surveys did not measure what respondents paid in taxes; whether they contributed to private, public, or no pension funds; the returns in their private pension funds; or what they expected to or did receive in retirement. As an alternative, I briefly describe the impact of the more broadly defined but relevant individual-level characteristics mentioned in Chapter 3: age, gender, and wealth. I estimate two models of support for pension privatization for each available year: one for countries that had already privatized and one for all Latin American countries. The statistical results are reported in Table 5.6 in the Chapter 5 Appendix.

The conventional wisdom among many pension reform proponents holds that active and especially young workers should be the primary supporters of privatization because they have reasons to doubt the long-term financial solvency of a public system. In Latin America, however, these same individuals have shouldered and will continue to shoulder the burden of the fiscal transition costs. The statistical results on the impact of age are ambivalent. In 1995 and 1998, age had a negative impact on pro-privatization sentiments, suggesting that concerns about transitions costs held sway among younger citizens. In 1999, however, age actually had a *positive* impact in countries that privatized (but no impact throughout the whole sample). Moreover, retired individuals, who do not have to cover transition costs but may interpret privatization as a weakening of the financial backing of their current monthly benefits, were *less enthusiastic* about privatization, although this finding is statistically significant in only one year.

Chapter 3 listed a number of reasons why pension privatization has reinforced income inequalities. Wealthy and educated individuals are less likely to be in the formal sector and thus are less likely to absorb a disproportionate share of transition costs. They are also better placed to absorb risk from private pension funds and afford administrative costs. Results conform to these expectations: Wealth and education exerted consistent and robust effects on public opinion. Both variables have statistically significant and positive coefficients in every single model; the wealthiest and best-educated citizens were typically about five to ten percentage points more likely to support pension privatization than the poorest and least educated. Moreover, although its impact was weaker, the effect of education even worked through family units, as the education of chief wage earners is statistically significant in every hypothesis test.

A common refrain among critics of pension privatization is that it disadvantages women. The statistical model confirms that women were typically (in 1995 and 1999) less likely to support pension privatization than men. Finally, capitalist values affected pension reform beliefs, although, as with the other policies, their effects were sporadic (statistically significant in four of eight hypothesis tests).

The Relative Size of Top-Down and Bottom-Up Influences

The evidence compiled in this and the preceding chapter highlights the two manners in which Latin Americans "consume" the Washington Consensus. As consumers of services provided by newly privatized firms, imported goods, and products sold by foreign-owned firms, citizens are highly attuned to market policies' impacts on prices, access, and variety. As political beings who selectively consume elite rhetoric and argumentation about these new policy measures, citizens are frequently persuaded by their leaders.

The totality of findings demonstrates, however, that the net impact of these two sources of public opinion varies. The bottom-up, consumption-based factors are important for establishing aggregate trends *and* for shaping individual-level differences over economic policy. In contrast, top-down elite influences contribute heavily to the latter by opening certain mass-level cleavages, but they merely tweak the aggregate popularity of each market policy.

Chapters 4 and 5 have established the primacy of bottom-up concerns in explaining both aggregate and individual-level patterns in public opinion. Chapter 4 established that economic factors, namely the bottom-up impacts a policy has on consumer interests (as well as on the macroeconomy), are responsible for the popularity of each policy. Recall that globalization has been more popular than privatization because the former has produced much more beneficial results for consumers than the latter. Moreover, support for privatization fell because of utility rate hikes in the second half of the 1990s. Chapter 5 has demonstrated that varying consumer tastes and interests explain some of the individual-level variance in policy attitudes.

In contrast, analyses have shown that elite opinion leadership only accounts for individual-level attitudinal differences. The balance of elite opinion did not have a notable influence on aggregate opinions, as revealed by statistical tests in Chapter 4. Further evidence from this chapter indicates why elites have only a limited ability to set aggregate levels of support for various market policies. The most likely case to illustrate a sizable top-down effect on aggregate opinion is the issue of free trade in 1996, but I show here that the substantive impact was quite weak. Elites were united on this issue, inducing a strong mainstreaming effect (revisit Figure 5.4, Panel A) and thus clearly convincing many politically aware individuals to support a policy that they might not have supported if elites were divided or opposed to trade. Highly aware individuals were fifteen percentage points more favorable toward trade than highly unaware ones. The quantitative impact on aggregate opinion of this mainstreaming effect, however, was *not* fifteen percentage points. This number quantifies elite influences only among a minority slice, the highly aware, of the population. To quantify the impact of elites on aggregate opinion, consider the counterfactual scenario of no elite influence on 1996 trade attitudes. Because the least aware are untouched by elite influence, I use this group as the point of reference to define what attitudes would have been in lieu of elite influence. In other words, if elites had had no influence, then the slopes on awareness for all three political groups would have been zero, and the level of support within each group would have matched that among the politically unaware. Simulating probabilities from the statistical models, predicted mean support would have been 79% instead of 84% among rightists, 75% instead of 81% among leftists, and 78% instead of 80% among independents. Overall mean support, according to the statistical model, would have dropped from 78% to 74%. In other words, the real-world elite consensus increased aggregate support for free trade by a mere four percentage points.

Another useful example is the series of privatization attitudes. Overall, the central tendencies of the three political groups' opinions moved in lockstep with one another through time. (Revisit Figure 5.3.) Most importantly, when support for privatization fell for bottom-up reasons from 1999 to 2003, it fell among *all* groups at all levels of awareness. By 2001, the most aware rightists were only as supportive of privatization as the most aware leftists in 1999. By 2003, the most aware rightists were eleven percentage points less supportive of privatization than highly aware leftists in 1999. All citizens shifted together in response to privatization's concrete material consequences; elites merely shaped the contours of cleavages around these central tendencies.

Discussion and Conclusion

This chapter has used the crucial individual-level variables of wealth and political awareness to organize the discussion of consumption- and elite-based effects, respectively, on mass attitudinal cleavages over the Washington Consensus. The findings on wealth challenge the widely held impression that Latin American leaders implemented market policies to the widespread approval of the rich and in the face of rigid resistance from the poor. Instead, the affluent in Latin America have been only slightly more supportive of market reforms (by about five to ten percentage points) than the impoverished, and at times no such wealth gap existed at all. A crucial implication of this finding is that the poor, like the wealthy, have supported globalization and opposed privatization. In other words, the popularity gap has existed among all wealth groups.

The claims that wealth gaps have been small may appear to contradict the consumption-based argument. On the one hand, I argue that consumer tastes have forged attitudinal cleavages over market policies and that these consumer tastes are closely linked to, and even measured by, wealth. On the other hand, I also conclude that wealth gaps have been modest in size (albeit statistically significant). For two reasons, however, these seemingly competing claims are not only compatible but wholly expected. First, the consumption-based argument predicts a nonlinear relationship between wealth and privatization attitudes, with middle-income groups voicing the most antimarket beliefs. This chapter demonstrates that once utility privatization had become widespread, the wealthy were as opposed to privatization as the very poor, and only middle-income groups expressed greater opposition. In other words, evidence of a closing wealth gap in privatization attitudes is most compatible with a consumer-interest argument. Second, the consumption-based argument does predict a linear relationship between wealth and pro-trade attitudes, but the size of this wealth gap *is supposed to be modest.* Consumer tastes vary across individuals in meaningful ways, yet they are more similar across different social groups, and especially wealth levels, than are labor-market criteria. Citizens from starkly different social backgrounds prefer lower prices to higher ones, yet their income sources are highly varied. I provide more specific evidence for this claim in subsequent chapters on Brazil.

Elite rhetoric has also opened cleavages in mass beliefs about market reforms. Most importantly, *the attitudinal cleavage between those who have been exposed and those who have not been exposed to elite discourse in Latin America has been just as large as the cleavage between the haves and the have-nots.* The pro-market bias in the balance of elite discourse has caused individuals who have been exposed to this discourse to look more favorably on the Washington Consensus than individuals who have not been exposed.

The hegemony effect, however, has not been constant across policies, time, and partisan groups. For issues on which elites themselves have been favorably united, namely free trade and regional trade pacts, this hegemony effect has existed among groups with all types of political predispositions. For other issues, namely privatization, the FTAA, and foreign investment, elites have been less unanimous. This has opened up partisan cleavages among the masses, yet these cleavages have tended to exist only among politically aware partisans. Moreover, elite divisions have not always erased the overall hegemony effect, as the antimarket Left has not always been large enough to counterbalance the amount of pro-market rhetoric emanating from market proponents.

What do these findings suggest about the Latin American Left's capacity as an opinion leader? Recall from Chapter 2 that many scholars alleged a decline in the Left's opinion-shaping power in the 1990s. This chapter demonstrates that, despite the divisiveness of privatization, the Left's influence was indeed limited to politically aware leftist partisans in the mid-1990s. Because of its diminutive size, the Left clearly lost the battle with the Center and Right to be opinion shapers of independents (typically the electorate's biggest prize). Moreover, while the Left leadership was also an effective opinion shaper of its highly aware mass copartisans on the globalization issue in the mid-1990s, *this was in a pro-trade, not a protectionist, direction.* In other words, the Left failed to forge antitrade opinions not because of a lack of capacity but because of a lack of will.

Patterns shifted after 1999, however, as the apparent posthegemonic era settled in. Most importantly, antiprivatization sentiments grew among elites of all political stripes, and antiprivatization elites saw gains in their ability to shape mass opinion. Awareness gaps closed, especially among independents but also among rightists. In fact, by 2002, it was the turn of pro-privatization elites to experience failures in shaping public opinion. The winds of overall elite discourse had clearly shifted in a more skeptical direction, and the extensive propaganda campaigns sponsored by the pro-market governments of the 1990s were long past as many privatization programs were exhausted by the early 2000s. Again, globalization was an exception. The posthegemonic era still featured mostly free-trade-promoting politicians of both the Left and Right, and the awareness gaps on regional trade attitudes and the FTAA existed because of this. Only on the FTAA issue did leftist leaders stoke protectionist passions among highly aware mass copartisans.

Despite elites' abilities to shape these various cleavage patterns, I conclude that politicians can only fine-tune the aggregate popularity of economic policies. Most citizens develop opinions more by assessing the material consequences of reforms than by elite attempts to persuade them. Citizens are not easily duped. Far from being merely "blown about by whatever current of information manages to develop the greatest intensity," the hard facts of market reforms, and especially their consequences for consumer interests, have mattered most (Zaller 1992, 311).

Chapter 5 Appendix: Multiple Regression Results

The multiple regression results discussed in the "Explaining Individual-Level Attitudes" and "Results" sections of this chapter are reported in Tables 5.1 through 5.6. Except where indicated, entries in these tables are ordered probit or binary probit maximum likelihood estimates with robust standard errors in parentheses. Standard errors are corrected for clustering within countries. I use OLS regression in a few instances when the dependent variable is a continuous indicator constructed from a principal components analysis. Dependent variables are identified at the bottom of each table. Dependent variables are coded so that higher values indicate greater support for the market policy in question. All nondummy independent variables are z-scores, so coefficients are x-standardized and can be compared across coefficients in the same model. An asterisk (*) denotes $p < .05$. Most hypothesis tests are one-tailed (with the expected direction indicated in the text), so coefficients that are not in the hypothesized direction, even if greater than twice the standard error, are not statistically significant. Blank entries indicate that a variable is not included in the model because of unavailability in the designated survey.

"Capitalist values" questions are coded so that higher numbers mean greater support for capitalist principles. Capitalist values are potentially endogenous to the other independent variables. To estimate the impact of all other variables without possible bias from these endogeneity effects, all coefficients reported in the tables and all results discussed in the text are estimated in models *without* capitalist values included (except obviously for the reported coefficients of capitalist values themselves). I estimate the reported coefficients on capitalist values from equivalently specified models save the inclusion of capitalist values. The results of these more fully specified models are not shown but are available from the author upon request and differ little from those reported in the tables. A dotted line in the tables between the capitalist values coefficients and all others indicates that I estimate the former separately.

All models contain parameter estimates that are not shown: country fixed effects (country dummy variables), a constant, ordered probit cutpoints (when applicable), and dummy variables for *Chief wage earner* and *Non-EAP* (when available). The last two dummy variables are needed to properly estimate the interaction effect of chief wage earner's education and employment insecurity, because the impact of these two variables is estimated only among non–chief wage earners and the non-EAP, respectively. Missing data are multiply imputed across ten datasets (King et al. 2001; Royston 2004). I weight cases in the estimation to correct for different country-level sample sizes: Each country is weighted equally for the final estimation results.

To allow the impact of awareness in these cross-national models to be different across the political groups, the *Party ideology* scale, coded from zero (leftist) to four or ten (rightist), is multiplied by awareness to create the following interaction term: *Awareness* × *Party ideology*. I also create a dummy variable for *Leftist*, which is also multiplied by awareness: *Awareness × Leftist*. This interactive approach allows the model to isolate the precise impact of awareness among leftists rather than constraining this impact to be a linear function of the party ideology ordinal scale. The precise impact of awareness among leftists is $\beta_{(Awareness)}$ + $\beta_{(Awareness \times Leftist)}$. *Independents* are coded as zero on the party ideology scale but are also interacted separately with awareness. The precise impacts of awareness among this group is $\beta_{(Awareness)}$ + $\beta_{(Awareness \times Independent)}$. The statistical significance of the awareness effects within each group is found in Figures 5.3 through 5.5, *not* in these appendix tables. For these top-down variables, the statistical significance tests in the tables are largely irrelevant to the main hypotheses.

Table 5.1. *Determinants of Individual-Level Attitudes toward Privatization in Latin America, 1990–2000*

Independent Variables	Privatization in General				Private Ownership of Utility Sectors		
	1990 WVS	1996 WVS	1998 *WSJA*	2000 WVS	1995 LB	1998 *WSJA*	1999 LB
Bottom–Up Factors: Consumer Interests							
Wealth	.138* (.025)	.148* (.040)	.110* (.029)	.013 (.026)	.142* (.034)	.086* (.034)	.103* (.026)
Wealth^2	−.011 (.019)	−.034* (.018)	−.007 (.005)	.037 (.026)	−.017 (.023)	.000 (.007)	.034* (.014)
Consumption security					.104* (.021)		.082* (.028)
Bottom–Up Factors: Labor–Market Interests							
Education	.026 (.030)	.025 (.028)	.131 (.024)	.072 (.024)	.160 (.032)	.121 (.019)	.128 (.018)
Chief wage earner's education					−.004 (.038)		.061 (.022)
Class	.070* (.025)	.025 (.019)		.032* (.009)	.001 (.028)		.025* (.015)
Unemployed	−.003 (.047)	.019 (.074)	−.092* (.050)	−.121* (.032)	.026 (.101)		.037 (.065)
Employment insecurity					−.011 (.028)	−.096* (.034)	−.083* (.035)
Public-sector employee					.103 (.062)		.165* (.034)
Top–Down Factors							
Political awareness			−.063 (.042)		.044 (.137)	.051 (.056)	.159* (.091)
Awareness × Party ideology			.019* (.007)		.050 (.049)	.012 (.008)	−.004 (.028)

(continued)

Table 5.1 (continued)

Independent Variables	Privatization in General				Private Ownership of Utility Sectors		
	1990 WVS	1996 WVS	1998 WSJA	2000 WVS	1995 LB	1998 WSJA	1999 LB
Awareness × Leftist			.110 (.100)		-.150 (.143)	.024 (.091)	-.083 (.128)
Awareness × Independent			.155* (.045)		.128 (.143)	-.013 (.052)	-.050 (.093)
Party ideology	.014 (.015)	-.001 (.023)	.016* (.010)	.001 (.021)	.071 (.060)	.031 (.009)	.040 (.038)
Leftist	-.201* (.109)	-.227* (.092)	-.120* (.065)	-.159* (.100)	-.044 (.167)	.066 (.018)	-.166 (.012)
Independent	.082 (.091)	.036 (.104)	.016 (.060)	.063 (.077)	.139 (.167)	.149* (.059)	.016 (.111)
Other							
Woman	-.223* (.072)	-.115* (.032)	-.098* (.032)	-.085* (.032)	-.183* (.066)	-0.024 (.044)	-.184* (.043)
Age	.092* (.022)	.068* (.020)	-.017 (.020)	.065* (.018)	-.039 (.032)	.010 (.021)	.043 (.019)
Town size			.006 (.019)			.066* (.018)	
Capitalist Values							
Capitalist values 1	.303* (.031)	.018 (.041)	.028* (.013)	.021 (.022)	.097* (.034)	.080* (.017)	.013 (.019)
Capitalist values 2	.016 (.047)	-.064 (.031)		-.126 (.042)			.021 (.020)
N	5,361	8,020	11,239	4,715	7,176	11,400	14,659

Note: Entries are probit and OLS regression coefficients with standard errors in parentheses. Some predicted values from these models are reported in Figures 5.2 and 5.3.

Sources: Dependent variables for "Privatization in General" are *Private ownership should be increased* (WVS) and *Change to privatization is good for country* (WSJA). Dependent variable for "Private Ownership of Utility Sectors" is *Index of support for utility privatization* (LB/WSJA) (OLS estimation).

158

Table 5.2. *Determinants of Individual-Level Attitudes toward Privatization in Latin America, Continued, 1999–2003*

Independent Variables	1999 LB	2000 LB	2001 LB	2002 LB	2003 LB
Bottom-Up Factors: Consumer Interests					
Wealth	.050* (.021)	.088* (.015)	.004 (.016)	.032* (.019)	-.010 (.017)
Wealth^2	.046* (.015)	.028* (.010)	.056* (.012)	.045* (.013)	.027* (.009)
Consumption security	.074* (.023)	.087* (.017)	.067* (.018)	.038* (.017)	.085* (.014)
Bottom-Up Factors: Labor-Market Interests					
Education	-.004 (.013)	.011 (.012)	-.016 (.016)	-.031* (.016)	-.013 (.018)
Chief wage earner's education	.017 (.011)	.013 (.020)	-.009 (.013)	-.030 (.020)	-.001 (.014)
Class	.023* (.012)	.018* (.010)	.015 (.010)	.013 (.010)	.016 (.012)
Unemployed	.008 (.028)	.002 (.049)	.003 (.035)	-.001 (.040)	.008 (.043)
Employment insecurity	-.017 (.018)	.019 (.016)	-.064* (.019)	-.030* (.011)	.011 (.021)
Public-sector employee	.042 (.038)	.026 (.032)	.050 (.030)	-.015 (.023)	.051 (.033)
Top-Down Factors					
Political awareness	.005 (.062)	-.050 (.040)	.023 (.038)	.060 (.055)	-.001 (.057)
Awareness × Party ideology	.018 (.019)	.014* (.007)	.005 (.013)	-.020 (.021)	.005 (.008)
Awareness × Leftist	-.050 (.058)	-.094 (.064)	-.116 (.089)	-.117 (.069)	-.137* (.069)
Awareness × Independent	.007 (.054)	.080* (.048)	-.017 (.045)	-.050 (.056)	.001 (.062)
Party ideology	.047 (.033)	.040* (.016)	.054 (.029)	.049* (.018)	.025* (.011)

(continued)

159

Table 5.2 (continued)

Independent Variables	1999 LB	2000 LB	2001 LB	2002 LB	2003 LB
Leftist	−.135 (.141)	.167 (.124)	−.144 (.159)	−.122 (.111)	−.106 (.098)
Independent	.096 (.094)	.202* (.092)	.064 (.079)	.059 (.068)	.067 (.082)
Other					
Woman	−.011 (.022)	.010 (.020)	−.021 (.021)	−.021 (.031)	−.005 (.018)
Age	−.006 (.013)	−.022 (.012)	−.051* (.012)	−.049* (.013)	−.036* (.015)
Capitalist Values					
Capitalist values 1	−.051 (.016)	−.044 (.022)	−.040 (.017)	−.020 (.018)	−.026 (.018)
Capitalist values 2	.051* (.014)		.071* (.018)		
N	14,155	16,663	15,460	15,200	15,865

Note: Entries are probit coefficients with standard errors in parentheses. Some predicted values from these models are reported in Figures 5.2 and 5.3.

Source: Dependent variable is *Privatization is good for country* (LB).

Table 5.3. *Determinants of Individual-Level Attitudes toward North–South Trade in Latin America, 1996–2001*

Independent Variables	Free Trade in General			Free Trade Agreement of the Americas	
	1996 LB	*w/ Durables*	1998 *WSJA*	1998 *WSJA*	2001 LB
Bottom-Up Factors: Consumer Interests					
Wealth	.056* (.023)	−.058 (.043)	.085* (.033)	.080* (.030)	.067* (.024)
Wealth^2	−.021 (.013)	−.028 (.013)	−.006 (.005)	−.015* (.006)	−.020 (.017)
Propensity to consume durables		.127* (.042)			
Consumption security	.020 (.016)	.018 (.016)			.037* (.015)
Bottom-Up Factors: Labor-Market Interests					
Education	.064* (.017)	.064* (.017)	.096* (.034)	.047* (.021)	.019 (.013)
Education^2	.036* (.019)	.037* (.019)	.012 (.010)	−.003 (.012)	−.028 (.014)
Chief wage earner's education	.018 (.025)	.017 (.025)			−.010 (.015)
Chief wage earner's education^2	−.025 (.015)	−.024 (.015)			−.014 (.014)
Class	.014 (.014)	.014 (.014)			.007 (.014)
Unemployed	−.018 (.046)	−.014 (.046)	−.159* (.046)	−.130 (.094)	.033 (.040)
Employment insecurity	−.093* (.040)	−.093* (.039)			.050 (.018)
Top-Down Factors					
Political awareness	.233* (.065)	.233* (.065)	−.023 (.088)	−.049 (.045)	.049 (.067)

(continued)

Table 5.3 (continued)

Independent Variables	Free Trade in General		Free Trade Agreement of the Americas	
	1996 LB	1998 WSJA	1998 WSJA	2001 LB
Awareness × Party ideology	-.029 (.022)	.014 (.013)	.011 (.007)	.023 (.020)
Awareness × Leftist	-.104 (.113)	.037 (.137)	.044 (.046)	-.160* (.080)
Awareness × Independent	-.177* (.061)	.082 (.095)	.089* (.049)	.020 (.063)
Party ideology	.017 (.022)	.006 (.010)	.017* (.006)	.012 (.013)
Leftist	-.067 (.110)	.009 (.066)	.037 (.054)	-.118 (.117)
Independent	-.083 (.067)	-.019 (.058)	.053 (.039)	-.138* (.051)
Other				
Woman	-.092* (.023)	-.095* (.030)	-.116* (.036)	-.013 (.017)
Age	-.000 (.015)	-.010 (.023)	.027* (.013)	.009 (.012)
Town size		.070 (.034)		
Capitalist Values				
Capitalist values 1	.015 (.014)	-.022 (.012)	-.006 (.012)	.028 (.020)
Capitalist values 2				-.001 (.015)
N	14,566	11,073	10,414	14,607

Note: Entries are probit coefficients with standard errors in parentheses. Some predicted values from these models are reported in Figures 5.2 and 5.4, Panel A.

Source: Dependent variables for "Free Trade in General" models are *Free trade helps country* (LB) in 1996 and *Free trade helps country* (*WSJA*) in 1998. Dependent variable for "FTAA" models is *In favor of FTAA* (LB) in 2001.

Table 5.4. *Determinants of Individual-Level Attitudes toward Foreign Investment in Latin America, 1995–2001*

Independent Variables	1995 LB	1998 *WSJA*	1999 LB	2001 LB
Bottom-Up Factors: Consumer Interests				
Wealth	.036* (.018)	.072* (.025)	.051* (.018)	.057* (.022)
Wealth^2	.047 (.017)	−.003 (.004)	.020 (.011)	−.005 (.015)
Consumption security	.060* (.029)		.019 (.017)	−.019 (.017)
Bottom-Up Factors: Labor-Market Interests				
Education	.050* (.022)	.071* (.026)	.065* (.012)	−.005 (.013)
Education^2	−.041 (.023)	.019 (.013)	.021* (.010)	−.002 (.010)
Chief wage earner's education	−.032 (.027)		.026 (.020)	−.002 (.012)
Chief wage earner's education^2	−.032 (.025)		.008 (.017)	.008 (.015)
Class	−.008 (.021)		.001 (.013)	.024* (.014)
Unemployed	−.076 (.117)	−.104* (.053)	−.002 (.033)	.001 (.045)
Employment insecurity	−.068 (.048)		.017 (.019)	.034 (.023)
Top-Down Factors				
Political awareness	.129* (.055)	−.058 (.064)	.114* (.061)	.112* (.033)
Awareness × Party ideology	.007 (.015)	.019 (.010)	.012 (.019)	−.010 (.011)
Awareness × Leftist	−.114* (.060)	−.010 (.073)	−.033 (.062)	−.181 (.058)
Awareness × Independent	−.070 (.060)	.087 (.066)	−.036 (.059)	−.061* (.035)
Party ideology	.084* (.036)	.001 (.013)	−.022 (.025)	.030 (.019)
Leftist	−.165 (.160)	−.172* (.087)	−.133 (.135)	−.028 (.081)
Independent	.109 (.122)	−.007 (.067)	−.092 (.071)	.014 (.049)
Other				
Woman	−.088* (.040)	−.150* (.030)	−.117* (.027)	−.062* (.021)
Age	.029 (.026)	.060* (.022)	.030* (.015)	−.012 (.013)
Town size		.021 (.018)		
Capitalist Values				
Capitalist values 1	.044* (.024)	−.005 (.013)	−.051 (.019)	.014 (.015)
Capitalist values 2			.027 (.019)	−.024 (.018)
N	6,951	11,031	14,538	15,481

Note: Entries are probit coefficients with standard errors in parentheses. Some predicted values from these models are reported in Figure 5.5.

Source: Dependent variables are *Foreign investment is good for country* (LB) in 1995, *Foreign investment is good for economy* (*WSJA*) in 1998, and *Foreign investment should be encouraged* (LB) in 1999 and 2001.

Table 5.5. *Determinants of Individual-Level Attitudes toward Regional Trade Pacts in Latin America, 1995–2003*

Independent Variables	1995 LB	1996 LB	1997 LB	1999 LB	2001 LB	2003 LB
Bottom-Up Factors: Consumer Interests						
Wealth	−.088 (.033)	.007 (.013)	−.003 (.024)	.041* (.017)	.044* (.022)	−.001 (.019)
Wealth²	.000 (.025)	.009 (.009)	.008 (.011)	.008 (.011)	−.003 (.011)	−.007 (.011)
Consumption security	.067* (.027)	.064* (.021)	.196* (.020)	.055* (.015)	.046* (.019)	.061* (.019)
Bottom-Up Factors: Labor-Market Interests						
Education	.064* (.031)	.034* (.019)	.004 (.016)	.009 (.020)	.011 (.016)	−.024 (.021)
Education²	−.039 (.024)	.016 (.011)	−.012 (.012)	−.021 (.017)	−.004 (.013)	−.016 (.013)
Chief wage earner's education	.084* (.038)	.020 (.023)	.029 (.015)	−.003 (.019)	−.012 (.017)	.018 (.017)
Chief wage earner's education²	.002 (.028)	−.007 (.016)	.015 (.016)	.002 (.016)	.012 (.011)	.009 (.015)
Class	.057* (.025)	.024* (.012)	.003 (.012)	.001 (.005)	−.006 (.011)	−.006 (.010)
Unemployed	−.131 (.111)	−.076 (.065)	.061 (.049)	−.006 (.056)	.009 (.042)	.008 (.039)
Employment insecurity	−.068* (.036)	−.010 (.021)	.018 (.020)	.074 (.028)	.043 (.020)	.030 (.018)
Top-Down Factors						
Political awareness	−.010 (.117)	.048 (.057)	.135* (.068)	.124* (.055)	−.025 (.088)	.085 (.060)
Awareness × Party ideology	.026 (.041)	.002 (.015)	−.019 (.020)	−.018 (.022)	.024 (.026)	−.005 (.009)
Awareness × Leftist	.191 (.122)	−.022 (.060)	−.021 (.070)	−.096* (.056)	.015 (.101)	.046 (.084)

Awareness × Independent	.058 (.129)	−.022 (.050)	−.039 (.061)	−.054 (.064)	.076 (.076)	−.000 (.059)
Party ideology	.030 (.037)	.005 (.020)	−.014 (.035)	−.036 (.020)	−.028 (.026)	.039* (.008)
Leftist	−.349 (.232)	−.062 (.062)	−.184 (.135)	−.279* (.099)	−.216* (.116)	.107 (.090)
Independent	−.027 (.113)	−.119* (.058)	−.180* (.087)	−.163* (.059)	−.234* (.073)	.093* (.053)
Other						
Woman	.057 (.055)	−.061* (.024)	−.041 (.028)	.010 (.026)	−.054* (.027)	−.005 (.031)
Age	.041 (.039)	.005 (.017)	−.002 (.012)	−.005 (.019)	−.017 (.012)	−.007 (.033)
Capitalist Values						
Capitalist values 1	.033 (.026)	−.000 (.017)		−.042 (.022)	−.002 (.015)	−.041 (.019)
Capitalist values 2				.061* (.018)	.018 (.016)	
N	5,305	11,526	11,936	12,926	12,540	11,477

Note: Entries are probit coefficients with standard errors in parentheses. Some predicted values from these models are reported in Figure 5.4., Panel B.

Source: Dependent variable is *Regional trade agreement benefits country* (LB).

Table 5.6. *Determinants of Individual-Level Attitudes toward Pension Privatization in Latin America, 1995–1999*

Independent Variables	1995 LB		1998 *WSJA*		1999 LB	
	Privatizers	Full Sample	Privatizers	Full Sample	Privatizers	Full Sample
Bottom-Up Factors: Fiscal-Channel Interests						
Age	−.011* (.006)	−.039* (.020)	−.031 (.021)	−.032* (.016)	.040* (.022)	−.000 (.020)
Retired	−.038 (.258)	−.006 (.100)			−.119 (.083)	−.131* (.062)
Wealth	.130* (.020)	.125* (.024)	.117* (.071)	.102* (.043)	.047* (.022)	.073* (.021)
Wealth^2	−.010 (.049)	−.013 (.025)	−.009 (.012)	−.010 (.008)	−.018 (.018)	−.005 (.012)
Education	.113* (.032)	.094* (.019)	.162* (.027)	.120* (.021)	.105* (.029)	.074* (.025)
Chief wage earner's education	.069* (.028)	.050* (.024)			.063* (.019)	.050* (.020)
Woman	−.164* (.066)	−.111* (.051)	−.006 (.027)	−.000 (.020)	−.132* (.038)	−.119* (.031)
Bottom-Up Factors: Labor-Market Interests						
Class	−.029 (.028)	−.015 (.016)			.039* (.017)	.028* (.015)
Unemployed	−.090 (.079)	.039 (.076)	.013 (.080)	.055 (.084)	.219* (.063)	.188* (.048)
Employment insecurity	.002 (.038)	.041 (.029)			−.009 (.035)	−.007 (.021)
Public-sector employee	−.035 (.130)	.062 (.057)			.077 (.052)	.095 (.027)
Top-Down Factors						
Political awareness	−.071 (.172)	.018 (.081)	.024 (.063)	.009 (.052)	.016 (.096)	.060 (.082)

	(1)	(2)	(3)	(4)	(5)	(6)
Awareness × Party ideology	.041 (.063)	.023 (.028)	.010 (.009)	.012 (.007)	.019 (.024)	.004 (.023)
Awareness × Leftist	.040 (.063)	-.090 (.070)	.019 (.225)	.086 (.112)	.036 (.137)	.021 (.096)
Awareness × Independent	.109 (.197)	.033 (.078)	-.016 (.077)	.024 (.053)	.028 (.086)	.000 (.079)
Party ideology	.159* (.035)	.036 (.035)	-.000 (.011)	.003 (.010)	.040 (.027)	.022 (.018)
Leftist	.349 (.359)	.003 (.143)	-.285* (.126)	-.106 (.076)	-.049 (.148)	-.117 (.089)
Independent	.286* (.079)	.032 (.071)	-.053 (.062)	-.028 (.053)	.024 (.088)	.036 (.058)
Other						
Consumption security	.076* (.026)	.059* (.013)		.062* (.021)	.049 (.037)	.013 (.022)
Town size			.060 (.039)			
Capitalist Values						
Capitalist values 1	.107* (.053)	.082* (.024)	.069* (.013)	.048* (.013)	.008 (.025)	.005 (.016)
Capitalist values 2					.012 (.022)	.013 (.017)
N	3,046	7,376	5,705	11,348	8.340	15,096

Note: Entries are probit coefficients with standard errors in parentheses. Privatizers (1995): Argentina, Chile, Peru. Privatizers (1998): Argentina, Bolivia, Chile, Colombia, Mexico, Peru, Uruguay. Privatizers (1999): Argentina, Bolivia, Colombia, Costa Rica, Chile, El Salvador, Mexico, Peru, Uruguay (Gill et al. 2005).

Source: Dependent variables are *Privatization by sectors: Pensions* (LB) in 1995 and 1999 and *Privatization by sectors: Pensions* (*WSJA*) in 1998.

Mass Support for Reform in Brazil

6

The Economic Consequences and Elite Rhetoric of Market Reform in Brazil

> When the Workers Party was born, it was a tiny baby. It grew up, became a teenager, then an adult, then it got married, and with marriage came the responsibility of governing.
> – Luiz Inácio Lula da Silva, as Brazilian president in 2005 (Branford et al. 2003, 10)

The three chapters of Part III focus on a single country: Brazil. The case study conducted in these chapters parallels the regionwide analysis conducted in the preceding three chapters. Chapter 6 summarizes the relevant economic consequences and elite rhetoric of reform in Brazil, Chapter 7 describes the sources of aggregate support for market policies, and Chapter 8 analyzes the determinants of individual-level variation in mass beliefs. These chapters, however, do not merely repeat the analyses and findings of Chapters 3 through 5 for the Brazilian case. Although they use some of the same data sources and methods of analysis, I advance the overall argument by presenting different, and typically more precise, forms of evidence. In particular, I provide even more convincing evidence for the consumption- and elite-based explanations by describing (1) Brazilians' rationales, provided in open-ended survey questions, for their beliefs about market reforms, (2) Brazilians' beliefs about how market policies have affected consumption- and labor-market criteria, (3) the impact of consumer tastes, as captured by precise and varied measures of consumption behavior, and (4) the nature of elite opinion, as measured not only by surveys of legislators but also by the volume of media coverage and the specific pronouncements of various presidents.

Moreover, the context in which Brazilians answered these survey questions makes the country a particularly fruitful case for in-depth analysis. For at least two reasons, Brazil is a "hard" or "critical" case, meaning that if a particular hypothesis holds in Brazil, it probably holds in other Latin American countries. First, Brazil is a critical case for testing the consumption-based explanation of globalization's popularity because it is the region's largest economy. As demonstrated in Chapter 4, large economies tend to have the most protectionist citizenries in Latin America; large economies are more capable than small ones of satisfying consumer demands with locally produced goods. If Brazilians are still found to be overwhelmingly pro-trade and, more importantly, if they justify this sentiment by citing trade's consumer benefits, then it is likely that citizens in smaller economies would give consumer rationales to an even greater degree. Similarly, if Brazilians' trade policy attitudes are stratified by consumer tastes, as measured by extensive batteries querying consumption behavior, then it is likely that such measures would yield even stronger findings in other Latin American countries.

Second, Brazil is a critical case to test for elite influences because Brazilians hold their politicians in comparatively low regard. According to Latinbarometer results, Brazilians nearly always rank in the lowest quartile (among Latin American countries) in their aggregate levels of trust in congress and in political parties, and they typically rank last in the extent of mass partisanship (Mainwaring 1999; Samuels 2006). Because of this, if Brazilians' opinions about market reforms show signs of being influenced by elites, then it is likely that elite influences exist in all other Latin American countries. (Of course, Chapter 5 demonstrated that elite influence occurs *on average* across all Latin American countries, but this is distinct from the finding that it occurs in every country.)

This portrayal of Brazil as a critical case, however, does not mean that the country is an anomaly from which one should avoid generalizing. As mentioned in Chapter 4, cross-national heterogeneity in aggregate opinions toward market reforms is minimal. In particular, the most crucial finding, the existence of a popularity gap between globalization and privatization, holds throughout Latin America and thus in Brazil.

Moreover, Brazil's general experience with regard to the primary independent variables, the economic consequences of and elite rhetoric about reform, has been typical. First, SOE privatization has had a negative but, in the aggregate, minimal impact on labor markets, yet utility-sector privatizations have led to higher prices for telecommunications and electricity services. In contrast, globalization has destroyed countless jobs in Brazil's industrial sector and raised overall unemployment rates, yet it has lowered consumer prices on tradable goods. The distributional consequences of these policies have also been typical: Globalization has placed regressive pressures on income distribution through both the labor-market and consumer channels, while the effects of privatization have been nonlinear. Second, Brazil's political scene throughout the 1990s featured a pro-market elite nagged by a minority Left that launched vociferous critiques of most market reforms. The 2000s, however, saw an ascendant Left that eventually won the presidency.

This chapter describes these economic and political developments. In doing so, it provides the context for the analyses of Brazilian public opinion data conducted in Chapters 7 and 8. Like Chapter 3, it focuses on the consequences of reforms for workers and consumers, as well as the nature of elite rhetoric and conflict. The first section of this chapter describes Brazil's reform process and its economic consequences. (Because Brazil's pension reforms were more modest than those of most of its neighbors, stopping well short of privatization, I do not focus on this issue in the case study.) The second section describes various aspects of elite opinion toward market reforms, including the nature of rhetorical frames that elites employed and the distribution of opinions by partisan camp.

Market Reforms and Their Economic Consequences in Brazil

Privatization

President Fernando Collor de Mello (1990 to 1992) launched Brazil's National "Destatization" Program (PND: *Programa Nacional de Destatização*) soon after his inauguration in 1990 with the ambition of privatizing most SOEs in Brazil's manufacturing sector.[1] During his tumultuous three-year tenure, small- and medium-scale privatizations occurred in three sectors: steel, petrochemicals, and fertilizers. Because of his political travails and shortened stay in office, however, the number of sell-offs fell far short of the administration's original goal. Collor's successor, Itamar Franco (1993 to 1994), had a much weaker personal commitment to privatization, yet he sold more combined assets in his two-year tenure than Collor had. Franco

---

[1] Privatization actually began under President João Figueiredo (1979 to 1985) and José Sarney (1985 to 1990) in the 1980s, but they sold a mere forty firms with combined assets of only US$737 million (Couto 1998). By comparison, despite its disappointing pace, privatization in just two years under Collor netted about US$5 billion.

even oversaw the sale of one of Brazil's most visible and symbolic "national champions": The aircraft company Embraer was an important exporter and supplier to the country's armed forces.

The pace and size of the process accelerated substantially under the subsequent Fernando Henrique Cardoso administration (1995 to 2002). Cardoso tackled the largest sell-offs, collecting almost 70% of all revenues from Brazil's privatization program in 1997 and 1998 alone. Moreover, almost all privatizations occurring on Cardoso's watch were in the most politically sensitive, or hard, sectors: electricity, telecommunications, mining, and petroleum (Murillo 2009). During his first term (1995 to 1998), Cardoso oversaw sales of electricity distributors, the large and highly symbolic state-owned mining company (Companhia Vale do Rio Doce, CVRD), and numerous ports and railroad networks. He also privatized in 1998 the US$30 billion telecommunications sector, which was the largest privatization sell-off in Latin American history and among the largest in any country ever. Many state-level administrations also carried out some parallel privatizations in the electricity and energy sectors during this time. The process reached a near standstill in Cardoso's second term (1999 to 2002), however, despite the continued existence of around 100 SOEs. Sales of shares in Petrobrás, the monopolistic petroleum giant, did occur in 2000, but the company remained under majority state control. Sizable SOEs remained in the financial and electricity sectors, and no privatization occurred under Cardoso's successor, Luiz Inácio Lula da Silva.

The consequences of these measures for workers and consumers have been typical of those (discussed in Chapter 3) occurring in Latin America as a whole: Job losses and utility rate hikes have been balanced by gains in consumer access. As elsewhere, most SOEs were indebted and unprofitable because they engaged in overemployment and charged below-market prices (Pinheiro and Giambiagi 1997). Firms, especially those in the manufacturing sectors, substantially improved their productivity and profitability after privatization occurred. However, "much of the income gain from increased efficiency was captured by the new owners," because productivity gains were largely the result of "reduced direct employment and more rewarding prices" (Baer 2001, 292; Macedo 2005, 255; see also Pinheiro 1996). I describe these two effects, on employment and consumer prices, in turn.

Scholars conclude that "a share of the costs of privatization have been borne by some of the workers directly employed by the former SOEs who lost their jobs either in the process of adjustment for the sale or thereafter" (Anuatti-Neto et al. 2005, 165). According to some estimates, median employment levels have fallen by about 1,000 workers in privatized firms (Anuatti-Neto et al. 2005; see also Souza 2000). Moreover, most SOE jobs were highly desirable because SOE employees were better paid than private-sector workers with equivalent skills (Macedo 1985; Schneider 1992). That said, the number of laid-off workers summed across all newly privatized firms was tens of thousands, not the hundreds of thousands that might have had a noticeable impact on the labor market in a country of Brazil's size. The sum total of all workers in sectors in which privatizations were concentrated barely exceeds 1 million. Moreover, many firms eventually expanded and hired new workers or outsourced certain activities to outside individuals and firms, potentially re-creating some of the employment opportunities that had been lost. Remaining workers have also enjoyed wage increases and a lucrative acquisition of shares in many newly privatized firms. In sum, while producing a net negative impact, the aggregate and distributional impacts of privatization on Brazil's labor market have been minimal.

The unrealistically low and often politically motivated prices that SOEs charged for their services harmed their profitability. For example, in the early 1990s, Brazil's state-owned telecommunications monopoly Telebrás charged some of the lowest monthly subscription (about US$0.65 per month) and per-unit local-call rates for residential users in the world (Novães 1999). Electricity rates under state ownership in the 1980s and early 1990s also subsidized residential and industrial users, as various state and federal administrations used their ability to control electricity prices as an anti-inflationary device. The state also subsidized manufacturing firms and consumers by not allowing petrochemical and steel prices to rise as quickly as inflation during the 1980s (Schneider 1992).

In part because of their low starting point, prices for telephone and electricity[2] services soared to "excessively high rates" throughout the late 1990s and early 2000s (Macedo 2005, 268). Figure 6.1 illustrates these trends. Although the privatization of fixed-line providers occurred in 1998, the Cardoso administration allowed tariff rebalancing to begin in 1996 in order to encourage investor interest and a higher selling price. Two major

---

[2] Brazil has made little progress in privatizing water utilities, but it did privatize a number of federal highways that resulted in toll increases, some of which exceeded inflation by a factor of three (Castro 1999).

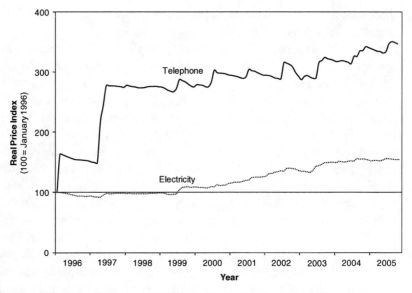

Figure 6.1 The Evolution of Utility Prices in Brazil, 1996–2005.
Source: IBGE (2006).

increases of around 100% each occurred in 1996 and 1997. Prices then remained steady until privatization took place in late 1998, after which they gradually increased over the subsequent seven years. Overall, from 1996 to 2003, subscription rates for monthly service rose over three times the overall rate of inflation (Baer 2001; Macedo 2005). Many citizens stopped paying for services under the burden of higher prices, and by the early 2000s some 6 million lines lay available but disconnected because of unpaid bills. A gradual and piecemeal privatization process in the electricity distribution sector began in 1996, and prices rose about 1.5 times faster than the overall inflation rate thereafter (Baer 2001; Macedo 2005).

Despite higher prices, the quality of services has improved only slowly and in some cases has worsened. In fact, Brazil has struggled with several major postprivatization breakdowns in the provision of telephone and electricity services. Changes implemented pursuant to privatization in the telecommunications sector led to widespread consumer outrage in the late 1990s. Telecommunications firms were inundated with customer complaints, and Brazil's consumer protection agencies found themselves devoting most of their time to customer grievances over telephone quality. Complaints of failed connections, dropped lines, and charges for unmade calls were commonplace. Widespread confusion existed over the new long-distance system, which required citizens to make a choice by dialing extra numbers each time they called. Quality breakdowns were so salient that one firm adopted the following marketing slogan: "The inconvenience is temporary, but the benefits are permanent" (Rhodes 2006, 142).

Service failures in the electricity sector were also common. The first major privatization in this sector occurred in 1996, when the state government of Rio de Janeiro sold to a foreign conglomerate its electricity retailer, Light. Numerous blackouts and shortages ensued. Consumer complaints spiked, and the sector's regulator levied fines against the company (Epstein 1999). Similar problems emerged on a nationwide scale after electricity distributor privatizations elsewhere. Customer complaints of power surges, burned-out appliances, and sporadic, localized power outages were frequent, taxing consumer protection agencies that were already swamped by telephone-related grievances. The problem grew particularly acute in 2001. Because of Brazil's heavy reliance on hydroelectric power, a drought severely diminished the electricity supply. The government responded by mandating a rate hike and a rationing scheme targeted at customers who did not curtail usage by 20% or more. Such users were penalized with higher per-unit rates and a threatened (although never implemented) three-day power outage.

Strictly speaking, neither the Light nor the rationing fiascoes were due to privatization. Light inherited the largely antiquated equipment of its state-owned predecessor, and sporadic blackouts were frequent throughout the country well before privatization occurred. Similarly, the shortages of 2001 occurred at the generation stage, which was actually dominated by state-owned firms. Many of these subtleties, however, were lost on consumers. The 2001 shortages were enough to derail numerous other planned privatizations in the electricity sector.

As in other Latin American countries, the one success on the consumer side has been a rapid expansion of access to telephone and electricity services (Macedo 2005, 266). The cost of acquiring a fixed line fell dramatically, and the number of such lines doubled between 1998 and 2004 (ITU 2005). Mobile phone usage has grown exponentially, and many consumers have adapted to rising fixed-line prices by substituting cellular phones for fixed lines. Access to electricity networks has also expanded, with gains concentrated among the lowest income groups. For example, coverage in rural areas grew from 63% to 80% between 1995 and 2003 (IDB 2006).

The distributional effects of privatization through the consumer channel have been nonlinear. Lower-income groups benefited disproportionately from the expansion in access, while the wealthy more easily absorbed price hikes. In contrast, middle-income groups were the ones most harmed by postprivatization rate increases. They were more likely than lower-income groups to have access already, yet they devoted a larger share of their incomes to such expenditures than high-income groups. In the few years following telecommunications privatization, middle-income consumer advocacy groups sounded a constant refrain of disgust at how existing users bore the cost of expanded access (Rhodes 2006).

Globalization

In the late 1980s, Brazil was one of the most closed economies in the developing world, featuring a trade-weighted average tariff of over 50%, numerous nontariff barriers, and constitutionally codified discrimination against foreign investors. The Collor and Cardoso presidencies, however, reversed decades of import substitution.[3] Collor lowered average tariffs to 15%, abolished most nontariff barriers, lowered taxes on foreign profit remittances, and legalized foreign ownership of SOEs. He also signed the Treaty of Asunción in 1991 to establish the blueprint for Mercosul, a free-trade area comprised of Argentina, Brazil, Paraguay, and Uruguay, which became one of the largest trading blocs in the world. During his first year in office, Cardoso secured the passage of constitutional amendments that (1) revoked the legal distinction between international and domestic capital and (2) repealed the prohibition on foreign (and private) ownership in the mining, natural gas, petroleum, and telecommunications industries. He also embraced negotiations over the FTAA and in 1995 oversaw the growth of Mercosul from a free-trade area to a customs union, a move that established a common external tariff with mostly unrestricted trade among the four members.

While these direct policy measures were significant, the secondary effects of the Cardoso administration's macroeconomic policies were even more crucial in opening Brazil to global markets. First, Cardoso propped up a severely overvalued currency throughout much of his first term, *encouraging imports* and thus heightening the competition that Brazil's firms

[3] Like privatization, trade liberalization actually began under Collor's predecessor, Sarney. Again, however, Collor's achievements were much more substantial.

faced from foreign exporters. Demand for imports surged while export volumes fell, converting long-held trade surpluses into deficits. Between 1989 and 1998, Brazil's foreign trade as a percent of GDP grew from 13% to 17%, but *all of this growth was in imports.* Imports as a percent of GDP rose from 5% to 10%, and exports fell from 8% to 7% (World Bank 2006). Second, an explosion in foreign direct investment (FDI) inflows also occurred during Cardoso's first term, largely because of his privatization efforts. FDI inflows rose from less than US$1 billion per year in the early 1990s to US$24 billion in 1998 and US$30 billion in 1999, ranking Brazil as one of the top five destinations for FDI in the developing world in the late 1990s. A large portion of FDI inflows in these two years created new capital stock on Brazilian soil. However, 40% occurred through the acquisition of existing assets vended in the privatization process, and almost 60% of privatization proceeds were from foreigners (Baer 2001; ECLAC 2000a).

Even as the role of international markets expanded, the beginning of Cardoso's second term (1999 to 2002) marked a conceptual break with the first decade of Brazil's new trade policy. First, the Cardoso administration's 1999 decision to let the currency float and devalue by 50% curtailed the effective favoritism bestowed on imports at the expense of exporters. Export volumes ballooned thereafter, turning the trade deficit into a surplus by 2002. Exports continued to boom during Lula's first term, rising to 18% of GDP in 2004 and creating a record trade surplus of over US$30 billion. Brazil's total trade that year was 31% of GDP, almost 2.5 times the 1989 figure.

Second, Brazil adopted an aggressive stance in multilateral trade negotiations after 1999 that stalled, although it did not reverse, further trade liberalization measures. Cardoso's second term and Lula's first (2003 to 2006) were characterized by sporadic conflict between Brazil and several of its trading partners. In a variety of multilateral negotiating venues, Brazil refused to lower further its protective tariffs because of alleged protectionism on the part of developed countries. Cardoso filed disputes with the World Trade Organization (WTO) against Canada and the United States for their barriers to certain Brazilian imports, and he refused to move up the implementation date of the FTAA from 2005 to 2003. Under Lula, three major commercial agreements that were initially scheduled to come into effect in 2005 missed their deadlines and were unlikely to be revived: a Mercosul–EU agreement, the FTAA, and the Doha round of the WTO. Brazil's refusal to lower tariffs on its manufactured goods, in the face of

U.S. and EU intransigence, stalled negotiations in all three venues. Lula did sign, however, bilateral accords easing trade with China, India, and South Africa, and he expanded Mercosul's membership with the hope of eventually forming a South American free trade area. Overall, Brazil remained as open in 2005 to foreign inflows of goods and capital as it was in 1995.

The economic consequences of Brazil's newfound exposure to global competition have been substantial. Many firms have folded. The ones that have survived have done so by increasing per-worker productivity, often through layoffs and the incorporation of laborsaving technological advances. As a result, the number of jobs in tradable goods sectors has declined (Berg et al. 2006; Dias and Amaral 2002; Thomas 2006). FDI has reinforced these trends, boosting productivity but creating a minimal net gain in job opportunities: "The employment impact of multinationals has been minimal" (Baer 2001, 245). For example, FDI in the motor vehicles sector intensified after 1990, and total production doubled by 2001. During this time, however, employment in the automotive assembly sector declined by nearly 30% (Ferraz et al. 2004). Moreover, a large share of foreign investment inflows went toward the acquisition of newly privatized assets, a job-deleting process. Because of globalization, the aggregate number of individuals employed in industry declined every year in the 1990s: "Shrinking employment in industry stems from the establishment of unfettered trade and the increased competition ensuing from this structural change" (Camargo et al. 2002, 236). The number of individuals working in industry fell by almost 50% between 1990 and 1999 (IBGE 2006). The most rapid declines occurred in the first two years after the implementation of Collor's tariff restructuring and during the years of currency overvaluation.

Historically, Brazil's informal sector absorbed a fair portion of such layoffs, and during the 1990s the share of the workforce employed in the informal sector did grow by more than ten percentage points (ILO 2005). However, the informal sector and the expanding services sector were insufficient to soak up all the workers who lost jobs in a tradable goods sector. Unemployment rates in the 1990s more than doubled, increasing from 4% to 10% (IDB 2006). Largely due to discouragement over the inability to find well-paying jobs, the labor-force participation rate fell from 64% to 57% during the 1990s and the total number of work hours per person also declined (Berg et al. 2006).

Even the more positive labor-market consequences have had regressive distributional effects. Because of enhanced productivity, real wages in the industrial sector have grown (Amann and Baer 2002; ILO 2005). Similarly, the growth of FDI has boosted wages because workers employed in foreign-owned corporations enjoy higher remuneration. Only 5% of the labor force, however, is employed by foreign-owned corporations. Furthermore, the gradually increasing wages enjoyed by industrial laborers have accrued to the ever-shrinking pool of workers fortunate enough to have maintained industrial employment (Berg et al. 2006, 111). The technological upgrades introduced by foreign-owned firms have replaced many unskilled workers who were unqualified to operate the more modern capital equipment. The expansion of capital-intensive technologies has increased Brazil's already high skill premium (Blom et al. 2001; Camargo et al. 2002; Neri and Camargo 2002). Returns to schooling for university-educated workers have increased. In 1990, the average wages of a college graduate were 85% higher than those of a secondary-school graduate. By 2001, the difference was 103% (IDB 2004).

Despite these negative labor-market trends, the devaluation of the currency in 1999 laid the possible groundwork for some export-led job growth. Between 1998 and 2004, exports as a percent of GDP swelled from 8% to 18%. Brazil asserted itself as a leading agro-exporter, yet even these developments have had mixed reverberations. Most of Brazil's exports have low labor intensity: ". . . Brazil [has] remained specialized in low-value and low to medium labor-intensive primary and semiprocessed products, creating little employment" (Berg et al. 2006, 88). Aggregate employment did rebound, however, both in the industrial sector and overall. Industrial employment increased by 25% after 1999, and urban unemployment fell from 12% to 10% in the two years following 2003 (IBGE 2006). Overall, while they have trended in a positive direction in the new millennium, labor markets after 2005 still did not meet the demand for employment as well as they did in 1990.

In contrast to these mostly negative developments in the labor market, globalization has had a far-reaching and mostly positive influence on consumer options. During the days of import substitution, Brazil imported less than 10% of its finished consumer goods because protection was concentrated in this sector (Baer 2001). Enterprises that were insulated from global competition filled the demand for consumer products such as clothing, domestic appliances, automobiles, and food. These firms did so, however, by selling goods at prices above those set in international markets and below international standards of quality. After the liberalizing reforms of the Collor and Cardoso presidencies, consumers substituted domestically produced goods with competitively priced imports. Moreover, many surviving domestic enterprises enhanced their productivity and lowered their sales prices by deploying foreign-made capital equipment acquired at new lower prices.

Systematic evidence on prices indicates how the relative price of tradable goods fell (Camargo et al. 2002; Thomas 2006). Figure 6.2 plots the evolution of real price indices for three classes of tradable goods: food and beverages, household durables, and clothing. To provide a point of comparison, the figure also shows the real price of a composite index of services, such as education, personal services (such as haircuts), health services, public transportation, and telecommunications.[4] The average real price for each tradable goods category fell substantially in the years following the initial liberalization measures of 1990. Prices for clothing and household durables fell most rapidly. By 2006, their average real prices were less than half those in 1989. Relative food prices also fell but did so more slowly. In contrast, the relative price of services rose by more than 50%. The bulk of this recalibration of Brazil's price structure occurred quite rapidly, with most of the eventual relative price shifts occurring in the two to three years following the 1990 reforms. The relative prices of tradable goods and services, however, did continue to diverge gradually during the overvaluation years and even thereafter.

The upward-sloping line in Figure 6.2 may give the impression that the costs of services increased because of trade liberalization, but this would be an incorrect conclusion. Trade reforms merely caused inflation for tradables to slow vis-à-vis that for services. In other words, the rise in the *relative* price of services did not cancel out the net gains to consumers caused by lower prices for tradables. In fact, trade liberalization can also indirectly slow service price inflation since tradable inputs used by service providers become less expensive.

Figure 6.2 also has implications for the distributional consequences of globalization through the consumer channel. On average, consumers experienced net static gains as trade barriers fell and real prices for tradable goods declined. Among tradable goods categories, however, the relative price of food fell most slowly because Brazil exported a large share, about 25%, of its agricultural production (Dias and Amaral 2002). As a result, poor consumers experienced slightly smaller net gains from trade

---

[4] The service index is a weighted average of price changes for each item. Each service class item is weighted by its share in the average consumer's consumption basket.

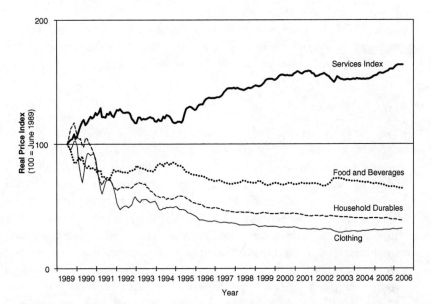

Figure 6.2 The Evolution of Pre- and Postliberalization Prices for Tradable Goods and Services in Brazil, 1989–2006.
Source: IBGE (2006).

liberalization because the relative price of food did not fall as sharply as that of the tradable goods that comprise higher shares of middle-income and high-income consumption budgets. For example, in 2003 the wealthiest quintile devoted 21% of its monthly consumption budgets to clothing and household durables, while the poorest quintile devoted only 13% to such purchases. In contrast, the poorest quintile spent 35% of its consumption budgets on food and beverages, while the wealthiest quintile devoted only 15% of its expenditures to these needs (IBGE 2006). In sum, expanded trade helped all consumers, but it helped middle- and upper-income ones the most.

Elite Opinion in Brazil

As in Chapter 3, I use surveys of elites, namely legislators, to discern the balance and partisan distribution of elite opinion. However, I provide even greater detail on elite opinion by describing (1) some specific rhetorical devices and frames used by elites in their public pronouncements and (2) shifts through time in the volume of elite discourse about market policies. The first subsection describes some of the rhetorical frames employed by Brazil's presidents, and the second subsection looks at the opinions of legislators and the volume of media coverage.

Rhetorical Frames

From the 1950s to the late 1980s, "developmentalist" ideologies and dependency theory had a strong grip on Brazil's elite (Sikkink 1991). Protectionism, state ownership of heavy industry, subsidies for large business, and strict regulation of FDI were widely practiced and even deemed hegemonic: ". . . antiliberal ideas such as corporatism, import substituting industrialization, dependency theories, and structuralism have held a sturdier hegemony in Brazil than in most other developing countries" (Schneider 1992, 235). Further cementing statist convictions was the fact that developmentalist policies were employed with ostensible success, as average living standards rose dramatically between 1945 and 1980.

Brazil's 1989 presidential election, its first democratic one in twenty-nine years, marked a fundamental change. Merely a year after the promulgation of a highly statist constitution, developmentalism had fallen out of fashion. Nonleftist candidates and parties competed to be seen as the leading critic of bloated and inefficient bureaucracies, irresponsible fiscal behavior, and subsidized businesses. Collor, the eventual winner, attacked statism with a populist slant. His campaign slogan, "*caçador de marajás*," or "hunter" of corrupt and overpaid public-sector workers, implicated privatization and other bureaucratic reforms as an equity-enhancing issue. Although Collor did not explicitly push privatization itself as a proposal during his campaign, he planted its seeds by repeatedly hammering away at an alleged class of privileged yet undeserving public-sector elites that benefited from overemployment at taxpayers' expense (Schneider 1992). Collor insisted that the public sector had become a place where individuals were hired and maintained for political and not economic reasons, a so-called "*cabide de emprego*" (literally, an "employment peg," but best translated as a "patronage mill"). In the end, his rants set the stage for privatization by portraying SOEs as hovels of indebtedness, inefficiency, and especially corruption.

The Cardoso government also framed privatization as an equity issue, painting opponents as defenders of privileged, retrograde groups that wanted to maintain the inequality in access to basic services and nonessential jobs. Cardoso emphasized the need for the state to focus on its "core" functions of providing health, housing, education, and security, and it posed utility privatization as a means to expand access, especially to the poor. Cardoso's administration also promised to devote revenues from sell-offs to social spending. To promote its pro-privatization arguments during the country's most controversial sell-offs, the administration purchased commercial spots on television and radio and organized a scheme to have highly visible but otherwise apolitical media icons paid to stump for privatization.

During the Collor and Cardoso administrations, the PT and its perennial presidential candidate, Lula, expressed vocal opposition to these claims and to the privatization process in general. Along with elements from civil society that included labor unions, parts of the Catholic Church, peasant movements, and consumer advocacy groups, the Left presented a highly visible rhetorical challenge that was backed by public protest, legal challenges, strikes, invasions of government property, and, occasionally, violence and vandalism. A common ideological refrain bemoaned the sale to private interests of the *patrimônio do povo* – that is, the "people's patrimony" or "inheritance." The socialist logic behind this complaint held that economic activity, especially in sectors that relied on the exploitation of natural resources, should be state-owned so that revenues could be applied to social spending or deliberate overemployment and overpayment of workers. Privatization's opponents also frequently invoked the need to maintain national sovereignty over strategic sectors, protesting the sale to foreign investors of industries considered crucial to economic development and national security. Large, profitable natural resource companies, such as the CVRD mining firm and the petroleum giant Petrobrás, had long been pride-evoking symbols. Finally, the claim that privatization would reduce corruption was turned on its head when tape-recorded telephone conversations revealed that the sitting minister of communications, Luis Carlos Mendonça de Barros, may have collaborated with potential buyers in the privatization of Telebrás. Mendonça de Barros resigned, and many privatization opponents used the incident to call for a review and even a reversal of the telecommunications sell-off. In the end, however, a legal process cleared him of all charges, and the privatization process in Brazil was actually far cleaner than those that occurred in many other Latin American countries.[5]

Regarding globalization, Collor's decision to liberalize trade had pragmatic roots. With inflation out of control, the Collor administration

---

[5] Corruption in the privatization process surfaced in Argentina, Mexico, Panama, Peru, and elsewhere.

promoted lower tariffs as a means to stem spiraling prices. Collor also touted hopes that trade and foreign investment would modernize Brazil's industry by breaking its dependency on the state, expanding the capital stock, and lowering the price of inputs. Cardoso also advocated for globalization on several fronts. He claimed that foreign investment would bring more modern technology, knowledge, and experience to Brazil, increasing productivity and global competitiveness. He added that the Brazilian business class and the state did not have the savings to invest on the scale that foreigners could. By the end of his second term, however, Cardoso had become slightly more skeptical toward globalization. He was publicly critical of the developing world's agricultural subsidies and the perceived unwillingness of the United States to make concessions in the FTAA negotiations.

As with privatization, the PT and left-leaning elements of Brazilian civil society criticized the globalizing policies of incumbent administrations. Early in the decade, the Left met Collor's and Cardoso's liberalization measures with criticism, decrying the potential loss of national sovereignty and the transfer of decision-making power abroad. Similar claims of First World "imperialism" and a "neocolonial" exploitation of labor were also common. The PT was especially critical of Brazil's trade policy and overvalued currency in 1998, as Lula made these issues a central plank of his election campaign. Complaining of "predatory" and "superfluous" imports, Lula and the PT claimed that Brazil was exporting jobs because of its rapid and indiscriminate liberalization process. As the starting date for the FTAA loomed, Lula and the PT described it as a potential "economic annexation" by the United States. The Left was also highly critical of certain measures designed to attract FDI, such as tax exemption and subsidized plant assembly. Criticisms of foreign portfolio investors as "speculators" who treated Brazil as a "casino" were also commonplace.

Elite and Media Survey Results

Using surveys of national legislators, Figure 6.3 summarizes Brazilian elites' beliefs about the two sets of policies that are the focus of this book: privatization (Panel A) and globalization (Panel B). The figure summarizes attitudes among three different groups between 1995 and 2005. First, the gray "All" markers represent the mean (weighted by party size) across all legislators. This is the estimate of the overall balance of elite opinion. Second, the black "CC" markers depict the mean (weighted by party size) among "Cardoso coalition" parties – that is, the centrist and rightist parties

Consequences of Market Reform in Brazil

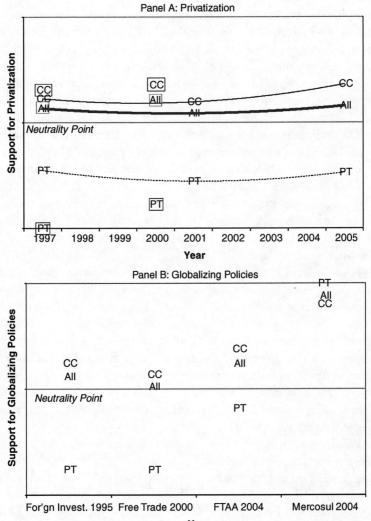

Figure 6.3 Elite Opinion toward Market Reforms in Brazil, 1995–2005.
Note: "CC" = mean (weighted by party size) among Cardoso coalition legislators; "All" = mean (weighted by party size) across all legislators; "PT" = mean among *petista* legislators. Labels with boxes around them in Panel A represent means that were *not* used to estimate the time trend.
Sources: Alcántara (2005) (2004 entries in Panel B); Power (2005) (entries in Panel A connected by lines); Hagopian (2001) (all others).

that provided the core legislative support for Cardoso's reform proposals during his two terms.[6] Finally, the black "PT" markers represent the mean among *petista* (as PT affiliates and sympathizers are called) legislators. Lines connect means in Panel A of the only survey question that was repeated at multiple time points. Markers with boxes around them in Panel A represent means from two nonrepeated questions. In addition, as indicated on the *x*-axis, none of the questions in Panel B was repeated.

The summaries shown do not suffer from the question-wording problems inherent in some of the queries used in Chapter 3. They are based on survey items with balanced response sets that provide respondents with equal opportunities to express opposition to and support for each policy. The *y*-axis spans the entire range of the response set, and each panel contains a horizontal line indicating the "neutrality point," or the midpoint of the scale. (The Survey Data Appendix contains details on question wordings and calculations.)

Four findings are evident. First, Brazilian legislative elites were, on balance, pro-market, albeit slightly so. Every "All" marker, with the exception of free trade in 2000, is above the neutrality point. Second, deep partisan divisions existed. On average, members of the Cardoso coalition favored all market reforms at all times and members of the PT opposed all of them, with the exception of Mercosul, at all times. Third, *petistas* were more favorable toward certain aspects of trade liberalization. They were unanimous in support of Mercosul and not as opposed to the FTAA as they were to other policies. Finally, average beliefs about privatization remained steady through time.

From one perspective, these findings confirm existing knowledge about elite preferences. Collor and especially Cardoso relied on legislative majorities, albeit bare and fractious ones, to implement market-friendly reforms. Moreover, PT legislators unanimously opposed in roll call votes almost every reform proposed by these two administrations (Figueiredo and Limongi 1999; Mainwaring et al. 2000). The PT was one of the most well-organized and programmatic antimarket parties in Latin America during the 1990s.

---

[6] These Cardoso coalition parties are the Brazilian Social Democracy Party (PSDB), the Party of the Brazilian Democratic Movement (PMDB), the Liberal Front Party (PFL), the Brazilian Progressive Party (PP/PPB), and the Brazilian Labor Party (PTB). Some of these parties shuffled in and out of the Cardoso government, and they certainly did not vote unanimously in favor of Cardoso's market reform proposals. Moreover, the PMDB entered Lula's governing coalition in 2004. Overall, however, these parties provided the core of elite support for Cardoso's market measures.

Missing from these findings, however, is any evidence of the PT's alleged moderation; Figure 6.3 shows that the PT was just as opposed to privatization in 2005 as it was in 1997, and it nearly unanimously opposed free trade in 2000. The PT's move toward the ideological center is one of the most well-documented and widely accepted phenomena in Brazilian politics. A multitude of data sources – the party's manifestoes (Bruhn 2004), its candidates' campaign pronouncements (Samuels 2004), interviews with the party leadership (Hunter 2007), surveys of other parties' leaders (Power 2008) – seemingly prove that the party has cultivated a more moderate image and adopted a more centrist ideological orientation since its loss in the 1994 election. So, has the PT "matured" (in Lula's words from the epigraph) by moderating its rhetoric or not?

Unpacking the reform process helps to reconcile these ostensibly contradictory claims. The PT has fostered a more moderate image in ways that do not necessarily touch directly and explicitly on the privatization and globalization issues. In part, characterizations of the new PT typically reflect shifts in labeling and imagery rather than in policy positions. Existing studies of PT moderation find the party to be less oriented toward "socialism," emphasizing clean and competent government over "radical" economic change (Hunter 2007; Samuels 2004). The party is viewed as less "leftist" and more "social democratic" (Power 2008). To be sure, the PT did shift its stances on issues such as pension reform, fiscal discipline, monetary policy, land reform, and foreign debt servicing, especially once in power. Its shifts on the privatization and globalization issues, however, were much less drastic, if they existed at all. As late as 2002 during his presidential campaign, Lula referred to the proposed FTAA as "economic annexation," and he effectively followed through on an anti-FTAA policy once in office, pursuing expansions only of South–South trade. Moreover, although Lula and much of the PT leadership did not advocate outright reversals of the major privatizations after 1998, his presidency did stall the privatization process despite the continued existence of over 100 SOEs.

Perhaps most importantly, the PT was able to maintain its moderate image alongside its ongoing distaste for privatization and globalization because the visibility and salience of these issues declined after 1998.[7] To

[7] I conducted these counts with the search engine at http://www1.folha.uol.com.br/folha/arquivos/. For privatization, I counted the number of stories that mentioned "*privatização*" or "*privatizações*." For globalization, I counted the number that mentioned "*investimento estrangeiro*," "*investimentos estrangeiros*," "*abertura comercial*," "*livre comércio*," "*globalização*,"

report one measure of salience, Brazil's leading newspaper (*Folha de São Paulo*) had over 3,200 stories per year that mentioned privatization in 1997 and 1998, and in Cardoso's second term the paper published 1,700 stories on the topic per year. In Lula's first three years, however, it averaged only 550 stories on privatization per year. Moreover, between 1997 and 2001, the paper published 3,900 stories per year that mentioned some aspect of globalization besides the FTAA, but between 2002 and 2005 the average per year dropped by 33%. The only concrete issue of relevance that received substantial attention after 2000 was the FTAA. The average number of stories about the FTAA increased after 2000 from about 200 per year to over 800 per year.

In sum, the findings in this section add important nuance to the conventional wisdom that the PT has moderated. I claim that its moderation has not been as extensive and visible in the areas of privatization and globalization as it has been in other areas. Despite their ongoing opposition to these market policies, however, Lula and the PT have been able to foster a more moderate image because these issues have not been as central to the country's policy agenda as they were during the Cardoso administration.

Conclusion

The consequences of market reforms in Latin America's largest country, Brazil, have been similar to those incurred elsewhere in the region. Consumers have been able to purchase lower-priced tradable goods, but many have also found well-paying formal-sector jobs scarcer. Privatization has expanded access to telecommunications and electricity networks, yet it has done so through layoffs and higher prices. In the midst of these economic developments, elites have spoken out on reform, exhibiting a slight pro-market bias. The PT, however, has voiced rigid opposition to privatization and globalization. This opposition has largely remained, although it has grown quieter as voters' and the media's attention has shifted to other issues. Using this contextual information about bottom-up and top-down factors, I test a series of hypotheses about Brazilian public opinion in the following two chapters.

or "*Mercosul*." For FTAA, I counted the number that mentioned "*alca*" or "*área livre comércio américas*."

7

How Many Brazilians Support Market Reforms?

> Brazilians do not want renationalization, the end of the market, or the closing of the country!
> – Cristóvam Buarque, as Workers Party (PT) governor of Brasília (1999 to 2002), in a plea made to his party to moderate its stance on economic issues[1]

According to conventional scholarly wisdom, Lula's historic election victory in 2002 was the culmination of a successful journey by him and much of his party to the center of Brazil's political spectrum: "Lula Light" finally seduced the median voter by advocating moderate economic policies in his fourth try at the presidency. Existing scholarship, however, provides only a one-sided view of this process. Lula and the PT's moderation is well-documented (Bruhn 2004; Hunter 2007; Samuels 2004). In contrast, little is known about what Brazil's median voter thinks about the country's new economic policies, despite their status as the main source of elite contestation in the New Republic (Mainwaring et al. 2000). This chapter addresses that gap by describing the contours of aggregate opinion toward the various market policies in Brazil, focusing on differences in popularity across policies and time. In other words, I describe how many Brazilians, or more precisely what proportion of Brazilians, have supported each market reform. I also provide further evidence to support the bottom-up, consumption-based argument about why some policies have been more popular than others. (This chapter does not focus on top-down influences because of the finding in Chapter 4 that they have a weak influence on aggregate beliefs.)

[1] Quoted in *Veja* On-line, November 8, 2000, edition 1674.

This chapter establishes the existence of a popularity gap in Brazil. Like all Latin Americans, Brazilians have been more enthusiastic about globalization than about privatization. They have also, like other Latin Americans, grown increasingly disenchanted with the latter after utility sell-offs occurred in the late 1990s. I uncover the precise reasons for these patterns and trends by analyzing open-ended survey questions that recorded the self-expressed rationales behind citizens' beliefs. Rather than inferring citizens' motivations indirectly from statistical analysis, as I did in Chapter 4, these open-ended results directly measure the thought processes and justifications that underlie citizens' expressed policy attitudes. In the end, they provide convincing evidence that the consequences of reforms for consumer interests have weighed more heavily in citizens' perceptions of reforms than other considerations, especially labor-market criteria. The average voter that Lula pursued supported trade liberalization with enthusiasm because it placed downward pressures on prices. In contrast, average support for privatization was lower and became decreasingly so for the opposite reason: Utility privatizations precipitated price increases as well as declines in the quality of service.

Aggregate Support for Market Reforms in Brazil

Does Brazilian public opinion, like that in Latin America as a whole, feature a popularity gap between globalization and privatization? Because of their country's large economy and historical ability to produce a diversified array of finished consumer goods, Brazilians may be less likely to support globalization with the same enthusiasm expressed elsewhere in the region. Despite this propensity, I show in this section that, on balance, Brazilians have enthusiastically supported globalization while opposing privatization, thus exhibiting the same popularity gap found elsewhere in Latin America.

I present the results in a series of figures that parallel those presented in Chapter 4. Figures 7.1 and 7.2 illustrate aggregate patterns of support for privatization in general and the privatization of various sectors, respectively. Figure 7.3 displays aggregate support for free trade in general, the FTAA, and the Mercosul (South–South) trade agreement. Figure 7.4 depicts aggregate beliefs about foreign investment. I also briefly describe attitudes toward the welfare state in the text. The figures use three types of survey data. First, I report results from the Brazil components of the cross-national surveys used in previous chapters. Second, I display the results of nationwide surveys (without cross-national components) carried out by

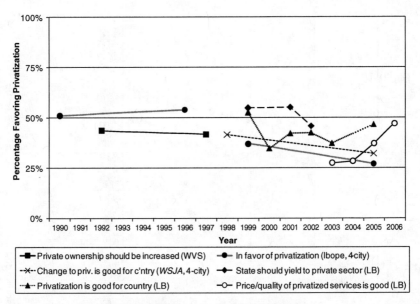

Figure 7.1 Support for Privatization in Brazil, 1990–2006.
Sources: LB, *WSJA*, WVS, and four-city survey.

two leading Brazilian survey firms: Datafolha (DTF) and Ibope. Finally, I report the findings from a survey that I designed and conducted in 1999 and 2005 in four of Brazil's largest cities: Belém, Porto Alegre, Recife, and São Paulo.[2] While this "four-city survey" is more limited in geographical scope than the nationally representative polls, it provides advantages in the measurement of attitudes and in the breadth of its conceptual coverage. Moreover, in 2005 the survey repeated several questions from the 1998 *WSJA* survey, thereby providing more measures of time trends than the cross-national surveys alone.

Results

Between 1990 and 2006, Brazilians were, on average, lukewarm toward privatization, and the number of its proponents dwindled gradually throughout most of these years. First, as demonstrated in Figure 7.1, about

---

[2] These cities draw from the entire range of Brazil's regional, economic, and political variation.

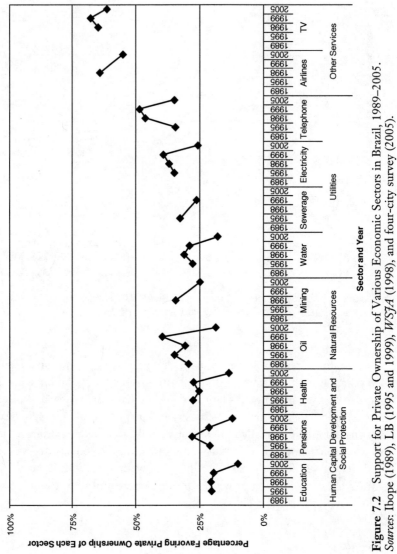

Figure 7.2 Support for Private Ownership of Various Economic Sectors in Brazil, 1989–2005.
Sources: Ibope (1989), LB (1995 and 1999), *WSJA* (1998), and four-city survey (2005).

194

half (40% to 55%) of Brazilians supported privatization in the 1990s, making them more enthusiastic (by a few percentage points) about privatization than their counterparts in the rest of Latin America. In other words, during the early stages of the process when sell-offs were occurring in easy sectors, such as steel and petrochemicals, the pro- and anti-privatization camps were roughly balanced. Second, once policymakers turned to more politically sensitive sectors in the late 1990s, the number of privatization advocates fell. Due to a lack of question-wording continuity, it is difficult to tell whether a sharp drop-off in support occurred when the bulk of these hard sell-offs took place between 1996 and 1999. It is beyond doubt, however, that support for privatization declined steadily between 1998 and 2003. By 2003, at most 37% of Brazilians supported privatization, and just 27% believed that it had improved the quality and prices of services. Figure 7.1 gives conflicting results as to what happened after 2003. Two series show a rebound in privatization's popularity after 2003, but two others show a definite decline between the late 1990s and 2005.

Survey items querying mass support for private ownership in eleven sectors confirm that only minorities supported privatization. These results, shown in Figure 7.2, also suggest that support declined between 1999 and 2005. During the 1990s, 30% to 40% of Brazilians supported private ownership in the natural resource and utility sectors. Average support for private ownership in most sectors dropped after 1999 by about fifteen percentage points.

Still, important and revealing nuances exist across sectors. In the telecommunications sector, 35% of Brazilians supported private ownership in 1995, yet this number jumped to 50% in 1998 *after two years of sharp price increases under state ownership*. The popularity of telecommunications privatization then fell sharply between 1999 and 2005 as gradual post-privatization price increases took hold. Support for private ownership in the electricity sector also fell by fifteen percentage points between 1999 and 2005, a period that straddled the electricity blackouts of 2001. In sum, fewer Brazilians expressed support for private ownership once the effects of the hard privatizations became evident after 1999.

In contrast to privatization, trade liberalization has been persistently popular among Brazilians. Figure 7.3 shows aggregate support for various forms of North–South (Panel A) and South–South (Panel B) trade. Large majorities supported free trade in general. Between 1996 and 2005, 68% to 81% believed that free trade had helped the country. Three-quarters thought that imports had helped the country, and 63% even agreed that the

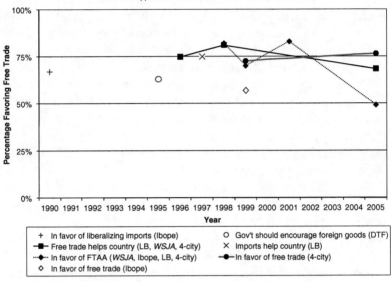

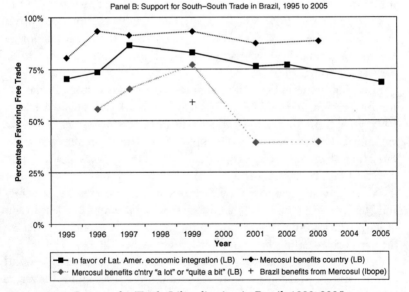

Figure 7.3 Support for Trade Liberalization in Brazil, 1990–2005.
Sources: Ibope, Datafolha (DTF), LB, *WSJA*, and four-city survey.

government should facilitate the entrance of foreign products. The enthusiasm for openness existed as early as 1990, when 67% favored the liberalization of import inflows. Brazilians extended this enthusiasm to South–South trade as well. More than 70% of respondents favored Mercosul and greater Latin American economic integration in nearly every year between 1995 and 2005. Most of these percentages are not as high as those for Latin America as a whole; as discussed in Chapter 4, Brazilians have been less favorable toward globalization because of their economy's large size and their distance from the United States. The differences, however, amount to a few percentage points and do not alter the fundamental fact that Brazilians have overwhelmingly embraced free trade.

Some deviations from this seemingly unbridled support for trade liberalization exist, and they reveal much about the sources of mass support for globalization. In particular, support for free trade seems to have peaked in the late 1990s and early 2000s, either when the currency was overvalued, showering consumers with inexpensive imports, or when memories of the overvaluation were still fresh in consumers' minds. Evidence for this is threefold. First, support for free trade in general (Panel A) was lower in the early to mid-1990s than in the late 1990s. In turn, between 1998 and 2005, the percent believing that "free trade helps the country" fell from 82% to 68% (Panel A). Second, a large number of Brazilians turned against the FTAA after 2001; the percentage "in favor of FTAA" fell from 83% in 2001 to 49% in 2005 (Panel A). Finally, enthusiasm for Mercosul unequivocally peaked in 1999. The vertical gaps between the diamond-marked dark and gray lines in Panel B indicate a rise and then a decline in the intensity of pro-Mercosul attitudes during the period depicted. In particular, many respondents moved from weak support ("a little") to especially strong support ("a lot" or "quite a bit") between 1996 and 1999. Even more respondents, however, moved from strong to weak support in the two subsequent years.

These conclusions about time trends, however, must remain tentative and highly qualified. Observed trends in the percentage of Brazilians believing that "free trade helps the country" are based on differently worded questions. Questions from the early and mid-1990s that showed lower levels of support were never repeated, and the post-1998 downward trend connects results from surveys with different sampling frames. Moreover, a slight rise (from 73% to 77%) between 1999 and 2005 in the number of Brazilians who were generally "in favor of free trade"

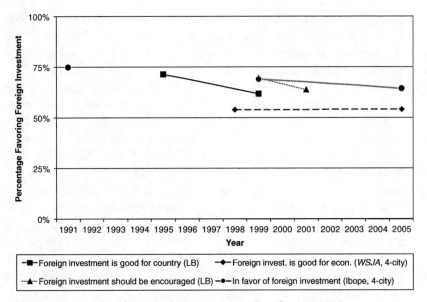

Figure 7.4 Support for Foreign Investment in Brazil, 1991–2005.
Sources: Ibope, LB, *WSJA*, and four-city survey.

contradicts the claim that support peaked in the late 1990s. Finally, Brazilians did grow less intense in their support for Mercosul, but they were certainly not more negative toward the regional trade pact in the early 2000s. The safest overall conclusion is that more than two-thirds of Brazilians persistently supported free trade in the fifteen years following the implementation of Collor's trade liberalization measures.

As with trade liberalization, most Brazilians approved of foreign investment, with pro-trade majorities ranging from 54% to 72%. Figure 7.4 shows patterns of support for foreign investment between 1991 and 2005. These majorities were not as large as the pro-trade majorities, and they again were a few percentage points smaller than the pro-foreign-investment majorities in other Latin American countries. (This again was due to the domestic economy's large size, as described in Chapter 4.) Moreover, the evidence seems to indicate a gradual decline in support during the period analyzed, although the different data series are not unanimous in this finding. In the end, foreign investment clearly commanded persistent majority support, and if it existed at all, the downward trend was not substantial (five to ten percentage points).

What do Brazilians think about fiscal policy and the welfare state? The beliefs of Brazilians, and for that matter of Latin Americans in general, about the proper size of the welfare state remain unclear due to poor instrumentation in cross-national surveys. For example, the 1999 Latin-barometer asked respondents if they preferred more or less spending in a number of different realms: health, education, unemployment insurance, pensions, and others. The question, however, did not mention that this would be "public" spending, nor did it pose a trade-off between higher spending and higher taxes/deficits. As a result, huge majorities of more than 90% expressed a preference for more spending in nearly every realm. To improve on this, the four-city survey in 2005 asked the following question:

Now I'm going to describe two types of political systems and I want to know which of them you would prefer. Would you prefer to live in a country with high taxes that provides many social services, such as health, education, and unemployment insurance? Or would you prefer to live in a country with low taxes where people are more responsible for their own economic situation?

Despite the explicit mention of a trade-off, a majority (59%) still favored the tax-and-spend state, with the remaining 41% preferring to reside in a society of "rugged individuals." These findings are corroborated by a 1993 nationwide survey that found that 71% disagreed, almost all of them strongly so, with the following statement: "The government should offer fewer public services, including things such as health and education, to reduce taxes."[3] In short, a majority of Brazilians appreciated publicly funded services, even when recognizing the need to pay for them with higher taxes.

Although they privatized firms and liberalized trade, neither Collor nor Cardoso aimed to remove the Brazilian state from the health and education sectors. Therefore, attitudes toward general welfare state retrenchment do not capture specific support for any of Brazil's actual policy reforms. Only in the area of retirement pensions did some retrenchment occur. While Figure 7.2 showed support for pension privatization to be minuscule, such a drastic measure never reached Brazil's legislative agenda. Instead, the key planks of the reforms were to require a minimum number of contribution years (implemented in 1998) and to raise the minimum retirement age

---

[3] This survey conducted by Datafolha is archived at the *Centro de Estudos de Opinião Pública* (CESOP) as study #00322.

(implemented for the public sector in 2003). Substantial minorities, rising from 38% in 1999 to 48% in 2005, expressed support for the *Change to a contribution time minimum* in the four-city survey. Fewer, just 34% in 2005, approved of the Lula administration's shift to a *Minimum age requirement* for the public sector. Despite the funding shortfalls in Brazil's pension regime, a majority of citizens opposed the stricter standards and more austere measures implemented by the Cardoso and Lula administrations.

In conclusion, the following findings are central. First, as in the rest of Latin America, Brazilian public opinion has featured a popularity gap between globalization and privatization. Brazilians have been free traders who oppose private ownership in many economic sectors. Due to slightly lower levels of opposition to privatization and support for globalization, this popularity gap has been somewhat smaller than the gap for the region as a whole. Still, it has been a yawning one. Second, support for privatization and globalization probably trended downward after 1998. Finally, most Brazilians have been social democratic in their orientations toward the welfare state, favoring state-funded social protections and opposing the Cardoso and Lula administrations' efforts to make retirement pensions less generous. Overall, Brazilians have evaluated the Washington Consensus like other Latin Americans.

Considering Methodological Counterarguments

The conclusions about public opinion in this and previous chapters are based on a variety of differently worded survey questions. This lends credibility to the claims about aggregate patterns and trends. Methodological doubts may remain, however, especially regarding the crucial claim that a popularity gap exists. In this subsection, I refute the following two methodological counterarguments: (1) response sets in the cross-national surveys are not comparable across policies and (2) expressed opposition to privatization is shallow.

First, the four-city survey is particularly useful in evaluating the robustness of the assertion that there is a popularity gap between privatization and globalization because it contained a series of questions that offered interviewees an equivalent list of response options for each policy: "Are you in favor, against, or do you not have an opinion about [this policy]? Are you strongly or slightly [in favor/against]?" (This was read after a short description of each policy.) This simple approach used to measure if respondents were *In favor of privatization, In favor of free trade,* and *In favor of foreign investment* offers several advantages. First, the common response set enables more valid comparisons of aggregate support across the different policies. Second, the response set offered interviewees an "easy out" by mentioning "no opinion" as an explicit option. While this approach surely encouraged some opinionated respondents to opt out and not offer a valid answer (Berinsky 2004; Gilljam and Granberg 1993), it also discouraged unopinionated respondents from reporting "nonattitudes" that were invented to avoid embarrassment or to satisfy interviewers (Converse 1964). This is particularly important given the perception among some observers that Latin American citizens are too poorly educated or too politically ignorant to understand and evaluate the complexities of economic policy issues (Silveira 1998). Third, asking citizens whether they were in "favor" of or "against" each policy provides much more general measures of issue attitudes than many of those employed in the cross-national datasets. Many questions in the cross-national surveys asked citizens to assess whether a policy had been good or bad for the country. While useful, this approach encouraged respondents to invoke a particular kind of criterion – retrospective and macroeconomic – in evaluating market policies. Finally, the measure of trade policy attitudes omitted the word "free." Because it has a positive connotation, the description of trade liberalization as "free" may artificially drive down aggregate levels of protectionist sentiment.

Results from these more comparable response sets strongly confirm both the existence of the popularity gap and the temporal decline in support for privatization. Panel A of Figure 7.5 presents the full distribution of responses to these three policy questions in 1999 and 2005. The figure is particularly useful for identifying the median citizen's beliefs because the horizontal "50% line" (emerging from the 50% marker on the *y*-axis) runs through the median respondent's answer. Free trade and foreign investment were highly popular in both years, while privatization was unpopular. The median citizen was slightly favorable toward the two globalizing policies in 1999 and 2005, although the "strongly favor" camp claimed 40% or more of respondents at each juncture. In contrast, the median citizen was against privatization in 1999 and strongly against it in 2005. Most of the decline in support for privatization was caused by a net shift from "strongly favor" to "strongly against." Overall, these findings confirm without equivocation the robustness of the popularity gap. Moreover, despite being offered the easy out, only small minorities of between 15% and 25% failed to offer

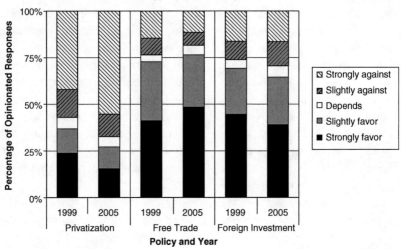

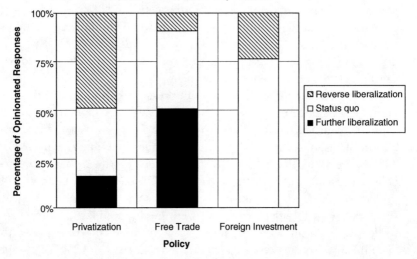

Figure 7.5 A Comparison of Beliefs about Three Economic Policies in Brazil, 1999 and 2005.
Source: Four-city survey.

opinions, suggesting that the aggregate popularity totals reflect real rather than nonexistent attitudes.

Second, I consider whether citizens' overall assessments of a policy are divorced from their perception of (1) how the policy was implemented and (2) what the future of that policy should be. Some economists interpret mass opposition to privatization from the following viewpoint:

> Latin American publics seem to want not the renationalization of privatized firms so much as proper legal and ethical control over the privatization process and the firms already privatized. . . . Latin Americans take a jaundiced view of badly conducted privatization, but not of privatization as such. (Lora and Panizza 2003, 126, 134–135)

Low levels of support for privatization may thus be an expression of mass frustration with the way privatization was carried out (too corrupt or too cheaply sold) and how newly privatized firms are regulated. (See also Shifter and Jawahar 2005.) Citizens' orientations toward the overall goals of the privatization process and private ownership per se may be more positive. In other words, citizens may prefer regulation to renationalization, finding the latter option far too drastic a response to easily solvable problems. The widespread expressions of negativity toward privatization thus may be irrelevant to citizens' preferences about future policy directions. Even Lula and other PT moderates, as seen in the epigraph to this chapter, considered a wholesale reversal of privatization to be too far away from the average Brazilian's preference.

Have Brazilians supported privatization in principle while opposing the way it was carried out? Have they been squeamish about full-scale renationalization, even if frustrated with the material consequences of privatization? Public opinion data reveal that the answer to both questions is definitely "no." *A majority of Brazilians desire the renationalization of some newly privatized firms.* Figure 7.2 provided initial support for this claim because it indicated that most Brazilians opposed private ownership in recently privatized sectors, namely mining, telecommunications, and electricity. In fact, the percentage opposing privatization *increased* after the sell-offs occurred.

Panel B of Figure 7.5 presents this case even more convincingly by showing with alternative data that Brazilians were not meek in expressing their advocacy of renationalization. The four-city survey asked citizens about the *Future direction of privatization*, the *Future direction of trade*, and the *Future direction of foreign investment policy*. For example, the wording of the privatization question was as follows: "Some people think that more state-owned businesses should be privatized, while others think that the privatizations of recent years should be reversed. Do you think that more businesses should be privatized, the number of privatized businesses should be maintained, or the privatizations of recent years should be reversed?" For Panel B of Figure 7.5, the possible responses for the three questions were renamed to reflect the "further liberalization" response, the "status quo" response, and the "reverse liberalization" response. (A "further liberalization" option was not offered in the foreign investment question.)

In 2005, almost 50% of respondents favored a wholesale reversal of the privatizations of recent years. This is slightly less than the 67% who were against privatization (from Panel A of Figure 7.5), but the modal belief was to renationalize. Those who were against privatization (from the Panel A question) but who opposed reversals, presumably the combination of responses expected by the economists cited earlier, comprised less than 20% of respondents. As a point of comparison, Panel B of Figure 7.5 indicates that only a small minority of Brazilians wanted to reverse trade and capital account liberalization measures, consistent with the reports of pro-globalization attitudes in earlier figures. In short, Brazilians have *not* disconnected previous policy effects from future policy preferences. Instead, they have supported the reversal of policies with perceived negative consequences.

Explaining Attitudes toward Market Reforms

The bottom-up theoretical framework stresses that the manner in which citizens encounter policy-relevant information in their everyday lives influences their evaluation of economic policies. Because of the degree and visibility of their impact on consumer options, market reforms have cued consumer-oriented considerations and have triggered individuals to evaluate them along these lines. While Chapters 4 and 5 revealed numerous observable implications in Latin America that are consistent with this claim, I have not yet presented direct evidence to confirm that citizens have consumption in mind when they evaluate the Washington Consensus.

In fact, the immediate reasons and rationales underlying Latin Americans' responses to market policies remain objects of speculation in the broader literature on public opinion in the region. Recall from Chapter 4 that some economists have ventured into the realm of public opinion to attempt to

explain why privatization is so unpopular when it has been, in their evaluation, so beneficial. The list of reasons they offer is extensive. Some assert that
labor-market considerations drive mass beliefs about privatization: "The
public is persuaded . . . that the distributional effects of privatization through
employment are large and negative. . . . Privatization, it is claimed, throws
masses of people out of work or forces them to accept jobs with lower
pay, less security, and fewer benefits" (Birdsall and Nellis 2005, 1, 22; see also
IDB 2004, 167, 170). Others attribute disillusionment with privatization to
corruption and corporate greed: "Suspicions that shares in public enterprises
were diverted to cronies of political elites or that privatization proceeds
have not been used in the public interest likely fueled the discontent"
(McKenzie and Mookherjee 2005, 76). Similarly, "one popular suspicion
highlighted is that . . . the capitalized enterprises have only the best interests
of the majority (foreign owners) in mind. . . . The recent worldwide focus on
corporate malfeasance has helped bring these concerns to the forefront"
(Barja et al. 2005, 123).

A few scholars also speculate about the causes of beliefs toward other
policies. Some impute a labor-market frame to citizens' assessments of
globalizing policies (and, noticeably, misperceive Latin Americans' preferences for free trade):

It is possible that the impact of [trade] liberalization on employment was initially –
and still is – the main reason for political and public opposition to this reform.
There may be many reasons for such a rejection. Perhaps it is thought that imports
displace domestic production, prompting companies to lay off workers, or that,
although liberalization promotes exports, there may not be enough jobs created to
offset the losses in the sectors that compete with imports. (IDB 2004, 146)

All of these scholarly claims are mere conjectures, unsupported by any
investigations into the underlying rationales behind citizens' beliefs.
Closed-ended survey responses are a blunt instrument for discerning the
rationales and subjectivity behind simple expressions of support for or
opposition to a policy. I propose "open-ended, retrospective probes" as a
means to gauge these rationales (Zaller 1992).

In the four-city survey, after recording each respondent's closed-ended
beliefs about privatization, free trade, and foreign investment,[4] interviewers asked "And what are your reasons for being [in favor of/against]
this policy?" Interviewers then wrote down everything the respondent

---

[4] These are the closed-ended questions reported in Figure 7.6, Panel A.

said and asked "Anything else?" until the respondent was finished. Coders read all of these texts and identified distinct rationales that were mentioned by multiple respondents.[5] A single rationale characterizes thoughts and phrases of a nearly identical ilk. For example, a statement by respondent A that "Foreign investors bring employment" would be coded as the same rationale as respondent B's assertion that "Foreign investment creates jobs." On the other hand, respondent C's belief that "Foreign firms provide higher-paying jobs," although it also evokes a labor-market criterion, would be categorized as a separate rationale. In short, a single rationale unites responses that conveyed an identical message and belief about the policy. Because respondents said as much as they wanted about the reforms, many made multiple statements invoking multiple rationales.

To summarize these rationales, I group them into a small number of "frames" or categories that convey a main topic or criterion (e.g., consumption, the labor market, the macroeconomy). Political communications about a single issue can present and describe it in a variety of ways, and economic policies can influence well-being through various channels or roles. As a result, different individuals absorb or formulate varying interpretations of the same issue. Despite this, the number of different interpretations tends to be finite because large groups of individuals absorb similar frames (Gamson 1992; Just et al. 1996). Common frames are even identifiable across different issues. Describing and tallying rationales and frames thus provides an optimal means for knowing the content of what populations consider when evaluating an issue and for understanding the building blocks of aggregate support for a particular policy. Quite simply, if it is true that "Privatization is not popular because of corruption," then many individuals should justify their opposition to privatization by saying that it was a corrupt process or that it has increased corruption. In line with the theory and findings developed thus far, I expect consumption-related rationales to occur with high frequency.

Tables 7.1 through 7.6 in the Chapter 7 Appendix paraphrase the most frequently mentioned rationales and report the relative frequency of each frame and rationale. The discussion will make occasional reference to these tables, but the most important findings are discussed in the text and depicted graphically in Figures 7.6 (privatization), 7.7 (free trade), and 7.8 (foreign investment).

---

[5] I coded the 1999 data, and a research assistant coded the 2005 data.

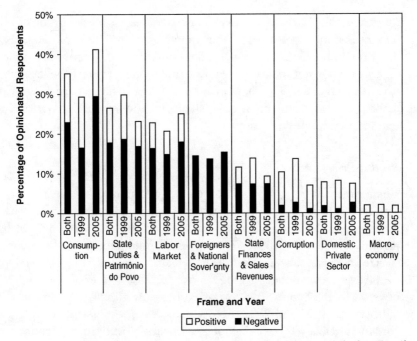

Figure 7.6 Frames in Open-Ended Rationales for Privatization Beliefs in Brazil, 1999 and 2005: Relative Frequencies.
Source: Four-city survey.

Each figure lists the entire set of frames for the relevant issue from left to right on the *x*-axis. They are shown in descending order of frequency. For example, Figure 7.6 indicates that the relevant frames for the privatization issue are "consumption," "state duties and *patrimônio do povo*," "labor market," "foreigners and national sovereignty," "state finances and sales revenues," "corruption," "domestic private sector," and "macroeconomy." The overall height of each bar is the percentage of respondents that mentioned a rationale falling within a given frame. The figure shows three bars for each frame: one for the average over "Both" survey years, one for 1999, and one for 2005. For example, the "Consumption: Both," or leftmost, bar in Figure 7.6 shows that 35% of respondents in both years rationalized their belief about privatization by referring to the policy's impact on consumers. The figure divides each bar into white and black portions to indicate the share of rationales within each frame that were positive (favorable to the policy) and the share that were negative

207

(critical of the policy), respectively. For example, the black portion of the leftmost bar indicates that 23% of respondents mentioned a rationale that described privatization's impact on consumers in a negative light. The white portion indicates that 12% mentioned a positive consumer-oriented rationale. The sum of all percentages for a particular year exceeds 100% because many respondents mentioned multiple rationales that fell into multiple frames.

Results: Privatization

The most frequently provided rationales for privatization beliefs invoked consumer interests. Across both survey years, a plurality of 36% mentioned some aspect of the availability, quality, or price of services provided by privatized industries. About 62% of these consumption-related responses referred to quality, while most of the remainder referred to prices.

A close look at the building blocks of these aggregate percentages reveals why the popularity of privatization in Brazil was weak and why it fell between 1999 and 2005. Across both years, respondents invoking a consumer frame were overwhelmingly critical of privatization. Mentions of negative rationales within this frame outnumbered positive ones by almost 2:1. Moreover, *the decline of about ten percentage points from the late 1990s to the mid-2000s in support of privatization* (see Figure 7.5, Panel A) *was solely due to an increase in the negative assessments of privatization's impact on consumer welfare and, more specifically, disappointment with utility price increases.* In 2005, 42% of all respondents mentioned a consumption-oriented rationale, up from 29% in 1999. This upward shift was driven exclusively by a *doubling* from 1999 to 2005 of the share of respondents mentioning negative rationales. This pushed the ratio of negative to positive mentions from 1:1 to 3:1, a change that single-handedly drove the ten percentage point decline in overall aggregate support for privatization. Figure 7.6 clearly shows that the consumer frame was the only category to undergo such a large negative shift.

Privatization-induced price changes caused these shifts in public opinion. The 1999 interviews occurred six months after the privatization of the telecommunications sector and on the heels of three years of rate hikes by a *state-owned* company. In the next seven years, the real price of phone usage increased every year. Similarly, numerous price increases by newly privatized electricity distributors also occurred during this time. As a result, utility prices grew to dominate the consumption-oriented considerations mentioned by respondents.[6] Between 1999 and 2005, the share of respondents complaining of higher prices increased *fivefold*, while the share of Brazilians reporting a corresponding improvement in service quality fell.[7] (See Table 7.2.) The rising tide of discontent with privatization in Brazil was due to the growing perception that it caused higher utility prices without corresponding improvements in quality. These qualitative results from open-ended questions thus confirm the statistical findings in Chapter 4 (from the pooled time series model) about the causal impact of price changes on temporal shifts in mass opinions about privatization.

After consumption, the second most frequently mentioned category was "State Duties and the *Patrimônio do Povo*." This ideologically toned frame captures some of the main arguments disseminated by elites on both sides of the issue. It contains rationales that evaluate privatization according to the respondent's vision of the state's proper role in society. For example, a common rationale falling into this frame, one that matches a frequent refrain of the Cardoso government, is that the "state should focus on health, education, and security" rather than on utility provision or natural resource extraction. In contrast, many privatization opponents lamented the sale of the "people's" or "our" resources, with many explicitly naming the loss of the *patrimônio do povo* (people's patrimony). A quarter of the respondents in both years mentioned a rationale of this type. Across both years, negative mentions within this frame outnumbered positive ones 2:1, and this ratio grew between 1999 and 2005. A near halving, from 11% to 6%, of positive responses within the frame occurred during this six-year period. Citizens may have repudiated these ideologically motivated positive assessments because of (1) their disgust with the consumer consequences of privatization and/or (2) the fact that the Cardoso administration was no longer in office propagating such sentiments.

The third most frequently mentioned frame represents labor-market concerns. Rationales with a "Labor Market" frame, mentioned by 24% of respondents, typically evoked the perceived job creation or destruction resulting from privatization. Brazilian citizens were generally accurate in their perceptions of privatization's labor-market effects, as they were more

---

[6] Coders also recorded when respondents explicitly mentioned a particular sector in their response. Almost three-quarters of all references to a particular sector were to the telecommunications or the electricity sector.

[7] Improved service quality, however, was the most frequently mentioned rationale among privatization supporters in both years.

than twice as likely to claim that the process generated unemployment as they were to say that privatization mitigated unemployment. Little movement occurred through time. The small three percentage point boost in negative assessments between 1999 and 2005 indicates that the employment consequences of the privatizations of the late 1990s did not resonate much with citizens, especially in comparison to the consumer consequences. In short, while labor-market concerns were far from negligible and clearly contributed to the weak support for privatization, respondents did not mention them as frequently as they mentioned consumption concerns. Moreover, trends in labor-market mentions cannot explain the temporal shift in aggregate support.

The fourth most frequently mentioned frame indicates that, despite the popularity of globalization, economic nationalism is not entirely dead in Brazil. A significant portion of respondents (15%) justified their anti-privatization attitudes by lamenting that foreigners owned many controlling shares in newly privatized industries. Almost all responses within this "Foreigners and National Sovereignty" frame complained of the sale of "our" or the "people's" resources to foreigners, a rationale that differs from the *patrimônio do povo* argument only in that the respondent made explicit reference to the transfer of the people's patrimony to foreigners. No respondents hailed the sale of these assets to foreigners as a positive thing.

These four most frequently mentioned frames dominated the considerations about privatization, as the four remaining ones were mentioned by only 2% to 12%. Still, the remaining results reveal some interesting findings. Because the Cardoso administration touted sales revenues as a source of income for greater social spending, the relative dearth of rationales in the "State Finances and Sales Revenues" frame is telling. Only 12% of respondents weighed in with such a rationale, and the majority of these registered a criticism of privatization. About 5% were on the negative side, asserting that these revenues disappeared or never benefited the Brazilian people, and almost no respondents reiterated the Cardoso administration's argument on this issue. (See Tables 7.1 and 7.2.)

A few scholars claim that beliefs about corruption have driven mass preferences for privatization. Some adhere to a modified "Collor claim": Citizens supported privatization prior to its implementation because leaders framed it as an anticorruption measure (Reis and Cheibub 1993; Sola 1994). Other scholars make the reverse argument: Corruption in the privatization process has been the primary reason for mass discontent (Frye 2006; Lora and Panizza 2003). The open-ended rationales show that a

"Corruption" frame has *not* weighed heavily in the minds of Brazilians. Just 14% in 1999 and 7% in 2005 offered a corruption-oriented rationale. Citizens were more likely to mention the Collor claim than the converse: Concerns about corruption actually provided a net boost to the policy's popularity. This was (statistically tied for) the second most frequently mentioned frame among privatization proponents. Many proponents mentioning this frame remembered the reputation of SOEs as *cabides de empregos*. Because of the Cardoso government's relatively clean oversight and administration of the privatization process, few Brazilians believed that privatization had worsened corruption.

Results: Free Trade

While privatization has been unpopular in Latin America because it has raised prices, I have argued throughout this book that trade liberalization has been popular because it has lowered prices. Figure 7.7 provides the most direct and convincing evidence that positive assessments of trade's impact on consumer interests have driven the overall popularity of free trade. As with privatization, the modal frame across both years was a consumer-oriented one: A plurality of 34% mentioned a consumption-oriented rationale. The vast majority of respondents that invoked this frame, about 85%, were favorable toward free trade, claiming that the relaxation of trade barriers had (1) lowered prices, (2) raised the quality of consumer items, and/or (3) increased the variety of options. In 1999, an impressive 53% of all trade proponents and 39% of all respondents invoked at least one of these three rationales. Thoughts about prices were primary: 27% of respondents justified their pro-trade opinions by saying that free trade had improved prices, compared to 11% mentioning higher quality and 13% praising greater variety. (See Table 7.3.) In contrast to these overwhelmingly positive consumer orientations, only 15% of those invoking a consumer frame opposed free trade, complaining that imports were expensive and/or that the highest-quality products were exported.

The frequency of consumer-oriented rationales did drop between 1999 and 2005, falling from 43% to 26%. In 2005, fewer citizens said that trade had lowered prices, although the relative frequency of negative consumer claims remained stable over this six-year period. This decline in the rate of positive consumer rationales highlights the importance of cognition in shaping attitudes. The 1999 interviews occurred closer in time to the most important and most visible changes in Brazil's trade regime: Collor's trade

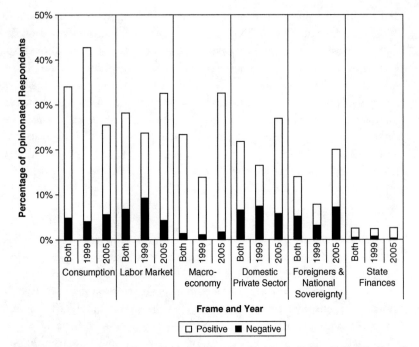

Figure 7.7 Frames in Open-Ended Rationales for Trade Policy Beliefs in Brazil, 1999 and 2005: Relative Frequencies.
Source: Four-city survey.

liberalization measures in the early 1990s and the currency overvaluation of the late 1990s. These events "primed" positive consumption-based considerations by subsidizing an import-buying spree. By 2005 these events had faded from many memories, so the novelty of free trade and its impact on consumer options in Brazil had begun to wear off.

Interestingly, however, the aggregate level of support for free trade did *not* fall over this time. Figure 7.7 indicates that positive considerations with a variety of frames filled the gap: "Labor Market," "Macroeconomy," "Domestic Private Sector," and "Foreigners and National Sovereignty." The relative movements within and across these categories reveal the value added of recording and analyzing these self-reported, open-ended motivations. Between 1999 and 2005, the aggregate level of support for free trade did not change, but its building blocks did. Whereas overvaluation and the recentness of trade liberalization primed consumption and its benefits in 1999, the revival of the macroeconomy and Brazil's export sector filled the gap in 2005. The distribution of rationales underlying trade attitudes was more balanced in 2005 because concerns about economic growth, private-sector vibrancy, and especially labor-market health took a place alongside consumption as determinants of public opinion.

First, labor-market concerns were mentioned only half as frequently as consumer concerns in 1999, but they surged in importance over the subsequent six years. While this seems to contradict my earlier claims about the limited visibility of trade's impact on labor markets, the fact that positive responses within this category were more numerous than negative responses in 1999 actually confirms it. Lower protectionist barriers and an overvalued currency had decimated Brazil's industrial goods sectors by the late 1990s. If ever trade was exerting a visible impact on employment opportunities, it was at this time. This process, however, went largely unnoticed by Brazilians. About 60% of those mentioning a labor-related consideration in 1999 were *positive* toward free trade. Less than 10% of all respondents mentioned a negative labor-market consideration. Perceived labor-market trends affected some citizens' beliefs, yet *actual* trends shaped those of only a few. Cardoso's gamble to effectively subsidize consumers at the expense of industrial producers and workers paid off because he won reelection in late 1998. The psychology of mass opinion explains why Cardoso was successful in this endeavor: The positive impact of trade and currency overvaluation on consumer prices was much more visible than the negative impact on job opportunities.

While few Brazilians blamed trade for the 1999 employment crisis, positive assessments of trade's impact on the labor market did increase with real job growth thereafter. Labor-market concerns increased in frequency by 2005. The share of individuals mentioning that trade had a positive impact on the labor market (almost all suggesting that it created jobs) increased, doubling in frequency by 2005. The percentage of respondents saying that free trade increased unemployment also fell by two-thirds, and the positive-to-negative ratio within the labor-market category jumped from 60:40 to 85:15. In short, by 2005, many citizens had become cognizant of Brazil's emergence as an export power and of the resulting job growth.

Second, the resurgence of the Brazilian economy and the rise in export volumes led an increasing number of citizens to attribute macroeconomic growth to free trade in 2005. Over 30% of respondents in 2005 said that free trade had helped the macroeconomy, mentioning that it had spurred

213

economic growth, encouraged greater investment, and/or improved access to new technologies. The frequency of positive macroeconomy statements, like those of positive labor-market rationales, doubled between 1999 and 2005. Negative statements remained rare.

Third, perceptions of trade's impact on the domestic private sector were important in both years, and the 16% of respondents mentioning this frame in 1999 grew to 27% in 2005. Again, a more than doubling in the frequency of positive rationales drove all of this growth. The most frequently mentioned positive rationales attributed increased business competitiveness and expanded export markets to free trade. Negative considerations – primarily statements that Brazilians should resist buying foreign products and value Brazilian goods, services, and businesses (*valorizar o produto nacional*) – were less frequent at around 6% per year.

Finally, foreigners and national sovereignty are the point of reference for the last important category. As with the other nonconsumption-oriented categories, the frequency of mentions within this frame increased from 1999 (8%) to 2005 (20%), and this rise was mostly driven by an increase in the frequency of positive statements. A substantial portion of respondents reported that "Exchange with foreigners and foreign countries is a good thing." Negative considerations, which actually doubled over time, include traditional nationalist fears that foreigners exploit Brazil or expropriate profits and capital from Brazil. Only about 1% of respondents mentioned the protectionism of foreign countries, despite the frequent complaints of Cardoso and Lula. In short, the *enthusiasm* for engaging with foreigners and the limited number of nationalist claims are striking given the length and depth of Brazil's protectionist past.

Results: Foreign Investment

Consumer concerns have been the most important determinants of attitudes toward privatization and trade policy. In contrast, Figure 7.8 demonstrates that beliefs about foreign investment were overwhelmingly justified with positive labor-market (59%) and macroeconomy rationales (35%). Consumer-oriented rationales were relatively rare (10%), although these too were predominantly positive. In both years, 50% of all respondents mentioned that foreign investment was good because it had generated jobs, while just 9% claimed that it had erased jobs or had been bad for workers in other ways. Over a quarter of respondents cited foreign

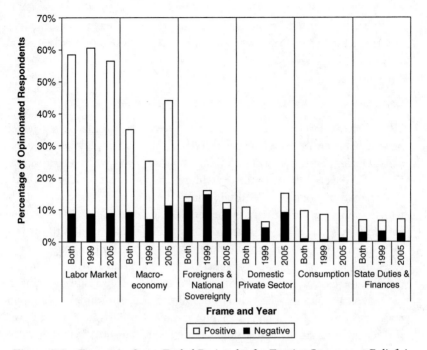

Figure 7.8 Frames in Open-Ended Rationales for Foreign Investment Beliefs in Brazil, 1999 and 2005: Relative Frequencies.
Source: Four-city survey

investment's beneficial impact on the macroeconomy, with just 9% saying that it had achieved the reverse.

A mostly nationalistic "Foreigners and National Sovereignty" frame was the largest source of negative rationales toward foreign investment. Many different sentiments were popular within this realm: "Foreign investment gives foreigners too much power over our economy," "Brazil has enough capital to get by without foreigners," "Brazil must break its dependency on foreigners or it will become a colony," and "Foreign firms are committed to profits, not Brazil." Only 12% of respondents mentioned such considerations across both years, although this group comprised 35% of all foreign investment opponents. Overall, as in the case of free trade, the relative infrequency of these traditional nationalistic and dependency sentiments is more striking than their importance among the opponents of foreign investment. Citizens have evaluated the control that foreigners have over certain aspects of their economy with much more

215

pragmatism than with nationalistic dogmatism. In fact, fewer Brazilians mentioned such rationales when assessing these globalizing policies than when assessing privatization.

Cognition and Consumption: Understanding Exceptions

Why did the importance of consumer interests to trade policy beliefs decline between 1999 and 2005? Moreover, why did employment, and not consumption, dominate mass thinking about foreign investment in Brazil? Both of these exceptions to the overriding empirical pattern emphasize the importance of cognition in establishing the parameters and criteria by which economic policies are evaluated. Recall from Chapter 2 that consumption has played the primary role in shaping mass attitudes toward the Washington Consensus not because of some inherent preeminence of consumer interests per se, but because the material impacts of market policies on consumption criteria have been especially visible to citizens with, typically, limited knowledge of politics and economics. The open-ended results presented in this chapter merely demonstrate that, in Brazil, not all reforms at all times have created such obvious causal linkages between policy and consumer interests.

First, the post-1999 decline in the frequency of consumption-oriented rationales for trade policy beliefs highlights the role of cognition. In the late 1990s, the abrupt influx of foreign goods, caused by the static gains to consumers from trade liberalization and currency overvaluation, was still fresh in citizens' minds. The visibility of this process heightened citizens' sensitivity to their interests, and the benefits they were reaping, as consumers. By 2005, however, the novelty of being able to buy higher-quality foreign goods had faded.[8] The consumer gains from trade registered with fewer individuals as foreign goods became a part of the status quo.

Second, the clear importance of labor-market frames to beliefs about foreign investment, and especially the frequency with which respondents cited the beneficial impact of foreign corporations on job growth, underscores the role of cognition and, particularly, cognitive limitations. Recall from Chapters 3 and 6 that multinational corporations (MNCs) have *not* fomented widespread improvements in labor markets because of their laborsaving technologies and crowding-out effects. Because citizens have

---

[8] This was a prediction made in Baker (2003, 452): ". . . the novelty of being able to buy higher quality foreign goods may eventually wear off."

observed and thought about the material impact of foreign investment in bounded or narrow ways, they have overemphasized and even over-estimated its job-creating effects. In other words, while the perception of labor-market criteria has been important for attitudes about foreign investment in Brazil, *objective* labor-market trends have played a weak role. If actual employment trends had mattered, the frequency of negative labor-market rationales would have been higher. Therefore, the overwhelmingly positive response to foreign investment on employment-channel grounds in Brazil confirms the theoretical claim that the connection between labor-market interests and mass political and policy beliefs is weak (even if it does not confirm the constancy of the consumer lens). Because of the clearer signals that policies have sent regarding consumption criteria, mass policy attitudes based on such criteria are more realistic – that is, more linked to actual trends in prices, quality, and access.

Why have citizens overemphasized and overestimated the net job-creating effects of foreign investment? Foreign-owned companies in Brazil employ a large number of workers and thus appear to increase the number of available jobs: The seemingly mundane sight of MNC employees trig-gers positive thoughts about employment opportunities and possibilities. This cognitive experience, however, fails to reveal the possible dismissal of workers in competing firms, the crowding out of local investors, and the increased inequality caused by more capital-intensive production pro-cesses. Indeed, the high esteem with which citizens hold the employment effects of MNCs implies that, when asked, they assess the issue by con-sidering just one form of foreign investment: FDI through asset creation. Had citizens alternatively or also considered the other two forms – FDI through asset transfer, typically through privatization, and foreign port-folio investment (FPI) – support for foreign investment and its employ-ment effects would have been lower. FDI through privatization has been a job-deleting process, and, strikingly, citizens have been more likely to rail against foreigners when rationalizing their privatization beliefs than when rationalizing their foreign investment beliefs. FPI is an esoteric process that has had few direct and visible influences on the common citizen's life.

Discussion and Conclusion

This chapter has demonstrated that the cross-policy and temporal varia-tion in beliefs about the Washington Consensus among Brazilians has been roughly similar to the general patterns seen in Latin America as a whole:

Globalization has commanded persistent majority support, while privatization has been less popular and that popularity has declined through time. Open-ended questions confirmed the central role that consumer interests have played in forging this popularity gap.

Despite the overall similarities between Brazilians' attitudes and Latin Americans' attitudes, some minor but interesting differences exist. Support for privatization is about five to ten percentage points higher in Brazil than in the region as a whole, while that for foreign investment and free trade is about five to fifteen percentage points *lower* in Brazil. The findings in this chapter and in Chapter 4 provide some insight into why Brazil's aggregate levels of support have deviated somewhat from Latin America's central tendencies. In other words, why has the popularity gap been smaller in Brazil?

Privatization was slightly more popular in Brazil after the mid-1990s than it was in the rest of Latin America for two reasons. First, in comparison to many of his Latin American presidential counterparts, Cardoso oversaw a deliberate, negotiated, transparent, and relatively clean privatization process. A notable "dog that didn't bark" in the open-ended rationales was corruption. While concerns about a corrupt privatization process were not the primary reason for privatization's unpopularity in Brazil, the lack of overt corruption scandals may have boosted pro-privatization attitudes by a few percentage points.

Second, utility rate hikes in countries with SOEs increased support for privatization, while utility rate hikes by privately owned companies reduced it. (See Chapter 4.) In the two years preceding the privatization of Brazil's telecommunications sector, prices rose dramatically, a shift that seemingly "primed the pump" by giving consumers the sense that state ownership could no longer keep the lid on prices. Ironically, this tariff rebalancing was meant to prepare the sector for privatization, a fact that the Cardoso administration successfully disguised from the public. Support for privatization did eventually decline as utility price hikes occurred, but it began from a relatively high level because of the preprivatization fee increases.

Mean support for globalizing policies in Brazil has been slightly lower than that seen throughout Latin America. (See Chapter 4.) The country's large, diversified tradable goods sector has provided consumers with many homemade options, making them slightly less supportive of free trade than other Latin Americans. Foreign investment has also been less popular in Brazil because of the sheer size of its economy. This may be due to the same consumer logic that underlies the comparatively lower level of support for free trade. However, the lack of consumer-oriented statements in open-ended rationales for foreign investment beliefs indicates that it may exist because Brazil's large economy is less starved for capital than those of Latin America's smaller states. Another reason, however, may be that a large share of FDI inflows have gone toward the acquisition of formerly state-owned assets. Foreign investment, in the minds of Brazilians, may be somewhat contaminated by its association with privatization. As mentioned earlier, foreign investment certainly invoked in most respondents the notion of asset creation, yet the transfer of assets to foreigners through the privatization process may also have influenced enough citizens to lower the aggregate percentages.

Evidence from other nationwide surveys confirms that foreign investment has been less popular when framed as asset transfer through privatization. In 1993, 62% of respondents preferred *Government monopolies* in energy and natural resource sectors, while just 38% favored foreign-business participation. In the same survey, however, 72% said foreign investment was welcome in Brazil because it generated wealth and new jobs, and a majority disagreed with the following statement: "The entry of foreign capital is dangerous because it threatens national sovereignty." Similarly, just 25% of respondents in a 1995 nationwide survey agreed with constitutional amendments to allow *Private investment in the petroleum sector* and *Private investment in the telecommunications sector*, regardless of its national origin.

In the end, all of the findings in this chapter, especially those derived from the open-ended responses, yield one final and fundamental conclusion: The notion that the central economic issues affecting Brazilians are too esoteric and beyond their mental reach is categorically false. Brazilians' attitudes toward market reforms are nuanced and real: Almost all respondents who gave a closed-ended opinion offered an open-ended rationale that indicated at least a minimal understanding of each policy and its impact, and a large majority of citizens gave reasoned and frequently well-articulated rationales for why they supported or opposed various aspects of the Washington Consensus. Rates of nonopinionation are low. Most Brazilians hold meaningful, reasoned attitudes involving causal beliefs about market reforms and their material consequences.

Chapter 7 Appendix: Detailed Open-Ended Results

Tables 7.1 through 7.6 summarize the main results from the analysis of open-ended questions discussed in the "Explaining Attitudes toward

Market Reforms" section of this chapter. In the leftmost column, frames are italicized, while rationales are in roman type. The remaining four columns report the relative frequencies of each frame and rationale. For each year, these relative frequencies are defined over (1) the percentage of all opinionated respondents and (2) the percentage of respondents supporting or opposing (depending on the evaluative slant of the rationales) the policy. Tables show all rationales with at least 5% of supporters/ opponents in at least one year. Rationales are sorted from top to bottom by the average (across both years) percentage of opinionated respondents that mentioned them. Since respondents provided multiple justifications that fell into multiple frames, the sum of frame percentages typically exceeds that of the column heading. For this reason (and because rarely mentioned rationales are omitted), the sum of the rationale percentages does not equal their corresponding frame percentages.

Not all of the frames are mutually exclusive. Therefore, to categorize rationales into frames, I use the most immediate meanings in the respondents' statements rather than presuming connotations or implications that they did not explicitly mention. For example, the antiprivatization argument that the policy transfers the *patrimônio do povo* to private interests carries a number of connotations. Most immediately, it conveys the belief that the state should take an active role in socializing the benefits of the country's resource endowments, so references to this concept are tallied into a "State Duties and *Patrimônio do Povo*" frame. However, citizens might plausibly adhere to this viewpoint because they think that such measures would improve the country's economic performance ("Macroeconomy" frame) or create jobs through overemployment ("Labor Market" frame), yet the statement is not coded as such because these frames were not explicitly invoked.

How Many Brazilians Support Market Reforms?

Table 7.1. *Open-Ended Reasons for Supporting Privatization in Brazil, 1999 and 2005*

	1999		2005	
	Percentage of Opinionated Respondents	Percentage of Supporters	Percentage of Opinionated Respondents	Percentage of Supporters
Privatization Supporters	36.8	100	27.1	100
Consumption	*12.8*	*31.7*	*11.8*	*35.4*
It yields higher-quality services.	11.7	28.5	9.3	27.3
It yields better-priced/expanded access to services.	2.5	6.3	3.0	10.6
State Duties and the Patrimônio do Povo	*11.2*	*29.4*	*6.3*	*21.2*
State is poorer administrator than private sector.	7.8	20.4	4.4	14.7
State should focus on health, education, and security.	4.2	11.3	2.3	8.1
Corruption	*11*	*28.5*	*5.9*	*20.7*
SOE workers were in a *cabide de emprego*, overly privileged, or corrupt.	7.5	19.9	1.9	6.1
It reduces patronage and the political use of SOEs.	2.5	5.9	0.4	1.5
It reduces corruption in general.	1.8	4.5	2.7	10.1
Labor Market	*5.8*	*14.0*	*7.1*	*22.7*
It generates jobs.	3.8	9.5	6.2	19.2

(continued)

Table 7.1 (continued)

	1999		2005	
	Percentage of Opinionated Respondents	Percentage of Supporters	Percentage of Opinionated Respondents	Percentage of Supporters
It improves salaries and benefits for workers in the privatized firm.	2.3	5.4	1.4	4.6
Domestic Private Sector	*7.2*	*17.7*	*4.8*	*15.7*
Competition and the free market spur workers and owners.	4.8	12.2	2.5	8.1
Newly privatized businesses become more profitable and productive.	2.5	5.9	2.2	7.1
State Finances and Revenues from Sell-Offs	*6.5*	*14.5*	*1.9*	*6.6*
Indebted SOEs raised public deficit.	3.8	7.2	0.3	1.0
Macroeconomy	*2.0*	*5.0*	*1.8*	*5.6*

Source: Four-city survey.

Table 7.2. *Open-Ended Reasons for Opposing Privatization in Brazil, 1999 and 2005*

	1999		2005	
	Percentage of Opinionated Respondents	Percentage of Opponents	Percentage of Opinionated Respondents	Percentage of Opponents
Privatization Opponents	57.0	100	67.4	100
Consumption	*16.5*	*26.3*	*29.5*	*38.8*
It yields lower-quality services.	12.5	19.6	10.0	13.0
It yields higher prices.	4.7	7.9	24.4	32.5
State Duties and the Patrimônio do Povo	*18.7*	*29.2*	*16.9*	*24.0*
Those resources belong to the people.	8.7	14.9	8.6	12.4
The *patrimônio do povo* was sold.	7.7	12.6	3.3	4.7
Labor Market	*14.8*	*24.6*	*18.0*	*23.8*
It generates unemployment.	14.0	23.4	16.4	21.5
Foreigners and National Sovereignty	*13.7*	*23.7*	*15.3*	*21.5*
The people's resources are sold to foreigners	12.2	21.0	13.2	18.5
State Finances and Revenues from Sell-Offs	*7.3*	*11.1*	*7.4*	*10.4*
Revenues disappeared, did not benefit the people.	5.2	8.2	3.6	5.1
Corruption	*2.7*	*4.1*	*1.1*	*1.4*
Domestic Private Sector	*1.0*	*1.8*	*2.6*	*3.7*
Depends	*4.8*	NA	*4.9*	NA

Source: Four-city survey.

Table 7.3. *Open-Ended Reasons for Supporting Free Trade in Brazil, 1999 and 2005*

	1999		2005	
	Percentage of Opinionated Respondents	Percentage of Supporters	Percentage of Opinionated Respondents	Percentage of Supporters
Free Trade Supporters	72.8	100	76.5	100
Consumption	*38.7*	*52.7*	*19.9*	*24.1*
It yields better-priced goods and services.	27.6	37.4	10.7	13.8
It yields higher-quality goods and services.	11.3	15.0	8.9	10.7
It yields a greater variety of goods and services.	12.6	17.3	6.2	7.5
Macroeconomy	*12.8*	*17.6*	*30.8*	*38.0*
It spurs the economy and economic growth.	8.9	12.2	23.5	29.0
It increases the availability and use of technology.	3.9	5.3	3.9	4.9
It brings in more investment and foreign capital.	0.4	0.5	7.8	9.8
Labor Market	*14.4*	*19.3*	*28.2*	*34.3*
It generates jobs.	14.4	19.3	28.2	34.3
Domestic Private Sector	*9.0*	*12.2*	*21.2*	*27.3*
It increases exports/foreign markets for Brazil.	8.7	11.7	9.9	12.8
It makes Brazil more competitive.	0.2	0.3	9.7	12.4
Foreigners and National Sovereignty	*4.6*	*6.4*	*12.8*	*16.2*
Exchange with foreign countries is a good thing.	2.6	3.6	8.8	11.3
State Finances	*1.7*	*2.0*	*2.3*	*2.8*

Source: Four-city survey.

Table 7.4. *Open-Ended Reasons for Opposing Free Trade in Brazil, 1999 and 2005*

	1999		2005	
	Percentage of Opinionated Respondents	Percentage of Opponents	Percentage of Opinionated Respondents	Percentage of Opponents
Free Trade Opponents	23.5	100	18.5	100
Labor Market	*9.3*	*28.4*	*4.3*	*18.0*
It generates unemployment.	9.1	27.6	3.2	14.1
Domestic Private Sector	*7.4*	*28.4*	*5.8*	*22.7*
The people should value Brazilian goods, services, and businesses. (*Desvaloriza o produto nacional.*)	7.0	27.6	4.9	19.6
Foreigners and National Sovereignty	*3.2*	*11.0*	*7.2*	*28.1*
Other countries are protectionist or subsidize their goods and services.	0.6	2.4	2.6	5.5
Foreigners exploit Brazil.	0.2	0.8	2.3	12.5
It sends capital and profit to foreigners.	0.3	1.6	1.9	8.6
Consumption	*4.1*	*12.6*	*5.6*	*22.6*
It yields higher prices; imports are expensive.	0.7	3.2	3.8	15.6
It yields lower-quality goods and services because those of highest quality are exported.	0.6	2.4	1.4	6.3
Miscellaneous	*3.5*	*13.4*	*2.6*	*12.5*
Brazil has enough to survive on its own.	3.5	13.4	2.6	12.5
Depends	*3.9*	*NA*	*3.9*	*NA*
Brazil should only import what it needs.	1.7	NA	0.1	NA

Source: Four-city survey.

Table 7.5. *Open-Ended Reasons for Supporting Foreign Investment in Brazil, 1999 and 2005*

	1999		2005	
	Percentage of Opinionated Respondents	Percentage of Supporters	Percentage of Opinionated Respondents	Percentage of Supporters
Foreign Investment Supporters	69.2	100	64.5	100
Labor Market	*51.9*	*72.6*	*47.6*	*69.7*
It generates jobs.	51.5	72.0	46.8	68.6
Foreign firms treat and pay workers better.	1.9	2.7	3.4	5.0
Macroeconomy	*11.0*	*15.5*	*24.0*	*35.1*
It spurs the economy and economic growth.	12.6	17.9	21.7	31.2
It brings in more investment and foreign capital.	0.2	0.0	11.3	16.5
It increases the availability and use of technology.	5.1	6.8	6.3	8.9
Domestic Private Sector	*12.0*	*16.6*	*20.7*	*29.4*
It forces Brazilian business to work better.	0.2	0.3	4.0	5.8
Consumption	*7.1*	*9.8*	*9.0*	*13.4*
It yields higher quality goods and services.	3.4	4.9	5.2	7.8
It yields better priced goods and services.	3.0	4.4	3.2	4.8
State Finances	*3.4*	*4.6*	*4.5*	*6.7*
It generates tax revenues to devote to social spending.	3.4	4.6	4.5	6.7

Source: Four-city survey.

Table 7.6. *Open-Ended Reasons for Opposing Foreign Investment in Brazil, 1999 and 2005*

	1999		2005	
	Percentage of Opinionated Respondents	Percentage of Opponents	Percentage of Opinionated Respondents	Percentage of Opponents
Foreign Investment Opponents	26.1	100	29.5	100
Foreigners and National Sovereignty	*14.7*	*43.9*	*10.1*	*27.0*
It gives foreigners too much power over the economy.	4.5	10.8	2.0	4.7
Brazil has investment to get by without foreigners.	4.0	15.1	2.8	7.1
Brazil must break its dependency on foreigners, will become a colony.	3.0	8.6	3.8	10.4
Foreign firms have no commitment to Brazil itself, just want profits.	1.7	5.8	1.8	5.7
Labor Market	*8.7*	*25.2*	*8.8*	*24.6*
It generates unemployment.	6.0	18.0	6.8	19.0
Foreigners exploit workers, pay low salaries.	2.8	7.9	2.1	6.2
Macroeconomy	*7.0*	*16.6*	*11.2*	*31.3*
Foreigners leave with capital and profits.	7.0	16.6	11.2	31.3

(continued)

Table 7.6 (continued)

	1999		2005	
	Percentage of Opinionated Respondents	Percentage of Opponents	Percentage of Opinionated Respondents	Percentage of Opponents
Domestic Private Sector	*4.3*	*10.1*	*9.1*	*22.3*
It slows the growth of Brazilian businesses.	0.2	0.7	4.1	10.4
Foreign firms receive benefits from the government that Brazilian firms do not.	1.9	2.2	2.7	6.2
The people should value Brazilian goods, services, and businesses. (*Desvaloriza o produto nacional.*)	2.4	7.2	3.4	8.5
State Finances	*3.2*	*7.2*	*2.5*	*6.2*
These businesses evade taxes, or pay fewer taxes.	2.6	5.0	0.7	1.9

Source: Four-city survey.

8

Which Brazilians Support Market Reforms?

> The socialist character of the PT is . . . revealed in the fact that the basis of our platform is workers' demands. Workers' demands are the fundamental force behind our mobilization and electoral struggle.
> – Workers Party (PT) platform in 1989 (*Diretório Nacional do PT* 1998, 384)

> Leaders of the popular classes, intellectuals, artists, and religious people with a variety of ideological stripes have spontaneously declared their support for a project of change in Brazil. Significant portions of the business community are also joining our project. This is a vast coalition – in many respects a "supra-party" coalition – that is looking for new horizons for the country.
> – Luiz Inácio Lula da Silva, as presidential candidate of the Workers Party in 2002, excerpted from his "Letter to the Brazilian People" (Silva 2002, 1)

Brazil has one of the most unequal distributions of income in the world. Some observers describe Brazil as "Belindia," where a few million citizens enjoy the living standards of Belgium and tens of millions suffer through those of India. Amid this inequality, most parties are devoid of ideology and programmatic orientations, geared instead to municipal-level pork-barrel politics and particularistic benefits (Ames 2001; Samuels 2003). Moreover, the degree of partisan identification is low, and citizens hold their elected officials in low regard (Mainwaring 1999; Samuels 2006). Because of these circumstances, one might expect bottom-up factors such as wealth rather than top-down factors such as political predispositions and elites to shape public opinion about the most crucial issues of the day.

In this chapter, I find this expectation to be incorrect. Wealth has been only a moderate source of stratification in mass attitudes because consumer interests unify different income groups in their attitudes toward market

229

policies more than they divide them. Consumer interests and tastes are more homogeneously distributed across the population than labor-market assets, mitigating the relevance of concrete economic disparities to public opinion. Moreover, top-down influences occur in Brazil. With their rhetorical appeals, even Brazil's allegedly nonprogrammatic elites have forged at times an important attitudinal cleavage between the politically attentive and the politically unaware. That said, Brazil's most well-organized party, the leftist PT, has counterbalanced the dominance of pro-market elites in shaping public opinion by generating opposition to market policies among certain mass groups. By the time the PT ascended to power in 2003, however, neither it nor the conservative camp was effective in shaping mass opinion on economic reform because these issues had faded from elite rhetoric.

As in Chapter 5, I first establish basic descriptive facts about the size of wealth gaps and hegemony effects. The remainder of the chapter exploits the advantages of the Brazilian data to build on the straightforward conclusions presented in Chapter 5 about the merits of the consumption-based and top-down frameworks. In a section on bottom-up effects, I illustrate how consumption patterns account for the observed relationships between wealth and policy attitudes. In a subsequent section on top-down effects, I describe patterns of elite influence both before and after the Left's rise to power in Brazil.

Wealth Gaps and Hegemony Effects in Brazil

The sizes of Brazil's wealth gaps and hegemony effects dispute much conventional wisdom about the country: Wealth has not been a substantively significant stratifier of market attitudes, and elite opinion leadership has taken place. Figure 8.1 depicts the wealth gaps and hegemony effects for each issue from 1990 to 2003. The circles in the left half of the figure are the wealth gaps: the estimated differences in the probability of taking a pro-market stance between the 95th and 5th percentiles of wealth. The right half of the figure shows hegemony effects, the estimated attitudinal differences between the 95th and 5th percentiles of awareness. The vertical lines connect the upper and lower bounds of the 95% confidence intervals.

As in the rest of Latin America, the wealth gaps in Brazil were moderate in size. The wealthy were more pro-market than the poor in nearly every instance, but only a minority of wealth gaps are statistically distinguishable from zero. Wealthy Brazilians were typically just five to thirteen percentage points more likely to support market reforms than the poor. In the mid- to

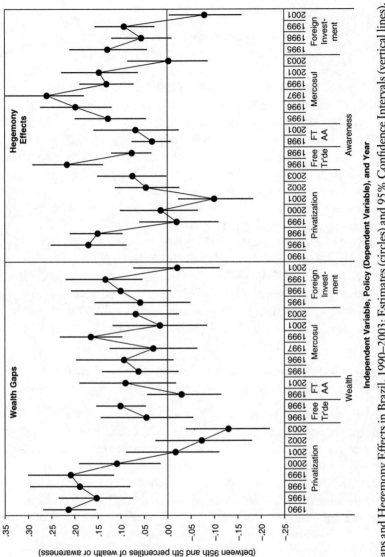

Figure 8.1 Wealth Gaps and Hegemony Effects in Brazil, 1990–2003: Estimates (circles) and 95% Confidence Intervals (vertical lines). *Note:* Circles represent the estimated difference between the 95th and 5th percentiles (of wealth or awareness) in the probability of supporting the corresponding market policy. The vertical lines sweep out the 95% confidence intervals. Estimates are derived from probit models containing only wealth and awareness as independent variables. *Sources: WSJA* (1998). All others years: LB.

231

late 1990s, the wealth gap in privatization attitudes was larger than this, between fifteen and twenty percentage points. By 2001, it had disappeared. (In 2003, the wealthiest were even thirteen percentage points more likely than the poor to *oppose* privatization.) The wealth gap in foreign investment attitudes also declined through time, falling from a peak of thirteen percentage points in 1999 to effectively zero throughout the 2000s.

Hegemony effects were slightly larger and more likely to be statistically significant. In most instances, the politically aware were more pro-market than the politically unaware. For several policies, hegemony effects were substantively as well as statistically significant. The awareness gaps in privatization attitudes were more than fifteen points in 1995 and 1998, and they were between seventeen and twenty-three percentage points for the issues of free trade and Mercosul in the mid-1990s. For most policies, however, hegemony effects were smaller in the 2000s than they were in the 1990s.

Overall, exposure to elite rhetoric has been slightly *more* important than income disparities in shaping Brazilians' attitudes toward market reforms. Surprisingly, in a country where political parties and politicians are discredited but where economic inequalities run deep, elite rhetoric has been slightly more important than wealth in stratifying public opinion.

Bottom-Up Influences: Consumption and the Stratification of Policy Attitudes in Brazil

What accounts for these observed relationships between wealth and economic policy attitudes in Brazil? In this section, I consider three topics that elucidate the nature of wealth's relationship with public opinion. First, I briefly describe the role of wealth and consumer interests in shaping privatization attitudes. Second, I take a microscope to the concept of wealth as a causal variable by contrasting its impact with the influence of precisely measured consumer tastes. Third, I assess whether the impact of wealth varies more with assessments of the consumer consequences of reforms than the labor-market consequences. This illustrates whether citizens are more unified across income groups when they think as consumers than when they think as workers.

Consumption and Privatization Attitudes

To test a variety of hypotheses about mass-level attitudinal cleavages in Brazil, I estimate a series of multiple regression models using the Brazilian

232

components of the Latinbarometer data. I use a list of dependent and independent variables nearly identical to that used in Chapter 5 (with a few exceptions described in the Chapter 8 Appendix). Tables 8.1 through 8.3 in the Chapter 8 Appendix report the full results. In this subsection, I focus on the findings relating to wealth and privatization attitudes (reported in Table 8.1). I then return to these regression results in a later section on top-down influences.

Recall from Figure 8.1 that wealth gaps in privatization attitudes disappeared rapidly after 1999; the modest linear impact that existed in the 1990s no longer existed in the 2000s. This does not mean, however, that wealth no longer exerted a causal influence on privatization beliefs. The multiple regression results in Table 8.1 indicate that the linear relationships of the 1990s gave way to U-shaped ones in the 2000s: middle-income citizens were less enthusiastic about privatization than low- and upper-income citizens were. Not coincidentally, the privatization of the telecommunications provider and many electricity distributors occurred in the late 1990s, instigating consumer-channel effects that led to these now-familiar nonlinear patterns in mass beliefs.

These nonlinearities were deep. $Wealth^2$ was statistically significant in every year from 2000 to 2003 (but not in 1995 or 1999). More importantly, the attitudinal gaps between *middle-* and *extreme*-income (meaning low- and high-income) groups were substantively large. In 2000, the wealthiest individuals (95th percentile) were twenty-five percentage points more likely to favor privatization than were those of median wealth. Similarly, in 2001 and 2002, these differences were ten and sixteen percentage points, respectively, as were the gaps between median-wealth individuals and the poorest (5th percentile). In short, the utility privatizations of the late 1990s in Brazil caused wealth gaps to disappear. However, wealth still mattered thereafter, as it exerted a nonlinear impact because of citizens' consumptive experiences with newly privatized services.

Consumer Tastes, Wealth, and Trade Policy Beliefs

This book has relied heavily on the claim that the existence and at times nonexistence, as exemplified in the preceding subsection, of wealth gaps are explained solely by varying consumer tastes. The relative unavailability thus far (save one exception in Chapter 5) of direct measurements of consumer tastes may leave some doubts as to whether wealth is indeed a consumption variable – that is, if wealth is relevant to policy attitudes

(1) because of variation in consumption budgets and (2) *only* because of variations in consumption budgets. To alleviate these concerns, I establish both of these facts with highly precise measures of consumer tastes from the four-city data.

The 2005 four-city survey contained more detailed questions on relevant consumption patterns than are usually available in public opinion surveys of political attitudes. In particular, it queried respondents' propensities to consume (1) foreign entertainment and (2) durable goods, the two aspects of consumer tastes that Chapter 2 hypothesized to be positively correlated with pro-trade beliefs. First, to measure each respondent's *Preference for foreign entertainment*, I created a single index from the following four variables: (1) the number of foreign films and (2) the number of foreign television programs watched in the preceding month, (3) the number of times the respondent listened to foreign music on the radio in the preceding month, and (4) the number of tapes, records, and CDs of foreign music the respondent owned. Second, to capture more accurately the propensity to consume durable goods (which are more likely to be imported than services and food products), the survey contained a battery of asset indicators that was far more extensive than those available in the cross-national surveys used in Chapters 4 and 5. The battery included a long list of consumer electronics (such as a VCR or DVD player and a dishwasher) and other durables. Respondents' self-reported ownership of all of these items was combined into an index of *Preference for durable goods*.

In building a statistical model to determine the extent to which these variables can explain trade policy attitudes, I include two crucial sets of control variables. First, I create a highly detailed and precise measure of overall *Wealth* that is calculated from the two aforementioned tastes batteries as well as novel measures of household savings and service consumption, including domestic assistance, cable television, cellular phone subscriptions, school tuition, and private health insurance. If wealth explains trade attitudes because it captures differences in relevant consumer tastes and *only* for this reason, then wealth should (1) be positively correlated with pro-trade attitudes when *not* controlling for either of the two measures of consumer tastes and (2) *not* be correlated with trade attitudes when controlling for either of the two measures of consumer tastes.

Second, I control for two different labor-market characteristics. As always, I control for skill level with *Education* and *Education*^{2}. More importantly, I also control for the international competitiveness of the respondent's employment sector. Unlike the cross-national surveys, the four-city data contain measures of *Sectoral competitiveness*. This variable measures labor-market assets that are far more specific to a particular job, occupation, or sector than workers' skill level. Workers in export-oriented, internationally competitive sectors (coded +1) should be more pro-trade than those employed in sectors that are not as competitive as imports (−1) (Frieden 1991). Attitudes among workers employed in a nontradables sector (0) or not in the EAP (0) should fall somewhere in between (Mayda and Rodrik 2005). Finally, I control for the potentially confounding hegemony effect with *Political awareness*.

I measure the dependent variable, trade policy beliefs, with an *Index of support for free trade* constructed from the shared variation of three different questions about trade policy. (See the Survey Data Appendix for details on all variables.) The year of the survey sets up a critical case test of whether consumer tastes explain this dependent variable; as demonstrated in the previous chapter, for cognitive reasons, fewer citizens recognized the beneficial impact of trade liberalization on consumer interests in 2005 than in previous years. If analysis nonetheless reveals that consumer tastes mattered in 2005, then it is likely that they mattered in other years and countries as well.

I estimate five multiple regression models, varying slightly the set of independent variables in each to test (1) if the two direct measures of nonhomothetic tastes explain attitudes and (2) if wealth was related to beliefs merely because of its relationship to these tastes. Table 8.4 in the Chapter 8 Appendix reports the full numerical results, but I convey the main substantive results graphically and in the text. Figure 8.2 plots predicted values (solid lines) of the dependent variable (expressed as standard deviations from the variable's mean) as a function of one independent variable of interest in each of the five models. The two tastes variables range from the "Weakest" (5th percentile) preference for foreign entertainment/durable goods to the "Strongest" (95th) preference, and wealth ranges from "Poorest" (5th) to "Richest" (95th). Lines generated by statistically significant coefficients (see Table 8.4) are thick; those generated by insignificant coefficients are thin. The figure also reports 95% confidence intervals (dashed lines) for the predicted values.

Figure 8.2 plots five predicted value lines in five separate columns, one for each regression model in Table 8.4. The Model 1 column in Figure 8.2 plots predicted support for free trade as a function of the preference for foreign entertainment with no control for wealth. If this aspect of consumer tastes matters, then the slope should be positive. The Model 2 column plots the impact of wealth when controlling for the preference for

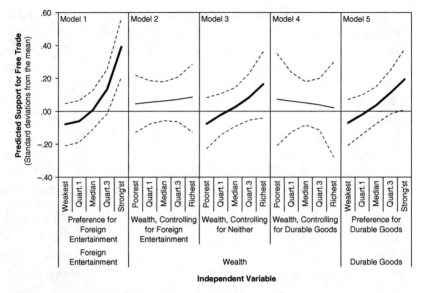

Figure 8.2 Consumer Tastes and Trade Policy Preferences in Brazil, 2005: Predicted Values and 95% Confidence Intervals.
Note: The figure depicts predicted values from regression models reported in Table 8.4. Dependent variable is *Index of support for free trade* (4-city). "Quart." is quartile.
Source: Four-city survey.

foreign entertainment. I expect this line to be flat because, if wealth is solely a proxy for tastes, then wealth should not influence trade policy attitudes when controlling for tastes. The Model 3 column plots the impact of wealth when not controlling for either of the two consumer tastes variables. Because tastes are not present in this model, the wealth proxy should show its relevance in this instance. The Model 4 column plots the impact of wealth when controlling for the preference for durables. Similar to the Model 2 column, I expect this line to be flat because wealth should not influence attitudes when a precise measure of tastes is included. Finally, the Model 5 column shows the impact of the preference for durables with no controls for wealth. Similar to the Model 1 column, a positively sloped line here would indicate the relevance of this aspect of consumer tastes.

The results conform exactly to these expectations. First, the statistically significant results in the leftmost and rightmost columns (Models 1 and 5, respectively) illustrate the impact of the more precise measures of consumer tastes. The Model 1 result demonstrates that the preference for foreign entertainment was a substantively and statistically significant cause of support for free trade. Individuals who spent much time and money consuming foreign entertainment were almost one-half of a standard deviation more enthusiastic about free trade than those who spent no time and money on such recreation. The Model 5 result illustrates the importance of durable consumer goods. Although not as strong substantively, the preference for durable goods had a statistically significant impact (about one-quarter of a standard deviation) on support for free trade.

Second, the shifting influence of wealth is just as revealing. When there was no control for either foreign entertainment preference or durable goods preference (Model 3), wealth had a positive and statistically significant impact on support for free trade. Once consumer tastes were held constant, however, wealth drops out: When controlling for the preference for foreign entertainment (Model 2) and durable goods (Model 4), wealth had no statistically discernible impact on attitudes toward Brazil's trade policy. Moreover, the two consumer tastes variables are statistically significant even when controlling for wealth (not pictured, but see Table 8.4, Models 2 and 4).

A final set of relevant findings provides further evidence of the irrelevance of labor-market factors. Skill level and sectoral competitiveness did not shape attitudes toward trade liberalization in Brazil. (See Table 8.4.)

In sum, wealth is related to trade policy attitudes only because it correlates with meaningful differences in consumer tastes. In other words, *the part of wealth that is correlated with consumer tastes leads citizens to be more or less enthusiastic about trade liberalization*. No other component of wealth relates to issue attitudes. From a methodological standpoint, this confirms that wealth is a decent proxy for consumer tastes in lieu of more specific measures like those used here. More substantively, the mass politics of wealth in Brazil has become the politics of consumer tastes.

Consumer Interests and the Leveling of Horizontal Economic Cleavages

What are the implications of this new politics of consumer tastes? While the attitudinal and political relevance of varied consumer tastes is interesting in its own right, the fact that tastes are closely tied to wealth makes differences in consumption budgets a variable that carries potentially important implications for economic and political cleavages. In particular, I argue that consumption concerns are actually a great societal leveler. Consumer interests unify policy preferences across horizontally defined

237

economic cleavages, namely wealth and class divides, more than they divide them. After all, citizens at all wealth levels prefer lower prices to higher ones. Moreover, while consumer tastes vary with wealth, labor-market assets differ far more markedly across individuals than consumer tastes do. As a result, wealth gaps in attitudes exist, but they are smaller when citizens evaluate market policies as consumers than when citizens evaluate them as workers.

If consumer interests do cut across income differences, then wealth gaps should be smaller when citizens evaluate the consumption-related impact of economic policies than when they evaluate their impact on other types of factors. The 2005 four-city survey contained a battery of questions that asked respondents to assess the impact of privatization, trade liberalization, and foreign investment on a number of economic criteria, including the prices they paid, the number of jobs in the economy, and the quality of the macroeconomy. I report nine (three policies × three economic criteria) of these *Focused policy assessments*. For each of these, Figure 8.3 reports the wealth gap: the estimated difference in the probability of positively evaluating the policy's impact between an individual at the 95th percentile of wealth and one at the 5th percentile of wealth. For example, the *rightmost* result indicates that the wealthy had a .21 higher probability than the poor of believing that foreign investment had exerted a positive impact on the macroeconomy. The 95% confidence interval for this result spans from .11 to .31.

The figure clearly demonstrates that when Brazilians thought about market policies as consumers, they were united across wealth levels in their evaluations. When they thought about market policies as workers or as members of a broader national collective, they were divided by wealth. The three smallest wealth gaps existed when citizens evaluated the impact of each policy on consumer prices. The wealthiest and the poorest were unified in their (largely negative) assessments of postprivatization price changes. In contrast, the wealthy were ten percentage points more likely than the poor to positively evaluate the labor-market and macroeconomic consequences of privatization. A similar pattern characterizes beliefs about the economic consequences of foreign investment, although here the wealth gaps in labor-market and macroeconomic attitudes were even larger (.18 and .21, respectively). Finally, a small (.08) and statistically significant wealth gap did exist in attitudes toward free trade's impact on prices, as would be expected given the results discussed in the preceding subsection. However, wealth gaps in the labor- and macroeconomy-related beliefs

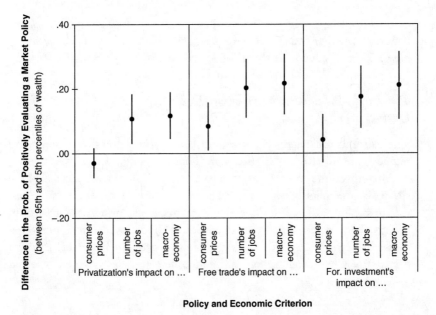

Figure 8.3 Wealth Gaps in Focused Policy Assessments in Brazil, 2005: Estimates (circles) and 95% Confidence Intervals (vertical lines).
Note: The circles represent the estimated difference between the 95th and 5th percentiles of wealth in the probability of positively assessing the impact of the corresponding market policy. The vertical lines sweep out the 95% confidence intervals.
Source: Four-city survey.

about trade were nearly three times as large (.20 and .22, respectively). Wealth influences trade policy attitudes for consumption-related reasons (as confirmed repeatedly throughout this book), but it matters less than if labor-market concerns shaped attitudes.[1]

In sum, the rise in Brazil of consumer-driven beliefs about the main economic policy issues has crucial consequences for the politicization of the country's deep inequalities. Consumer concerns mitigate the relevance of concrete economic disparities to policy attitudes by unifying the interests of

---

[1] In results not shown, I do find that wealth gaps existed in Brazilians' assessments of the effects of these three policies on the *quality* of goods and services; the impact of market reforms on quality was more beneficial in the eyes of the wealthy than in those of the poor. In Figure 8.3, however, I focus on prices as the main criterion of consumer welfare because the open-ended responses clearly indicated that citizens were more focused on the price consequences of policies (especially in 2005) than on their quality consequences.

citizens from vastly different material backgrounds. *Wealth gaps are moderate in Brazil, and thus presumably throughout Latin America, because the politics of economic reform has become the politics of consumption, not production.*

Top-Down Influences: Nurturing Hegemony and Counterhegemony

The existence of hegemony effects in Brazil attests to elite influence on public opinion. (Revisit Figure 8.1.) These hegemony effects, however, declined through time and varied across policies. Moreover, because of the sharp disagreement between the PT leadership and all other major parties, it is possible that hegemony effects were not constant across all partisan groups. In this section, I assess top-down effects by plotting predicted values from the multiple regression models reported in Tables 8.1 through 8.3 in the Chapter 8 Appendix. Figures 8.4 and 8.5 portray expected

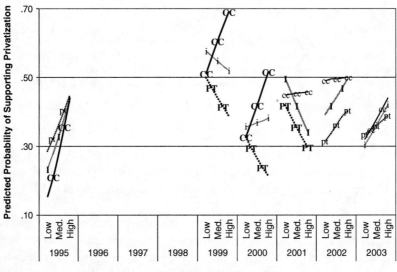

Year and Political Awareness

Figure 8.4 Attitudes toward Privatization in Brazil by Political Predispositions, Awareness, and Year, 1995–2003.
Note: Lines are predicted probabilities from statistical models reported in Table 8.1. Lines labeled with bold and uppercase letters have slopes that are statistically distinguishable from zero. "**CC**" and "cc": Cardoso coalition partisans. "**PT**" and "pt": PT partisans. "**I**" and "i": independents.
Source: LB.

support for privatization and various globalizing policies, respectively, as a function of political awareness and year for three mass-level political groups: *petistas*, *Cardoso coalition partisans*, and *Independents*.

The analysis of elite opinion data from Chapter 6 indicated that, except on the issue of Mercosul, reform attitudes have been highly partisan, dividing *petista* legislators from the more market-friendly legislators of Cardoso's coalition. Moreover, in contrast to its stance on other policies, PT elites' attitudes on globalization and privatization did *not* seem to moderate through time. That said, its antimarket stance on many aspects of these issues was less visible after 1999. What impact did these somewhat ambivalent trends have on mass attitudinal cleavages?

The overriding difference between, on the one hand, the results for privatization (Figure 8.4), North–South trade, and foreign investment (Figure 8.5, Panel A) and, on the other hand, those for Mercosul (Figure 8.5, Panel B) confirms that elite influence on public opinion existed in Brazil. Recall that at the elite level, information flows for the issues of privatization, foreign investment, free trade, and the FTAA were two-sided, while those for Mercosul were one-sided. At the mass level, attitudes toward the first set of policies typically exhibited the expected polarizing effect, whereby divergences in beliefs between the two partisan groups increased with awareness. In contrast, attitudes toward Mercosul between 1995 and 2001 exhibited signs of the mainstreaming effect. Political awareness produced greater support for Mercosul within most of the political groups at most times: Positive and statistically significant awareness gaps exist for eleven of the fifteen instances. Not once did awareness have a negative and statistically significant impact on the probability of supporting Mercosul. In short, the elite consensus in favor of Mercosul produced a strong hegemony effect that was, for the most part, constant across independents and both types of partisans.

Numerous exceptions and temporal changes exist underneath these overarching findings. Most importantly, patterns in mass opinion were more fluid and dynamic than those in elite opinion. While Chapter 6 showed elite opinions toward privatization to be relatively stable through time, Figure 8.4 shows constantly shifting mass-level cleavages that roughly fall into the following three eras: a hegemonic era (1995), a two-sided era (1999 to 2001), and a convergence era (2002 to 2003). First, in 1995, large and positive awareness gaps on the privatization issue existed among all three groups. *This included petistas* (although the gap among *petistas* is not statistically significant), which suggests that the party

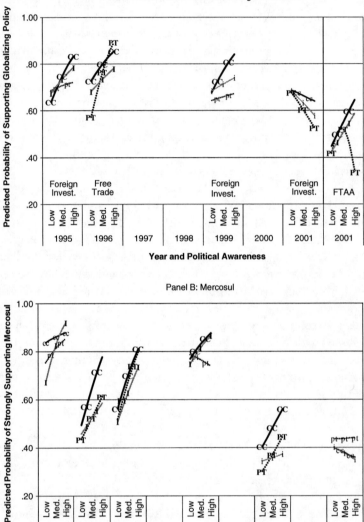

Figure 8.5 Attitudes toward Globalizing Polices in Brazil by Political Predispositions, Awareness, and Year, 1995–2003.
Note: Lines are predicted probabilities from statistical models reported in Tables 8.2 and 8.3. Lines labeled with bold and uppercase letters have slopes that are statistically distinguishable from zero. "**CC**" and "cc": Cardoso coalition partisans. "**PT**" and "pt": PT partisans. "**I**" and "i": independents.
Source: LB.

leadership was not successful in the mid-1990s in reaching even its highly aware supporters with an antiprivatization message. Overall, mass *petistas* were on average just as likely to support privatization as the two other political groups. Second, by 1999 and 2000, these hegemony effects had disappeared among independents and *petistas*, and a pattern more consistent with the actual two-sided flows emanating from elites emerged. The PT leadership was effective at mobilizing antiprivatization sentiments among its highly aware supporters, and it even provided an effective counterbalance to the pro-market rhetoric emanating from the Cardoso coalition, as no awareness gap existed among independents. Third, by 2002 and especially 2003, elites no longer seemed to exert much influence on mass opinion. Awareness had a statistically significant impact in just one of six instances, and in 2003 attitudes were not stratified by either partisanship or awareness.

Some of these patterns, although not all, are also evident in attitudes toward North–South trade and foreign investment (Figure 8.5, Panel A). Most importantly, hegemony effects on mass globalization attitudes were substantial in the mid-1990s. In 1995 and 1996, elites induced awareness gaps in attitudes toward free trade and foreign investment among five of the six political groups. In fact, the largest such awareness gap existed among *petistas* in 1996! Despite the party leadership's opposition to trade liberalization, highly aware *petistas* were thirty-two percentage points more likely to favor trade free trade in general than highly unaware ones. By the early 2000s, however, a more partisan era had emerged. In 2001, PT leaders *were* effective in mobilizing antiglobalization sentiments on foreign investment policy and the FTAA among their highly aware supporters. Cardoso coalition politicians achieved the converse, mobilizing their highly aware mass partisans in favor of the FTAA (although not foreign investment). These efforts also spilled over to influence independents' attitudes toward the FTAA (although again not toward foreign investment).

Why did these patterns in mass opinion shift so quickly compared to the relatively stable beliefs of elites? In particular, why was the PT leadership an effective shaper of antimarket opinion only during Cardoso's second term, despite its steadfast opposition to privatization and most globalizing policies? Most peculiarly, why did the PT fail to foster antiprivatization attitudes when in government in 2003?

The PT struggled to forge antimarket beliefs in the mid-1990s, even among its supporters, because of its diminutive size. During Cardoso's first term, the PT was a marginal party that held less than 10% of gubernatorial and national legislative seats. Lula himself was a visible figure, winning 27% of the presidential vote in 1994. His high profile, however, was limited to election years, and he himself was fast becoming one of the most moderate leaders of the party. In contrast to the PT, the pro-market parties in the Cardoso government accounted for more than 60% of national legislative seats and almost all gubernatorial posts. Members of the government, especially cabinet ministers and the president himself, aggressively promoted through the media their efforts to privatize and to allow foreign investment in key sectors (Rhodes 2006). This period was thus characterized by vigorous persuasive efforts on the part of pro-market elites that overwhelmed those of the country's largely marginalized Left. Even many highly aware *petistas* were roped in by the pro-market skew to elite rhetoric.

In contrast, both conservative and leftist elites failed to shape public opinion in 2002 and 2003 because these particular reform issues had faded from view in Brazil. Political awareness had almost no impact on privatization or even Mercosul attitudes among any mass political groups in these years (Figure 8.5, Panel B). Even the PT, while occupying the bully pulpits of the presidency and the government, failed to forge antiprivatization sentiments among its highly aware supporters. Recall from Chapter 6 that the *volume* of media coverage about privatization (and other reforms) fell dramatically in Lula's second term, despite relative persistence in elites' beliefs. As information flows about these reforms diminished, so too did elites' impact on mass opinion. In short, elites must constantly nurture hegemony, as well as *counterhegemony*, effects on mass opinion.

Conclusion

The two epigraphs to this chapter contrast the rhetoric of the electorally unsuccessful PT of 1989 with that of the successful PT of 2002. The party's well-documented ideological moderation and self-labeled "maturation" are evident. The youthful PT of 1989 was unabashed about identifying itself with socialism; the elderly PT of 2002 failed to do so. The 1989 version pursued a strictly working-class constituency; the 2002 version pursued a cross-class strategy.

While this change in posture took place among PT elites, in many ways the PT of 1989 encountered a very different society from that of 2002. Free-market policies had become the status quo, creating winners and losers across all social groups. Rich and poor consumers saw themselves as winners from trade liberalization, and these same consumers saw themselves as losers from privatization. The priming of consumer interests thus united citizens' interests by wealth more than it divided them. Had Lula and the PT attempted to appeal to citizens with criticisms of extant economic policy that cued class or wealth differences, their efforts would have fallen on deaf ears.

Not all of their appeals, or those of other elites for that matter, were ignored. Despite evoking disgust in most citizens, Brazilian politicians have managed to sway the economic policy beliefs of many constituents. Elites' ability to shape mass opinion, however, can be ephemeral; declines in elite attention to certain market policies diminish their persuasive impact. Top-down effects, while extant in Brazil at various times, must be constantly nurtured.

Chapter 8 Appendix: Multiple Regression Results

Full Models of Individual-Level Attitudes

Tables 8.1 through 8.3 report the multiple regression results discussed in the "Consumption and Privatization Attitudes" subsection and in the "Top-Down Influences: Nurturing Hegemony and Counterhegemony" section. I only use Latinbarometer surveys in these models because (1) the *WSJA* does not identify *petistas*, (2) the Ibope, Datafolha, and WVS surveys contain no useful measures of political awareness, and (3) the four-city survey is not comparable to the Latinbarometer because of its narrower sampling frame. The specification of the multiple regression models in Tables 8.1 through 8.3 is similar to those reported in Chapter 5. All entries are ordered probit, binary probit, or OLS regression estimates with robust standard errors in parentheses. Dependent variables and *Capitalist values* questions are coded so that higher values mean greater support for market policies and/or capitalist principles. Models with capitalist values variables included are run separately, as described in the Chapter 5 Appendix. A "*" denotes $p < .05$. All models also contain parameters that are not shown: a constant, ordered probit cutpoints (when applicable), and dummy variables for *Chief wage earner* and *Non-EAP*.

The models contain two partisan groups not depicted in Figures 8.4 and 8.5. (These are included largely as an accounting mechanism.) *Other conservative* parties are small parties like the Liberal Party (PL) and Party of the Reconstruction of the National Order (PRONA) that, while never a formal part of the Cardoso government, fell on the conservative side of Brazil's political spectrum. *Other leftist* parties are those that were not the PT but still provided consistent opposition to Cardoso's legislative agenda from a statist or socialist perspective: the Democratic Labor Party (PDT), Brazilian Socialist Party (PSB), Socialist People's Party (PPS), Communist Party of Brazil (PCdoB), Green Party (PV), and United Socialist Workers' Party (PSTU). For a number of survey years, there are not enough observed partisans in the other conservative or other leftist camp to estimate properly the coefficients for these variables. In these instances, "—" denotes that a coefficient is not estimated for this reason.

As indicated by the variable names, the precise impact of awareness in each group *can* be read directly from the corresponding coefficients. The impact of awareness among *petistas*, Cardoso coalition supporters, and independents is $\beta_{(Awareness\ among\ petistas)}$, $\beta_{(Awareness\ among\ Cardoso\ coalition\ supporters)}$, and $\beta_{(Awareness\ among\ independents)}$, respectively.

Consumer Tastes, Wealth, and Trade Policy Beliefs

The predicted values reported in Figure 8.2 are generated from the multiple regression models of Table 8.4. Entries in Table 8.4 are OLS regression coefficients with robust standard errors in parentheses. Higher values on the dependent variable mean more support for free trade. Boldface entries correspond to the coefficients plotted in Figure 8.2. All variables are defined in the Survey Data Appendix.

Table 8.1. *Determinants of Individual-Level Attitudes toward Privatization in Brazil, 1995–2003*

Independent Variables	1995 LB	1999 LB	2000 LB	2001 LB	2002 LB	2003 LB
Bottom-Up Factors: Consumer Interests						
Wealth	.235* (.078)	.157* (.046)	.164* (.047)	.005 (.050)	.021 (.050)	−.059 (.046)
Wealth^2	−.040 (.042)	.027 (.038)	.107* (.029)	.064* (.034)	.101* (.033)	.059* (.030)
Consumption security	.019 (.056)	.029 (.039)	−.018 (.039)	.088* (.039)	.034 (.042)	−.002 (.041)
Bottom-Up Factors: Labor-Market Interests						
Education	.218 (.076)	−.054 (.048)	−.003 (.054)	−.029 (.054)	−.108* (.055)	−.081 (.050)
Chief wage earner's education	−.225* (.082)	.021 (.051)	−.119* (.052)	.047 (.059)	−.032 (.061)	.021 (.052)
Class	.140* (.063)	.077* (.044)	.051 (.043)	.008 (.094)	.034 (.044)	.066 (.043)
Unemployed	.040 (.194)	.044 (.150)	−.057 (.143)	.092 (.154)	.121 (.154)	.103 (.124)
Employment insecurity	−.028 (.066)	−.013 (.046)	.026 (.048)	.067 (.045)	−.115* (.049)	−.045 (.049)
Public sector employee	.203 (.163)	.138 (.114)	.057 (.106)	−.012 (.109)	−.052 (.118)	.100 (.115)
Top-Down Factors						
Awareness among Cardoso coalition partisans	.316* (.095)	.167* (.078)	.178* (.091)	.009 (.094)	.005 (.103)	.123 (.105)
Awareness among *petistas*	.164 (.148)	−.100* (.077)	−.130* (.082)	−.118* (.084)	.116 (.083)	.059 (.082)
Awareness among independents	.247* (.085)	−.051 (.071)	.023 (.061)	−.144* (.061)	.115* (.065)	.122 (.105)
Awareness among other conservative partisans	1.322* (.369)	−1.690 (.608)	−.256 (.301)	−.117 (.277)	—	—
Awareness among other leftist partisans	−.482* (.242)	.130 (.173)	−.311* (.183)	.064 (.163)	−.239 (.209)	—
Cardoso coalition partisan	−.308 (.264)	.372* (.168)	.127 (.226)	.285 (.234)	.235 (.217)	.048 (.112)

(continued)

Table 8.1 (continued)

Independent Variables	1995 LB	1999 LB	2000 LB	2001 LB	2002 LB	2003 LB
Petista	−.010 (.290)	.039 (.170)	−.189 (.221)	.069 (.235)	−.103 (.209)	−.010 (.089)
Independent	−.176 (.263)	.291 (.171)	.048 (.215)	.251 (.227)	.111 (.203)	0 (0)
Other conservative partisan	−.671 (.449)	−.481 (.567)	−.399 (.455)	.202 (.390)	—	—
Other leftist partisans	0 (0)	0 (0)	0 (0)	0 (0)	0 (0)	—
Other						
Woman	−.028 (.128)	−.053 (.088)	−.051 (.084)	−.149* (.085)	.171 (.092)	.063 (.080)
Age	−.197* (.072)	.149* (.056)	−.077 (.048)	−.047 (.051)	−.085 (.051)	−.053 (.049)
Capitalist Values						
Capitalist values 1	.053 (.053)	−.082 (.039)	−.055 (.039)	.051 (.042)	.064 (.040)	−.001 (.039)
Capitalist values 2		−.052 (.039)		.053 (.041)		
N	909	822	865	870	832	961

Note: Entries are probit coefficients with standard errors in parentheses. Some predicted values from these models are reported in Figure 8.4.
Sources: Dependent variables are *Index of support for utility privatization* (LB) in 1995 (OLS estimation) and *Privatization is good for country* (LB) in 1999–12003.

248

Table 8.2. *Determinants of Individual-Level Attitudes toward Globalization in Brazil, 1995–2001*

Independent Variables	Foreign Investment			Free Trade	FTAA
	1995 LB	1999 LB	2001 LB	1996 LB	2001 LB
Bottom-Up Factors: Consumer Interests					
Wealth	.039 (.070)	.093* (.049)	.004 (.054)	.053 (.058)	.136* (.051)
Wealth²	.045 (.046)	−.015 (.035)	−.007 (.036)	−.035 (.041)	.019 (.037)
Consumption security	.030 (.053)	.012 (.039)	.054 (.042)	−.014 (.050)	.063 (.044)
Bottom-Up Factors: Labor-Market Interests					
Education	.038 (.077)	.017 (.049)	.003 (.068)	.059 (.063)	−.098 (.072)
Education²	.030 (.054)	.039 (.037)	−.015 (.037)	.130* (.047)	.056 (.042)
Chief wage earner's education	−.007 (.090)	−.014 (.063)	.028 (.066)	−.025 (.069)	−.078 (.063)
Chief wage earner's education²	−.022 (.060)	−.064 (.051)	.040 (.058)	−.086 (.071)	.000 (.060)
Class	.003 (.049)	−.019 (.039)	.102* (.040)	−.023 (.050)	.074* (.044)
Unemployed	.061 (.163)	.112 (.130)	−.151 (.176)	.065 (.181)	.123 (.173)
Employment insecurity	−.069 (.058)	.106 (.049)	.032 (.049)	−.123* (.056)	.075 (.051)
Top-Down Factors					
Awareness among Cardoso coalition partisans	.216* (.093)	.195* (.070)	−.047 (.086)	.153* (.107)	.177* (.085)
Awareness among *petistas*	.029 (.131)	.027 (.072)	−.143* (.091)	.350* (.112)	.063 (.112)
Awareness² among *petistas*					−.187* (.089)
Awareness among independents	.118* (.074)	.062 (.065)	−.099 (.063)	.095* (.076)	.147* (.067)
Awareness among other conservative partisans	.671 (.536)	−.723 (.650)	.126 (.378)	.742* (.378)	.222 (.243)
Awareness among other leftist partisans	−.046 (.229)	−.097 (.158)	.002 (.159)	.314* (.180)	−.173 (.200)
Cardoso coalition partisan	−.059 (.232)	.042 (.168)	.268 (.218)	.084 (.176)	.372 (.230)

(continued)

Table 8.2 (continued)

	Foreign Investment			Free Trade		FTAA
Independent Variables	1995 LB	1999 LB	2001 LB	1996 LB	2001 LB	
Petista	–.115 (.252)	–.237 (.169)	.143 (.222)	–.024 (.176)	.366 (.247)	
Independent	–.070 (.227)	–.099 (.168)	.203 (.210)	–.132 (.1560)	.273 (.225)	
Other conservative partisan	–.208 (.518)	–1.377* (.512)	.274 (.391)	–.054 (.414)	–.294 (.347)	
Other leftist partisan	0 (0)	0 (0)	0 (0)	0 (0)	0 (0)	
Other						
Woman	–.210* (.117)	–.110 (.092)	–.092 (.088)	–.066 (.109)	–.002 (.093)	
Age	.009 (.065)	–.006 (.050)	–.041 (.054)	.041 (.060)	–.154* (.054)	
Capitalist Values						
Capitalist values 1	.012 (.047)	.005 (.040)	.003 (.043)	.016 (.047)	.116* (.044)	
Capitalist values 2		–.017 (.041)	–.010 (.043)		–.030 (.041)	
N	898	836	849	905	776	

Note: Entries are probit coefficients with standard errors in parentheses. Some predicted values from these models are reported in Figure 8.5.
Sources: Dependent variables are *Foreign investment is good for country* (LB) in 1995 and *Foreign investment should be encouraged* (LB) in 1999 and 2001.
Dependent variables are *Free trade helps country* (LB) in 1996 and *In favor of FTAA* (LB) in 2001.

Table 8.3. Determinants of Individual-Level Attitudes toward Mercosul in Brazil, 1995–2003

Independent Variables	1995 LB	1996 LB	1997 LB	1999 LB	2001 LB	2003 LB
Bottom-Up Factors: Consumer Interests						
Wealth	−.060 (.079)	−.020 (.049)	.024 (.049)	.081 (.050)	.004 (.052)	.028 (.051)
Wealth²	.030 (.052)	−.049 (.035)	.009 (.034)	−.019 (.034)	.003 (.036)	−.012 (.039)
Consumption security	−.032 (.060)	.085* (.044)	−.034 (.046)	.091* (.045)	.081* (.042)	.026 (.045)
Bottom-Up Factors: Labor-Market Interests						
Education	.267* (.092)	.161* (.048)	−.013 (.068)	.229* (.052)	.024 (.074)	.057 (.066)
Education²	.072 (.066)	.029 (.038)	.009 (.037)	−.003 (.040)	.085* (.043)	−.029 (.046)
Chief wage earner's education	.088 (.108)	.004 (.056)	−.054 (.079)	.045 (.065)	−.044 (.070)	−.032 (.058)
Chief wage earner's education²	.020 (.068)	.076 (.060)	−.054 (.058)	−.045 (.049)	.025 (.060)	−.048 (.053)
Class	−.005 (.055)	.064* (.039)	.028 (.045)	−.012 (.039)	.053 (.043)	.013 (.046)
Unemployed	−.325* (.170)	.189 (.160)	.185 (.163)	.056 (.158)	.030 (.156)	.081 (.152)
Employment insecurity	−.088 (.071)	−.000 (.042)	.008 (.050)	.022 (.051)	.025 (.052)	−.005 (.050)
Top-Down Factors						
Awareness among Cardoso coalition partisans	.069 (.104)	.255* (.085)	.255* (.087)	.151* (.077)	.142* (.087)	−.047 (.119)
Awareness among *petistas*	.135 (.156)	.149* (.100)	.274* (.094)	−.056 (.076)	.146* (.095)	−.001 (.087)
Awareness among independents	.338* (.095)	.109* (.067)	.211* (.061)	.159* (.078)	.030 (.065)	−.051 (.065)
Awareness among other conservative partisans	1.333* (.800)	.644* (.337)	—	−.246 (.797)	.475* (.230)	—
Awareness among other leftist partisans	−.173 (.253)	.275* (.131)	.250* (.189)	.236 (.236)	−.167 (.160)	—
Cardoso coalition partisan	−.268 (.284)	.415* (.143)	−.037 (.204)	.286 (.197)	−.018 (.206)	.008 (.123)

(continued)

Table 8.3 (continued)

Independent Variables	1995 LB	1996 LB	1997 LB	1999 LB	2001 LB	2003 LB
Petista	−.481 (.302)	.091 (.143)	−.122 (.210)	.112 (.197)	−.315 (.212)	.176 (.101)
Independent	−.500 (.278)	.084 (.128)	−.225 (.196)	.225 (.197)	−.303 (.199)	0 (0)
Other conservative partisan	−1.728* (.749)	1.225* (.380)	—	.356 (.381)	−.283 (.328)	—
Other leftist partisan	0 (0)	0 (0)	0 (0)	0 (0)	0 (0)	—
Other						
Woman	−.097 (.137)	−.157* (.092)	−.341* (.089)	−.244* (.093)	−.227* (.092)	−.131 (.088)
Age	.149* (.079)	.073 (.051)	−.015 (.050)	−.065 (.053)	−.066 (.057)	.079 (.062)
Capitalist Values						
Capitalist values 1	.006 (.054)	−.012 (.043)		.012 (.043)	−.050 (.045)	−.076 (.043)
Capitalist values 2				.077* (.041)	.028 (.042)	
N	826	811	751	806	749	746

Note: Entries are probit coefficients with standard errors in parentheses. Some predicted values from these models are reported in Figure 8.5.

Source: Dependent variables is *Regional trade agreement benefits country* (LB) in 1995–2003.

Table 8.4. *The Impact of Consumer Tastes on Beliefs about Trade Policy in Brazil, 2005*

Key Independent Variable: Model Number in Figure 8.2:	Preference for Foreign Entertainment		Wealth Only	Preference for Consume Durable Goods	
	Model 1	Model 2	Model 3	Model 4	Model 5
Bottom-Up Factors: Consumer Tastes					
Preference for foreign entertainment	**.212* (.042)**	.206* (.046)		.089[a] (.062)	
Preference for consume durable goods		**.009 (.029)**		**−.013 (.053)**	**.075* (.032)**
Wealth			**.048* (.027)**		
Bottom-Up Factors: Labor–Market Interests					
Education	.050 (.039)	.046 (.042)	.057 (.042)	.056 (.042)	.054 (.041)
Education^2	−.011 (.028)	−.011 (.028)	−.016 (.027)	−.017 (.027)	−.018 (.027)
Sectoral competitiveness	−.045 (.113)	−.043 (.113)	−.046 (.117)	−.054 (.117)	−.052 (.117)
Top-Down and Other Factors					
Political awareness	.105* (.038)	.102* (.038)	.092* (.038)	.089* (.039)	.088* (.039)
Age	−.001 (.002)	−.001 (.002)	−.003 (.002)	−.003 (.002)	−.003 (.002)
Woman	−.057 (.065)	−.058 (.065)	−.092 (.065)	−.089 (.065)	−.089 (.065)
Porto Alegre resident	−.308* (.090)	−.313* (.090)	−.282* (.089)	−.306* (.092)	−.305* (.092)
Recife resident	.183* (.078)	.183* (.078)	.177* (.078)	.169* (.079)	.170* (.079)
São Paulo resident	−.101 (.098)	−.103 (.098)	.018 (.096)	−.025 (.096)	−.026 (.096)
Constant	.171 (.130)	.149 (.162)	.113 (.161)	.128 (.163)	.114 (.148)
N	944	944	953	953	953

Note: Entries are OLS regression coefficients with standard errors in parentheses. Bold coefficients are plotted in Figure 8.2. * $p < .05$, one-tailed.
[a] $p < .10$, one-tailed.

Source: Dependent variable is *Index of support for free trade* (4-city) in 2005.

PART IV

Conclusion

9

The Politics of Consumismo in Latin America

> The "left" in Latin America committed many sins. . . . But it kept the issue of poverty on everyone's mind, and it held out a dream of a more egalitarian society, where basic needs were met. Maybe it even served as a check on the most blatant displays of consumerism. It was noisy and persistent. But now the left has all but vanished, having been swallowed by electoral politics, consumerism, and nihilism. There is no one "stirring things up," asking hard questions about state and society. The social Christian political parties have in the past committed themselves to many of the same ends (via different means), but they seem now to have strayed from their mission. Today they, too, are "at the mall."
> – Forrest Colburn in *Latin America at the End of Politics* (2002, 65)

> Consumers need to be citizens, too.
> – Julio María Sanguinetti, Uruguayan president (1985–1990, 1995–2000) (Colburn 2002, 37)[1]

The economic and attitudinal trends of Latin America described throughout this book are akin to portrayals of the world economy's "McDonaldization" or "Wal-martization" (Ritzer 1996). The lower political and physical barriers to international exchange have diminished labor's bargaining power, decimating trade unions and making employment more precarious. At the same time, globalization has dramatically decreased the costs of consumer goods. Consumers have thus gone shopping, more lured by the consumption benefits of globalization than repelled by the labor-market damage. The allure of consumption is the engine of globalization.[2]

---

[1] Both quotations are from Colburn (2002, 65, 37).
[2] This sentence is a quotation from Baker (2005, 924).

Two sets of indicators from Brazil exemplify these trends. On the one hand, in the 1990s, the average length of job tenure fell by 12%, the number of unionized workers dropped by 40%, and the number of strikes fell by an order of magnitude (from about 1,000 to about 100 per year).[3] Increases in the rate of job churning generated a "market-induced fragmentation," weakening labor organizations and thus chipping away at the associational vibrancy of state-led development (Kurtz 2004, 274; see also Roberts 1998). On the other hand, the number of shopping malls in Brazil more than tripled between 1990 and 2006, rising from 90 to 315.[4] Market reforms initiated the "mall decade," as "the twentieth century in Latin America ended ... with a shopping spree" (Colburn 2002, 65). Citizens went shopping amid the employment flux, often for flashy new foreign goods and services.

A central claim of this book is that Latin Americans in this new era think about the most important economic issues of their time as consumers and not as workers. Increased labor-market volatility and the weakening of labor-based organizations have reduced the influence of specific worker interests on policy preferences. Meanwhile, the vast and visible impact that the new policies have had on prices has cued the citizenry to their consequences for consumption. The low prices caused by globalization have lured Latin Americans into supporting their governments' efforts to expand foreign trade and investment.

These strict consumer orientations, however, have not made Latin Americans advocates of all market reforms. What the Washington Consensus has given to consumers with one hand it has taken away with another. Privatization has increased electricity, water, and telephone bills across the region, and citizens have again responded as consumers and not as workers. They have opposed privatization and often demanded its reversal, despite the fact that it has had a far less detrimental impact on labor markets than globalization.

These aggregate trends, however, only represent central tendencies. Not all consumers have the same tastes, so the new consumer orientations have led some Latin Americans to express more enthusiasm for the

---

[3] Union density data are from IDB (2004) and are based on a comparison of averages from the 1985–1990 period and the 1990–1995 period. Number of strikes data are from the *Encyclopedia of Nations* (2006) and Antunes and Wilson (1994) and correspond to 1986 and 2000, respectively. Job tenure data are from IDB (2006) and refer to the change from 1993 to 2000.

[4] Shopping mall data are from ABRASCE (2007).

Washington Consensus than others. Wealthy consumers have benefited more from trade liberalization than poor consumers because the former purchase more imports and foreign entertainment than the latter. In contrast, middle-income groups have borne the heaviest burden of post-privatization price increases. They were more likely than the poor to have access to these services before privatization occurred and less likely than the rich to have to devote a large share of their incomes to subsequent price increases. All of these patterns have resonated in public opinion.

Consumer tastes have not been the only factor differentiating individual-level attitudes. Elite rhetoric, different levels of attention to it, and different propensities to accept it have also forged intranational cleavages over economic policy beliefs. Throughout the 1990s, elite rhetoric was over-whelmingly favorable toward market policies, so individuals of all political stripes who were attentive to elite appeals were more pro-market than individuals who were not. With the revival of the Left in the new millen-nium, however, a posthegemonic era in elite opinion has emerged. The shift in elite rhetoric has stratified opinions not just by awareness of elite discourse but also by political predispositions. These top-down, elite-led effects have thus been important in forging new mass-level cleavages in beliefs about reforms. They have been, however, far less important than bottom-up consumer considerations for setting the overall popularity of reforms.

In this concluding chapter, I discuss the implications of these findings for comparative political economy, the rise of the Latin American Left, and the structure of political cleavages in the region. First, I point out that scholars of comparative political economy must "bring the consumer in." The conventional wisdom on mass preferences in the small states of the developed world holds that citizens accept international openness only if they receive compensation from their governments in the form of guaranteed incomes and social spending. Latin Americanists can learn from these small-state contexts by noting how citizens unpack the issues of foreign and domestic economic policy in a manner similar to that in Latin America. At the same time, scholars of the developed world's small states can learn from Latin Americans' obsession with prices that consumption-based, and not solely producer-based, interests often underlie mass preferences.

Second, this propensity for Latin American citizens to unpack reforms makes them ambivalent about the Washington Consensus: They support globalization but oppose privatization. This ambivalence explains why the

Left in Latin America has turned out to be moderate. In line with voters' preferences, the Left has stalled or reversed some privatizations but it has not reversed the process of trade liberalization. Because of voters' obsession with low prices, the Left is empowered to reverse privatization but constrained from raising protectionist barriers. In other words, the Left has received and carried out a mandate that is moderate because of electorates' sharp ambivalence across different policies.

Finally, I consider whether the new consumer-based preferences of Latin Americans have reoriented the region's political cleavages around tastes. Disparities in consumption patterns, especially ones that are wealth-related, may now provide the basis for political competition and contestation. In the end, however, I argue that these nonhomothetic tastes have minimal potential to forge domestic political cleavages because consumer tastes unify citizens across different income groups more than they divide them. In fact, the rise of the new consumer politics is one of the reasons why class-based political cleavages in Latin America are so weak.

Latin American States (and Consumers) in World Markets

Most depictions of elite and mass preferences toward the new market model in Latin America still cling to the notion that various economic policies fit a single market-versus-statist dimension and are evaluated as a monolithic whole. The evidence presented throughout this book demonstrates that Latin American citizens are more discerning than this. On average, they are favorably inclined toward their region's newfound engagement in global markets. In contrast, they still favor state ownership of natural resources as well as state provision of utilities and more traditional welfare-state services.

That scholars of Latin America remain so wedded to a unidimensional conception of market reform indicates a failure to learn lessons from political economies elsewhere. In particular, the manner in which most Latin Americans unpack reforms is reminiscent of alleged configurations in Europe's small states. According to some scholars, citizens in these countries support international economic openness, but they also demand a thick welfare safety net and state provision of many other services to protect against the income volatility caused by this openness: "[T]he link between the case for free trade and the case for laissez-faire [is] broken" in these countries (Katzenstein 1985, 48). According to Peter Katzenstein (1985), small economies resist protectionist policies because such measures

(1) would raise the prices of intermediate inputs necessary for producing exports and (2) might evoke protectionist retribution from larger states. In return for accepting this openness, citizens in small states expect and receive a cushion from the vicissitudes of international markets: income and employment guarantees; generous state-funded health, education, and pension systems; and nationalization of a large portion of economic production (see also Rodrik 1998). In the end, Katzenstein concludes, "the small European states are clear exceptions to the generalization that liberalism in the international economy and interventionism in the domestic economy are incompatible" (1985, 57). Scholars of Latin America have thus failed to notice that the "the small European states' important contribution to the repertoire of modern capitalism" is now present in Latin America as well (Katzenstein 1985, 58). After all, most Latin American states are also small.

Admittedly, important differences between the European and Latin American states exist. Latin Americans support globalizing policies in lieu of significant compensation from their limited welfare states because they deem sufficient the consumption gains from trade. While they certainly favor larger and more effective welfare states, compensation through price subsidies, rather than income transfers or guaranteed employment, drives their preference for a large state presence in economic production. Historically, Latin America's SOEs provided only a limited number of jobs, yet citizens oppose privatization because SOEs guaranteed low prices for many basic services. In the end, Latin Americans look like small-state Europeans but for slightly different reasons.

That said, Katzenstein and other political economy scholars might not entirely grasp the motivations underlying the policy configurations and preferences of citizens in small states. Katzenstein betrays the common export or producer-oriented bias because he claims that the need for open foreign markets and inexpensive inputs in export-oriented sectors drives the openness of small states. Small economies, however, are also dependent on foreign producers to fill their demand for consumer goods because they cannot manufacture everything themselves. As a result, consumers as well as producers drive the need for small states to maintain international openness.[5] Scholars of political economy and Latin America too often

[5] Political economists typically ignore consumer interests on the presumption that the masses do not notice and mobilize in favor of the diffuse benefits of lower prices. For example, a spate of research suggests that freer trade is more likely to exist in democracies

overlook the seemingly obvious and noncontroversial fact that citizens support policies that they believe to have lowered prices.

The Latin American Left's Ambivalent Mandate

The public opinion findings in this book finally provide some data on mass preferences that can help elucidate the nature of Latin America's new governing Left and its mandate. Many observers criticize the Left for being too moderate in power. A typical claim holds that the Left has violated the antimarket mandate that voters have granted it. I argue that public opinion *has* constrained the new Left and that the new leadership *has* largely pursued the mandate voters granted to it. Substantive policy changes under the new Left match voters' pro-globalization, antiprivatization preferences. Leftist leaders have stalled and reversed privatizations, but they have maintained and in some instances even increased their country's openness to international markets. Overall, Latin America's new Left is moderate because democracy has tied leaders to voters' *ambivalence* toward the Washington Consensus.

Despite their often fiery campaign rhetoric, the new governing Left in Latin America has not overturned the new market-oriented model. Trade continues to be relatively free, most foreign investors are still welcome, and many former SOEs remain under private ownership. To explain this moderation, observers cite the constraints imposed by international financial institutions, foreign investors and multinational corporations, earmarked expenditures and other fiscal commitments, fractious governing coalitions, and well-organized domestic beneficiaries of the new model. Although not always mentioned explicitly, these explanations evoke the "mandate violations" or "policy switches" of the reform implementation years: Candidates campaign from the statist Left, then elected politicians govern from the market-friendly Right (Stokes 2001a).

Latin America's newly enfranchised citizens and the preferences of its median voters, however, are missing from this list of possible reasons for the Left's moderation. I argue that Latin American governments have not

not because of its consumption benefits but because of its presumed macroeconomic or labor-market benefits (Milner and Kubota 2005). This book demonstrates that consumers do notice and prefer lower prices as well as the policies that lead to them, so consumers should be the most obvious constituency in favor of trade liberalization. Because mass enfranchisement empowers consumers relative to well-organized rent-seeking producer groups, consumer interests are the reason more trade follows democracy.

implemented a wholesale reversal of market reforms *because their citizens have not called for one.* Latin American governments and even the new Left have followed and been constrained by the mandate that voters have granted them: Maintain free trade but curb privatization. In voting for the Left, citizens are not calling for a return to protectionism or developmentalism. Moreover, citizens are not ideologues committed to statism. Instead, they are consumers who have granted a mandate for low prices. In recent experiences, this has meant stalling or even reversing the privatization process while keeping protectionist barriers low.

Most concrete reversals of market policies have been concentrated in the areas of privatization, addressing the outcry against private ownership and the resulting price increases. Governments of widely varying ideological stripes have stalled, blocked, or reversed privatizations in a number of utility sectors, often in response to protests and even public opinion. Although many SOEs remain candidates for the auction block, the privatization process has been largely defunct in Latin America since 2000.

Privatization has been a particular whipping boy of the region's new Left. In 2001, Hugo Chávez halted what he saw as the creeping privatization of Venezuela's enormous gas and petroleum industry, requiring the state to hold a majority stake in all future deals and raising taxes on existing private investors in the sector. In his third inauguration speech six years hence, Chávez announced the re-nationalization of the electricity and telecommunications sectors. During his first year in office, Evo Morales followed the lead of his political mentor and declared the "nationalization" of Bolivia's natural gas and mining sectors. In 2006, Néstor Kirchner canceled a large and long-standing contract with the private owners of Aguas Argentinas after the company was prohibited from raising prices and produced contaminated drinking water.

Such abrupt policy shifts stoked rancor between these left-of-center presidents and the almost exclusively *foreign* investors and statesmen who stood to lose from the breaking of existing contracts. Kirchner butted heads with the French, Morales did so with Brazil, and Chávez thumbed his nose, as always, at the United States (among other countries). These incidents, along with the vitriolic nationalist rhetoric of these and other left-leaning leaders, incline many observers to interpret reversals of privatization as a regional backlash against globalization as well.

Outbursts against foreign investors, however, have focused on those who have acquired existing assets (asset transfer) through the privatization process, not those who have created new assets with greenfield investment.

Moreover, this interpretation of an antiglobalization backlash does not correspond to the region's or even the new Left's orientation toward trade. The Left's refusal to reverse trade liberalization measures is not a mandate violation but rather wholly in line with voters' preferences. Presidents have hesitated to raise protectionist barriers because such measures would lead to inflation. Leftists, even overzealous ones with nationalist intentions, remain hamstrung by consumer demands.

For example, free trade agreements with the United States continued to proliferate well after the left turn began. While the failure of the FTAA fueled interpretations of a backlash against globalization, by 2008 *most* Latin American countries either had or were pursuing free trade deals with the United States.[6] Moreover, Mercosul countries Argentina and Brazil were aggressively seeking trade links with other developing countries, and they did not raise average tariffs. In his first year in office, Morales himself pushed for enhanced economic integration with the EU and trade preferences from the United States, and he refused to pull out of the Andean Pact at Chávez's urging (Cameron 2006). Even Chávez, despite withdrawing from the Andean Pact because of Colombia's and Peru's agreements with the United States, oversaw expanded trade with his imperial nemesis. In Chávez's first eight years in office (1999 to 2007), the dollar value of imports from the United States to Venezuela doubled, with one observer citing Venezuela's "*de facto* free trade agreement with the United States" (Naím 2006, 42). During this time, Chávez also left his country's overall average tariff level in the low teens.[7]

That mandates, median voters, and moderation are now the order of the day in Latin America's new democracies is not to be taken for granted. According to scholars, the 1980s and 1990s were characterized by not just mandate violations but also by "radical new economic policies" and "delegative" presidencies in which voter preferences were ignored (O'Donnell 1994; Weyland 2002). Hyperinflationary crises and fragile new democratic institutions afforded sitting presidents much leeway in addressing economic ills (Stokes 2001a; Weyland 1998a). However, while

---

[6] These countries were Chile (through a bilateral deal), Colombia (seeking a bilateral deal), Costa Rica (through the Dominican Republic–Central American Free Trade Agreement, DR-CAFTA), Dominican Republic (through DR-CAFTA), El Salvador (through DR-CAFTA), Guatemala (through DR-CAFTA), Honduras (through DR-CAFTA), Mexico (through NAFTA), Nicaragua (through DR-CAFTA), Panama (seeking a bilateral deal), and Peru (through a bilateral deal).

[7] Trade data are from the U.S. Census Bureau: http://censtats.census.gov/sitc/sitc.shtml.

The Politics of Consumismo

Latin America in the 2000s remains rife with economic problems, the severity and immediacy of crisis are gone. In *most* countries, democratic institutions are in place and stable, even if imperfect. The democratic politics of incrementalism and moderation are now the standard means of governing, especially as politicians compete for the loyalties of centrist voters. As in established democracies, voters would punish leaders who implement drastic policy swings (Stimson 2004). Although the extraordinary times of the transitional decades have left their imprint on voters, a more normal politics is establishing itself in the new millennium.

The limited capacity of elites to shape public opinion is a reassuring part of this new setting. Elite rhetoric takes a back seat to voters' perceptions of material consequences in establishing the aggregate levels of support for various policies. Leaders, no matter how charismatic, cannot persuade citizens to accept or support policies that do not exert a positive and visible impact on economic well-being. This puts the Left in a catch-22. It is unable to implement a wholesale reversal of the Washington Consensus because it has no mandate to do so, yet this forced moderation weakens its ability to generate public opposition to the market. This is, however, the nature of democratic politics.

Consumption and Cleavages in Latin America

Latin American citizens have had a variety of experiences as consumers of newly privatized utility services and imported goods and capital. Many made their first-ever phone calls from their own private lines. Many saw their monthly electricity bills increase dramatically. Some bought their first VCRs to enjoy foreign films, and others decided to start shopping exclusively in grocery stores with foreign names. For these reasons, consumption concerns have overtaken labor-market interests as the dominant shaper of Latin Americans' attitudes toward the primary economic issues of the day.

Although seemingly idiosyncratic, the frequency of different types of consumptive experiences like these has been related to wealth. In recent years, the poor have been more likely than the rich to make their first-ever phone calls. In contrast, the rich have been more likely than the poor to shop in foreign-owned shopping malls and hypermarkets. Because of the visible and intense relevance these experiences have for incumbent economic policies, one might expect the region to experience a reorientation of its politics and political cleavages around differences, and especially wealth-related differences, in consumer tastes.

Is the region heading toward a politics of nonhomothetic tastes, where disparities in consumption patterns and not labor-market assets structure political competition and contestation? I argue that differences in consumer tastes have only limited potential to forge deep and lasting political cleavages because consumer tastes unify citizens across wealth levels more than they divide them.[8] In fact, the rise of *consumismo* is a reason why wealth-related cleavages have grown weaker in Latin America in the new market era.

One might reasonably expect the newfound relevance of consumer interests to forge deeper class-based political cleavages than those existing when labor-market interests held sway. Differences in wealth-related consumer tastes *have* played a role in structuring consumer-protection movements that sprang up around the issues of utility privatization. Middle-income groups who already had phones spurred movements against telecommunications privatization (Rhodes 2006). Poor individuals who spent a relatively large share of their income on potable water spearheaded movements concerned with the cost and quality of water (Olivera 2004).

Moreover and more generally, nonhomothetic tastes pervade daily life in ways that reinforce perceptions of economic differentiation, thus potentially increasing the politicization of group disparities (Bourdieu 1986; Edwards 2000). Citizens know where wealthy and poor consumers shop, dine, and play. A heightened focus on consumption can reinforce wealth-based distinctions and perceptions of social exclusion if the two groups rarely meet in these venues. When they do encounter one another, the "conspicuous consumption" by the wealthy of "positional" goods and services – that is, the acquisition of goods and services solely to convey status – may also deepen feelings of resentment and marginalization among those who cannot afford such luxuries (Hirsch 1976; Veblen 1899). Globalization itself may exacerbate such divisions: The entrance of a new set of flashy foreign goods, many of which are geared toward upper-income consumers, may trigger new but largely frustrated consumption desires among the poor (Ger and Belk 1996; James 2000; Nurkse 1953).

---

[8] In a study of consumer protection movements in Argentina, Brazil, and Chile, Rhodes (2006, 7) agrees: "It would be premature to claim that much of Latin America has undergone a full and irreversible swing toward consumer-based politics." She does conclude, however, that the rise of such movements is a sign that the region has switched from the labor-based corporatist style of interest representation to a more pluralist one.

Moreover, the amount one can consume, not the amount one can produce, ultimately defines individual well-being. On this point, theorists as different as Karl Marx and Adam Smith agreed:

Consumption is the sole end purpose of all production. (Smith 1776, 376)

The ultimate cause of all real crises is always the . . . restricted consumption of the masses. (Marx 1894, 615)

The new consumption-based thinking may orient individuals toward the most fundamental aspect, rather than the intermediate causes, of economic well-being. The fact that individuals can diversify their income sources by supplementing the returns to their employable assets with investment returns, rental incomes, transfer payments, and familial support may further mitigate the politicization of labor-market factors.

In the end, however, I conclude that the relevance of consumer interests to economic policy attitudes is unlikely to forge new and lasting political cleavages in Latin America. The primary reason for this is that consumer interests vary less across individuals than producer interests do. Most individuals benefit from lower prices for a particular good or commodity. In contrast, far fewer individuals benefit from wage increases in a particular firm or sector because wage changes and negotiations are often a zero-sum game. Moreover, all consumers must devote a certain share of their incomes to certain necessities, giving individuals from various income groups a common denominator of shared consumer interests. In contrast, income-earning sources are atomized into myriad economic sectors and investment options. Overall, differences in consumer tastes are less likely than differences in labor-market assets to mobilize and pit one group against another in political contestation. The rise of *consumismo* thus contributes to the puzzling political irrelevance of class in a region where objective economic disparities are vast (Roberts 2002).

This book has provided substantial support for this claim. All consumers, save the relatively few who actually work in or have assets in a utility sector, want lower-priced electricity and telecommunications services. Once utilities were privatized in Latin America, citizens' opposition was rather uniform across income groups. (See Chapter 5.) Similarly, all consumers prefer less expensive, higher-quality tradable goods to more expensive ones. In fact, the fascination with foreign goods itself cuts across income groups. While this book highlights the hold that foreign goods and

entertainment have on middle- and upper-income Latin Americans, poor
consumers are not far behind in their propensity to create a "fetish of
foreignness" (Tinsman 2006, 19):

A century ago, a fairly narrow elite was fascinated by the expensive furniture,
elegantly tailored clothes, and the fine wines of London and Paris. Today the pole
of attraction is mainly the popular material culture of the United States, and the
appeal of these goods reaches much deeper into Latin American society than
before. All manner of things from the global market, but especially from the United
States, wash into the new shopping centers and trickle even into the most remote
niches of rural Latin America. (Bauer 2001, 202)[9]

For these reasons, globalization has *weakened*, rather than strengthened,
feelings of frustration due to unfulfilled consumption goals among lower-
income groups. The conspicuous consumption of positional goods, especially those whose status intensity is conveyed by their foreign name, is
certainly *not* a creation of the current globalization wave in Latin America
(Bauer 2001; Needell 1987). Moreover, many of the foreign-made positional goods from the import substitution era – athletic shoes, cosmetics,
satellite televisions, consumer electronics – are now within the reach of
even low-income consumers precisely because of the price declines caused
by globalization. Consumption has been "democratized" (Guedes and
Oliveira 2006). As a result, rather than creating or intensifying them,
globalization has merely shifted what constitutes status-conveying goods
or services; the rich now seek out nonnecessities, such as expensive automobiles, foreign travel, and private education, that differ from the acqui-
sitions of poor people merely in terms of quality.

Another reason why Latin America may not be heading toward the
permanent politics of consumer tastes lies in the cognitive underpinnings
of citizens' perceptions of the Washington Consensus. The new consumer
orientations may be transient. The major economic changes occurring
between the 1980s and the early 2000s may have induced a "perfect storm"

[9] In a study of how wage increases produced new consumption patterns among unskilled
workers in Chile's export-oriented fruit industry, Tinsman (2006, 19) concurs: "It was a
commodity's *foreignness* that made it explicitly esteemed and coveted. . . . Fruit workers,
like other Chileans, increasingly measured their advances or failures in terms of the ability
to make individual purchases of imported goods" (emphasis in the original). Some observers view these preferences among the poor (and thus globalization in general) with disdain,
criticizing imports and multinational corporations for "distorting" the consumption
structure of lower-class individuals who should not be "wasting" precious income and
foreign exchange on luxury items and other nonnecessities (Cardoso and Faletto 1979; Ger
and Belk 1996; Needell 1987).

of developments that delivered an overwhelming amount of consumption-oriented information to Latin America's mass publics. Developments such as hyperinflationary crises and their solutions, abrupt influxes of new foreign goods and foreign investment, overvalued currencies, and abrupt changes in the quality and cost of widely used utility services heightened citizens' sensitivities toward consumer interests during these two decades. These sensitivities, however, may eventually fade as the novelty and static impact of these changes become a thing of the distant past. In short, the implementation of market-friendly policies may have created an acute but ephemeral "consumptive moment" in Latin American history.

A final reason consumer-oriented cleavages are unlikely to develop is that consumption patterns are less "sticky," or specific to a particular usage, than employable assets. A redeployment of labor-market skills upon loss of employment typically mandates an income loss during job search and retraining. This loss is far more costly than the search for a consumption alternative. The end of monopolies and oligopolies gives consumers the opportunity to "substitute away" from high-priced or low-quality consumer options (Porto 2006). For example, millions of Latin Americans in recent years have chosen to substitute away from their monopolistic fixed-line telephone providers by turning to mobile telephone services that are offered in more competitive markets. The number of mobile phone subscriptions surpassed the number of fixed lines in 2005, a year in which, perhaps not coincidentally, mass support for privatization began to rebound (ITU 2005). (Revisit Figure 4.1.) Similarly, poor individuals who cannot afford foreign-owned supermarket or shopping mall commodities can still purchase necessities in traditional markets. As a result, the relative lack of consumer "option specificity" allows citizens to substitute away from unattractive consumer options and works against the wholesale politicization of consumer concerns. Just as a decrease in the specificity of employable assets works against their politicization, an increase in consumer options works against the politicization of consumer concerns (Frieden 1991). Overall, *consumer interests typically fail to structure political contestation not because they are diffuse and imperceptible*, as economists and political economists so often think, *but because they unify more than they divide*.

There are thus elements of truth in claims by some observers that Latin American citizens are "co-opted by *consumismo*." Market reforms in Latin America *have* politically demobilized many individuals and weakened economic civil society because they tend to separate workers' political consciousness from their labor-market interests and reorient them toward their consumer goals (Kurtz 2004; Roberts 1998). Consumption-oriented citizens are not entirely quiescent politically: The rise of consumer protection movements attests to this (Rhodes 2006). Overall, however, consumption-minded individuals are less likely to be active, participating citizens, as implied in the epigraphs to this chapter (Colburn 2002; Silva 1995; Tinsman 2006). The reasons for this are now clear: A nation of consumers is less politically divisive than a nation of producers.

Survey Data Appendix

QUESTION WORDINGS AND SAMPLING FRAMES

Measures of Elite Support for Market Reforms in Latin America

Figure 3.3

Elite Support for Privatization of Public Services (PELA, 1994 to 2004): "Which of the following statements best summarizes your personal attitude toward the issue of the privatization of public services? (2) I would privatize all public services. (1) I would only privatize services of low profitability. (1) I would privatize all public services except for those that are used by a majority of the population." Although not offered explicitly, interviewers also coded the following two responses: (0) "I would leave things in their current state." (0) "I wouldn't privatize any public services." The failure to offer these two as explicit options probably results in an overestimation of support for privatization, although many respondents offered these answers nonetheless. The neutrality point is 0.5.

Elite Support for Free Trade in General (PELA, 1998 to 2001): "Of the different regional integration schemes that I will show you, which would be, in your opinion, the most adequate for your country? (0) One that includes countries in our immediate geographic and cultural area. (0) One that, besides including countries in our immediate geographic and cultural area, also has privileged relations with the United States. (0) One that groups together the largest number of Latin American countries. (1) One that, besides grouping together the largest number of Latin American countries, has preferential trade agreements with other non–Latin American countries." Because these zero-coded responses are not necessarily explicit expressions of protectionism, treating the last item as the only pro-trade response may underestimate elite support for trade liberalization. The neutrality point is 0.5.

Elite Support for Regional Trade Pacts (PELA, 1998 to 2004): "Are you in favor of your country's membership in [Andean Pact/CACM/Mercosul/ NAFTA]? (1) Yes. (0) No." The neutrality point is 0.5.

Elite Support for the FTAA (PELA, 2002 to 2004): "Regarding the different international forums of which your country is a member, what is, in your opinion, the degree of interest in being a member of each? Membership in a future FTAA. (1) A lot, (1) somewhat, (0) little, (0) none." The neutrality point is 0.5.

Elite Support for Foreign Investment (PELA, 1994 to 2001): "Keeping in mind the privatization process that is occurring in your country's economy, how high is your interest in the investment capital coming from each of the following places: (a) the United States, (b) Japan, (c) the European Union (excluding Spain), (d) Spain, (e) other Latin American countries? (5) Very high, (4) high, (3) medium, (2) low, (1) very low." For each respondent, I take the average answer over these five questions. The neutrality point is 3.

To derive the "Mean (Weighted by Party Size) Across all Countries" for each year, I first established each *party's* mean score by calculating the mean survey response among all legislators of each party. I then derived each *country's* mean score by calculating the *weighted* mean across all parties within a given country; in calculating the country mean score, each party's mean score was weighted by the party's seat share in the lower house.[1] (Parties with fewer than six respondents were excluded.) Weighting in this way simply ensures that large parties have greater weight than do small ones in establishing the estimated balance of elite opinion in a given country. I then calculated a *yearly* mean based on all available country means in each year. Each yearly mean, when available, is calculated from about three to six country means. (No country appears in the dataset more than once per legislative session, so most countries appeared only three times between 1994 and 2004.) Finally, the actual lines depicted in the figures are smoothed values (fitted with a third-order polynomial in long time series or a straight line in short ones) of these yearly means.

---

[1] Legislative seats data are from the Election Results Archive at http://cdp.binghamton.edu/ era/index.html.

To derive the "Mean among Right-of-Center Parties" and the "Mean among Left-of-Center Parties," I calculated the mean of all *party* means for all appropriate parties. Parties were *not* weighted for their size.

Figure 6.3

Foreign Investment (Hagopian, 1995) and Privatization (Hagopian, 1997): "Independently of your party's position, what was your position on the following government proposals? (a) Change in the definition of national capital (revoking Article 171). (b) Privatization of CVRD. (1) Total opposition, (2) partial opposition, (3) neutral, (4) partial support, (5) total support." Both questions were asked in 2000, but I plot them in the respective years in which these policies were voted on in the National Congress. The neutrality point is 3.

Privatization (Hagopian, 2000) and Free Trade (Hagopian, 2000): "How would you classify the effects of the following government policies on the well-being of the country? (a) The program of privatizing federal industries. (b) The international commercial opening (*abertura comercial internacional*). (1) Very negative, (2) negative, (3) neutral, (4) positive, (5) very positive." The neutrality point is 3.

Privatization (Power, 1997, 2001, 2005): "I would like to ask for your general evaluation of these aspects of Brazilian democracy since 1985. Using a scale that goes from 1 (most negative evaluation) to 10 (most positive evaluation), indicate your opinion about the following items. The privatization (*desestatização*) of the economy in recent years." The neutrality point is 5.5.

For weighted means, I first established each *party's* mean score by calculating the mean survey response among all legislators of each party. I then derived the overall mean (for "All" legislators or "CC" legislators) score by calculating the *weighted* (by the party's seat share in the lower house) mean across all relevant parties. Parties with fewer than six respondents were excluded.

Measures of Mass Support for Market Reforms in Latin America

The percentages favoring market reforms, as measured by these questions, appear in figures and text throughout Chapters 4 and 7. Many are also used as dependent variables in Chapters 5 and 8. Questions are listed below by figure.

Figure 1.1

Free Trade Helps Country (LB, 1996): "In general, do you think that trade with other countries, like the buying and selling of products, (1) helps or (0) hurts the economy of this country?" Figure plots the predicted percent answering "helps."

Foreign Investment Should Be Encouraged (LB, 1999): "Foreign investment should be encouraged. Do you (4) strongly agree, (3) agree, (2) disagree, or (1) strongly disagree with this statement?" Figure plots the predicted percent answering "strongly agree" or "agree."

Privatization Is Good for Country (LB, 2001): "The privatization of state-owned enterprises has been beneficial to the country. Do you (4) strongly agree, (3) agree, (2) disagree, or (1) strongly disagree with this statement?" Figure plots the predicted percent answering "strongly agree" or "agree."

Privatization by Sectors: Pensions (LB, 1999): "From the following list of activities, which do you think should be (0) majority-owned by the state and which do you think should be (1) majority-owned by private hands? Retirement pensions."

Figures 4.1 and 7.1

Private Ownership Should Be Increased (WVS, 1990, 1996, and 2000; DV in Chapter 5): "Now I'd like you to tell me your views on various issues. How would you place your views on this scale? 1 means you agree completely with the statement on the left ("Government owner-ship of business and industry should be increased"); 10 means you agree completely with the statement on the right ("Private ownership of business and industry should be increased"); and if your views fall somewhere in between, you can choose any number in between." Figures plot the percentage of opinionated respondents answering "7" through "10."

Change to Privatization Is Good for Country (WSJA, 1998; DV in Chapters 4 and 5): "Do you think that the change toward privatization is good or bad for the country?" Figures plot the percentage of opinionated respondents answering "good." This variable is coded (1) bad, (2) both good and bad or neither, (3) good.

State Should Yield to Private Sector (LB, 1999, 2001, and 2002): "The state should leave productive activity to the private sector. Do you strongly agree, agree, disagree, or strongly disagree with this statement?" Figures plot the percentage of opinionated respondents answering "strongly agree" or "agree."

Privatization Is Good for Country (LB, 1999, 2000, 2001, 2002, 2003, and 2005; DV in Chapters 4, 5, and 8): "The privatization of state-owned enterprises has been beneficial to the country. Do you (4) strongly agree, (3) agree, (2) disagree, or (1) strongly disagree with this statement?" Figures plot the percentage of opinionated respondents answering "strongly agree" or "agree."

Price/Quality of Privatized Services Is Good (LB, 2003, 2004, 2005, and 2006): "State-owned services like water, light, etc., have been privatized. Taking into account the price and the quality, are you currently much more satisfied, satisfied, less satisfied, or much less satisfied with privatized services?" Figures plot the percentage of opinionated respondents answering "much more satisfied" or "satisfied."

In Favor of Privatization (Ibope, 1990): "Now I'm going to read some measures that President Collor has taken or is taking. I would like you to tell me if you are against or in favor of these measures. Privatization of state-owned businesses." Figure 7.1 plots the percentage "in favor." This survey is archived at the Centro de Estudos de Opinião Pública (CESOP) as study #00229.

In Favor of Privatization (Ibope, 1996): "The National 'Destatization' Program is privatizing some state-owned businesses. Privatizing a state-owned business means transferring or selling the business from the government to the private sector. Are you in favor of or against the privatization of state-owned businesses, or do you not have an opinion on the issue?" Figure 7.1 plots the percentage "in favor." (CESOP #00555)

In Favor of Privatization (4-City, 1999 and 2005):   "In the last ten/ fifteen years, many state-owned businesses, which were directed by the state, were sold to the private sector in a process called 'privatization.' People have different opinions about privatization. Are you in favor, against, or do you not have an opinion on privatization? Are you strongly or slightly in favor/against?" Figure 7.1 plots the percentage of opinionated respondents answering "strongly favor" or "slightly favor."

Change to Privatization Is Good for Country (4-City, 2005):   Question wording is equivalent to that of *Change to privatization is good for country* (*WSJA*). Figure 7.1 plots the percentage of opinionated respondents answering "good."

Figures 4.2 and 7.2

Privatization by Sectors (LB, 1995 and 1999):   "From the following list of activities, which do you think should be (0) majority-owned by the state and which do you think should be (1) majority-owned by private hands?" These were coded (1) state and (3) private in chapter 4. Figures plot the percentage of opinionated respondents answering "private hands." The *Index of support for utility privatization* (DV in Chapters 5 and 8) variable is each respondent's score on the first dimension extracted from a principal components analysis conducted on the four utility sector variables: water, sewerage, telecommunications, and electricity. *Privatization by sectors: Pensions* is also used as a dependent variable in Chapter 5.

Privatization by Sectors (WSJA, 1998):   "Please tell me which activities should be the property of the (1) government and which should be (3) private?" Volunteered responses of "mixed" or "both" were coded as 2. Figures plot the percentage of opinionated respondents answering "private." The *Index of support for utility privatization* (DV in Chapter 5) variable is each respondent's score on the first dimension extracted from a principal components analysis conducted on the three utility sector variables: water, telecommunications, and electricity. The *Privatization by sectors: Pensions* question is also used as a dependent variable in Chapter 5.

Privatization of Oil Sector (Ibope, 1989): "Petrobrás is a state-owned business – that is, the federal government is responsible for its administration. Recently, much has been said about privatizing state-owned businesses – in other words, transferring the administration of Petrobrás to private groups. In your opinion, should Petrobrás continue to be a state-owned business, should it be a private business, are you indifferent as to whether it's private or state-owned, or do you not have an opinion on this issue?" Figure 7.2 plots the percentage of opinionated respondents answering "private business." (CESOP #00204)

Privatization by Sectors (4-City, 2005): Question wordings are equivalent to those of *Privatization by sectors (WSJA)*. Figure 7.2 plots the percentage of opinionated respondents answering "private."

Figures 4.3 and 7.3

Free Trade Helps Country (LB, 1996; DV in Chapters 5 and 8): "In general, do you think that trade with other countries, like the buying and selling of products, (1) helps or (0) hurts the economy of this country?" Figures plot the percentage of opinionated respondents answering "helps."

Imports Help Country (LB, 1996): "From what you know or have heard, how do you think imports influence the national economy? Help a lot, help a little, hurt a little, hurt a lot." Figures plot the percentage of opinionated respondents answering "help a lot" or "help a little."

Free Trade Helps Country (WSJA, 1998; DV in Chapter 5): "Over the last few years the country has had more and more business and trade with other countries. This tendency is called 'free trade.' Do you think that free trade is good or bad for the country? Very or somewhat?" (4) Very good, (3) somewhat good, (2) somewhat bad, (1) very bad. Figures plot the percentage of opinionated respondents answering "very good" or "somewhat good."

In Favor of FTAA (WSJA, 1998; DV in Chapter 5): "The presidents of North and South America are talking about forming a single free trade zone for the entire continent. Are you in favor of or against this idea? Very or slightly?" (4) Very in favor, (3) slightly in favor, (2) slightly against, (1) very in favor. Figures plot the percentage of opinionated respondents answering "very in favor" or "slightly in favor."

In Favor of FTAA (LB, 2001; DV in Chapters 5 and 8):   "As you may know, an agreement has been reached for a Free Trade Area of the Americas, which would include Latin America, the United States, and Canada. Do you think that the establishment of the Free Trade Area of the Americas will (4) help a lot, (3) help somewhat, (2) help a little, or (1) not help the economic development of your country?" Unless otherwise noted, figures plot the percentage of opinionated respondents answering "a lot," "somewhat," or "a little."

Regional Trade Agreement Benefits Country (LB, 1995; DV in Chapters 5 and 8):   "All things considered, would you say your country (1) benefits or (0) not from its future links to [name of regional trade agreement]?" Figures plot the percentage of opinionated respondents answering "benefits."
(1996, 1997, 1999, 2001, 2003; DV in Chapters 5 and 8):   "All things considered, would you say your country (4) benefits a lot, (3) quite a bit, (2) a little, or (1) not at all for being part of [name of regional trade agreement]?" Unless otherwise noted, figures plot the percentage of opinionated respondents answering "a lot," "quite a bit," or "a little."

In Favor of Latin American Economic Integration (LB, 1995 and 1996):   "In general, are you in favor of or against the economic integration of Latin American countries, even when this implies some costs and sacrifices for people in your country?"
(1997, 1999, 2001, and 2002):   "In general, are you in favor of or against the economic integration of Latin American countries?" Figures plot the percentage of opinionated respondents answering "in favor."

In Favor of Liberalizing Imports (Ibope, 1990):   "Now I'm going to read some measures that President Collor has taken or is taking. I would like you to tell me if you are against or in favor of these measures. Liberalizing imports." Figure 7.3 plots the percentage of opinionated respondents answering "in favor." (CESOP #00229)

Government Should Encourage Foreign Goods (DTF, 1995):   "In your opinion, should the government discourage or encourage the sale of foreign goods in the country?" Figure 7.3 plots the percentage of opinionated respondents answering "encourage." (CESOP #00432)

In Favor of Free Trade (4-City, 1999 and 2005):   "In the last ten/fifteen years, Brazil's trade with foreign countries grew. This increase in trade is known as 'trade opening.' Some people favor and others oppose this trade opening. Are you in favor, against, or do you not have an opinion on trade opening? Are you strongly or slightly in favor/against?" Figure 7.3 plots the percentage of opinionated respondents answering "strongly favor" or "slightly favor." This question is part of the *Index of support for free trade* created from a principal components analysis and used as a DV in Chapter 8.

In Favor of Free Trade (Ibope, 1999):   "Some countries favor free trade – that is, few restrictions on the ability of countries to buy and sell to each other so as to encourage trade. Other countries favor restrictions on trade in order to protect their own products from foreign competition. Which policy do you personally favor – free trade or restrictions?" Figure 7.3 plots the percentage of opinionated respondents answering "free trade." This survey is archived at the Roper Center as USIA Poll #1999-I199021.

In Favor of FTAA (Ibope, 1999):   "Some people say that economic integration among countries of the Americas is a good idea because open markets help to create jobs and lift living standards. Other people say that economic integration is not a good idea because the costs for Brazil outweigh the benefits. Which view is closer to your own, or haven't you heard enough to say?" Figure 7.3 plots the percentage of opinionated respondents answering "It is a good idea. . . ." (Roper USIA Poll #1999-I199021)

In Favor of FTAA (4-City, 2005):   "The presidents of North America and South America are talking about forming a free trade area for the entire continent. Are you in favor of or against this idea? Are you strongly or slightly in favor/against?" Figure 7.3 plots the percentage of opinionated respondents answering "strongly favor" or "slightly favor."

Free Trade Helps Country (4-City, 2005):   Question wording is equivalent to that of *Free trade helps country (WSJA)*. This question is part of the *Index of support for free trade* created from a principal components analysis and used as a DV in Chapter 8.

Brazil Benefits from Mercosul (Ibope, 1999): "Taking all into account, how much would you say that Brazil benefits from belonging to Mercosul? A great deal, a fair amount, not very much, or not at all?" Figure 7.3 plots the percentage of opinionated respondents answering "a great deal" or "a fair amount." (Roper USIA Poll #1999-I199021)

Figures 4.4 and 7.4

Foreign Investment Is Good for Country (LB, 1995 and 1999; DV in Chapters 5 and 8, except for 1999): "In general, do you consider foreign investment to be (1) beneficial or (0) harmful for the development of the country?" Figures plot the percentage of opinionated respondents answering "beneficial."

Foreign Investment Is Good for Economy (WSJA, 1998; DV in Chapter 5): "Which phrase is closer to your way of thinking? (1) 'Foreign investment is good because it helps the economy grow' or (0) 'Foreign investment is bad because it gives other countries too much influence over our economy.'" Figures plot the percentage of opinionated respondents choosing the former statement.

Foreign Investment Should Be Encouraged (LB, 1999 and 2001; DV in Chapters 5 and 8): "Foreign investment should be encouraged. Do you (4) strongly agree, (3) agree, (2) disagree, or (1) strongly disagree with this statement?" Figures plot the percentage of opinionated respondents answering "strongly agree" or "agree."

Large Foreign Companies Are Good (Pew, 2002 and 2007): "As I read a list of groups and organizations, for each, please tell me what kind of influence the group is having on the way things are going in the country. Is the influence of large companies from other countries very good, somewhat good, somewhat bad, or very bad in your country?" Figure 4.4 plots the percentage of opinionated respondents answering "very good" or "somewhat good."

In Favor of Foreign Investment (Ibope, 1991): "Now, considering foreign businesses and multinationals, are you in favor without restrictions; in favor but controlled by the government; or against them under any circumstances?" Figure 7.4 plots the percentage of opinionated respondents answering "in favor."

Foreign Investment Is Good for Economy (4-City, 2005): The question wording is equivalent to that of *Foreign investment is good for economy* (*WSJA*). Figure 7.4 plots the percentage of opinionated respondents answering "Foreign investment is good. . . ."

In Favor of Foreign Investment (4-City, 2005): "Much has been said about foreign businesses investing in Brazil, which has grown over the last ten/fifteen years. Are you in favor, against, or do you not have an opinion on this growth in foreign investment in Brazil? Are you strongly or slightly in favor/against?" Figure 7.4 plots the percentage of opinionated respondents answering "strongly favor" or "slightly favor."

Figure 4.6

Regional Trade Bloc's Effects (WSJA, 1998): "Do you think that [Andean Pact/CACM/Mercosul/NAFTA] helped or harmed (a) the prices of consumer goods, (b) employment, (c) salaries? A lot or a little?" (5) Helped a lot, (4) helped a little, (3) neutral, (2) hurt a little, (1) hurt a lot. Individuals who had never heard of their country's regional trade bloc (40%) were not asked these questions. They were also not asked in the Dominican Republic. In 1998, Chile was an associate member of Mercosul. Bolivia was an associate member of Mercosul and a full member of the Andean Pact, so Bolivians were queried about the latter.

Chapter 4 Text

Globalization's Impact on the Country (Pew, 2002): "What do you think about the growing trade and business ties between your country and other countries? Do you think it is a very good thing, somewhat good, somewhat bad, or a very bad thing for your country?" The text reports the percentage of opinionated respondents answering "very good" or "somewhat good."

Globalization's Impact on My Family (Pew, 2002): "Now thinking about you and your family, do you think the growing trade and business ties between your country and other countries are very good, somewhat good, somewhat bad, or very bad for you and your family?" The text reports the percentage of opinionated respondents answering "very good" or "somewhat good."

Globalization's Effect on My Family (Globescan, 2003):   "As you may know, there are both positive and negative impacts from increasing globalization occurring in the world. By 'globalization,' I mean the increased trade between countries in goods, services, and investment. Thinking of you and your family's interests, do you think the overall effect of globalization is very positive, somewhat positive, somewhat negative, or very negative?" The text reports the percentage of opinionated respondents answering "very positive" or "somewhat positive."

Figure 7.5: Panel B

Future Direction of Privatization (4-City, 2005):   "Some people think that more state-owned businesses should be privatized, while others think that the privatizations of recent years should be reversed. Do you think that more businesses should be privatized [further liberalization], the number of privatized businesses should be maintained [status quo], or the privatizations of recent years should be reversed [reverse liberalization]?"

Future Direction of Trade Policy (4-City, 2005):   "Do you think that (0) the government should prohibit the sale of foreign products in Brazil [reverse liberalization], (1) the government should prohibit the sale of some foreign products in Brazil [status quo], or (2) the government should allow Brazilians to purchase whatever foreign products they want [further liberalization]?" This question is part of the *Index of support for free trade* created from a principal components analysis and used as a DV in Chapter 8.

Future Direction of Foreign Investment Policy (4-City, 2005):   "With which of the following sentences about foreign investment do you agree more? The government should allow foreign investors to invest in Brazil [status quo]? Or the government should make foreign investors leave the country [reverse liberalization]?"

Chapter 7 Text

Change to a Contribution Time Minimum (4-City, 1999 and 2005): "Recently, the National Congress approved pension reform (*reforma da previdência*). This reform requires a minimum number of contribution years before a worker can retire. Are you in favor, against, or do you not have an opinion on this change to minimum 'contribution time'? Are you strongly or slightly in favor/against?" The text reports the percentage of opinionated respondents answering "in favor."

Minimum Age Requirement (4-City, 2005): "Another part of the pension reform was to raise the minimum age for retirement with full benefits to sixty years for men and fifty-five years for women. People have different views about this issue. Are you in favor, against, or do you not have an opinion on the increase in the minimum age? Are you strongly or slightly in favor/against?" The text reports the percentage of opinionated respondents answering "in favor."

Government Monopolies (Ibope, 1993): "Starting in October of this year, the National Congress is going to review the 1988 Constitution. Among the questions that will be discussed is the state monopoly in certain economic sectors, such as energy and national resources. In your opinion, should foreign-owned businesses be able to participate in the exploitation of natural resources or should only the government be able to conduct these activities?" The text reports the percentage of opinionated respondents answering "foreign-owned businesses should. . . ." (CESOP #00333)

Private Investment in the Petroleum Sector (Ibope, 1995): "The new Congress intends to amend the Constitution, the supreme law of the land. Among the issues that will be discussed is the federal state monopoly in some economic sectors. Currently, for example, only Petrobrás can explore, extract, and refine petroleum. In your opinion, what is best for the country? That the law does not change, so that only Petrobrás continues extracting and refining petroleum. That besides Petrobrás, national private businesses can also extract and refine petroleum. That besides Petrobrás and other national businesses, foreign firms can also extract and refine petroleum." The text reports the percentage of opinionated respondents answering "besides Petrobrás and other national businesses, foreign firms. . . ." (CESOP #00405)

Private Investment in the Telecommunications Sector (Ibope, 1995): "The federal government also has a monopoly on telecommunications, through Telebras and state-level telephone companies.

283

In your opinion, which is better for the country? That the law does not change so that only the government continues to be active in the area of telecommunications. That besides the government, national private businesses can also be active in the area of telecommunications. That besides the government and other national businesses, foreign firms can also be active in the area of telecommunications." The text reports the percentage of opinionated respondents answering "besides the government and other national businesses, foreign firms. . . ." (CESOP #00405)

Figure 8.2 (DVs)

Focused Policy Assessments: Consumer Prices (4-City, 2005): "Think about the prices of the goods and services that you buy. Has privatization/free trade/foreign investment lowered, raised, or not changed the prices of the goods and services that you buy? Has it lowered/raised prices a little or a lot?" (5) Lowered a lot, (4) lowered a little, (3) not changed, (2) raised a little, (1) raised a lot.

Focused Policy Assessments: Number of Jobs (4-City, 2005): "And now, thinking about the number of jobs in the country, has privatization/free trade/foreign investment lowered, raised, or not changed the number of jobs in the country? Has it lowered/raised the number of jobs a little or a lot?" (5) Lowered a lot, (4) lowered a little, (3) not changed, (2) raised a little, (1) raised a lot.

Focused Policy Assessments: Macroeconomy (4-City, 2005): "Do you think that privatization/free trade/foreign investment improved, worsened, or did not change the economic situation of the country? Did it improve/worsen it a little or a lot?" (5) Improved a lot, (4) improved a little, (3) not changed, (2) worsened a little, (1) worsened a lot.

Independent Variables

The following are independent variables used in the multiple regression models in Chapters 5 and 8.

Latinbarometer

Wealth: "Do you or some member of your household possess any of the following goods?" (0) "No," (1) "Yes" scored for each of the following: color television (D), refrigerator (D), own home, computer (D), washing machine (D), telephone, automobile (D), second home/vacation home, potable water, hot water, sewerage. Wealth is the sum over all items. Items marked with "(D)" are used to create the *Preference for durable goods* variable.

Consumption Security: "Do the salary or wages that you receive and your family income allow you to satisfactorily cover your necessities? In which of the following situations do you find yourself? (0) They don't cover necessities; we have great difficulties. (1) They don't cover necessities; we have difficulties. (2) They just cover necessities without great difficulties. (3) They cover necessities well; we can save."

Class: "What is your current occupational situation? (a) Self-employed; (b) public-sector wage earner; (c) private-sector wage earner; (d) temporarily does not work; (e) retired; (f) homemaker; or (g) student? If actively working [answered a, b, or c], what type of work do you do? If unemployed or retired [answered d or e], what type of work did you do? If not a worker [answered f or g], what type of work does/did the head of household do?" Based on these answers, Latinbarometer administrators coded workers into one of the following categories, with the class category (assigned by myself) in italics and the scoring on the class variable shown in parentheses: (0) "Wage-earning employee": *Proletariat*; (2) "Self-employed" and "Wage-earning professional": *Semiautonomous employee (Proletariat–Petty Bourgeoisie)*; (3) "Self-employed professional": *Technocrat (Bourgeoisie-Proletariat)*; (5) "Mid-range executive": *Middle manager (Bourgeoisie-Proletariat)*; (6) "Independent farmer": *Petty bourgeoisie*; (7) "Business owner" (<6 employees): *Small employer (Bourgeoisie–Petty Bourgeoisie)*; (8) "Manager/supervisor": *Top manager (Proletariat-Bourgeoisie)*; (9) "Business owner" (>5 employees): *Bourgeoisie*. The class categories and scoring are assigned based on the categories derived in Wright (1979) and Wright and Perrone (1977). These sources develop a classification scheme that expands on Marx's original threefold typology – bourgeoisie, proletariat, and petty bourgeoisie – by categorizing some individuals into "contradictory" class locations that have characteristics of two of Marx's three types. Wright (1979, 40) in Table 2.3 classifies each group as having (0) "no control," (1) "minimal control," (2) "partial control," or (3) "full control" over each of the three factors of production. I use these scores, summed across the three different factors of production, to produce the scoring of categories.

Unemployed: "What is your current occupational situation? (0) Self-employed, (0) public-sector wage earner, (0) private-sector wage earner, (1) temporarily do not work, (0) retired, (0) homemaker, or (0) student?"

Public-Sector Employee: "What is your current occupational situation? (0) Self-employed, (1) public-sector wage earner, (0) private-sector wage earner, (0) temporarily do not work, (0) retired, (0) homemaker, or (0) student?"

Employment Insecurity: "How worried are you about being without work or becoming unemployed during the next twelve months? (0) Not worried, (1) a little worried, (2) worried, (3) very worried."

Education: "What schooling have you had? What was the last year of schooling you had? (1) No studies. (2) One year. (3) Two years. (4) Three years. (5) Four years. (6) Five years. (7) Six years. (8) Seven years. (9) Eight years. (10) Nine years. (11) Ten years. (12) Eleven years. (13) Twelve years. (14) Technical institute incomplete. (15) Technical institute complete. (16) University incomplete. (17) University complete."

Chief Wage Earner: "Are you the member of the household that contributes the most to family income? (1) Yes. (0) No."

Party Ideology (1995, 1996, 1997, 1999, 2001, and 2002): "If elections were held this Sunday, for which party would you vote?" Using Coppedge (1998) and Roberts and Wibbels (1999), parties and movements are coded on to a *Party ideology* scale as follows: (0) Left, (1) Center-Left, (2) Center, (3) Center-Right, (4) Right. Individuals who said they "did not know" or "would not vote" are coded as *Independents*. Independents are coded as 0 on the party ideology variable, but they are identified with separate dummy variables in all regression models.

Party Ideology (2000 and 2003): "In politics, one normally speaks of the 'Left' and the 'Right.' On a scale where 0 is Left and 10 is Right, where would you place yourself?" Individuals who said they "did not know" or "would not vote" if elections were held on Sunday (based on responses to the aforementioned question) are *Independents*, as are individuals not self-placing on the 0 to 10 scale. Among the remaining respondents, original codes on the 0 to 10 scale are used to create *Party ideology*. *Leftists* are those answering "0" and *Rightists* are those answering "10."

286

Political Awareness: "From the list of institutions that are on this card, please evaluate each in general terms, scoring them a 0 through a 10 (0 is 'very bad' and 10 is 'very good') or tell me if you have not heard enough to have an opinion. Mercosul, FTAA, Central American Common Market, Andean Pact, International Monetary Fund, United Nations, World Trade Organization, EU." Respondent awareness is the number of entities the respondent scored.

Capitalist Values (1995 and 2002): "Imagine the following situation: Two people of the same age work as computer programmers doing the same job. One earns (the equivalent of) US$50 more than the other one, but he does his work faster and more efficiently, and he is more trustworthy than the other worker. In your opinion, do you consider it fair that in this situation, one programmer is better paid than the other? (2) I consider it to be fair. (1) I do not consider it to be fair."

(1996): "In general, do you think it should be the responsibility of the government to reduce differences between the rich and poor? (1) Absolutely yes, (2) perhaps yes, (3) perhaps no, (4) absolutely not."

(Capitalist values 1; 1999, 2000, 2003, and 2005): "It is said that the state can solve all the problems of our society because it has the means to do so. Would you say that the state can solve (1) all the problems, (2) the majority of the problems, (3) many problems, (4) only some problems, or (5) the state cannot solve any problems?"

(Capitalist values 2; 1999): "With which of the following phrases do you more strongly agree? (2) That the country should raise its production and productivity or (1) that the country should improve its distribution of wealth."

(Capitalist values 1; 2001): "People have different ways of thinking about how societies should be. This card shows two sentences. Please read them carefully and tell me, on a scale from 1 to 10, where you place yourself, with 1 being 'a society with lots of freedom and few rules so that everyone can earn all the money they can produce' and 10 being 'a society with less freedom and more rules that protects equality of earnings.'" Scale was reversed.

(Capitalist values 2; 2001):   "Some people believe that the state should solve all of the problems of society because it has the resources to do it, while others think the market can solve all the problems of our society because it distributes resources in a more efficient manner. Using a scale from 1 to 10, where 1 means 'the state should solve all problems' and 10 means 'the market should solve all problems,' where would you place yourself?"

Wall Street Journal Americas

Wealth: Survey administrators coded income into four categories: lower class (bottom 40% of the population); middle and lower middle (next 30%); middle–upper class (next 20%); upper class (top 10%). I converted these figures into income in 1997 US$1,000s using country-level data on GDP per capita and income distribution by decile. Sources for this were ECLAC (2000b) and World Bank (2006).

Education: From zero to twelve years, education is coded as the number of years of education. Beyond 12, (13) undergraduate incomplete, (14) undergraduate complete, (15) postgraduate incomplete, (16) postgraduate complete.

Party Ideology: "In politics, one normally speaks of the 'Left' and the 'Right.' On a scale where 1 is left and 10 is right, where would you place yourself?" Individuals who said they "did not know" or "would not vote" if elections were held on Sunday (based on responses to another question in the survey) are *Independents*, as are individuals not self-placing on the 1 to 10 scale. Among the remaining respondents, original codes on the 1 to 10 scale are used and recoded from 0 to 9. *Leftists* are those coded as 0 and *Rightists* are those coded as 9.

Political Awareness: Respondents were asked to describe their country's regional trade area (Andean Pact/CACM/Mercosul/NAFTA) and "fast-track" authority. Their score on this variable was the number (0 to 2) of which they had an accurate knowledge.

Capitalist Values: "With which phrase do you agree more? (0) 'Government should take care of the well-being of individuals' or (1) 'Each individual should take care of his own well-being.'"

Survey Data Appendix

Town Size: The town size variable is recoded from the manner in which survey administrators recorded it. The code is the middle number of inhabitants for the recorded category divided by 1,000,000: (.0075) rural zone (less than 15,000 inhabitants); (.0325) small city (15,000 to 50,000 inhabitants); (.075) medium-sized city (50,000 to 100,000 inhabitants); (.55) big city (100,000 to 1 million inhabitants), (2) metropolis (over 1 million inhabitants).

World Values Survey

Wealth: "Here is a scale of incomes. We would like to know in what group your household is, counting all wages, salaries, pensions, and other incomes that come in. Just give the letter of the group your household falls into, before taxes and other deductions." Categories were recoded into deciles (1 through 10) by WVS.

Education: "What is the highest education level that you have attained? (1) No formal education, (2) incomplete primary school, (3) complete primary school, (4) incomplete secondary school (technical/vocational type), (5) complete secondary (technical/vocational type), (6) incomplete secondary (university/preparatory type), (7) complete secondary (university/preparatory type), (8) some university-level education without degree, (9) university-level education with degree.

Class: "Are you employed now or not? (a) Yes, full time; (b) yes, part time; (c) yes, self-employed; (d) no, retired; (e) no, homemaker; (f) no, student; (g) no, unemployed. If actively working [answered a, b, or c], what type of work do you do? If unemployed or retired [answered d or g], what type of work did you do? If not a worker [answered e or f], in which profession does the chief wage earner in your household work?" Based on these answers, WVS administrators coded workers into one of the following categories, with the class category (assigned by myself) in italics and the scoring on the class variable shown in parentheses: (0) "Employed, nonmanual office worker (nonsupervisory)," "Employed, skilled manual worker," "Employed, semiskilled manual worker," "Employed, unskilled manual worker," "Employed agricultural worker," "Member of armed forces": *Proletariat*; (1) "Foreman/supervisor," *Foreman/Supervisor (Bourgeoisie-Proletariat)*; (2) "Self-employed, nonmanual office worker (nonsupervisory),"

"Self-employed, skilled manual worker," "Self-employed, semiskilled manual worker," "Self-employed, unskilled manual worker," "Self-employed agricultural worker," "Employed professional": *Semiautonomous employee (Proletariat–Petty Bourgeoisie)*; (3) "Self-employed professional": *Technocrat (Bourgeoisie-Proletariat)*; (5) "Office worker (supervisory)": *Middle manager (Bourgeoisie-Proletariat)*; (6) "Farmer with own farm": *Petty Bourgeoisie*; (7) "Employer/manager" (<10 employees): *Small employer (Bourgeoisie–Petty Bourgeoisie)*; (9) "Employer/manager" (>9 employees): *Bourgeoisie*. The class categories and scoring are assigned based on the categories derived in Wright (1979) and Wright and Perrone (1977). These sources develop a classification scheme that expands on Marx's original threefold typology – bourgeoisie, proletariat, and petty bourgeoisie – by categorizing some individuals into "contradictory" class locations that have characteristics of two of Marx's three types. Wright (1979, 40) in Table 2.3 classifies each group as having (0) "no control," (1) "minimal control," (2) "partial control," or (3) "full control" over each of the three factors of production. I use these scores, summed across the three different factors of production, to produce the scoring of categories.

Unemployed: "Are you employed now or not? (0) Yes, full time; (0) yes, part time; (0) yes, self-employed; (0) no, retired; (0) no, homemaker; (0) no, student; (1) no, unemployed."

Chief Wage Earner: "Are you the chief wage earner in your household? (1) Yes, (0) No."

Party Ideology: "In political matters, people talk of the 'Left' and the 'Right.' How would you place your views on this scale, generally speaking?" Respondents chose an integer from 1 ("Left") to 10 ("Right"). Individuals who said they "did not know" or "would not vote" if elections were held on Sunday (based on responses to another question in the survey) are *Independents*. Among the remaining respondents, original codes on the 1 to 10 scale are used and recoded from 0 to 9. *Leftists* are those coded as 0.

Capitalist Values (Capitalist Values 1): "Now I'd like you to tell me your views on various issues. How would you place your views on this scale? 1 means you agree completely with the statement on the left ('The government should take more responsibility to ensure that everyone is provided for'); 10 means you agree completely with the statement on the right ('People should take more responsibility to provide for themselves'); and if your views fall somewhere in between, you can choose any number in between."

(Capitalist Values 2): "How would you place your views on this scale? 1 means you agree completely with the statement on the left ('Incomes should be made more equal'); 10 means you agree completely with the statement on the right ('We need larger income differences as incentives for individual effort'); and if your views fall somewhere in between, you can choose any number in between."

Four-City Survey

Preference for Foreign Entertainment: All of the following were combined into a single wealth index using the first dimension extracted from a polychoric principal components analysis.

(A) Foreign films: "In the last month, how many times, more or less, did you watch a foreign film? In case you do not remember the exact number, please give me your best guess." Responses greater than 30 were recoded to 30.

(B) Foreign television: "In the last month, how many times did you watch some type of foreign television program, such as a drama or comedy series (*seriado*), news, or a soap opera (*novela*)? In case you do not remember the exact number, please give me your best guess." Responses greater than 30 were recoded to 30.

(C) Foreign radio music: "In the last month, how many times did you listen to foreign music on the radio? In case you do not remember the exact number, please give me your best guess." Responses greater than 100 were recoded to 100.

(D) Foreign music ownership: "And more or less how many tapes, records, and CDs of foreign music do you own? In case you do not remember the exact number, please give me your best guess." Responses greater than 100 were recoded to 100.

Wealth: All of the following were combined into a single wealth index using the first dimension extracted from a polychoric principal components analysis.[2]

---

[2] Filmer and Pritchett (2001) and Kolenikov and Angeles (2004) discuss how conducting such an analysis on a large battery of asset and expenditure indicators produces a highly accurate yet easy-to-obtain measure of long-term wealth.

(A) List of asset indicators: "Now, merely to classify your income, could you tell me if you or someone in your house has the following things?" (0) "No"; (1) "Yes" scored for each of the following: cable television, own home, computer, washing machine, fixed-line telephone, cellular telephone, automobile, second home/vacation home, potable water, hot water, sewerage, VCR or DVD player, dishwasher, maid.

(B) Amount of savings: "Do you and your family have savings that total more than two months of your family's income? If so, do you and your family have savings that total more than four months of your family's income?" Responses of "no" to the first question were coded 0, responses of "yes" to the first and "no" to the second were coded 1, and responses of "yes" to both were coded 2.

(C) Amount spent on tuition: "Do you or someone in your family have monthly tuition payments for someone in school or university right now? If so, how much does you family pay per month in tuition?" Zero was entered for responses of "no" to the first question; the actual amount was entered for all others.

(D) Type of health coverage: "How do you cover your health spending? Do you have a (1) private health insurance plan, (0) a public health insurance plan, or (0) do you not have a health insurance plan?"

(E) Preference for foreign entertainment: This is comprised of the four individual indicators mentioned above.

Preference for Durable Goods: All of the following were combined into a single index using the first dimension extracted from a polychoric principal components analysis: refrigerator, computer, washing machine, automobile, VCR or DVD player, dishwasher, and foreign music ownership.

Sectoral Competitiveness: Respondents were asked "What is the product or service made in the business in which you work?" Respondents working in a manufacturing sector that exported more than it imported were coded +1. Respondents working in a manufacturing sector that imported more than it exported were coded −1. All other respondents (0) were either employed in the service sector, unemployed, or not in the EAP. Trade data are from United Nations (2008).

Education: "What is your education level?" (1) No instruction. (2) First or second grade. (3) Third or fourth grade. (4) Fourth or fifth grade.

(5) Seventh or eighth grade. (6) Secondary school incomplete. (7) Secondary school complete. (8) University/college incomplete. (9) University/college complete. (10) Graduate studies.

Political Awareness: "Who is the vice-president of Brazil? Inocêncio de Oliveira, Marco Maciel, Iris Resende, or José Alencar [correct]?" "What is the party of President Lula? PFL, PMDB, PSDB, or PT [correct]?" "Who is the president of the Chamber of Deputies? Severino Cavalcanti [correct], João Paulo Cunha, Eduardo Suplicy, or Miro Teixeira?" "Who is currently the finance minister? José Genoino, Antônio Palocci [correct], Ciro Gomes, or José Serra?" "What is the most important power of the Central Bank? Set interest rates [correct], raise taxes, sell state-owned enterprises, or negotiate treaties with foreign countries?" Awareness is a count (from 0 to 5) of correct answers.

List of Countries Surveyed

Latin American Parliamentary Elites Project

1994: Chile, Costa Rica, El Salvador, Honduras
1995: Dominican Republic, Mexico, Peru, Venezuela
1996: Argentina, Bolivia, Ecuador, Paraguay, Uruguay
1998: Argentina, Bolivia, Chile, Colombia, Costa Rica, Ecuador, El Salvador, Guatemala, Honduras, Nicaragua, Paraguay, Mexico
2000: Dominican Republic, El Salvador, Venezuela
2001: Mexico, Peru, Uruguay
2002: Chile, Costa Rica, Dominican Republic, Honduras, Nicaragua, Panama
2003: Bolivia, Colombia, Ecuador, El Salvador, Guatemala, Mexico, Paraguay
2004: Argentina, Brazil

World Values Survey[3]

1990: Argentina, Brazil, Chile, Mexico

[3] *Bibliographic Citation:* European Values Study Group and World Values Survey Association. EUROPEAN AND WORLD VALUES SURVEYS FOUR-WAVE INTEGRATED DATA FILE, 1981–2004, v.20060423, 2006. Aggregate File Producers: Análisis Sociológicos Económicos y Políticos (ASEP) and JD Systems (JDS), Madrid, Spain/Tilburg

1995 to 1997: Argentina, Brazil, Chile, Dominican Republic, Mexico, Peru, Uruguay, Venezuela
1999 to 2000: Argentina, Chile, Mexico, Venezuela

Latinbarometer

1995: Argentina, Brazil, Chile, Mexico, Paraguay, Peru, Uruguay, Venezuela
1996 to 2003: Argentina, Bolivia, Brazil, Chile, Colombia, Costa Rica, Ecuador, El Salvador, Guatemala, Honduras, Mexico, Nicaragua, Panama, Paraguay, Peru, Uruguay, Venezuela
2004 to 2007: Argentina, Bolivia, Brazil, Chile, Colombia, Costa Rica, Dominican Republic, Ecuador, El Salvador, Guatemala, Honduras, Mexico, Nicaragua, Panama, Paraguay, Peru, Uruguay, Venezuela

Wall Street Journal Americas

Argentina, Bolivia, Brazil, Chile, Colombia, Costa Rica, Dominican Republic, Ecuador, Guatemala, Mexico, Panama, Paraguay, Peru, Venezuela

Pew Global Attitudes Project

2002: Argentina, Bolivia, Brazil, Guatemala, Honduras, Mexico, Peru, Venezuela
2007: Argentina, Bolivia, Brazil, Chile, Mexico, Peru, Venezuela

Globescan

Argentina, Brazil, Chile, Mexico, Uruguay

University, Tilburg, the Netherlands. *Data Files Suppliers*: Analisis Sociologicos Economicos y Politicos (ASEP) and JD Systems (JDS), Madrid, Spain/Tillburg University, Tillburg, the Netherlands/ Zentralarchiv fur Empirische Sozialforschung (ZA), Cologne, Germany:) *Aggregate File Distributors*: Análisis Sociológicos Económicos y Políticos (ASEP) and JD Systems (JDS), Madrid, Spain/Tillburg University, Tilburg, the Netherlands/ Zentralarchiv fur Empirische Sozialforschung (ZA) Cologne, Germany.

References

Achen, Christopher, and Larry Bartels. 2006. "It Feels Like We're Thinking: The Rationalizing Voter and Electoral Democracy." Paper presented at the annual meeting of the American Political Science Association, Philadelphia.

Alcántara, Manuel. 2005. *Proyecto de Elites Parlamentarias Latinoamericanas (PELA)*. Available at http://americo.usal.es/oir/Elites/ [accessed May 12, 2008].

Alvarez, R. Michael, and John Brehm. 2002. *Hard Choices, Easy Answers: Values, Information, and American Public Opinion*. Princeton, NJ: Princeton University Press.

Amann, Edmund, and Werner Baer. 2002. "Neoliberalism and Its Consequences in Brazil." *Journal of Latin American Studies* 34(4): 945–959.

Ames, Barry. 2001. *The Deadlock of Democracy in Brazil*. Ann Arbor: University of Michigan Press.

Anderson, Benedict R. 1983. *Imagined Communities: Reflections on the Origin and Spread of Nationalism*. London: Verso.

Antunes, Ricardo, and Sabrina E. Wilson. 1994. "Recent Strikes in Brazil: The Main Tendencies of the Strike Movement of the 1980s." *Latin American Perspectives* 21(1): 24–37.

Anuatti-Neto, Francisco, Milton Barossi-Filho, Antonio Gledson de Carvalho, and Roberto Macedo. 2005. "Costs and Benefits of Privatization: Evidence from Brazil." In *Privatization in Latin America: Myths and Reality*, eds. Alberto Chong and Florencio López-de-Silanes, 145–196. Washington, DC: World Bank.

Arce, Moisés. 2005. *Market Reform in Society: Post-Crisis Politics and Economic Change in Authoritarian Peru*. University Park: Pennsylvania State University Press.

Armijo, Leslie Elliott, and Philippe Faucher. 2002. "'We Have a Consensus': Explaining Political Support for Market Reforms in Latin America." *Latin American Politics and Society* 44(2): 1–40.

Associação Brasileira de Shopping Centers [ABRASCE]. 2007. "ABRASCE." Available at http://www.abrasce.com.br/ [accessed February 15, 2007].

Avelino, George, David S. Brown, and Wendy Hunter. 2005. "The Effects of Capital Mobility, Trade Openness, and Democracy on Social Spending in Latin America, 1980–1999." *American Journal of Political Science* 49(3): 625–641.

Baer, Werner. 2001. *The Brazilian Economy: Growth and Development*, 5th ed. Westport, CT: Praeger.

Baker, Andy. 2003. "Why Is Trade Reform So Popular in Latin America? A Consumption-Based Theory of Trade Policy Preferences." *World Politics* 55(3): 423–455.

Baker, Andy. 2005. "Who Wants to Globalize? Consumer Tastes and Labor Markets in a Theory of Trade Policy Beliefs." *American Journal of Political Science* 49(4): 924–938.

Baker, Andy, Barry Ames, and Lucio R. Renno. 2006. "Social Context and Campaign Volatility in New Democracies: Networks and Neighborhoods in Brazil's 2002 Elections." *American Journal of Political Science* 50(2): 382–399.

Barber, Benjamin R. 1995. *Jihad vs. McWorld*. New York: Times Books.

Barja, Gover, David McKenzie, and Miguel Urquiola. 2005. "Bolivian Capitalization and Privatization: Approximation to an Evaluation." In *Reality Check: The Distributional Impact of Privatization in Developing Countries*, eds. John Nellis and Nancy Birdsall, 123–178. Washington, DC: Center for Global Development.

Bauer, Arnold J. 2001. *Goods, Power, History: Latin America's Material Culture*. New York: Cambridge University Press.

Bayliss, Kate. 2002. "Privatization and Poverty: The Distributional Impact of Utility Privatization." *Annals of Public and Cooperative Economics* 73(4): 603–625.

Behrman, Jere R., Nancy Birdsall, and Miguel Székely. 2003. "Economic Policy and Wage Differentials in Latin America." *Center for Global Development Working Paper Series 29*.

Berg, Janine, Christoph Ernst, and Peter Auer. 2006. *Meeting the Employment Challenge: Argentina, Brazil, and Mexico in the Global Economy*. Boulder, CO: Lynne Rienner.

Berinsky, Adam J. 2004. *Silent Voices: Public Opinion and Political Participation in America*. Princeton, NJ: Princeton University Press.

Berinsky, Adam J. 2007. "Assuming the Costs of War: Events, Elites, and American Public Support for Military Conflict." *Journal of Politics* 69(4): 975–997.

Berry, Albert, ed. 1998. *Poverty, Economic Reform, and Income Distribution in Latin America*. Boulder, CO: Lynne Rienner.

Bertranou, Fabio M. 2001. "Pension Reform and Gender Gaps in Latin America: What Are the Policy Options?" *World Development* 29(5): 911–923.

Biersteker, Thomas J. 1995. "The 'Triumph' of Liberal Economic Ideas in the Developing World." In *Global Change, Regional Response: The New International Context of Development*, ed. Barbara Stallings, 174–198. New York: Cambridge University Press.

Birdsall, Nancy, and John Nellis. 2003. "Winners and Losers: Assessing the Distributional Impact of Privatization." *World Development* 31(10): 1617–1633.

Birdsall, Nancy and John Nellis. 2005. "Privatization Reality Check: Distributional Effects in Developing Countries." In *Reality Check: The Distributional Impact of Privatization in Developing Countries*, eds. John Nellis and Nancy Birdsall, 1–30. Washington, DC: Center for Global Development.

References

Birdsall, Nancy, Augusto de la Torre, and Rachel Menezes. 2001. *Washington Contentious: Economic Policies for Social Equity in Latin America*. Washington, DC: Carnegie Endowment for International Peace.

Blom, Andreas, Lauritz Holm-Nielsen, and Dorte Verner. 2001. "Education, Earning, and Inequality in Brazil, 1982–1998: Implications for Education Policy." *Peabody Journal of Education* 76(3&4): 180–221.

Blomstrom, Magnus, and Ari Kokko. 1997. "Regional Integration and Foreign Direct Investment: A Conceptual Framework and Three Cases." *World Bank Policy Research Working Paper 1750*.

Bound, John, and George Johnson. 1992. "Changes in the Structure of Wages in the 1980's: An Evaluation of Alternative Explanations." *American Economic Review* 82(3): 371–392.

Bourdieu, Pierre. 1986. *Distinction: A Social Critique of the Judgement of Taste*. London: Routledge and Kegan Paul.

Branford, Sue, Bernardo Kucinski, and Hilary Wainwright. 2003. *Lula and the Workers Party in Brazil*. New York: New Press.

Bratton, Michael, Robert B. Mattes, and Emmanuel Gyimah-Boadi. 2004. *Public Opinion, Democracy, and Market Reform in Africa*. New York: Cambridge University Press.

Broda, Christian, and John Romalis. 2008. "Inequality and Prices: Does China Benefit the Poor in America?" Chicago: University of Chicago, working paper.

Broda, Christian, and David E. Weinstein. 2006. "Globalization and the Gains from Variety." *Quarterly Journal of Economics* 121(2): 541–585.

Brody, Richard A. 1991. *Assessing the President: The Media, Elite Opinion, and Public Support*. Stanford, CA: Stanford University Press.

Brody, Richard A., and Paul M. Sniderman. 1977. "From Life Space to Polling Place: The Relevance of Personal Concerns for Voting Behavior." *British Journal of Political Science* 7(3): 337–360.

Brooks, Sarah M., and Marcus J. Kurtz. 2007. "Capital, Trade, and the Political Economies of Reform." *American Journal of Political Science* 51(4): 703–720.

Brown, David S., and Wendy Hunter. 1999. "Democracy and Social Spending in Latin America, 1980–92." *American Political Science Review* 93(4): 779–790.

Bruhn, Kathleen. 2004. "Globalization and the Renovation of the Latin American Left: Strategies of Ideological Adaptation." Paper presented at the annual meeting of the Midwest Political Science Association, Chicago.

Buendia, Jorge. 2001. "Economic Reforms and Political Support in Mexico, 1988–1997." In *Public Support for Market Reforms in New Democracies*, ed. Susan C. Stokes, 131–159. New York: Cambridge University Press.

Bulmer-Thomas, Victor. 1994. *The Economic History of Latin America Since Independence*. New York: Cambridge University Press.

Bulmer-Thomas, Victor, ed. 1996. *The New Economic Model in Latin America and Its Impact on Income Distribution and Poverty*. Basingstoke, U.K.: Macmillan.

Camargo, José, Marcelo Neri, and Maurício Cortez Reis. 2002. "Employment and Productivity in Brazil in the Nineties." In *Brazil in the 1990s: An Economy in Transition*, ed. Renato Baumann, 233–261. New York: Palgrave Macmillan.

297

Cameron, Maxwell A. 2006. "A False and Damaging Dichotomy." Available at http://commentisfree.guardian.co.uk/maxwell_a_cameron/2006/06/ the_rightwrong_left_shibboleth.html [accessed May 12, 2008].

Campbell, Angus, Philip E. Converse, Warren E. Miller, and Donald Stokes. 1960. *The American Voter*. New York: Wiley.

Cardoso, Fernando Henrique, and Enzo Faletto. 1979. *Dependency and Development in Latin America*. Berkeley: University of California Press.

Castañeda, Jorge. 2006. "Latin America's Left Turn." *Foreign Affairs* 85(3): 28–44.

Castañeda, Jorge, and Patricio Navia. 2007. "The Year of the Ballot." *Current History* 105(2): 51–57.

Castro, Newton de. 1999. "Privatization of the Transportation Sector in Brazil." In *Privatization in Brazil: The Case of Public Utilities*, eds. Armando Castelar Pinheiro and Kiichiro Fukasaku, 177–218. Rio de Janeiro: Banco Nacional de Desenvolvimento Econômico e Social.

Chang, Won, and L. Alan Winters. 2002. "How Regional Blocs Affect Excluded Countries: The Price Effects of MERCOSUR." *American Economic Review* 92(4): 889–904.

Chisari, Omar, Antonio Estache, and Catherine Waddams Price. 2003. "Access by the Poor in Latin America's Utility Reform: Subsidies and Service Obligations." In *Utility Privatization and Regulation: A Fair Deal for Consumers?* eds. Cecilia Ugaz and Catherine Waddams Price, 25–53. Northampton, MA: Edward Elgar.

Chong, Alberto, and Florencio López-de-Silanes. 2005. "The Truth about Privatization in Latin America." In *Privatization in Latin America: Myths and Reality*, eds. Alberto Chong and Florencio López-de-Silanes, 1–66. Washington, DC: World Bank.

Cohen, Youssef. 1989. *The Manipulation of Consent: The State and Working-Class Consciousness in Brazil*. Pittsburgh: University of Pittsburgh Press.

Colburn, Forrest D. 2002. *Latin America at the End of Politics*. Princeton, NJ: Princeton University Press.

Collier, David, ed. 1979. *The New Authoritarianism in Latin America*. Princeton, NJ: Princeton University Press.

Collier, Ruth Berins, and David Collier. 1991. *Shaping the Political Arena: Critical Junctures, the Labor Movement, and Regime Dynamics in Latin America*. Princeton, NJ: Princeton University Press.

Converse, Philip E. 1964. "The Nature of Belief Systems in Mass Publics." In *Ideology and Discontent*, ed. David E. Apter, 206–261. London: Free Press of Glencoe.

Coppedge, Michael. 1998. "The Dynamic Diversity of Latin American Party Systems." *Party Politics* 4(4): 547–568.

Cornelius, Wayne A. 1973. "Nation Building, Participation, and Distribution: The Politics of Social Reform under Cárdenas." In *Crisis, Choice, and Change: Historical Studies of Political Development*, eds. Gabriel A. Almond, Scott C. Flanagan, and Robert J. Mundt, 392–498. Boston: Little, Brown.

Couto, Cláudio Gonçalves. 1998. "A Longa Constituinte: Reforma do Estado e Fluidez Institucional no Brasil." *Dados* 41(1): 51–86.

References

Currie, Janet, and Ann Harrison. 1997. "Sharing the Costs: The Impact of Trade Reform on Capital and Labor in Morocco." *Journal of Labor Economics* 15(3): S44–S71.

Dalgin, Muhammed, Vitor Trindade, and Devashish Mitra. 2008. "Inequality, Nonhomothetic Preferences, and Trade: A Gravity Approach." *Southern Economic Journal* 74(3): 747–774.

de Soto, Hernando. 1989. *The Other Path: The Invisible Revolution in the Third World*. New York: Harper and Row.

de Soto, Hernando. 2000. *The Mystery of Capital: Why Capitalism Triumphs in the West and Fails Everywhere Else*. New York: Basic Books.

Deaton, Angus. 1989. "Rice Prices and Income Distribution in Thailand: A Non-Parametric Analysis." *The Economic Journal* 99(395): 1–37.

Delli Carpini, Michael X., and Scott Keeter. 1996. *What Americans Know About Politics and Why It Matters*. New Haven, CT: Yale University Press.

Dias, Guilherme Leite Da Silva, and Cicely Moitinho Amaral. 2002. "Structural Change in Brazilian Agriculture, 1980–1998." In *Brazil in the 1990s: An Economy in Transition*, ed. Renato Baumann, 204–232. New York: Palgrave Macmillan.

Diretório Nacional do PT. 1998. *Partido dos Trabalhadores: Resoluções de Encontros e Congressos*. São Paulo: Editora Fundação Perseu Abramo.

Dix, Robert H. 1989. "Cleavage Structures and Party Systems in Latin America." *Comparative Politics* 22(1): 23–37.

Domínguez, Jorge I. 1998. "Free Politics and Free Markets in Latin America." *Journal of Democracy* 9(4): 70–84.

Domínguez, Jorge I., and James A. McCann. 1996. *Democratizing Mexico: Public Opinion and Electoral Choices*. Baltimore: Johns Hopkins University Press.

Dore, Elizabeth. 2003. "In the National Interest." *NACLA: Report on the Americas* 36(4): 20–23.

Downs, Anthony. 1957. *An Economic Theory of Democracy*. New York: Harper.

Duch, Raymond M. 1993. "Tolerating Economic Reform: Popular Support for Transition to a Free Market in the Former Soviet Union." *American Political Science Review* 87(3): 590–608.

Duckett, Jane, and William L. Miller. 2006. *The Open Economy and Its Enemies*. New York: Cambridge University Press.

Easton, David. 1965. *A Systems Analysis of Political Life*. New York: Wiley.

Echegaray, Fabian, and Carlos Elordi. 2001. "Public Opinion, Presidential Popularity, and Economic Reform in Argentina, 1989–1996." In *Public Support for Market Reforms in New Democracies*, ed. Susan C. Stokes, 187–214. New York: Cambridge University Press.

Economic Commission on Latin America and the Caribbean [ECLAC. 2000a]. *Foreign Investment in Latin America and the Caribbean*. Santiago, Chile: United Nations.

Economic Commission on Latin America and the Caribbean [ECLAC]. 2000b. *Statistical Yearbook for Latin America and the Caribbean*. Santiago, Chile: United Nations.

Economic Commission on Latin America and the Caribbean [ECLAC]. 2001. *America Latina: Índices de Precios al Consumidor*. Santiago, Chile: United Nations.

Economic Commission on Latin America and the Caribbean [ECLAC]. 2005. *Economic Survey of Latin America and the Caribbean*. Santiago, Chile: United Nations.

Economist, The. 2005a. "Trade and Poverty: Tired of Globalisation." *The Economist*, November 5:11.

Economist, The. 2005b. "The Summit of the Americas: Uncle Sam Visits His Restive Neighbours." *The Economist*, November 5:41.

Economist, The. 2005c. "Bolivia: Mob Rule, Not People Power." *The Economist*, June 18:17.

Economist, The. 2005d. "Chile's Conservatives: Out in the Cold." *The Economist*, October 29:38.

Economist, The. 2008. "Brazil: Happy Families." *The Economist*, February 9:39–40.

Edwards, Sebastian. 1995. *Crisis and Reform in Latin America: From Despair to Hope*. New York: Oxford University Press.

Edwards, Tim. 2000. *Contradictions of Consumption: Concepts, Practices and Politics in Consumer Society*. Philadelphia: Open University Press.

Encyclopedia of Nations. 2006. "Brazil: Labor." *Encyclopedia of Nations*. Available at http://www.nationsencyclopedia.com/Americas/ Brazil-LABOR [accessed April 19, 2006].

Engel, Ernst. 1857. "Die Productions: Und Consumtionsverhaltnisse des Konigreichs Sachsen." *Zeitschrift des Statistischen Bureaus des K. Sachsischen* 8:27–29.

Epstein, Jack. 1999. "Light's Out." *Latin Trade* 7(6): 61–68.

Estache, Antonio. 2005. "Latin America's Infrastructure Experience: Policy Gaps and the Poor." In *Reality Check: The Distributional Impact of Privatization in Developing Countries*, eds. John Nellis and Nancy Birdsall, 281–294. Washington, DC: Center for Global Development.

Estache, Antonio, and Ana Goicoechea. 2005. "A 'Research' Database on Infrastructure Economic Performance." *World Bank Policy Research Working Paper 3643*.

Estache, Antonio, and Martin Rossi. 2004. "Have Consumers Benefited from the Reforms in the Electricity Distribution Sector in Latin America?" *World Bank Policy Research Working Paper 3420*.

Estevadeordal, Antoni, Dani Rodrik, Alan M. Taylor, and Andrés Velasco, eds. 2004. *Integrating the Americas: FTAA and Beyond*. Cambridge, MA: Harvard University David Rockefeller Center for Latin American Studies.

Evans, Peter B. 1979. *Dependent Development: The Alliance of Multinational, State, and Local Capital in Brazil*. Princeton, NJ: Princeton University Press.

Ferranti, David M. de. 2003. *Closing the Gap in Education and Technology*. Washington, DC: World Bank.

Ferraz, João Carlos, David Kupfer, and Mariana Iootty. 2004. "Industrial Competitiveness in Brazil: Ten Years after Economic Liberalization." *CEPAL Review* 82:91–119.

References

Figueiredo, Argelina Maria Cheibub, and Fernando Papaterra Limongi. 1999. *Executivo e Legislativo Na Nova Ordem Constitucional*. Rio de Janeiro: Editora FGV.

Filmer, Deon, and Lant H. Pritchett. 2001. "Estimating Wealth Effects without Expenditure Data – or Tears: An Application to Educational Enrollments in States of India." *Demography* 38(1): 115–132.

Fiorina, Morris P. 1981. *Retrospective Voting in American National Elections*. New Haven, CT: Yale University Press.

Fishman, Charles. 2006. *The Wal-Mart Effect: How the World's Most Powerful Company Really Works and How It's Transforming the American Economy*. New York: Penguin Press.

Forero, Juan. 2002. "Still Poor, Latin Americans Protest Push for Open Markets." *The New York Times*, July 19: A1.

Forero, Juan. 2005. "Latin America Fails to Deliver on Basic Needs." *The New York Times*, February 22: A1.

Foster, Vivien, Erwin R. Tiongson, and Caterina Ruggeri Laderchi. 2005. "Utility Reforms." In *Analyzing the Distributional Impact of Reforms: Volume One*, eds. Aline Coudouel and Stefano Paternostro, 73–143. Washington, DC: World Bank.

Frieden, Jeffry A. 1991. *Debt, Development, and Democracy: Modern Political Economy and Latin America, 1965–1985*. Princeton, NJ: Princeton University Press.

Frye, Timothy. 2006. "Original Sin, Good Works, and Property Rights in Russia." *World Politics* 58(4): 479–504.

Gabel, Matthew J. 1998. *Interests and Integration: Market Liberalization, Public Opinion, and European Union*. Ann Arbor: University of Michigan Press.

Gabel, Matthew, and Kenneth Scheve. 2007. "Estimating the Effect of Elite Communications on Public Opinion Using Instrumental Variables." *American Journal of Political Science* 51(4): 1013–1028.

Galiani, Sebastian, Paul Gertler, Ernesto Schargrodsky, and Federico Sturzenegger. 2005. "The Benefits and Costs of Privatization in Argentina: A Microeconomic Analysis." In *Privatization in Latin America: Myths and Reality*, eds. Alberto Chong and Florencio López-de-Silanes, 67–116. Washington, DC: World Bank.

Gallup, John Luke, Alejandro Gaviria, and Eduardo Lora. 2003. *Is Geography Destiny? Lessons from Latin America*. Stanford, CA: Stanford University Press.

Gamson, William. 1992. *Talking Politics*. New York: Cambridge University Press.

Garrett, Geoffrey. 2004. "Globalization's Missing Middle." *Foreign Affairs* 85(6): 84–96.

Geddes, Barbara, and John Zaller. 1989. "Sources of Popular Support for Authoritarian Regimes." *American Journal of Political Science* 33(2): 319–347.

Ger, Güliz, and Russell W. Belk. 1996. "'I'd Like to Buy the World a Coke: Consumptionscapes of the 'Less Affluent World.'" *Journal of Consumer Policy* 19(3): 271–304.

Gervasoni, Carlos. 1995. "El Impacto Electoral de las Políticas de Estabilización y Reforma Estructural en América Latina." *Journal of Latin American Affairs* 3(1): 46–50.

Gill, Indermit Singh, Truman Packard, and Juan Yermo. 2005. *Keeping the Promise of Social Security in Latin America*. Stanford, CA: Stanford University Press and the World Bank.

Gilljam, Mikael, and Donald Granberg. 1993. "Should We Take 'Don't Know' for an Answer?" *Public Opinion Quarterly* 57(3): 348–357.

Globescan Research Partners. 2003. *19 Nation Poll on Global Issues: Questionnaire*. College Park: University of Maryland: Program on International Policy Attitudes.

Goldberg, Pinelopi Koujiano, and Nina Pavcnik. 2004. "Trade, Inequality, and Poverty: What Do We Know?" In *Brookings Trade Forum 2004*, eds. Susan M. Collins and Carol Graham, 223–269. Washington, DC: Brookings Institution Press.

Gomez, Brad T., and J. Matthew Wilson. 2006. "Cognitive Heterogeneity and Economic Voting: A Comparative Analysis of Four Democratic Electorates." *American Journal of Political Science* 50(1): 127–145.

Graham, Carol, and Stefano Pettinato. 2002. *Happiness and Hardship: Opportunity and Insecurity in New Market Economies*. Washington, DC: Brookings Institution Press.

Graham, Carol, and Sandip Sukhtankar. 2004. "Does Economic Crisis Reduce Support for Markets and Democracy in Latin America? Some Evidence from Surveys of Public Opinion and Well Being." *Journal of Latin American Studies* 36 (2): 349–377.

Gramsci, Antonio. 1971. *Selections from the Prison Notebooks of Antonio Gramsci*. New York: International Publishers.

Greene, Kenneth F. 2007. *Why Dominant Parties Lose: Mexico's Democratization in Comparative Perspective*. New York: Cambridge University Press.

Gregory, Mary, Wiemer Salverda, and Ronald Schettkat, eds. 2007. *Services and Employment: Explaining the U.S.–European Gap*. Princeton, NJ: Princeton University Press.

Guedes, Patrícia, and Nilson Vieira Oliveira. 2006. "Democracy 5: Progress and Aspirations in São Paulo's Periphery." *Braudel Papers* 38:1–17.

Haggard, Stephan, and Robert R. Kaufman. 1995. *The Political Economy of Democratic Transitions*. Princeton, NJ: Princeton University Press.

Hagopian, Frances. 2001. *Brazil Congressional Survey, 1999–2000*. Unpublished dataset, cited with permission.

Hainmueller, Jens, and Michael J. Hiscox. 2006. "Learning to Love Globalization? Education and Individual Attitudes Toward International Trade." *International Organization* 60:469–498.

Haltiwanger, John, Adriana Kugler, Maurice Kugler, Alejandro Micco, and Carmen Pagés. 2004. "Effects of Tariffs and Real Exchange Rates on Job Reallocation: Evidence from Latin America." *Journal of Policy Reform* 7(4): 191–208.

Harris, Clive, John Hodges, Michael Schur, and Padmesh Shukla. 2003. "Infrastructure Projects: A Review of Canceled Private Projects." *Public Policy for the Private Sector* 252:1–6.

References

Harsanyi, John C. 1953. "Welfare Economics of Variable Tastes." *The Review of Economic Studies* 21(3): 204–213.

Hellwig, Timothy, and David Samuels. 2007. "Voting in Open Economies: The Electoral Consequences of Globalization." *Comparative Political Studies* 40(3): 283–306.

Hirsch, Fred. 1976. *Social Limits to Growth*. Cambridge, MA: Harvard University Press.

Hiscox, Michael J. 2002. *International Trade and Political Conflict: Commerce, Coalitions, and Mobility*. Princeton, NJ: Princeton University Press.

Hojman, David E. 1994. "The Political Economy of Recent Conversions to Market Economics in Latin America." *Journal of Latin American Studies* 26(1): 191–219.

Hoogeveen, J. G. M. 2002. "Income Risk, Consumption Security and the Poor." *Oxford Development Studies* 30(1): 105–121.

Houthakker, H. S. 1957. "An International Comparison of Household Expenditure Patterns, Commemorating the Centenary of Engel's Law." *Econometrica* 25 (4): 532–551.

Huber, Evelyne, and John D. Stephens. 2000. "The Political Economy of Pension Reform: Latin America in Comparative Perspective." *Occasional Paper Series* 7. Geneva: United Nations Research Institute for Social Development.

Hunter, Linda C., and James R. Markusen. 1988. "Per-Capita Income as a Determinant of Trade." In *Empirical Methods for International Trade*, ed. Robert C. Feenstra, 89–109. Cambridge, MA: MIT Press.

Hunter, Wendy. 2007. "The Normalization of an Anomaly: The Workers' Party in Brazil." *World Politics* 59(3): 440–475.

Inglehart, Ronald. 1990. *Culture Shift in Advanced Industrial Society*. Princeton, NJ: Princeton University Press.

Instituto Brasileiro de Geografia e Estatística [IBGE]. 2006. "Sistema IBGE de Recuperação Automática – SIDRA." Available at http://www.sidra.ibge.gov.br/ [accessed June 10, 2006].

Inter-American Development Bank [IDB]. 1997. *Latin America after a Decade of Reforms: Economic and Social Progress in Latin America, 1997 Report*. Washington, DC: Inter-American Development Bank.

Inter-American Development Bank [IDB]. 1998. *Facing Up to Inequality in Latin America: Economic and Social Progress in Latin America, 1998–1999 Report*. Washington, DC: Inter-American Development Bank.

Inter-American Development Bank [IDB]. 2002a. *Beyond Borders: The New Regionalism in Latin America: Economic and Social Progress in Latin America, 2002 Report*. Washington, DC: Inter-American Development Bank.

Inter-American Development Bank [IDB]. 2002b. "The Privatization Paradox." *Latin American Economic Policies* 18:1–3.

Inter-American Development Bank [IDB]. 2004. *Good Jobs Wanted: Labor Markets in Latin America: 2004 Economic and Social Progress Report*. Washington, DC: Inter-American Development Bank.

Inter-American Development Bank [IDB]. 2006. "Sociómetro: Version 0.8." Available at http://www.iadb.org/sociometro/ [accessed May 12, 2006].

International Labour Office [ILO]. 2005. *2005 Labour Overview: Latin America and the Caribbean*. Lima, Peru: International Labour Organization.

International Telecommunication Union [ITU]. 2005. *America's Telecommunication Indicators, 2005*. Geneva: International Telecommunication Union.

International Telecommunication Union [ITU]. 2007. *World Telecommunication Indicators Database, 9th ed.* Geneva: International Telecommunication Union.

Irwin, Douglas A. 2005. *Free Trade under Fire*, 2nd ed. Princeton, NJ: Princeton University Press.

Irwin, Timothy, and Penelope J. Brook. 2003. "Private Infrastructure and the Poor: Increasing Access." In *Infrastructure for Poor People: Public Policy for Private Provision*, eds. Penelope J. Brook and Timothy C. Irwin, 1–19. Washington, DC: World Bank.

Jacobs, Meg. 2005. *Pocketbook Politics: Economic Citizenship in Twentieth-Century America*. Princeton, NJ: Princeton University Press.

James, Estelle. 1998. "Pension Reform: An Efficiency–Equity Tradeoff?" In *Beyond Tradeoffs: Market Reforms and Equitable Growth in Latin America*, eds. Nancy Birdsall, Carol Graham, and Richard Sabot, 253–272. Washington, DC: Brookings Institution Press.

James, Jeffrey. 2000. *Consumption, Globalization, and Development*. Basingstoke, U.K.: Macmillan.

Jennings, M. Kent. 1992. "Ideological Thinking Among Mass Publics and Political Elites." *Public Opinion Quarterly* 56(4): 419–441.

Johnson, Scott. 2004. "Latin America Lags Behind." *Newsweek International* July 5: 36.

Just, Marion R., Ann N. Crigler, and W. Russell Neuman. 1996. "Cognitive and Affective Dimensions of Political Conceptualization." In *The Psychology of Political Communication*, ed. Ann. N. Crigler, 133–148. Ann Arbor: University of Michigan Press.

Kahneman, Daniel, Paul Slovic, and Amos Tversky, eds. 1982. *Judgment under Uncertainty: Heuristics and Biases*. New York: Cambridge University Press.

Kahneman, Daniel, and Amos Tversky. 1979. "Prospect Theory: An Analysis of Decision under Risk." *Econometrica* 47(2): 263–291.

Katzenstein, Peter J. 1985. *Small States in World Markets: Industrial Policy in Europe*. Ithaca, NY: Cornell University Press.

Kaufman, Robert R., and Alex Segura-Ubiergo. 2001. "Globalization, Domestic Politics, and Social Spending in Latin America: A Time-Series Cross-Section Analysis, 1973–97." *World Politics* 53(4): 553–587.

Kaufman, Robert R., and Leo Zuckermann. 1998. "Attitudes toward Economic Reform in Mexico: The Role of Political Orientations." *American Political Science Review* 92(2): 359–375.

Keele, Luke, and Nathan J. Kelly. 2006. "Dynamic Models for Dynamic Theories: The Ins and Outs of Lagged Dependent Variables." *Political Analysis* 14(2): 186–205.

Kiewiet, D. Roderick. 1983. *Macroeconomics and Micropolitics: The Electoral Effects of Economic Issues*. Chicago: University of Chicago Press.

References

Kinder, Donald R., and D. Roderick Kiewiet. 1979. "Economic Discontent and Political Behavior: The Role of Personal Grievances and Collective Economic Judgments in Congressional Voting." *American Journal of Political Science* 23(3): 495–527.

Kinder, Donald R., and D. Roderick Kiewiet. 1981. "Sociotropic Politics: The American Case." *British Journal of Political Science* 11(2): 129–161.

King, Gary, James Honaker, Anne Joseph, and Kenneth Scheve. 2001. "Analyzing Incomplete Political Science Data: An Alternative Algorithm for Multiple Imputation." *American Political Science Review* 95(1): 49–69.

King, Gary, Michael Tomz, and Jason Wittenberg. 2000. "Making the Most of Statistical Analyses: Improving Interpretation and Presentation." *American Journal of Political Science* 44(2): 347–361.

Kolenikov, Stas, and Gustavo Angeles. 2004. "The Use of Discrete Data in Principal Component Analysis with Applications to Socio-Economic Indices." *CPC/MEASURE Working Paper 85.*

Kono, Daniel Y. 2007. "When Do Trade Blocs Block Trade?" *International Studies Quarterly* 51(1): 165–181.

Krueger, Dirk, and Fabrizio Perri. 2006. "Does Income Inequality Lead to Consumption Inequality? Evidence and Theory." *Review of Economic Studies* 73(1): 163–193.

Krugman, Paul R. 1996. *Pop Internationalism.* Cambridge, MA: MIT Press.

Kuczynski, Pedro-Pablo. 2003. "Reforming the State." In *After the Washington Consensus: Restarting Growth and Reform in Latin America*, eds. Pedro-Pablo Kuczynski and John Williamson, 33–48. Washington, DC: Institute for International Economics.

Kurtz, Marcus J. 2004. "The Dilemmas of Democracy in the Open Economy: Lessons from Latin America." *World Politics* 56(2): 262–302.

Lakoff, George. 2004. *Don't Think of an Elephant! Know Your Values and Frame the Debate: The Essential Guide for Progressives.* White River Junction, VT: Chelsea Green.

Lane, Robert Edwards. 1962. *Political Ideology: Why the American Common Man Believes What He Does.* New York: Free Press of Glencoe.

Leamer, Edward E. 1984. *Sources of International Comparative Advantage: Theory and Evidence.* Cambridge, MA: MIT Press.

Leamer, Edward E. 1997. "Access to Western Markets and Eastern Effort." In *Lessons from the Economic Transition, Central and Eastern Europe in the 1990s*, ed. Salvatore Zecchini, 503–526. Dordrecht, the Netherlands: Kluwer Academic.

Leonardi, Marco. 2003. "Product Demand Shifts and Wage Inequality." IZA Discussion Papers *908.*

Levitsky, Steven. 2003. *Transforming Labor-Based Parties in Latin America: Argentine Peronism in Comparative Perspective.* New York: Cambridge University Press.

Li, Wei, and Lixin Colin Xu. 2004. "The Impact of Privatization and Competition in the Telecommunications Sector around the World." *Journal of Law and Economics* 47(2): 395–430.

Lipset, Seymour M., and Stein Rokkan. 1967. "Cleavage Structures, Party Systems, and Voter Alignments: An Introduction." In *Party Systems and Voter Alignments: Cross-National Perspectives*, eds. Seymour M. Lipset and Stein Rokkan, 1–64. New York: Free Press.

Lora, Eduardo, and Ugo Panizza. 2003. "Latin America's Lost Illusions: The Future of Structural Reform." *Journal of Democracy* 14(2): 123–137.

Lora, Eduardo, Ugo Panizza, and Myriam Quispe-Agnoli. 2004. "Reform Fatigue: Symptoms, Reasons, and Implications." *Economic Review* 9(2): 1–28.

Luna, Juan P., and Elizabeth J. Zechmeister. 2005. "Political Representation in Latin America: A Study of Elite–Mass Congruence in Nine Countries." *Comparative Political Studies* 38(4): 388–416.

Luskin, Robert C. 1987. "Measuring Political Sophistication." *American Journal of Political Science* 31(4): 856–899.

Macedo, Roberto. 1985. *Os Salários nas Empresas Estatais*. São Paulo: Nobel.

Macedo, Roberto. 2005. "Distribution of Assets and Income in Brazil: New Evidence." In *Reality Check: The Distributional Impact of Privatization in Developing Countries*, eds. John Nellis and Nancy Birdsall, 253–280. Washington, DC: Center for Global Development.

Madrid, Raúl L. 2003. *Retiring the State: The Politics of Pension Privatization in Latin America and Beyond*. Stanford, CA: Stanford University Press.

Madrid, Raúl L. 2006. "Cómo Funcionan los Sistemas de Pensiones Privados en América Latina?" *Panorama Social* 4(2): 21–31.

Madsen, Douglas, and Peter Snow. 1991. *The Charismatic Bond: Political Behavior in Time of Crisis*. Cambridge, MA: Harvard University Press.

Magaloni, Beatriz, and Vidal Romero. 2008. "Political Determinants of Mass Attitudes towards Free Trade and Privatization in Latin America." *Latin American Research Review* 43(2): 107–135.

Mahon, James E. 2003. "Good-bye to the Washington Consensus?" *Current History* 101(652): 58–64.

Mainwaring, Scott P. 1999. *Rethinking Party Systems in the Third Wave of Democratization: The Case of Brazil*. Stanford, CA: Stanford University Press.

Mainwaring, Scott P., Rachel Meneguello, and Timothy J. Power. 2000. "Conservative Parties, Democracy, and Economic Reform in Contemporary Brazil." In *Conservative Parties, the Right, and Democracy in Latin America*, ed. Kevin J. Middlebrook, 164–222. Baltimore: Johns Hopkins University Press.

Mainwaring, Scott P., and Timothy Scully, eds. 1995. *Building Democratic Institutions: Party Systems in Latin America*. Stanford, CA: Stanford University Press.

Malloy, James M., ed. 1977. *Authoritarianism and Corporatism in Latin America*. Pittsburgh: University of Pittsburgh Press.

Manzetti, Luigi. 1999. *Privatization South American Style*. New York: Oxford University Press.

Marx, Anthony W. 1998. *Making Race and Nation: A Comparison of South Africa, the United States, and Brazil*. New York: Cambridge University Press.

Marx, Karl. 1894 [1981]. *Capital: Volume 3*. New York: Penguin Books.

References

Mayda, Anna Maria, and Dani Rodrik. 2005. "Why Are Some People (and Countries) More Protectionist Than Others?" *European Economic Review* 49(6): 1393–1430.

McClosky, Herbert. 1964. "Consensus and Ideology in American Politics." *American Political Science Review* 58(2): 361–382.

McKenzie, David, and Dilip Mookherjee. 2005. "Paradox and Perception: Evidence from Four Latin American Countries." In *Reality Check: The Distributional Impact of Privatization in Developing Countries*, eds. John Nellis and Nancy Birdsall, 33–84. Washington, DC: Center for Global Development.

Megginson, William L., and Jeffry M. Netter. 2001. "From State to Market: A Survey of Empirical Studies on Privatization." *Journal of Economic Literature* 39 (2): 321–389.

Mesa, Alberto Arenas de, and Fabio Bertranou. 1997. "Learning from Social Security Reforms: Two Different Cases, Chile and Argentina." *World Development* 25(3): 329–348.

Mesa, Alberto Arenas de, and Veronica Montecinos. 1999. "The Privatization of Social Security and Women's Welfare: Gender Effects of the Chilean Reform." *Latin American Research Review* 34(3): 7–37.

Mesa-Lago, Carmelo. 1978. *Social Security in Latin America: Pressure Groups, Stratification, and Inequality.* Pittsburgh: University of Pittsburgh Press.

Mesa-Lago, Carmelo. 2005. "Evaluation of a Quarter Century of Structural Pension Reforms in Latin America." In *A Quarter Century of Pension Reform in Latin America and the Caribbean: Lessons Learned and Next Steps*, ed. Carolin Crabbe, 43–82. Washington, DC: Inter-American Development Bank.

Milner, Helen V., and Keiko Kubota. 2005. "Why the Move to Free Trade? Democracy and Trade Policy in the Developing Countries." *International Organization* 59: 107–143.

Moreno, Alejandro. 1999. "Campaign Awareness and Voting in the 1997 Mexican Congressional Elections." In *Toward Mexico's Democratization: Parties, Campaigns, Elections, and Public Opinion*, eds. Jorge I. Domínguez and Alejandro Poiré, 114–146. New York: Routledge.

Morley, Samuel. 2001. "The Income Distribution Problem in Latin America and the Caribbean." Santiago, Chile: Economic Commission for Latin America and the Caribbean.

Morley, Samuel, Roberto Machado, and Stefano Pettinato. 1999. "Indexes of Structural Reform in Latin America." *ECLAC Series: Economic Reforms* (12): 1–36.

Movimiento al Socialismo [*MAS*]. 2005. *Press Release*. Available at http://www.masbolivia.org/mas/mas.html [accessed September 14, 2006].

Müller, Katharina. 2000. "Pension Privatization in Latin America." *Journal of International Development* 12(4): 507–518.

Munck, Ronaldo. 2003. "Neoliberalism, Necessitarianism and Alternatives in Latin America: There Is No Alternative (TINA)?" *Third World Quarterly* 24(3): 495–511.

Murillo, Maria Victoria. 2001. *Labor Unions, Partisan Coalitions and Market Reforms in Latin America.* New York: Cambridge University Press.

Murillo, Maria Victoria. 2002. "Political Bias in Policy Convergence: Privatization Choices in Latin America." *World Politics* 54(4): 462–493.

Murillo, Maria Victoria. 2009. *Voice and Light: Political Competition, Partisanship, and Policymaking. Market Reforms in Latin American Public Utilities.* New York: Cambridge University Press.

Murillo, Maria Victoria, and Cecilia Martinez-Gallardo. 2005. "Political Competition and Policy Adoption: Market Reforms in Latin American Public Utilities." ISERP Working Paper *06*.

Murillo, Maria Victoria, and Cecilia Martinez-Gallardo. 2007. "Political Competition and Policy Adoption: Market Reforms in Latin American Public Utilities." *American Journal of Political Science* 51(1): 120–139.

Murphy, Kevin M., and Andrei Shleifer. 1997. "Quality and Trade." *Journal of Development Economics* 53(1): 1–15.

Mutz, Diana C. 1993. "Direct and Indirect Routes to Politicizing Personal Experience: Does Knowledge Make a Difference?" *Public Opinion Quarterly* 57 (4): 483–502.

Naím, Moisés. 1994. "Latin America: The Second Stage of Reform." *Journal of Democracy* 5(4): 32–48.

Naím, Moisés. 2006. "The Lost Continent." *Foreign Policy* 157: 40–47.

Narayan-Parker, Deepa, and Patti L. Petesch, eds. 2002. *From Many Lands.* Washington, DC: Oxford University Press and the World Bank.

Navia, Patricio, and Andres Velasco. 2003. "The Politics of Second Generation Reforms." In *After the Washington Consensus: Restarting Growth and Reform in Latin America*, eds. Pedro-Pablo Kuczynski and John Williamson, 265–304. Washington, DC: Institute for International Economics.

Needell, Jeffrey D. 1987. *A Tropical Belle Epoque: Elite Culture and Society in Turn-of-the-Century Rio de Janeiro.* New York: Cambridge University Press.

Nellis, John, Rachel Menezes, and Sarah Lucas. 2004. "Privatization in Latin America: The Rapid Rise, Recent Fall, and Continuing Puzzle of a Contentious Economy Policy." *Policy Brief: Center for Global Development* 3(1): 1–7.

Nelson, Thomas E., and Donald R. Kinder. 1996. "Issue Frames and Group-Centrism in American Public Opinion." *Journal of Politics* 58(4): 1055–1078.

Neri, Marcelo, and José Márcio Camargo. 2002. "Distributive Effects of Brazilian Structural Reforms." In *Brazil in the 1990s: An Economy in Transition*, ed. Renato Baumann, 262–312. New York: Palgrave Macmillan.

Novães, Ana. 1999. "The Privatization of the Brazilian Telecommunications Sector." In *Privatization in Brazil: The Case of Public Utilities*, eds. Armando Castelar Pinheiro and Kiichiro Fukasaku, 111–141. Rio de Janeiro: Banco Nacional de Desenvolvimento Econômico e Social.

Nurkse, Ragnar. 1953. *Problems of Capital Formation in Underdeveloped Countries.* New York: Oxford University Press.

O'Donnell, Guillermo. 1973. *Modernization and Bureaucratic-Authoritarianism: Studies in South American Politics.* Berkeley: University of California.

O'Donnell, Guillermo. 1978. "State and Alliances in Argentina, 1956–1976." *Journal of Development Studies* 15(1): 3–33.

References

O'Donnell, Guillermo. 1994. "Delegative Democracy." *Journal of Democracy* 5(1): 55–69.

O'Dougherty, Maureen. 2002. *Consumption Intensified: The Politics of Middle-Class Daily Life in Brazil.* Durham, NC: Duke University Press.

Olivera, Oscar. 2004. *Cochabamba! Water War in Bolivia.* Cambridge, MA: South End Press.

Olson, Mancur. 1982. *The Rise and Decline of Nations: Economic Growth, Stagflation, and Social Rigidities.* New Haven, CT: Yale University Press.

Orlove, Benjamin, and Arnold J. Bauer. 1997. "Giving Importance to Imports." In *The Allure of the Foreign: Imported Goods in Postcolonial Latin America,* ed. Benjamin Orlove, 1–30. Ann Arbor: University of Michigan Press.

Panizza, Ugo, and Mónica Yañez. 2005. "Why Are Latin Americans So Unhappy about Reforms?" *Journal of Applied Economics* 8(1): 1–29.

Petras, James F. 1999. *The Left Strikes Back: Class Conflict in Latin America in the Age of Neoliberalism.* Boulder, CO: Westview Press.

Pew Research Center for the People and the Press. 2003. *The Pew Global Attitudes Project: Views of a Changing World.* Washington, DC: Pew Research Center for the People and the Press.

Pew Research Center for the People and the Press. 2007. *The Pew Global Attitudes Project: World Public Welcomes Global Trade – But Not Immigration.* Washington, DC: Pew Research Center for the People and the Press.

Pierson, Paul. 1996. "The New Politics of the Welfare State." *World Politics* 48(2): 143–179.

Piñera, Jose. 1996. "Empowering Workers: The Privatization of Social Security in Chile." *Cato's Letters* 10: 1–18.

Pinheiro, Armando Castelar. 1996. "Impactos Microeconômicos da Privatização no Brasil." *Pesquisa e Planejamento Econômico* 26(3): 357–398.

Pinheiro, Armando Castelar, and Fabio Giambiagi. 1997. "Lucratividade, Dividendos e Investimentos das Empresas Estatais: Uma Contribuição para o Debate sobre Privatização no Brasil." *Revista Brasileira de Economia* 51(1): 93–131.

Popkin, Samuel L. 1991. *The Reasoning Voter: Communication and Persuasion in Presidential Campaigns.* Chicago: University of Chicago Press.

Porto, Guido G. 2006. "Using Survey Data to Assess the Distributional Effects of Trade Policy." *Journal of International Economics* 70(1): 140–160.

Poulantzas, Nicos Ar. 1973. *Political Power and Social Classes.* London: Sheed and Ward.

Power, Timothy J. 2005. *Surveys of the Brazilian National Congress, 1997–2005.* Oxford: Unpublished dataset.

Power, Timothy J. 2008. "Centering Democracy? Ideological Cleavages and Convergence in the Brazilian Political Class." In *Democratic Brazil Revisited,* eds. Peter R. Kingstone and Timothy J. Power. Pittsburgh: University of Pittsburgh Press.

Powers, Nancy R. 2001. *Grassroots Expectations of Democracy and Economy: Argentina in Comparative Perspective.* Pittsburgh: University of Pittsburgh Press.

Prebisch, Raúl. 1950. *The Economic Development of Latin America and Its Principal Problems*. Lake Success, NY: United Nations Department of Economic Affairs.

Price, Vincent, and John Zaller. 1993. "Who Gets the News? Alternative Measures of News Reception and Their Implications for Research." *Public Opinion Quarterly* 57(2): 133–164.

Przeworski, Adam. 1991. *Democracy and the Market: Political and Economic Reforms in Eastern Europe and Latin America*. New York: Cambridge University Press.

Przeworski, Adam. 1993. "Economic Reforms, Public Opinion, and Political Institutions: Poland in Eastern European Perspective." In *Economic Reform in New Democracies: A Social-Democratic Approach*, eds. Luiz Carlos Bresser Pereira, José Maria Maravall, and Adam Przeworski, 132–198. New York: Cambridge University Press.

Ramamurti, Ravi, ed. 1996. *Privatizing Monopolies: Lessons from the Telecommunications and Transport Sectors in Latin America*. Baltimore: Johns Hopkins University Press.

Reardon, Thomas A., and Julio A. Berdegue. 2002. "The Rapid Rise of Supermarkets in Latin America: Challenges and Opportunities for Development." *Development Policy Review* 20(4): 371–388.

Reel, Monte. 2006. "Turning the Taps Back to the States." *The Washington Post*, *March* 27: A10.

Reis, Elisa P., and Zairo B. Cheibub. 1993. "Pobreza, Desigualdade e Consolidação Democrática." *Dados* 36: 233–259.

Remmer, Karen L. 1991. "The Political Impact of Economic Crisis in Latin America in the 1980s." *American Political Science Review* 85(3): 777–800.

Remmer, Karen L. 1998. "The Politics of Neoliberal Economic Reform in South America, 1980–1994." *Studies in Comparative International Development* 33 (2): 3–29.

Rhodes, Sybil. 2006. *Social Movements and Free-Market Capitalism in Latin America: Telecommunications Privatization and the Rise of Consumer Protest*. Albany: State University of New York Press.

Ritzer, George. 1996. *The McDonaldization of Society: An Investigation into the Changing Character of Contemporary Social Life*, rev. ed. Thousand Oaks, CA: Pine Forge Press.

Robbins, Donald, and T. H. Gindling. 1999. "Trade Liberalization and the Relative Wages for More-Skilled Workers in Costa Rica." *Review of Development Economics* 3(2): 140–154.

Roberts, Kenneth M. 1998. *Deepening Democracy? The Modern Left and Social Movements in Chile and Peru*. Stanford, CA: Stanford University Press.

Roberts, Kenneth M. 2002. "Social Inequalities without Class Cleavages in Latin America's Neoliberal Era." *Studies in Comparative International Development* 36 (4): 3–33.

Roberts, Kenneth M. Forthcoming. *Party System Change in Latin America's Neoliberal Era*. New York: Cambridge University Press.

Roberts, Kenneth M., and Moisés Arce. 1998. "Neoliberalism and Lower-Class Voting Behavior in Peru." *Comparative Political Studies* 31(2): 217–246.

310

References

Roberts, Kenneth M., and Erik Wibbels. 1999. "Party Systems and Electoral Volatility in Latin America: A Test of Economic, Institutional, and Structural Explanations." *American Political Science Review* 93(3): 575–590.

Rodriguez, Elsa, Miriam Berges, Karina Casellas, Rosángela Di Paola, Beatriz Lupín, Laura Garrido, and Natacha Gentile. 2002. "Consumer Behaviour and Supermarkets in Argentina." *Development Policy Review* 20(4): 429–439.

Rodrik, Dani. 1997. *Has Globalization Gone Too Far?* Washington, DC: Institute for International Economics.

Rodrik, Dani. 1998. "Why Do More Open Economies Have Bigger Governments?" *Journal of Political Economy* 106(5): 997–1032.

Rodrik, Dani. 2001. "Why Is There So Much Economic Insecurity in Latin America?" *CEPAL Review* 73(1):7–30.

Rogowski, Ronald. 1989. *Commerce and Coalitions: How Trade Affects Domestic Political Alignments*. Princeton, NJ: Princeton University Press.

Rohter, Larry. 2005. "With New Chief, Uruguay Veers Left, in a Latin Pattern." *The New York Times*, February 28:A3.

Romer, Paul. 1994. "New Goods, Old Theory, and the Welfare Costs of Trade Restrictions." *Journal of Development Economics* 43(1): 5–38.

Rosas, Guillermo. 2005. "The Ideological Organization of Latin American Legislative Parties: An Empirical Analysis of Elite Policy Preferences." *Comparative Political Studies* 38(7): 824–849.

Royston, Patrick. 2004. "Multiple Imputation of Missing Values." *Stata Journal* 4 (3): 227–241.

Saavedra, Jaime. 2003. "Labor Markets during the 1990s." In *After the Washington Consensus: Restarting Growth and Reform in Latin America*, eds. Pedro-Pablo Kuczynski and John Williamson, 213–264. Washington, DC: Institute for International Economics.

Samuels, David. 2003. *Ambition, Federalism, and Legislative Politics in Brazil*. New York: Cambridge University Press.

Samuels, David. 2004. "From Socialism to Social Democracy: Party Organization and the Transformation of the Workers' Party in Brazil." *Comparative Political Studies* 37(9): 999–1024.

Samuels, David. 2006. "Sources of Mass Partisanship in Brazil." *Latin American Politics and Society* 48(2): 1–27.

Samuelson, Robert J. 2002. "Global Economics under Siege." *The Washington Post*, October 16: A25.

Scheiner, Ethan. 2006. *Democracy without Competition in Japan: Opposition Failure in a One-Party Dominant State*. New York: Cambridge University Press.

Scheve, Kenneth F., and Matthew J. Slaughter. 2001. *Globalization and the Perceptions of American Workers*. Washington, DC: Institute for International Economics.

Scheve, Kenneth F., and Matthew J. Slaughter. 2004. "Economic Insecurity and the Globalization of Production." *American Journal of Political Science* 48(4): 662–674.

Schneider, Ben Ross. 1992. "Privatization in the Collor Government: Triumph of Liberalism or Collapse of the Development State?" In *The Right and Democracy in*

Latin America, eds. Douglas A. Chalmers, Maria do Carmo Campello de Souza, and Atílio A. Boron, 225–238. New York: Praeger.

Schwentesius, Rita, and Manuel Angel Gomez. 2002. "Supermarkets in Mexico: Impacts on Horticulture Systems." *Development Policy Review* 20(4): 487–502.

Sears, David O., Richard R. Lau, Tom R. Tyler, and Harris M. Allen, Jr. 1980. "Self-Interest vs. Symbolic Politics in Policy Attitudes and Presidential Voting." *American Political Science Review* 74(3): 670–684.

Seligson, Mitchell A. 1999. "Popular Support for Regional Economic Integration in Latin America." *Journal of Latin American Studies* 31(1): 129–150.

Selvanathan, E. A., and S. Selvanathan. 2003. *International Consumption Comparisons: OECD versus LDC*. River Edge, NJ: World Scientific Publishing.

Selznick, Philip. 1951. "Institutional Vulnerability in Mass Society." *American Journal of Sociology* 56(4): 320–331.

Sen, Amartya Kumar. 2000. *Development as Freedom*. New York: Anchor Books.

Shifter, Michael, and Vinay Jawahar. 2005. "Latin America's Populist Turn." *Current History* 104(2):51–57.

Shirley, Mary. 2005. "Why Is Sector Reform So Unpopular in Latin America?" *The Independent Review* 10(2): 195–207.

Sikkink, Kathryn. 1991. *Ideas and Institutions: Developmentalism in Brazil and Argentina*. Ithaca, NY: Cornell University Press.

Silva, Luiz Inácio Lula da. 2002. "Carta ao Povo Brasileiro." Available at http://www2.fpa.org.br/portal/modules/news/article.php?storyid=2324 [accessed May 9, 2008].

Silva, Patricio. 1995. "Modernization, Consumerism, and Politics in Chile." In *Neoliberalism with a Human Face? The Politics and Economics of the Chilean Model*, ed. David E. Hojman, 118–132. Liverpool, U.K.: Institute for Latin American Studies.

Silveira, Flavio Eduardo. 1998. *A Decisão do Voto no Brasil*. Porto Alegre: Edipucrs.

Simon, Herbert Alexander. 1957. *Models of Man: Social and Rational: Mathematical Essays on Rational Human Behavior in a Social Setting*. New York: Wiley.

Singer, André. 1990. "Collor na Periferia: A Volta por Cima do Populismo?" In *De Geisel a Collor: O Balanço da Transição*, ed. Bolívar Lamounier, 135–152. São Paulo: Sumaré.

Smith, Adam. 1776 [1993]. *An Inquiry into the Nature and Causes of the Wealth of Nations*. Oxford: Oxford University Press.

Smith, Peter H. 2000. *Talons of the Eagle: Dynamics of U.S.–Latin American Relations*, 2nd ed. New York: Oxford University Press.

Sniderman, Paul M., Richard A. Brody, and Philip Tetlock, eds. 1991. *Reasoning and Choice: Explorations in Political Psychology*. New York: Cambridge University Press.

Sniderman, Paul M., and Sean M. Theriault. 2004. "The Structure of Political Argument and the Logic of Issue Framing." In *Studies in Public Opinion: Attitudes, Nonattitudes, Measurement Error, and Change*, eds. Willem E. Saris and Paul M. Sniderman, 133–165. Princeton, NJ: Princeton University Press.

Sola, Lourdes. 1994. "The State, Structural Reform and Democratization in Brazil." In *Democracy, Markets and Structural Reform in Latin America: Argentina*,

312

References

Bolivia, Brazil, Chile, and Mexico, eds. William Smith, Carlos Acuña, and Eduardo Gamarra, 151–181. New Brunswick, NJ: Transaction Publishers.

Souza, Juarez de. 2000. "Privatization in Brazil: Toward an Evaluation." In *The Impact of Privatization in the Americas*, eds. Melissa H. Birch and Jerry Haar, 177–202. Miami: North-South Center Press.

Stallings, Barbara, and Wilson Peres. 2000. *Growth, Employment, and Equity: The Impact of the Economic Reforms in Latin America and the Caribbean*. Washington, DC: Brookings Institution Press.

Stepan, Alfred C. 1978. *The State and Society: Peru in Comparative Perspective*. Princeton, NJ: Princeton University Press.

Stewart, Frances. 1977. *Technology and Underdevelopment*. Boulder, CO: Westview Press.

Stimson, James A. 1999. *Public Opinion in America: Moods, Cycles, and Swings*, 2nd ed. Boulder, CO: Westview Press.

Stimson, James A. 2004. *Tides of Consent: How Public Opinion Shapes American Politics*. New York: Cambridge University Press.

Stokes, Susan C. 2001a. *Mandates and Democracy: Neoliberalism by Surprise in Latin America*. New York: Cambridge University Press.

Stokes, Susan C., ed. 2001b. *Public Support for Market Reforms in New Democracies*. New York: Cambridge University Press.

Stolper, Wolfgang F., and Paul A. Samuelson. 1941. "Protection and Real Wages." *The Review of Economic Studies* 9(1): 58–73.

Structural Adjustment Participatory Review International Network [SAPRIN]. 2004. *Structural Adjustment: The SAPRI Report: The Policy Roots of Economic Crisis, Poverty and Inequality*. London: Zed Books.

Thomas, Vinod. 2006. *From Inside Brazil: Development in a Land of Contrasts*. Washington, DC: World Bank.

Tinsman, Heidi. 2006. "Politics of Gender and Consumption in Authoritarian Chile, 1973–1990: Women Agricultural Workers in the Fruit-Export Industry." *Latin American Research Review* 41(3): 7–31.

Tomz, Michael, Jason Wittenberg, and Gary King. 2003. *CLARIFY: Software for Interpreting and Presenting Statistical Results*. Version 2.1. Stanford University, University of Wisconsin, and Harvard University. January 5. Available at http://gking.harvard.edu/ [accessed September 5, 2003].

Tullock, Gordon. 1967. "Welfare Costs of Tariffs, Monopolies, and Theft." *Western Economic Journal* 5: 224–232.

Turner, Frederick C., and Carlos Elordi. 1995. "Economic Values and the Role of the Government in Latin America." *International Social Science Journal* 145:474–488.

Ugaz, Cecilia. 2003. "Consumer Participation and Pro-Poor Regulation in Latin America." In *Utility Privatization and Regulation: A Fair Deal for Consumers?* eds. Cecilia Ugaz and Catherine Waddams Price, 80–98. Northampton, MA: Edward Elgar.

Ugaz, Cecilia, and Catherine Waddam Price. 2003. "Introduction." In *Utility Privatization and Regulation: A Fair Deal for Consumers?* eds. Cecilia Ugaz and Catherine Waddams Price, 3–24. Northampton, MA: Edward Elgar.

United Nations. 2008. "UN Comtrade: United Nations Commodity Trade Statistics Database." *UN Comtrade*. Available at http://comtrade.un.org/ [accessed January 6, 2008].

Veblen, Thorstein. 1899. *The Theory of the Leisure Class: An Economic Study of Institutions*. Norwood, MA: Norwood Press.

Ventura-Dias, Vivianne, Mabel Cabezas, and Jaime Contador. 1999. "Trade Reforms and Trade Patterns in Latin America." *ECLAC Series: International Trade* (5): 1–53.

Verba, Sidney, Jae-on Kim, and Norman H. Nie. 1978. *Participation and Political Equality: A Seven-Nation Comparison*. New York: Cambridge University Press.

Waisman, Carlos. 1982. *Modernization and the Working Class: The Politics of Legitimacy*. Austin: University of Texas Press.

Wallerstein, Immanuel Maurice. 1976. *Capitalist Agriculture and the Origins of the European World-Economy in the Sixteenth Century*. New York: Academic Press.

Walton, John, and Charles Ragin. 1990. "Global and National Sources of Political Protest: Third World Responses to the Debt Crisis." *American Sociological Review* 55(6): 876–890.

Weyland, Kurt. 1996. "Neopopulism and Neoliberalism in Latin America: Unexpected Affinities." *Studies in Comparative International Development* 31(3): 3–31.

Weyland, Kurt. 1998a. "Swallowing the Bitter Pill: Sources of Popular Support for Neoliberal Reform in Latin America." *Comparative Political Studies* 31(5): 539–568.

Weyland, Kurt. 1998b. "The Political Fate of Market Reform in Latin America, Africa, and Eastern Europe." *International Studies Quarterly* 42(4): 645–673.

Weyland, Kurt. 2000. "A Paradox of Success? Determinants of Political Support for President Fujimori." *International Studies Quarterly* 44(3): 481–502.

Weyland, Kurt. 2002. *The Politics of Market Reform in Fragile Democracies: Argentina, Brazil, Peru, and Venezuela*. Princeton, NJ: Princeton University Press.

Weyland, Kurt. 2004. "Neoliberalism and Democracy in Latin America: A Mixed Record." *Latin American Politics and Society* 46(1): 135–157.

Weyland, Kurt. 2007. *Bounded Rationality and Policy Diffusion: Social Sector Reform in Latin America*. Princeton, NJ: Princeton University Press.

Williamson, John. 1990. "What Washington Means by Policy Reform." In *Latin American Adjustment: How Much Has Happened?* ed. John Williamson 7–20. Washington, DC: Institute for International Economics.

Wise, Timothy A., Hilda Salazar, and Laura Carlsen, eds. 2003. *Confronting Globalization: Economic Integration and Popular Resistance in Mexico*. Bloomfield, CT: Kumarian Press.

Wood, Adrian. 1997. "Openness and Wage Inequality in Developing Countries: The Latin American Challenge to East Asian Conventional Wisdom." *World Bank Economic Review* 11(1): 33–57.

World Bank. 1994. *Averting the Old Age Crisis: Policies to Protect the Old and Promote Growth*. New York: Oxford University Press.

World Bank. 2006. *World Development Indicators*. Washington, DC: World Bank.

References

Wright, Erik Olin. 1979. *Class Structure and Income Determination*. New York: Academic Press.

Wright, Erik Olin, and Luca Perrone. 1977. "Marxist Class Categories and Income Inequality." *American Sociological Review* 42(1): 32–55.

Yeats, Alexander J. 1998. "Does Mercosur's Trade Performance Raise Concerns about the Effects of Regional Trade Arrangements?" *World Bank Economic Review* 12(1): 1–28.

Zaller, John R. 1992. *The Nature and Origins of Mass Opinion*. New York: Cambridge University Press.

Index

aggregation issues, in public opinion
   studies, 25, 27–34
  cross-individual variation as, 27, 30–34
  intranational behavioral patterns as part
   of, 31
  unpack reforms as, 27
  wealth and, 31–33
  See also unpack reforms
Aguas Argentinas, 263
Andean Pact, 16, 69, 264
Argentina
  free trade policies in, public opinions
   on, 98
  supermarket revolution in, 74
  unemployment rates in, 62
  utility services privatization in, 63, 263
asset transfer, in foreign investment, 217
awareness gap, 125
  in Brazil, 232
  See also hegemony effects

Bauer, Arnold, 19
Bolivia
  oil and gas nationalization in, 119n9
  privatization in, 5, 263
  socialist party success in, 6
  See also Morales, Evo
bottom-up approach, 13
  in Brazil, 232–240
  citizens, 23, 34–44
  domestic monopolies and, 38
  framework for, 41–44
  globalization and, 38
  hypothesized role of, 53
  import tariff relaxation and, 39

  labor-channel effects and, 39–41,
   131–132
  labor market volatility and, 40
  partisanship and, 45n11
  privatization in, 43–44, 152
  in public opinion surveys, 34–44
  SOEs and, employment ratio of, 39
  top-down v., 23–24, 52–55, 150–152
  utility services in, 39
  Washington consensus and, 150–152
  wealth gap and, 122
  See also framework, for bottom-up
   approach
Brazil, 171–246
  awareness gap in, 232
  blackouts in, 114, 176–177
  bottom-up influences in, 232–240
  consumer interests in, 181–182, 216–217
  consumer protection agencies in,
   176–177
  consumer tastes in, 233–237, 246, 253
  consumption patterns in, 232–233,
   245–246
  corruption concerns within, 209n4,
   210–211
  dependency theory and, 184–186
  developmentalist ideologies in, 184
  distributional effects in, 178
  electricity providers in, 177
  elites in, 173, 183–190
  employment rate factors in, 217
  employment tenure changes in, 258
  fiscal policy opinions in, 199
  Folha de São Paulo in, 189–190
  foreign entertainment in, 234

Index

Carvalho, Cicero Péricles de, 86
Central American Common Market, 16
Central American Free Trade Agreement, 98n9
Chávez, Hugo, 6, 263
  trade policy under, 264
  See also Venezuela
Chile
  pension reforms in, 75, 78
  socialist party success in, 5–6
  supermarket revolution in, 74
citizens as consumers/producers, in Latin
    America, 21–23
  in bottom-up approach, 23, 34–44
  cognition and, 35, 216–217
  during corporatist era, 21
  in Marxism, 21
  political action as result of, 22–23
  as transfer-payment recipients, 37
cleavages, consumption and, 265–270
cognition, 35, 216–217
  globalization and, 38–39
Colburn, Forrest, 257
Collor de Mello, Fernando, 173
  Mercosul under, 178
  privatization under, 173–174, 184–185
  tariff reform under, 178
  trade liberalization under, 185–186
  Treaty of Asunción under, 178
Colombia
  privatization in, 5
  telecommunications access expansion
    in, 63
Companhia do Vale do Rio Doce, 185
consumer-channel effects, 25n4, 59
  on market reform attitudes, 102–113
  of utility services access expansion,
    66–67
consumerism. *See* consumismo
consumer protection agencies, 266n8
  in Brazil, 176–177
consumers, interests of
  in Brazil, 181–182, 216–217
  consumer-channel effects and,
    25n4, 59
  consumption patterns as facet of, 267
  globalization benefits for, 59–60,
    69, 87
  homogeneity of, labor market interests
    and, 22–23n2

import tariffs and, 70
  labor markets interests v., 41n6
  popularity gap and, 101
  under privatization, 62–63
  supermarket revolution and, 74
  under trade liberalization, 70
  Washington consensus and, 113
  wealth gap and, 237–240
  See also consumer tastes; consumismo;
    consumption; consumption patterns;
consumer tastes, 43, 123, 128, 258–259
  in Brazil, 233–237, 246, 253
  cleavages and, 265–270
  foreign culture and, 72
  in Latin America, 260
  measurement of, 129–131, 233–237
  privatization and, 66
  wealth gap and, 136–139
  See also consumers, interests of; con-
    sumption; consumption patterns;
consumismo, 15, 19–20, 257–270
  bottom-up approach and, 23, 34–44
  cleavages and, 15
  leftist leadership and, 15
  wealth gap and, 267
  See also consumers, interests of; consumer
    tastes; consumption; consumption
    patterns
consumption
  See also consumers, interests of; consumer
    tastes; consumismo; consumption
    patterns
  cleavages and, 265–270
  democratization of, 268
  purpose of, 267
  See also consumers, interests of; consumer
    tastes; consumismo; consumption
    patterns
consumption insecurity/security, 123, 128,
    131
  employment security and, 133
  market reforms and, 139
consumption patterns
  in Brazil, 232–233
  consumer interests and, 267
  foreign investment and, 111
  globalization and, 108–113
  individual-level attitudes and, in Brazil,
    245–246
  the left and, 15

319

Index

Index

substitution of, in Brazil, 178
wealth and access to, 70
wealth gap and, 123
import substitution, in Brazil, 178
import tariffs, 63
consumer choice and, after relaxation of, 70
incrementalism, 265
independents, 134n9
in Brazil, 241
market reform attitudes among, 144
political awareness of, 144
inflation
market reform and, 26
of prices, 26
privatization and, 107
See also price inflation; pricing
institutionalism. *See* new institutionalism
International Monetary Fund, 7
intertemporal theory, 27, 31, 34
issue constraint
economic policy and, 29
in public opinion, in Latin America, 29, 100

job churning, 40
job losses
from privatization of SOEs, 61, 174–175
See also employment rates; unemployment rates

Katzenstein, Peter, 260
Kirchner, Néstor, 5, 263

labor
supermarket revolution and, 74
See also labor markets
labor-channel effects, 39–41, 59, 60, 132, 149
wealth gap and, 131–132
labor hoarding, 61
labor markets
bottom-up approach and, 39–41, 131–132
in Brazil, 209–210
consumer homogeneity and, 22–23n2
consumer interests v., 41n6
education level and, 131–132, 140n13, 234–235
free trade and, 213

under globalization, 60, 68
job churning, 40
market reform and, attitudes influenced by, 25–26, 40–41, 122, 139–141
under privatization, 60, 62
public opinion influenced by, 124
public sector employees and, 141
social class and, 132–133, 140
in SOEs, as percentage of total workforce, 39
supermarkets and, 74
unemployment rates and, 133, 140–141
unionized jobs and, 68–69
volatility of, 40
wealth gap and, 122, 131–133
Lagos, Ricardo, 5
Latin America
citizens as consumers/producers, 21
consumer protection agencies in, 176–177, 266n8
consumer tastes in, 260
consumismo in, 15, 19–20, 257–270
consumption patterns within, 265–270
corporatist era in, 22
elites in, 25
E.U. states v., 261
export-centered approach toward, 21–23
food retailing in, 73–75
foreign culture as import into, 72, 267–268
foreign investment in, 68
globalization and, 16, 67–75, 260–262
hegemony effects, 126
imports into, 67–68
incrementalism in, 265
leftist parties' rise in, 3–4, 6n1, 262–265
libertarianism in, 29
market reforms throughout, 6
neoliberalism in, 5, 9, 30n5, 121–154, 262–265
new institutionalism in, 24
pension privatization within, 17, 60, 75–79, 149–150
petroleum sector nationalization in, 105
privatization in, 5, 10–12, 38, 59–60, 91, 93, 104
public opinion before surveys within, 20
public views on globalization within, 10–12

Index

PT opposition to, 243–244
in public opinion surveys, 100, 204–217
social class and attitudes toward, 8–9
socialism v., 6–7
SOE employment and, 32
unpacking of attitudes toward, 27–30,
259–260
wealth gap in attitudes toward, 122,
124–127, 137, 138n12
See also economic policy; foreign
investment; free trade; globalization;
privatization; trade liberalization
Marxism
economic production according to, 21
social class and, 128
Marx, Karl, 267
media, 79, 114
elite opinions and, 186–190
Folha de São Paulo, 189–190
politicians' use of, for foreign investment,
244
Mendonça de Barros, Luis Carlos, 185
Menem, Carlos, 27
economic reform policies of, 27
Mercosul (Southern Cone Common
Market), 16, 69, 178
Brazilians' opinions on, 192, 241, 242,
251–252
under Cardoso, 178
individual-level attitudes toward,
251–252
political awareness and, 241
Mexico
export-led job creation in, 110n15
petroleum sector nationalization
in, 105
privatization in, 5
supermarket revolution in, 74
MNCs. *See* multinational corporations
monopolies, 38
Morales, Evo, 5, 121, 263
free trade pacts under, 264
morselize. *See* issue constraint
multi-national corporations (MNCs), in
Brazil, 216

National Destatization Program (PND),
173
nationalism, 24
neoliberal hegemony, 33, 45–46, 50–52

market reform and, 124–127
united elites under, 50–52
unpacking reforms and, 52
neoliberalism, in Latin America, 5, 9, 30n5,
121–154, 262–265
foreign investor clashes under, 263
hegemony in, 45–46, 50–52
privatization and, 83
social class and, 12
voter mandates under, 262–263
wealth gaps and, 122
See also market reforms
new institutionalism, 24
Nicaragua
foreign investment support within, 112
free trade support within, 112
nonhomothetic tastes. *See* consumer tastes
North–South trade. *See* free trade;
globalization; trade liberalization

open-ended survey questions, 204–217

Paraguay, free trade in, public opinions on,
98
partisanship, 24, 33–34
in bottom-up approach, 45n11
within Brazil, 240
elites and, 49, 83, 133–135
foreign investment attitudes and,
145–147
FTAA attitudes and, 84, 144–145
privatization atitudes and, 142
in top-down approach, 24, 45, 46
trade attitudes and, 144–145
pay-as-you-go (PAYG) system, 75–76
PAYG system. *See* pay-as-you-go system
PELA. *See* Latin American Parliamentary
Elites Project
pension privatization, 17, 60, 75–79,
149–150
administrative costs under, 77
age eligibility changes under, 77–78
age of worker and, 149–150
distributional consequences of, 78–79
employment rates after, 77
females under, 78–79, 150
financial market development from,
76
financial solvency as result of, 76
future retiree concerns under, 78

Index

Index

Other Books in the Series *(continued from page iii)*

Catherine Boone, *Political Topographies of the African State: Territorial Authority and Institutional Change*

Michael Bratton and Nicolas van de Walle, *Democratic Experiments in Africa: Regime Transitions in Comparative Perspective*

Michael Bratton, Robert Mattes, and E. Gyimah-Boadi, *Public Opinion, Democracy, and Market Reform in Africa*

Valerie Bunce, *Leaving Socialism and Leaving the State: The End of Yugoslavia, the Soviet Union, and Czechoslovakia*

Daniele Caramani, *The Nationalization of Politics: The Formation of National Electorates and Party Systems in Europe*

Kanchan Chandra, *Why Ethnic Parties Succeed: Patronage and Ethnic Headcounts in India*

José Antonio Cheibub, *Presidentialism, Parliamentarism, and Democracy*

Ruth Berins Collier, *Paths toward Democracy: The Working Class and Elites in Western Europe and South America*

Christian Davenport, *State Repression and the Domestic Democratic Peace*

Donatella della Porta, *Social Movements, Political Violence, and the State*

Alberto Diaz-Cayeros, *Federalism, Fiscal Authority, and Centralization in Latin America*

Thad Dunning, *Crude Democracy: Natural Resource Wealth and Political Regimes*

Gerald Easter, *Reconstructing the State: Personal Networks and Elite Identity*

Margarita Estevez-Abe, *Welfare and Capitalism in Postwar Japan: Party, Bureaucracy, and Business*

M. Steven Fish, *Democracy Derailed in Russia: The Failure of Open Politics*

Robert F. Franzese, *Macroeconomic Policies of Developed Democracies*

Roberto Franzosi, *The Puzzle of Strikes: Class and State Strategies in Postwar Italy*

Geoffrey Garrett, *Partisan Politics in the Global Economy*

Scott Gehlbach, *Representation through Taxation: Revenue, Politics, and Development in Postcommunist States*

Miriam Golden, *Heroic Defeats: The Politics of Job Loss*

Jeff Goodwin, *No Other Way Out: States and Revolutionary Movements*

Merilee Serrill Grindle, *Challenging the State: Crisis and Innovation in Latin America and Africa*

Anna Grzymala-Busse, *Rebuilding Leviathan: Party Competition and State Exploitation in Post-Communist Democracies*